Milton S. Eisenhower

EDUCATIONAL STATESMAN

Milton S. Eisenhower

EDUCATIONAL STATESMAN

Stephen E. Ambrose
Richard H. Immerman

The Johns Hopkins University Press

BALTIMORE AND LONDON

The Johns Hopkins University Press, Baltimore, Maryland 21218
The Johns Hopkins Press Ltd, London

Library of Congress Cataloging in Publication Data

Ambrose, Stephen E.
  Milton S. Eisenhower, educational statesman.
  Bibliography: pp. 317–20
  Includes index.
  1. Eisenhower, Milton Stover, 1899—   . 2. College presidents—United States—Biography. 3. Educators—United States—Biography. I. Immerman, Richard H. II. Title.
LA2317.E37A64 1983   370'.92'4 [B]   83–4
ISBN 0–8018–2988–7

TO ALL THE GRADUATES of Kansas State University, Pennsylvania State University, and The Johns Hopkins University who have degrees signed by Milton Eisenhower. You are his legacy.

Contents

Preface ix

1. "We'll All Help Push!"
   RETURN TO JOHNS HOPKINS 1

2. "Opportunity Is All About You—Reach Out and Take It"
   STORYBOOK CHILDHOOD IN ABILENE 8

3. "I Would Lose All Nervousness"
   KANSAS STATE, RAMSAY LODGE, AND MARRIAGE 31

4. "Love Life of the Bullfrog"
   WASHINGTON BUREAUCRAT 42

5. "The Greatest Possible Speed Is Imperative"
   WASHINGTON ADMINISTRATOR 53

6. "Our Concern Is with the Education of Men and Women
   Determined to Be Free"
   RETURN TO KANSAS STATE 72

7. "Unsophisticated, Unspoiled, Eager to Learn"
   THE STUDENTS AT KANSAS STATE 94

8. "To Change the Character of the Institution"
   PENN STATE 108

9. "Days of Tension and Hysteria"
   DEANS, FACULTY—AND CIVIL LIBERTIES AT PENN STATE 125

10. "How Much I Have Valued Your Counsel"
    A BROTHER IN THE WHITE HOUSE 146

11. "Milton Eisenhower Is Not a Loner"
HELEN'S DEATH AND THE DECISION TO LEAVE PENN STATE *161*

12. "There Is Nothing Else Like It Anyplace"
THE JOHNS HOPKINS UNIVERSITY *170*

13. "The Whole Thing Is One Massive Personal Equation"
ASSISTANTS AND FACULTY AT JOHNS HOPKINS *193*

14. "When the Light Is On"
THE STUDENTS AT JOHNS HOPKINS *215*

15. "Goddammit, If I Had Moved to Palm Springs, This Wouldn't Be Happening!"
RETIREMENT AND RETURN *228*

16. "Democracy Contains the Seeds of Its Own Destruction"
ON THE STATE OF THE UNION *240*

17. "A Smile on His Face, a Twinkle in His Eyes, and a Forward-looking Attitude"
IN RETIREMENT *253*

Appendix A: Inaugural Address, Kansas State College, September 30, 1943 *263*

Appendix B: The Presidency: Can Anyone Do the Job? *270*

Appendix C: Eisenhower to Senator Charles McC. Mathias, October 12 and November 9, 1979 *274*

Appendix D: Violent Crime: An Overview *280*

Appendix E: Commencement Address, The Johns Hopkins University, June 13, 1967 *292*

Notes *299*

Selected Bibliography *317*

Index *321*

Preface

Nearly every one of the hundreds and hundreds of people who have known Milton Eisenhower can vividly recall their first meeting. Most remember that they had expected to be impressed and that he did not let them down. My first meeting, in the late winter of 1964, was no exception. I was at Hopkins to interview for the position of associate editor of the Eisenhower Project. Alfred D. Chandler, Jr., editor of the *Eisenhower Papers*, took me to Eisenhower's office at Homewood House.

High above me on a now barren hill, Homewood House was a magnificent colonial place set boldly against the gray winter sky. I imagined how it must look with all the trees in bloom. From wherever you were on the campus, you climbed up to get to Homewood House, which in its turn looked serenely down North Charles Street, its large manicured lawn providing just the right balance. The entryway was appropriately grand, the scene inside one of the hustle and bustle of a modern administrative staff running a great university. But however much people darted out of one door and in through another, the house's serenity and charm were secure. The president's office was modest in size, with good, strong wooden tables, desks, walls, and bookcases and old-fashioned, high-quality furniture. It had a sweeping view across the lawn.

Walking into Dr. Eisenhower's office, Chandler leading the way, sticking out my hand and trying to smile, I was struck—as so many people have been—by the similarities between Milton and Dwight Eisenhower. I had seen Ike countless times on television—he was almost one of the family—and I had loved him for, among other things, his mannerisms, which I had come to know well. Milton Eisenhower had them too—the ready grin, the hearty laugh, the extraordinarily lively face, dancing eyes, balding pate, full lips, and a strong, lithe body. I had heard Ike's voice—on the radio, on television, and in person—and Milton sounded exactly like him, in pitch, pace, and pronunciation. It was uncanny, and it took getting used to. As one of his former students said about his first meeting, "I just couldn't stop thinking, 'My God! That's Milton Eisenhower! Ike's brother!' "

It did not take Milton long to get you to see him as himself rather than merely as someone's brother. Although dressed in a severely conservative, perfectly fitting suit that had not a hint of a wrinkle in it, he was personally relaxed, and he was such a dominant personality that he set the mood for the room, and Chandler and I relaxed. Milton began talking about the Eisenhower Project. It was clear that he was completely prepared for our visit, that he knew what he was talking about. Even more impressive was the genuine personal interest he took in his visitors, really wanting to know our views on the current controversies. (Richard Immerman and I were to discover in doing the research for this biography that nearly all of his young friends had had this experience.) He talked freely about his own views; although his views were well thought-out and strongly held, one always sensed that he had had to change his mind in the past because of new information and that he expected that he would have to do so in the future. In short, he talked to his visitors on a basis of equality, ready to hear and learn, just as ready to instruct where and when he could.

This scholarly atmosphere of equality was a stunning discovery for many visitors; one former student recalled thinking, "Doesn't he know who he is? He really ought to put on more airs!"

But the most impressive thing about Milton Eisenhower was not that he looked like Ike, his title, nor his clothes or furnishings: it was what he had to say. His vocabulary and sentence structure, organization, and composition were overshadowed only by the content. He knew the history and background of so many issues and he had been personally involved in so many crisis situations that he could recall a personal anecdote about almost any event in the twentieth century. Many of these anecdotes would be of the "so President Roosevelt asked me to . . ." or the "so I told President Johnson . . ." variety. Fascinating material, especially for a budding young historian. I hoped he would never stop.

In a sense he didn't. In the six years that followed I interviewed him frequently—about his role in the aftermath of the Darlan deal, his relations with Ike in the thirties, Ike's letters to him from the Philippines, and other matters relating to Ike's career, which was my concern at the time. Questions often led to anecdotes about Henry Wallace, Rex Tugwell, Douglas MacArthur, or Franklin Roosevelt. What struck me most strongly was, first, that from the twenties to the present he knew on a personal basis nearly everyone who was anyone in the American political world and that in talking about them he was not name-dropping. They were simply the people with whom he had associated throughout his adult life, so naturally they were the ones about whom he told stories.

Second, that his memory was so sharp: he could recall details such as who said what to whom and facts such as the provisions of this or that piece of legislation. Third, his objectivity: he always told a story from all points of view. He knew, and could state with logic and precision, the arguments on both sides, and although he usually ended by rejecting one argument and adopting the other, he did so on the basis of facts and reason, never emotion. Fourth, his competence: not only did he know the facts and the history of an issue, and could relate the issue to its time, place, and the other issues of the day, but he could draw the lesson and apply it to the present in a new, imaginative way. Whether the subject was a specific New Deal bill, his brother's career, or the ills of democracy, his presentation was usually persuasive, and his insights often brilliant. After I left Hopkins I continued to interview Dr. Eisenhower on a regular basis throughout the seventies, as I extended my own study of Dwight Eisenhower to include his presidency, an area in which Milton was of enormous help because he had been so close to his brother during his administration. Several times during this period I urged him to keep a diary and to see to the systematic collection of his correspondence, as his biography would have to be written someday, not because he was Ike's brother but because of his own accomplishments. I knew that he had been a great success as president of Kansas State, Penn State, and Hopkins, three very different institutions, and I told him that his biography would be an important chapter in the history of higher education in the United States. He agreed with me, but unfortunately he failed to take my advice. He kept no diary, nor did he retain his correspondence, which he was in the habit of destroying after it was five years old.

In 1978, after an interview with Dr. Eisenhower for a book I was doing on Ike and the CIA, I decided to attempt the biography myself. I asked Dr. Eisenhower, and he was enthusiastic. I then asked Dr. Richard Immerman, of Princeton University, who had worked with me on the CIA book, if he would be willing to collaborate on the Milton Eisenhower biography. Immerman had already interviewed Dr. Eisenhower as a part of his own work on the Eisenhower presidency and had made a thorough search of the Eisenhower papers, both Dwight's and what remained of

Milton's in the Eisenhower Library in Abilene. Immerman agreed to collaborate, and we went to work immediately.

In January 1980 I was Dr. Eisenhower's house guest for a week. We talked incessantly on subjects ranging from his childhood memories to highly sophisticated cures for inflation, and we recorded twenty-five hours' worth of our conversation on tape. In the formal sessions we concentrated on his educational career, since I had determined from the start that his experiences at Kansas State, Penn State, and Hopkins would be the focus of the biography. He had already written a memoir of his public service, *The President Is Calling*, which covered his relations with every president from Coolidge to Nixon, and there was no point in repeating what he had already said so well. Immerman also returned to Baltimore to interview Dr. Eisenhower at length.

Eisenhower's eyes would sparkle when he talked about his mother. He laughed heartily at childish pranks remembered. He obviously enjoyed recalling his relationship with Roosevelt and other leaders. But most of all, he was pleased to remember and talk about his three schools, his assistants, his deans, his faculties, and his students. He was proud of what he had done.

Although these interviews constitute the heart of the book, this is not an "as told to" biography. Immerman and I interviewed scores of his associates and corresponded with many others. We also drew extensively from the appropriate written sources—office records, the archives at all three schools, Eisenhower's own writings and speeches, the numerous articles written about him over the decades, campus and local newspapers, and so on. Throughout, it seemed important to keep some distance between authors and subject. This was because, as one of our sources, Donald Ford, put it, "It's very easy and natural for Milton to let that big heart of his open up and encompass you." He certainly did that with Immerman and me, and we could not help responding. Thus, perhaps a bit of the objectivity that we so admire in Milton Eisenhower is missing in this biography. We are too fond of him to be objective. Still, we know that we see some issues and events differently than he does, and we have tried to be critical, at least to the extent of making certain that for better or for worse this is our biography of Milton Eisenhower, not his autobiography. In short, the point of view is ours, not his, and obviously the errors are our fault.

All royalties from this book have been assigned to the Hopkins Scholarship Fund. All transcripts from the tape-recorded interviews and all correspondence have been deposited with the Hopkins Archives, where they are available to interested scholars.

This biography is written with the people to whom it is dedicated in mind. They are the ones we hope to please and inform about this great man. If they like it, we will be satisfied. If Dr. Eisenhower likes it, we will be ecstatic.

S. E. A.

When Steve Ambrose first asked me to work with him on a biography of Milton Eisenhower, I had serious reservations. I am a historian of U.S. foreign policy, and the biography, he told me, would hardly touch on Eisenhower's diplomatic experiences. Moreover, my knowledge of the history of higher education was at best scanty; my knowledge of Kansas State, Penn State, and Johns Hopkins even less. Nevertheless, I could not refuse the offer. Having for years studied the diplomacy of the 1950s, I knew Milton Eisenhower and I liked him. Having collaborated with Steve Ambrose before, I liked him. I decided to accept.

My participation in the project turned out to be very different than I had expected. To begin with, I found myself totally immersed in the topic. And not just in Eisenhower, although he always came first. What surprised me was how interested I became in educational history and in the histories of the three institutions of which Eisenhower was president. I loved reading the secondary books and going through the archival depositories. Even more, I loved interviewing so many people who knew Eisenhower well—his associates, his friends, his students. Each helped make my research not just rewarding but thoroughly enjoyable.

Second, I had expected to work with Steve as I had done previously: I would help out with the research, and he would write the bulk of the manuscript. I would be his collaborator. Steve had hardly finished a rough draft, however, when he was off to Ireland for a year. Suddenly I was upgraded to the position of coauthor, and it would be up to me to see the book through publication.

I was a research associate at Princeton at the time, and as soon as I learned of my new responsibilities, draft in hand, I took the train to Baltimore. I would be the house guest of Milton S. Eisenhower. We talked for what seemed to be forty-eight straight hours, discussing everything that the book would cover, and much more. I had never written a biography, and I wanted to learn as much as possible about and from my subject. I also talked extensively with Jack Goellner, the director of The Johns Hopkins University Press. I slept during the entire trip home.

Shortly thereafter the movers came to take all my possessions to

Boulder, Colorado, where I would be teaching at the university. Much to my wife Marion's dismay, however, I would not let them take three huge cartons. They were filled with documents, books, and interview transcripts for the biography, and I would not let them out of my sight. So the two of us, two cats, one Irish setter, and the cartons made the drive to Colorado. There I began to revise the draft. I finished midway through the spring semester and sent it off to Jack. The next day I accepted an appointment to the University of Hawaii.

I planned to make the final revisions in Princeton, where I would spend the summer. By now there were more cartons. I loaded them into the car, and back across the country we drove, this time without the animals, who flew on ahead to Hawaii. But the referee's report was delayed. Jack and I decided that it would be best to send it directly to Hawaii. So I put the cartons back in the car for the return trek, this time all the way to California. We shipped the car. Marion and I flew; I carried the cartons.

A week after we arrived the referee's report came. It was exceptionally detailed. I made the final revisions just in time to fly back to Denver, where I was presenting a paper at the American Political Science Association meeting. I left the cartons in Hawaii but carried the manuscript with me. I delivered it by hand to Henry Tom, the Press's social sciences editor.

You have the end result of this saga. I hope you like it. Despite everything, I certainly liked doing it. Writing a biography of Milton Eisenhower has made my life richer. Getting to know him, and those who knew him long before I did, has made my life even more so. I do not like everything about Milton Eisenhower, nor do I like everything he did. This will become evident to the readers of this biography. Yet it will also become evident that I find him perhaps the most remarkable man I have ever known. What he is, what he represents, what he has accomplished, and what he has meant to so many people is almost impossible to describe. I have tried to do the best job I could. As to how well I have done, it will be up to the reader—and Milton—to judge.

The list of those whom I must thank is much too long for the allotted space. For all those who consented to be interviewed or to write letters, I refer the reader to the bibliography and notes. The archivists and staffs at the libraries were great. Jean Wiggs at Princeton and Ann Underwood in Boulder turned my scribble into hundreds of beautifully typed pages, and Joanne Allen made sense out of those pages. Ralph Ward and Jim Silvan painstakingly compiled the index. Ross Jones, Hopkins's vice-president for university affairs, caught an embarrassing number of factual errors. Steve and Jack, of course, gave me the opportunity, encouraged me every step of the way, and waited and waited for me to finish. But my greatest debt is to Milton Eisenhower and Marion Immerman. Milton patiently let me pester him unendingly with my questions and never once asked me what I was doing with his answers. Marion put up with much more than I would have. She read drafts, photocopied documents, and listened to my rantings. And while I carried the cartons she carried the bags.

R. H. I.

Milton S. Eisenhower

EDUCATIONAL STATESMAN

CHAPTER 1

"We'll All Help Push!"
Return to Johns Hopkins

I t was 4:00 P.M., April 15, 1971. All over the lovely rolling, wooded Homewood campus of The Johns Hopkins University tulips, dogwoods, and daffodils were in full bloom, replacing the winter grayness with welcome splashes of bright color. Inside the large auditorium of Shriver Hall, filled to capacity, there was an atmosphere of hope, a feeling that the new man in charge could do what had to be done. The audience comprised Hopkins's faculty, staff, and student body, as intelligent an audience as one could assemble anywhere in the United States. Nearly all the faculty were highly respected scholars, men and women with well-earned international reputations. The students ranked in the top 2 percent nationally, whether measured according to their high school records or their college entrance examinations.

They were an elite group, and terribly spoiled. The faculty expected to spend the remainder of their career at Hopkins, enjoying a handsome salary while being left free to pursue their often esoteric research projects. The students expected to finish their undergraduate or graduate work at one of the world's most prestigious institutions of higher learning and then use their Hopkins degree to vault themselves into correspondingly prestigious positions in finance, business, law, scholarship, medicine, or public service.

Increasingly over the past three years, however, this ideal situation had become threatened. Hopkins had long enjoyed a healthy financial surplus, encouraging the faculty to expect whatever funding was necessary

for new research projects. Now that surplus had turned into a huge deficit, and even ongoing projects were in jeopardy of losing support. Positions were being eliminated; hiring was at a standstill; salaries were being
frozen. An eroding sense of security accompanied the eroding budget.
Professors of all ranks began to look with a jaundiced eye towards other
colleges and universities.

Compounding the fiscal uncertainty was a widespread academic malaise. Across the country relations between administrators, faculty, and
students had never been so bad. The Vietnam War raged on, bringing
chaos to the campuses. Student protests against the war expanded into
protests against administrators, trustees, deans, and teachers. "Don't trust
anyone over thirty" became the watchword of youth. At Columbia and
Berkeley students occupied the president's office; at Cornell they carried
guns. Hopkins students were traditionally conservative, yet they were not
immune from the unrest. This was 1970, the year of Cambodia and Kent
State. Some embraced the radical movement; others began to thumb
through college catalogs, wondering, as were their teachers, whether they
could transfer to an institution that would provide the opportunities,
prestige, and serenity they had expected from Hopkins.

Both faculty and student discontent focused on Lincoln Gordon, the
new president. After all, most reasoned, his brief tenure had paralleled
Hopkins's eclipse, and the blame had to rest somewhere. Taking the lead,
the faculty demanded a meeting with Gordon. They wanted answers. The
president obliged, but he had no simple answers. Further frustrated, the
faculty elected a committee of five to speak as one voice. Without hesitation, the committee informed Gordon that it demanded his removal from
office. Faced with such unity of nonsupport, Gordon felt that he would
never be able to generate the confidence in his administration that the situation required. In March 1971 he submitted his resignation to the board
of trustees, effective immediately. At a critical juncture in its history Hopkins was leaderless.

As the crisis developed, veterans on the administrative staff thought
back to better days. "Thank God he [Milton Eisenhower] got out when he
did," they mused. "None of these old-timers could cope with the new
problems." Nevertheless, in desperation the trustees asked Milton Eisenhower to return to the post he had resigned in 1967, to turn back the clock
of his beloved university to the glorious eleven years during which he had
presided. For weeks Eisenhower hesitated. Then he agreed.

"Dr. Milton is coming back." The notice flashed across Hopkins on
April 5, 1971, brightening up the campus more than the blossoming flow-
ers. The majority of students knew of Eisenhower only through legend.
None of the trustees, faculty, or staff knew what he would or could do.

The situation had deteriorated so badly during the three years of his retirement that there was little reason for the Hopkins community to feel confident. But it did. Everyone agreed that only one man could save the university, and that was "Dr. Milton." Merely the announcement that Eisenhower would speak on April 15 generated hope and anticipation. The audience that settled into Shriver Hall fully expected to witness the rebirth of The Johns Hopkins University.[1]

Milton Eisenhower strode onto the stage, a few scribbled notes in his hand. He was seventy-one years old, but he could have passed for fifty. Impeccably dressed, as befitted a man previously voted one of the ten best-dressed men in America, he carried himself lightly, with a springy step. His round face, highlighted by his light complexion, a pair of over-size glasses, and a large, balding pate, was marvelously expressive. Broad of shoulder, solidly built, he exuded confidence. He had the air of a man who had been through countless crises in his lifetime and was sure he would get through this one.

It was the supreme moment in his distinguished career. Nevertheless, Eisenhower did not want to be there. When the group of trustees had come to him some weeks earlier, begging him to come back to his old post, he had asked, "Do you want me to return in a wheelchair?" When he did resume his place in his Homewood House office members of the group brought him a miniature, white plastic wheelchair mounted on a black onyx base. On the face of the base was a plate engraved with the words "We'll all help push!"

Eisenhower welcomed this promise of support; nevertheless, he did not want to be on the stage at Shriver Hall, looking down on all those hopeful faces. Never, however, had there been any real chance that he would not return. When he had made his decision, his mind had gone back to January 1956, when he was the most valued adviser to the president of the United States, his older brother. Dwight Eisenhower was then in the last year of his first term. It was less than six months since he had suffered a serious heart attack, and he was undecided about running for reelection. Republicans were literally begging him to run, telling him that no other Republican could win and insisting that it was his duty to serve his country for another four years.

Ike wanted Milton's advice. Milton gave him a long list of pros and cons and concluded, "Finally, may I point out the obvious, more personal, perhaps more selfish view: if you decline to run, you will clearly go down in history as one of our greatest military and political leaders, with no major domestic or international difficulty to mar your record. If you go on, you might enhance your standing . . . or you might face serious economic set-

backs at home and upheavals abroad. You might jeopardize your health
. . ."—and, by implication, his reputation.

Ike jotted in ink beside the paragraph that raised the question of protecting his reputation, "Of no great moment, even though history might
condemn a failure it cannot weigh the demand of conscience."[2]

The importance of duty. Robert E. Lee, himself a college president following his military service, once said that duty was the most beautiful
word in the English language. To the Eisenhowers it was the most compelling. From the cradle the Eisenhower boys had learned the importance of
duty. They had spent their lifetime doing their duty. And so it was that in
the spring of 1971 Milton Eisenhower's duty was clear to him, no matter
how distasteful, no matter how fraught with danger to his own reputation.

"I realized that there was no one else that I knew of who could do the
job, because it had to be done quickly and therefore you had to know the
place intimately, both personnel and finance and organization. So I said,
'All right. The institution is more important than any one individual. I'll
go back.' " Thus did he recall his decision ten years later. "But I assure you
that when I went back I thought that was going to be the end of Milton
Eisenhower's reputation."[3]

In preparing for his speech in Shriver Hall, in planning to turn around a
budget that had an "unconscionable" deficit, Eisenhower had much to
draw on, most of all his own decade of experience at Hopkins. Some of his
old staff were still there—Ross Jones in particular, along with a young,
personable, hard-driving new provost, Steven Muller, who had arrived
just as the old president had resigned. (Muller was still splitting his time
between Hopkins and Cornell, where he had classes to finish and administrative responsibilities to fulfill.)

Almost exactly two years before, Muller had been through a terrible
crisis at Cornell, and in his view the Hopkins people were overreacting to
their situation just a bit. Muller had a three-hour interview with Eisenhower at Eisenhower's Bishops Road home, from which he came away
"tremendously impressed." Muller was delighted that Eisenhower wanted
him to stay on as provost, and even though he expected that within the
year a new president would be appointed who would likely appoint his
own provost, he accepted. A major reason was the opportunity to work
with Eisenhower, the opportunity to watch and to learn. Muller knew
that Eisenhower "was venerated on this campus, and he would have the
skill to do what needed to be done in the short run to calm everybody
down."[4]

As soon as Eisenhower consented to come back the entire administration went to work. The budget deficit was the immediate problem, and

Eisenhower's strategy was to cut expenses and raise money, in that order. Drastic cuts had to be made. Again and again Eisenhower assured Muller, "I don't want to have to do mean things," but he would slash away nevertheless.

After his period of retirement, Eisenhower was surprised to find himself so eager to respond to the challenge. He should not have been so surprised. He was back in his element, making decisions. Muller was amazed at his "marvelous ability to decide what was right and then do it. He could make difficult decisions quickly, and usually—just about always—correctly."

While the people at Homewood and the medical institutions fretted, according to Muller, Eisenhower appeared not at all worried. Muller himself, new to Baltimore, could hardly believe that Eisenhower and about half his staff took off, in the middle of the crisis, for the Orioles' opening-day game. Eisenhower understood, as Muller would later, that an essential ingredient to recovery was to convey the impression that the situation was well in hand, that things were back to normal. "It was nice that spring and Milton arrived together, along with lacrosse and the Orioles," Muller was to comment in retrospect.

So, although Eisenhower did not want to be on that stage at Shriver Hall the afternoon of April 15, he was nonetheless well prepared, knowing exactly what needed to be done and prepared to do it. And he sensed the overwhelming support from the audience. "The mood was 'Thank God we have somebody in charge who knows what he's doing,' " Muller remembered. "I suspect if Milton had read from the Baltimore telephone directory he would have had a rising ovation. He must have been aware of that," because "there was a great sense of joy that was evident even when we walked in." Eisenhower was going to have to announce some "mean things" in the way of cuts, but Muller was not apprehensive. "It was what people had been longing to hear for a long time and hadn't heard."[5]

Eisenhower spoke without a microphone, but as always during his fifty-year career, his voice carried in loud, clear tones to the back of the auditorium. Seldom glancing at his notes, he spoke in perfect sentences and paragraphs. He seemed completely confident, totally in command.

Eisenhower began by showing his miniature wheelchair and reading the inscription, "We'll all help push!" "I fervently hope that is true," he continued, "for the current problems of this distinguished and pioneering institution are so serious, so ominous, that they can be solved only with the complete cooperation of all who make up the Hopkins community. But let me hasten to say that *with* cooperation they can be solved."

He promised to speak with "brutal candor," then outlined the state of the budget, giving details about the reserve fund (nearly exhausted) and the endowment (not touched) and explaining that the largest cost increases were in fund-raising staff (up 400 percent) and central administration (up 300 percent). Elsewhere the jumps had not been so high, but still they were serious.

"The crucial question now is, What can be done?" Raising tuition, already high, was out of the question. Eisenhower said that he had already made "extremely severe cuts" in administration, fund-raising, and other staffs, thereby saving $1.4 million. That was the major cut by far, and it came out of Eisenhower's own office, not faculty or student funds. Another $450,000 would be cut from the Arts and Sciences budget (which had tripled in three years). Auxiliary enterprises had been operating "seriously in the red." Eisenhower had eliminated the bookstore deficit by contracting with a management firm, and he had taken steps to fill the university-owned dorms and apartments in order to eliminate that deficit. Nothing could be overlooked. Counter service in Levering Hall was a luxury Hopkins could no longer afford. He was going to replace it with commercial vending machines, "an unhappy move" but a necessary one. His axe was sharp but fair. Eisenhower also eliminated a $100,000 appropriation for furniture for the new administration building.

In making cuts, Eisenhower said, he would never lose sight of the "purpose of this institution": to provide "high quality undergraduate, graduate and professional education and research. Everything else we do is designed to serve this purpose." He acknowledged "the traditional understanding" of the faculty that professors would teach one graduate and one undergraduate course each semester, using the other half of their time for research, but declared, "We must do more. On the basis of what faculty representatives said to me when I was torturing myself with the decision I had to make about a temporary return to the presidency, I believe that most members of the faculty will be willing to assume heavier responsibilities, at least until the present precarious situation has been overcome." Therefore, he asked all faculty to "offer more courses at the undergraduate level and thus enable us to accept more students." Ideally, he wanted every faculty member to teach two undergraduate courses per semester. (Years later Eisenhower remarked ruefully that this was the one request he made that produced no results: the attitude of the Hopkins faculty was, "Nothing doing!")

From the students Eisenhower asked for patience, especially in their oft-expressed desire to have a student union building. They would have to recognize that this "desperate need" was "out of the question for the time being." He hoped that the need could be met soon, but "I have little hope of performing a miracle while I am here."

Eisenhower's conclusion was personal. "It was a struggle for my conscience and feeling of duty to overcome my common sense and thus bring me for a time back to Johns Hopkins, where I can do nothing but cast a shadow over what modest reputation I may have left here four years ago," he said. "I'm probably the oldest man ever made president of an American university. My energy is not what it was when I left here. But now that I have returned, my reluctance is forgotten and I shall personally do all I can to forward the interests of this distinguished institution for the short time I am here."

He emphasized that throughout his career, spanning half a century in government and education, he had always maintained an open-door policy in his office. "I shall do that now. I'll see any faculty member, administrator, student, or alumnus who feels I should listen to him or help him."

He closed with an expression of faith: "Johns Hopkins has always been a pioneering institution of superb quality, earning and meriting an enviable reputation in this country and throughout the world. This reputation is due to the eminence of the faculties and the quality of the students who constitute the Hopkins community. It is a great university today. Current problems *can* be solved . . . *if all of you will get behind the wheelchair and push very hard.*"[6]

There was a moment of silence. Eisenhower later recalled that he did not know how the speech had been received, whether the Hopkins community was ready to accept the austere budget he proposed. "I stood there silently for about fifteen seconds," Eisenhower remembered. "Didn't even say thank-you or anything. And started to walk off the stage."[7]

His doubts were short-lived. As if one, the members of the audience rose, and there was tumultuous applause. The famous grin spread across his face.

CHAPTER 2

"Opportunity Is All About You—Reach Out and Take It"

Storybook Childhood in Abilene

His heredity was Pennsylvania Dutch, his environment small-town America. Both emphasized the traditional virtues of hard work, honesty, frugality, Christianity, service to others, and ambition. They provided the base from which Milton Eisenhower stepped onto the world stage, where he became an associate of some of the great men of the twentieth century, the chief executive officer of three famous universities, and an adviser to every president from Coolidge to Nixon. During that long and illustrious career he never saw cause to turn his back on either the Eisenhower heritage or Abilene, Kansas. He held to their ideals and their values. Their principles, rooted in the eighteenth and nineteenth centuries, were his, even when he was dealing with the most complex of modern problems, whether in the New Deal or World War II as a government administrator or in higher education from the end of World War II through the Vietnam War.

David and Ida Eisenhower and Abilene, Kansas, are inseparable. The couple lived most of their adult life in the little prairie town, where they raised their six sons. They were respected and trusted but never prominent. Neither held elective office, their names appeared only rarely in the local paper, their home was modest even by Abilene standards, and their role in Abilene's economy was a minor one. They did not mind their common life because they had common goals and values. They loved each other, their sons, their work, their home, and their town. In the American tradition, they wanted their sons to achieve more than they had. In Milton's eyes they were—and remained—model parents in a model setting. The temptation is to call them typical, a typical "Ma and Pa" in a typical American town. Indeed, one of their sons, Edgar, once told an interviewer, "There are many David and Ida Eisenhowers in this great country of ours."[1] But in fact they were exceptional, the sires of an exceptional family.

In Germany's hilly Odenwald, bordering on the Nekar, Main, and Rhine rivers, the name was spelled "Eisenhauer," literally "iron hitter," referring to the ancient heritage represented on the family crest. Hans Nicol Eisenhower made the leap across the ocean to the New World, arriving in 1741 aboard the *Europa*, bringing with him his Mennonite religion, his wife, and their three sons. He settled among his fellow German immigrants, or "Pennsylvania Dutch" as they were commonly called, in Lancaster County, on the frontier west of Philadelphia. He acquired a farm of 120 acres and built a house, only to have it burned to the ground by Indians in August of 1756. He rebuilt, and his progeny grew. They moved westward towards and then past Harrisburg, always on the edge of the frontier, acquiring new land. Like most Pennsylvania Dutch, they were outstanding farmers. Their hard work yielded barns full of sweet-smelling hay, fields beautifully tilled, abundant crops, and healthy livestock. In short, they lived the life of American folklore. They ate well, slept well, and praised God and America at every opportunity.

In the early nineteenth century the Eisenhowers joined the River Brethren sect of the Mennonites, or Dunkards, so-called because they held river baptisms. Milton's grandfather, Jacob Eisenhower, born in 1826, became the minister of the Lykens Valley River Brethren. Jacob, who was something of a scholar, attracted large audiences to his dynamic sermons, which he delivered in Pennsylvania German, a blend of several dialects, particularly Palatinate with some admixture of High German and English, still the first language of the River Brethren. He had a full beard, which emphasized his stern countenance and flashing eyes. In his old age Jacob lived with David and Ida; he died in 1906, when Milton was seven. Milton recalls that "he never seemed to lose his ministerial aspect," and indeed to the youngster old Jacob must have looked just a bit like God himself.[2]

As would be the case with his grandson, Jacob had an ability to talk, to persuade, to organize, to lead. After the Civil War he helped persuade a number of the River Brethren to push on to Kansas. In 1878 the farm in Pennsylvania sold for eighty-five hundred dollars. With his children, his congregation, and fifteen carloads of freight, Eisenhower began the trek.

The caravan stopped when it reached Dickinson County, a lush valley almost exactly in the middle of the state. Only forty miles further west were the flat, arid, treeless Great Plains of western Kansas. Just south of the Smoky Hill River, a couple of miles from the settlement known as Abilene, Jacob bought a farm. Eventually three hundred members of his congregation settled around him.[3]

The cowboys from Texas, who had spent months driving cattle up the Chisholm trail, called it "Sweet Abilene, prettiest town I've ever seen." Abilene's moment of glory was short—the few years right after the Civil War when the western terminus of the Kansas-Pacific Railroad was in Abilene and "Wild Bill" Hickok was the town marshal. The cowboys, sometimes just paid a year's wages, would gamble, drink, find girls, and shoot the town up. It all gave Abilene a lurid reputation, much romanticized since, but it lasted only until the Kansas-Pacific pushed on west. By 1878, when Jacob arrived, the open range was being turned into settled farmland, and Abilene was being turned into a community that served the farmers rather than the cowboys.

David Eisenhower, then fifteen years old, made the journey west with his father, along with two brothers and a sister. Jacob found that he did not have sufficient time to run the farm and attend to his ministry, so he tried to interest his son in the farm. But the young man found the work repetitious and back-breaking. David wanted an education instead; he wanted to be an engineer. Evidently Jacob put considerable pressure on David to take over the farm; there is a strong feeling in the Eisenhower family that because Jacob pushed his son so persistently to be something that he did not want to be, David never tried to influence his children in their career choices.[4]

David, who could be as Pennsylvania Dutch stubborn as his father (or, later, his sons), continued to refuse to accede to his father's wishes. It did not spoil their relationship. Jacob not only spent his last years living in David's house but even provided the money to make it possible for David to leave Abilene for Lecompton, Kansas, to attend Lane, a River Brethren college (now defunct) near Topeka. David studied mechanics, mathematics, Greek, rhetoric, and penmanship. He became proficient in mathematics, excellent in Greek (from his scholarly father he had learned perfect German), and he got a start on his engineering.

Then he met Ida Stover and, as if following a Hollywood script, lost his heart. They had much in common. She had been born a Lutheran, and her people also had come to America from Germany. They had settled on the Pennsylvania frontier in 1730 and then had moved down the Shenandoah Valley to Mt. Sidney, Virginia, where Ida had been born in 1862, a year earlier than David. Highly intelligent, she had concentrated on Biblical studies, almost the only outlet for scholarly interests available to a girl in Virginia. She once won a prize in Mt. Sidney for memorizing 1,365 Biblical verses in six months.[5]

Orphaned at age eleven and raised by an uncle, Ida had insisted on an education for herself. Higher education for young women was considered so improper in Virginia that she packed up her few belongings, bought a train ticket, and traveled to Topeka, where an older brother lived. "Kansas was still wild and woolly when mother came," one of her sons later observed. There, unlike in Virginia, "they didn't care if a woman went to college or not."[6] So Ida entered Lane, the same year as David.

In their own way, both David and Ida were rebels. David had rejected farming, while Ida had rejected the traditional role of a young woman in Virginia. They made a good-looking couple. David was tall and muscular, with the broad shoulders that characterized all Eisenhower men. He had a thin, hard-set mouth, thick black hair, dark eyebrows, deep-set, penetrating eyes, and a large, rounded chin. His legs were long, his hands large and expressive. For all his size and strength, however, he was quiet, a bit shy, and retiring.

More delicate than David, Ida had beautiful hair, which invariably was done to perfection, a ready grin which spread across her whole face, and a hearty laugh. Next to her grin, her most notable feature was her sparkling eyes, which signified a spontaneity and liveliness that complemented David's seriousness. It was from Ida that Milton—and all his brothers— inherited the sparkle and the ever-ready grin that one day would be recognized around the world.

David and Ida fell in love so quickly and so deeply that, despite all the effort they had made to get to Lane, they agreed to leave before finishing, get married, and raise a family. Ida converted to the River Brethren, and on September 23, 1885, in the Lane chapel, they exchanged vows.

Perhaps as one final effort to induce David to become a farmer, Jacob gave him a handsome wedding present—160 acres of land and two thousand dollars in cash. But David mortgaged the farm to an uncle and spent his capital on a general store in Hope, Kansas, twenty-eight miles south of Abilene. He took in a partner, Milton Good, who had been a salesman in a clothing store in Abilene and thus had some experience in business. The Goods and the Eisenhowers had adjoining apartments above the store, where they entertained and earned a reputation for living beyond their means.

Less than three years later financial disaster struck. David awoke one morning to discover Good gone, most of the inventory with him, and a stack of unpaid bills left behind. As Milton heard the story as a youngster,

Good had absconded, leaving the innocent David to face the creditors. But although Ida studied law textbooks on bankruptcy for a number of years thereafter, no suit was ever pressed. Kansas was in the midst of the worst agricultural depression in her history, a depression that was rapidly turning Kansas farmers, normally the most conservative of men, into agitated Populists eager to raise less corn and more hell. With wheat down to fifteen cents a bushel, they could not pay their bills. David and Good had been carrying them on credit, in the time-honored manner of American general stores. When the farmers went under, they took the business with them.[7]

Ida, who had already had one son, Arthur, born in 1886, was pregnant with her second child, Edgar, who was born in January 1889, a few months after the bankruptcy. When she became pregnant again, she went to Abilene to live with Jacob while her husband took a ten-dollar-per-week job with a railroad in Denison, Texas. He rented a small house by the tracks, where Ida joined him in time for the birth of Dwight, born in October 1890.

At this point the family rallied around the young couple. Cris Musser, David's brother-in-law, was foreman at the River Brethren–owned Belle Springs Creamery, a new plant and one of the biggest and most prosperous enterprises in Dickinson County. Musser offered David a job as a mechanic-engineer in the creamery, starting at fifty dollars per month. So in 1891 it was back to Abilene, where a fourth son, Roy, was born in 1892. Following Roy in 1894 was Paul, who died an infant. Then in 1898 came Earl, and on September 15, 1899, Ida gave birth to Milton Stover Eisenhower.

The world Milton entered was a small, white frame house on South Fourth Street. Although it had a basement, an upstairs, and a downstairs, all the rooms except the dining room were tiny, and the best room, the front room, or parlor, was reserved for entertaining and church activities. Thus there was barely enough living space. Here six active, healthy boys grew up, often fighting, sometimes brawling, usually shouting, always eating—all this in a household whose head never in his life had a spare five dollars in his pocket (in 1912 David's salary at the creamery was still under one hundred dollars per month). "I have found out in later years we were very poor," Dwight said when he returned to Abilene decades later to begin his presidential campaign. "But the glory of America is that we didn't know it then. All we knew was that our parents . . . could say to us: Opportunity is all about you. Reach out and take it."[8]

By most standards, David and Ida never reached out to take that opportunity for themselves. They concentrated on being parents, and they worked hard at it. They wanted their sons to be responsible, honest, and ambitious. They wanted them to succeed in a wider setting than Abilene or even Kansas. None of the boys disappointed them.

Basic to everything was the break with the narrowness of the Pennsylvania Dutch past, beginning with language. David wanted his boys to be Americans, and to that end he refused to speak German in the house, except with his father. The Eisenhowers had been in America for six generations by the time Milton was born, but David's sons were the first to grow up speaking only English.

They were also the first set of Eisenhowers to produce neither a farmer nor a minister. David and Ida encouraged them to choose whatever career they wanted. They were also the first to move outside the confines of the River Brethren community. Without ever saying so directly, David and Ida gave the boys the feeling, as Milton later put it, that "if you stay home you will always be looked upon as a boy."[9]

Breaking with the past did not mean abandoning religion. Indeed, as Milton recalled, "religion was as much a part of our home life as eating or sleeping." David would read from the Bible before every meal, then ask a blessing. After dinner he would bring the Bible out again. The boys would take turns reading. To keep them interested in the reading, David developed a game. As Milton explained it, "When it was my turn to read, I was permitted to read until I made a mistake; but if one of my brothers caught me in an error, then he was *privileged* to read."[10]

Indeed, next to their sons, the Bible and church activities were the center of David and Ida's life. David kept a copy of the Bible in Greek by his bedside for nighttime reading. Ida organized meetings of the Bible students of the Watchtower Society, which met on Sundays in the Eisenhower parlor. Ida played the piano and led the singing with her good, strong voice. Milton learned to play too, and found in music a lifelong source of joy and contentment.

David and Ida lived their religion, without shame, embarrassment, or apology. The River Brethren were pacifists, and despite the Eisenhower ancestry, the couple never abandoned their opposition to war. When America entered the First World War, Ida's articulate pacifism and German name nearly got her arrested. Only the intervention of an influential friend in town kept her out of jail. Yet they did not try to force their sons to accept their doctrines or their sect, and not one of the boys stayed with the River Brethren. Even when Dwight decided on a career in the military, neither parent ever objected, at least not outwardly.[11]

Partly as a result of practical necessity, mainly as a matter of principle, the parents developed in their sons a strong sense of responsibility. David had acquired the home from his uncle Abraham. While he never learned to like farming, the property had attracted him because three acres and a barn went with it. This meant that the Eisenhowers could raise nearly all their own food, as well as a small surplus to bring in extra money. They had a cow, a horse, a vegetable garden, chickens, and a fruit orchard. Each of the boys had chores to do. If they were not done—if the fire was not lit in the morning, if the chickens were not fed, or the cow was left unmilked—everyone suffered, but most of all the culprit, who would undergo a well-laid-on whipping.

A sense of fairness extended to all things, even dessert. When it was time to serve the pie, Ida solved the age-old problem of who got the biggest piece by having one of her sons cut it. Then all the others had the right to choose before the cutter. Edgar later recalled that "we got so good at this that there wasn't the slightest difference in the size of any of the pieces; and even to this day I can cut a pie in three, five, seven or nine pieces without a variance of a quarter of an ounce in any of them."[12]

It was a happy household. Although Ida could lay on a switching with a stick that would turn the boys' bottoms red and keep them red for hours, each son remembered that she did so only when he deserved it. When the antics were of the "boys will be boys" variety, she was tolerant and understanding. When they fought among themselves, which was frequent, especially among the older sons, she would stand back and let them fight. David, meanwhile, was a mild-mannered man who seldom raised his voice—Milton could hardly recall his ever doing so—and he took no notice at all of the youthful fistfights. When there was a question about whether some punishment was warranted, it was usually David who would decide. He always listened to all sides before reaching a judgment. "We weren't ever punished just on the spur of the moment by father," Milton later commented. "He thought things through." And if the two parents ever disagreed, the children never knew it. The boys never doubted that they had received a just hearing.[13]

Romanticized or not, the examples set by David and Ida unquestionably instilled in their sons a strong sense of fairness and objectivity. They also instilled a strong sense of service to others. As Edgar once explained, "Religion to my father and mother was a way of life; they lived it. They believed in the brotherhood of men . . . ." For four decades after he left the creamery David ran the savings plan for the employees of a public utilities complex. Never did he misplace a penny. Often one of the boys was awakened in the middle of a rainy or snowy night to accompany his mother to the house of a sick neighbor. Ida had what Edgar called "a certain amount of medical magic which always soothed a person in distress, and she would comfort her neighbor until a doctor could come." As adults, all the Eisenhower boys earned well-deserved reputations as friends and leaders who could be counted on.[14]

The Eisenhower parents believed in letting the boys make their own mistakes. When Earl was seven years old he informed his parents that he was going to run away from home and go to work. David advised him as to the best roads to take to nearby towns and the best kind of weather to travel in. He even suggested the best places to get a job. Ida told him to let her know when he got ready to go so she could make a big box lunch for his journey. Earl announced that he wouldn't need any of her sandwiches. He left the house, walked about a mile down the road, thought better of it, and returned home. No one said a word.[15]

"The fortunate thing for us boys is that father and mother complemented one another," Edgar said in summing up his parents. "Mother had the fire. Mother had the ambition. Mother had the personality. She had the joy. She had a song in her heart."

"Dad was the anchor. He was the one who kept everybody's feet on the ground. As I look back now, I realize Dad had a quiet influence on us that we didn't recognize until we got older and began to experience some of the responsibilities of life."[16]

Milton was the youngest of six boys, a fact that played a major role in his life. For one thing, it meant he wore hand-me-down clothes until he was out of high school. By the time the pants, shirts, socks, and shoes had worked their way down from Arthur through the others to Milton, they were at best in poor condition, and often they were out of style, even in a town that changed as slowly as Abilene. Milton grew up wearing knickers and long stockings that had originally been black but had been mended so often by the time Milton got them that they had become gray.

The other kids at school poked fun at him. When he complained to his mother, begging her for some new stockings, she said, "Well, the stockings are warm. They are all right. Pay no attention to what they say. The time may come when you'll laugh at them."[17] In a sense Milton did have the last laugh: in the 1950s he was named one of the ten best-dressed men in America.

To add to Milton's childhood discomfort, his being a boy—and the last of six—was a great disappointment to his parents. "My father was sorry he never had a girl," Earl later recalled. "He used to sit on our front porch and make friends with every little girl that came by. I know he was miserable because Milton wasn't a little girl."[18]

Ida, too, had wanted a girl, so much so that she let Milton's hair grow and put it in curls. He wore shoulder-length curls until he was five years old, when the kidding from his brothers and playmates got so bad—and by which time David had accepted the inevitable—that David took him out back and, without telling Ida, took out a scissors and cut the curls.[19]

Being the youngest, Milton was considered the "baby" by his older brothers, an attitude that was reinforced by the curls. Making matters worse, at the age of four he caught scarlet fever and was quarantined in his room for six weeks. He emerged from the ordeal with permanently weakened eyesight, and in comparison with his robust brothers, he looked frail and spindly.

The older boys enjoyed teasing Milton and making him cry, while at the same time they were determined to make him into a tough-guy imitation of themselves. One of his earliest and sharpest childhood memories was of an incident in 1903, when he was four years old. The Smoky Hill River overflowed its banks, flooding the town. "I came downstairs early in the morning," Milton remembered. "Father took me by the hand, led me to the head of the steps that led down to the cellar, and opened the door, and there was the water, within an inch of the kitchen floor." It frightened him so that he began to cry.

This so disgusted Edgar, then fourteen years old (and characterized by Arthur as "the meanest of the bunch"), that he set out on a personal campaign to toughen Milton up. He forced Milton into the attic, locked the door behind him, then howled with laughter as Milton screamed in terror of the total darkness. Another time, when Milton was romping among the bales in the hayloft, he slipped through an opening into a dungeonlike hole in the hay. Edgar quickly piled more bales onto the opening, leaving the little boy once again trapped in total darkness, unable to move. His screams could not be heard. Another brother eventually pulled the bales away, but the incident left Milton with a fear of the dark that he could not shake until he was in his twenties. Even as a high school student, when school activities kept him out late, he would run home, keeping to the middle of the street.[20]

But there were advantages to having older brothers. For one thing, he was able to share their playthings. And while older brothers can be cruel, they can also be kind, as when Dwight brought him "Flip," a stray dog that became Milton's constant companion throughout high school, long after all the other boys had left home. Flip, who by a stretch of the imagination could be called a fox terrier, was a quick learner, and Milton would pass the hours away teaching him to roll over, play dead, shake hands, and all the other tricks at which mongrels are so adept. While Milton was teaching Flip, Dwight was teaching Milton. He taught him to shoot a rifle and to swim, although Milton never mastered much beyond the sidestroke and the dog paddle. Dwight even instructed his baby brother in the rough-and-tumble art of Abilene boyhood. For example, he showed him how to dive from a rafter in the hayloft, headfirst toward the bales, then turn a somersault in mid-air to land feetfirst. Unfortunately, the first time Milton tried he came down on his head and knocked himself out. Milton could never be an athlete like his older brothers, the stars of local baseball and football teams. He would practice and practice, but he managed only to make the third team in baseball, while in football he was reduced to the lowly status of water boy.[21]

Although Milton idolized his brothers and wanted with all his heart to be like them, he soon realized that it would be impossible for him to match them in athletics. He wanted them to be as proud of him as he was of them. But how? He decided to be a scholar. None of them was a scholar—they were content just to get by in school. Here was an area in which he clearly could exceed their accomplishments. There was a healthy respect for scholarship among the Eisenhowers, and all the boys, especially Dwight, encouraged him. He promised Milton a dollar for every A grade he brought home on his report card. The first semester Milton got five A's. Dwight never paid up, but Milton was nevertheless grateful for the encouragement.[22]

Milton began to read everything he could get his hands on, but his favorites were the adventure stories of the Rover Boys. Then one day, when Milton was about eight and Dwight about seventeen, Dwight glanced over his shoulder as Milton was coming to the climax of a Rover Boy book. With a glance, Dwight, always an extraordinarily fast reader, took in the last paragraph. One of the Rover Boys was racing the town bully to reach a damsel in distress. If the Rover Boy got there first, she was saved; if the bully won the race, she was doomed. Both boys were running at top speed. One hundred yards before the end of the race, the Rover Boy put on a burst of speed and got to the girl first.

Dwight snorted. "Isn't that ridiculous," he exclaimed in disgust. "How could he put on a 'burst of speed' if he was already running at top speed?"

Milton looked up at his brother, thought about what he had said, looked down at the book, folded it shut, and never read another Rover Boys story. He did not try to defend his heroes from his brother's scoffing but instead considered Dwight's point, realized immediately that he was right, and came to the logical conclusion: the Rover Boys stories were not worth reading. Both boys obviously had quick and active minds.[23]

As Milton grew so did Abilene. In his youth, he recalled, "everyone was putting something in." David added electricity, then running water to the

Eisenhower family portrait, 1902: *top row*, Edgar and Arthur; *second row*, Dwight, Earl, and Roy; *bottom row*, David, Milton, and Ida. *(Courtesy of Dwight D. Eisenhower Library, Abilene, Kansas)*

David and Ida were married on September 23, 1885. *(Courtesy of Dwight D. Eisenhower Library, Abilene, Kansas)*

Milton never forgot Ida's recipes. *(Courtesy of Dwight D. Eisenhower Library, Abilene, Kansas)*

David and Ida aged gracefully, a family characteristic. *(Courtesy of Dwight D. Eisenhower Library, Abilene, Kansas)*

Milton *(right)* and Earl care for the family chickens. *(Courtesy of Dwight D. Eisenhower Library, Abilene, Kansas)*

At age thirteen, Milton received a new suit for his graduation from Lincoln Grade School. *(Courtesy of Dwight D. Eisenhower Library, Abilene, Kansas)*

The year the United
States entered World
War I, Milton graduated
from high school at the
top of his class.
*(Courtesy of Dwight D.
Eisenhower Library,
Abilene, Kansas)*

"Scoop," cub reporter for the *Abilene Reflector (Courtesy of Dwight D.
Eisenhower Library, Abilene, Kansas)*

Milton's caption for this 1920 photograph in the family album read, "My first date with Helen Eakin was a golf game. Knickers were then in style!" *(Courtesy of Dwight D. Eisenhower Library, Abilene, Kansas)*

As vice-consul in Edinburgh, Scotland, in 1924, Milton *(second from left)* was popular with the Ramsay Lodge crowd. *(Courtesy of Dwight D. Eisenhower Library, Abilene, Kansas)*

Milton on his honeymoon at Virginia Beach *(Courtesy of Dwight D. Eisenhower Library, Abilene, Kansas)*

Milton described his marriage to Helen as "ideal." *(Courtesy of Dwight D. Eisenhower Library, Abilene, Kansas)*

Milton and "Daddy Roy" Eakin became lifelong friends. *(Courtesy of Dwight D. Eisenhower Library, Abilene, Kansas)*

house. Milton helped him put in a serviceable gas water heater. Paved streets replaced the old gravel roads. When Milton was fourteen the town acquired a telephone system.

Still Abilene remained unsophisticated. "The isolation was physical, political, and economic," as Milton remembered it, "as well as just a prevailing state of mind.... Self-sufficiency was the watchcry; personal initiative and responsibility were prized; radicalism was unheard of."

Abilene seemed then—and always remained in the Eisenhower boys' memories—the ideal place to grow up. They hardly noticed the day-after-day heat of close to one hundred degrees in the summer or the freezing, biting winds of winter. That they almost never traveled outside Dickinson County, that Kansas City seemed like the end of the world, went unnoticed because no one they knew traveled either. They accepted as perfectly natural that everyone knew and gossiped about everyone else, or that if you leaned your bike against the wall at the soda fountain and didn't come back until hours later, it would still be there.

Abilene had only one intellectual, Mr. Charles Moreau Harger, the newspaper editor, who would have a decisive impact on Milton's development. Aside from Harger, almost no one read serious literature or engaged in meaningful political or economic debate. When wheat prices went up after the turn of the century, Populism around Abilene passed away and the area returned to its traditional Republicanism.

Milton was different. When he was eleven years old, Woodrow Wilson was inaugurated as governor of New Jersey. Wilson caught Milton's imagination because Ida had commented proudly that Wilson had been born in Staunton, Virginia, only a few miles from her hometown, Mt. Sidney. When Wilson made Colonel Edward M. House his principal adviser, David commented that House was from Texas, where the Eisenhowers had lived for a couple of years and where Dwight had been born.

Milton's interest in Wilson "became almost an obsession." He read the Kansas City, Topeka, and Abilene newspapers avidly for news of his hero, especially during the 1912 Democratic National Convention. Whenever he could get an adult to stop and take him seriously, Milton would argue politics, praising the virtues of Wilson and House. Abilene was solidly for President William Howard Taft, the regular Republican nominee, so in most cases the listener would scoff at Milton's firmly expressed views and then dismiss the boy.[24]

For Milton, Abilene's dullness was relieved by an excellent public school system. Most of his teachers were spinsters, old-time "school marms," dedicated to their pupils, and determined to make sure all their charges learned their reading, writing, and arithmetic. It was rote learning, but it stuck. Throughout his life Milton would amaze his colleagues by his ability to memorize and retain facts and figures.

There were some gifted teachers, women who recognized Milton's specialness and gave to him fully of their time and talents. When Milton entered high school, Ida arranged for one, Miss Annie Hopkins, to live in the Eisenhower home for a year, free of charge; her only obligation was to teach Milton how to study effectively. Each evening after the Bible reading, in each subject—English, history, mathematics, Latin, and science—Milton had to quickly review the lesson and then study the assignment in detail, making notes. When he had completed the study, Miss Hopkins would have him go back and review. It was a traditional method which Milton utilized all his life. Thanks to his own abilities and Miss Hopkins's guidance, Milton got straight A's all through high school.

Milton recalled that once his Latin teacher, Miss Ault (she was known only as Miss Ault, never by her first name), very young and very serious about her work, kept him after class and accused him of using a "pony," or book of translations. Indignantly he denied it. "Milton Eisenhower," Miss Ault charged, "your translations are too perfect. You must be using a pony." Getting red in the face, Milton repeated his denial. Miss Ault persisted, so that night Milton asked Miss Hopkins to talk to Miss Ault. She did, and the next day after class Miss Ault apologized to Milton.[25]

Miss Ruth Hunt taught English. She told Milton that his writing was grammatically correct and logical but devoid of feeling, that it had no dynamism, it did not touch the emotions. She told him to write not just what he saw but how he felt about what he saw. He tried. She read the result, looked at Milton, and declared, "Now you are overdoing it. Cross out those adjectives." She kept after him, giving him the kind of personal attention and guidance any aspiring writer would envy. In his own words, he "never became a great writer," but in his first year in college he entered a short-story writing contest and won first prize, for which he was given a six-ounce, pure gold medal. Eventually he became an accomplished speech writer, often for others, including that master orator Franklin Delano Roosevelt.

Miss Ruth Harger also taught English. Her father, a Harvard graduate, not only was editor of the *Abilene Reflector* but in addition contributed regularly to the *Atlantic Monthly, Harpers,* and the other leading magazines of the day. Harger had numerous opportunities to become an editor on New York or Washington papers, but he preferred life in Abilene, even though his fellow townsmen considered him a bit snobbish and arrogant.

"He was a complete intellectual who never stopped thinking," Milton explained in defense. "It would irritate people when they would pass him on the street and he wouldn't speak. He was always preoccupied with his thinking." When his daughter was grown and had taken a position in the high school English department, Harger decided to run for Congress. He was defeated by the Abilene vote; the townspeople thought him too much of a snob. His daughter, too, with her sophisticated literary tastes, was thought to be rather high-and-mighty. Perhaps she was, but, like her colleagues, Miss Harger recognized Milton's abilities and encouraged him to develop them.[26]

In 1917, when America entered World War I, Milton graduated. Because he had skipped a grade, he was five months short of being eighteen years old. Nevertheless, he announced his intention to lie about his age and join the army with his friends. When Miss Harger heard about it, she called Milton to her office, scolded him, and announced that her father wanted to see him.[27]

Milton reported at the *Reflector* office. Of course Harger knew Milton— he knew everyone in the town of five thousand—and had watched his progress. The tall, slender, intense editor looked at the ill-at-ease seventeen-year-old across his desk. The boy's thick, dark hair was precisely parted on the left side and severely cut three inches above the top of his ear. Like his mother, he had a rounded chin, dark, deep-set eyes, and full, sensuous lips. Of normal height, he was thin, almost skinny, but with David's broad shoulders. Harger knew that he was outspoken but that he

thought about what he said and usually did some research on a subject before saying his piece. Harger also knew, from his daughter and from Milton's reputation in town, that the boy had ability.

Milton grinned his Eisenhower grin, out of nervousness more than confidence, and practically blurted out that Miss Harger had said the editor
wanted to see him. Indeed he did, Harger responded. He dismissed Milton's plan to enlist with a wave of his hand, leaned forward, stated that his
daughter had recommended Milton highly, and then mentioned that he
needed a reporter for the *Reflector.* The pay was eight dollars per week.
Would Milton like the job?

The offer was all Milton needed to change his mind. He instantly accepted and lost no time beginning work. Soon he was a common sight on
Abilene's Main Street, notebook in hand, pencil behind his ear, searching
for stories. He earned the nickname "Scoop," after "Scoop, the Cub Reporter," a popular comic strip of the day.

To Milton then and now, Harger was "a great teacher." He encouraged
his young reporter to seek out local-interest stories. Milton, bursting with
eagerness, did so. He picked up a piece of gossip: some mysterious kegs
had been unloaded at midnight at the creamery. Abilene was a dry town.
Highly pleased with his scoop, Milton wrote the story and turned it in.
Within an hour it was back on his desk. Harger had made one minor
change. With his blue pencil, he had crossed out the word *creamery* and
simply written in that the kegs had been unloaded "at the home of David J.
Eisenhower." Milton was cured forever from reporting gossip.

In the summer of 1917 the great event in Abilene was the appearance of
William Jennings Bryan at the Redpath Chautauqua. The Great Com-
moner, three-time Democratic nominee for president and former secre-
tary of state, was scheduled to speak at three o'clock in the afternoon.
Since the *Reflector* went to bed at three, to be delivered at half past four,
Harger told Milton to go to the Union Pacific Hotel and get an advance on
Bryan's speech.

As Milton told the story

*Remember, I was not yet eighteen, a neophyte. With knees shaking, I
entered the lobby of the hotel and shuffled over to the desk. I asked for
Mr. Bryan. The clerk waved his hand toward the barber shop, just off
the lobby, and said, "He's in there." I peeked around the corner and
saw a barber with abandon splashing soap on the great man's face.
That gave me a modicum of courage. When Bryan came into the lobby
I went toward him and he said, "Do you want to see me, young man?"*

*I explained the problem at our paper and asked for an advance of his
speech. "Oh, I always speak extemporaneously," he said. "Can you*

*write shorthand?" I couldn't, but I assured Mr. Bryan that I could write
fast. So he dictated a two-column story in good newspaper form—
lead, direct quotes, indirect quotes, and so on. When he finished he
asked if we had a cut [photograph] of him. I explained that it was a
single-column cut, not very good. He went to his room and brought
me an excellent two-column cut.*

Milton turned in the story. When he got paid on Friday, his envelope
contained twelve dollars instead of the usual eight. He went to Harger to
report the error. Harger said, "Milton, that was a great story you wrote on
the Bryan speech. You deserve the raise. You are learning quickly."

Milton felt guilty. He brooded about the raise all weekend. On Monday
he explained to Harger that he had not really written the story and did not
deserve the raise. Harger leaned back in his chair, grinned, and said, "If
you can get the real authority to do much of the work for you, you deserve whatever pay you get!"

What Milton had not written, and did not tell Harger about, was a conversation he had had with Bryan after Bryan had dictated the story. Milton had asked Bryan's opinion of Wilson. Bryan, who had resigned as
secretary of state in protest over Wilson's stern notes to Germany about
submarine warfare, had treated the young reporter to a half-hour tirade
against Wilson's foreign policy, both with regard to Germany and
Wilson's imperialistic adventures in Mexico, Central America, and the
Caribbean. Milton listened, nodded, and wrote nothing.

Later, he concluded that "I would never have succeeded as a career
newspaper reporter." He had assumed that Bryan was speaking in confidence and thus had failed to file the interview.[28] Had he filed it, it would
have made the national press, bringing prestige and honor to Harger and
the *Reflector*. But that willingness and ability to keep a confidence, while
it may indeed have prevented Milton from becoming a famous reporter,
became one of his most appreciated characteristics as an adviser to Cabinet officials and presidents. Had he not been that way, he might never
have advanced as far in government service as he did.

Harger responded to Milton's articulateness and eagerness to learn as
his high school teachers had done, giving him unlimited attention, encouraging his ambitions, and guiding his intellectual development. He set
out a reading course for his protégé, lending him from his personal
library de Tocqueville, Locke, Shakespeare, Tolstoy, and other classics.
They would then discuss the material at length.

Harger may have gotten as much out of the relationship as Milton did.
Aside from his wife and daughter, Milton was almost the only person in
town with whom he could have a serious intellectual discussion. For Mil-

ton, Harger supplied the intellectual stimulation that his parents and his high school teachers had encouraged but could not give. Harger taught Milton how to read critically, both in literature and in political reporting. Gently but firmly he criticized President Wilson's foreign policies, forcing Milton to leave behind his unquestioning partisanship and adopt a more balanced, objective view.

Milton, still an admirer, albeit modified, of Wilson, told Harger he wanted to emulate the president and make a career in either higher education or government service. The editor, whom Milton later called a "second father," heartily approved and began to narrow the focus of Milton's reading program. He gave him history, political science, and biographies of former presidents and world leaders. They talked about the kind of education that would best serve Milton's aspirations. Harger suggested a broad liberal arts education with an emphasis on political science.

Harger was the chairman of the board of regents of higher education in Kansas, a body that governed, among other institutions, Kansas State College in Manhattan, just sixty miles east of Abilene. Kansas State had a school of journalism, which in fact taught only two courses, the History of Journalism and the Ethics of Journalism. All the other courses were in the liberal arts. Harger suggested that such a program would be perfect for Milton, as it would give him a chance to earn both a living and a broad education.

In the fall of 1918 Milton accordingly set off for Manhattan. He discovered that all male students were automatically inducted into the Student Army Training Corps and that nonmilitary education was drastically curtailed for the duration of the war. He was taught to drill on a parade ground, the rudiments of infantry tactics, and so on, the idea being that he would get an officer's commission and go to France in 1919. He found himself wearing a uniform to his "classes," sleeping on a cot in the gymnasium, and serving as mess sergeant.

This was a long way from the intellectual stimulation he had sought. Then the influenza epidemic that swept the world in the winter of 1918/19 came to Manhattan. Milton caught it. He was rushed to the YMCA, where row after row of sick young men were stretched out on cots. Many died, including the four students surrounding Milton's cot. By the time he recovered, the Armistice had been signed and the Student Army Training Corps had been demobilized. Milton returned to Abilene to go back to work for Harger, with the idea of saving enough money to try college again in the fall of 1919.

Being Harger's chief reporter did not take up all his time, so he took on the additional summer job of managing one of the Redpath Chautauquas. He rode the trains from Louisiana to South Dakota, soliciting contracts from the small towns for the Chautauqua to come the following year. Milton was becoming a man of the world. Now twenty years old, he began to develop sophisticated manners, to wear stylish clothes, and to date women he met during his travels. During his second summer on the job he almost proposed to an accordion player. But his work for the Chautauqua ended in late summer, at the same time that Harger went east to be with an ailing family member. He had Milton take over as managing editor of the *Reflector*. Milton introduced banner headlines to the paper. Harger, hearing about the change, was indignant. He told his business partner on the phone that he was going to board the next train for Kansas and straighten things out. "Stay where you are," Harger's partner told him. "Our circulation has increased by one hundred and twenty-eight."[29]

In the fall of 1919 Milton returned to Manhattan, this time as a real student. He had new clothes, a pocket relatively full of money, some experience in business and in affairs of the heart, a reputation as a newspaperman, and a head full of ambition. His legacy from his parents was a sense of responsibility, a basic honesty, common sense and decency, and the constant admonition to seize the opportunities America presented. From his brothers he had learned how to compete, from his teachers how to read and write, and from Mr. Harger how to think. He was ready to go out into the world.

CHAPTER 3

"I Would Lose All Nervousness"

Kansas State, Ramsay Lodge, and Marriage

Aproduct of the 1862 Morrill Act, Kansas State was a small school in 1919. The student body, even with the influx of World War I veterans, only slightly exceeded three thousand. Except for a smattering of liberal arts courses, Kansas State remained devoted to agriculture, the sciences, and engineering. In fact, not until 1912 had the requirements for admission been raised to the equivalent of a high school education. Most of the faculty did not hold the Ph.D. degree, and there were few distinguished scholars. Salaries were so notoriously low that by 1920, with the expansion of the national economy, the faculty turnover rate reached as high as 75 percent among the engineers alone. Perched above the town of Manhattan and the Kaw River Valley, Kansas State was the archetypical "cow college."[1]

The students resembled the young men and women Eisenhower had known all his life. Generally referred to pejoratively as "aggies" by those at the more prestigious University of Kansas, in Lawrence, they were almost exclusively middle-class or poorer, and most represented their family's first generation in college. Characteristic of his tendency to look for the bright side, Eisenhower felt that their background worked to their advantage. He described them as "homogeneous in character, wholesome, unsophisticated men and women, eager to learn." Moreover, like Eisenhower, many were paying their own way, which gave them a strong incentive to work hard. The flapper era, just beginning in the colleges in the East, was unknown at Kansas State.[2]

Not surprisingly, the industrious Eisenhower prospered in this environment. He became one of the most prominent students on the campus, winner of numerous prizes, a straight-A student (except in biology, where his aversion to cutting up frogs resulted in a B), editor of the student newspaper, confidant of the president of the college, and the man who courted and won the hand of the most sought-after girl in town. Furthermore, despite Kansas State's provincialism, he found his years there broadening. In his first week on campus Eisenhower joined a fraternity, Sigma Alpha Epsilon, and moved into the fraternity house. Mother Pasmore was the housemother. Eisenhower fondly remembered the sixty-five-year-old woman as having "beautiful white hair and a majestic stature." She lived on the first floor and never invaded the students' territory on the upper two floors; nevertheless, "she was always on hand to serve as hostess when we brought dates to the house." She bought the food and supervised its preparation, then sat at the head of the table when it was served. She required shirts, ties, and coats at meals. "From her," Eisenhower said, "we learned how to act at dinner." Her presence ensured that "there was no riotous behavior in the house."

Eisenhower stood out at the SAE house, largely because even as a freshman he would not allow the upperclassmen to haze him. Other pledges were paddled and harassed for minor infractions of the rules or for no reason at all, but Eisenhower would not tolerate a paddling. He made it clear that he would leave the fraternity if anyone tried such childish nonsense on him. When he became an upperclassman, still living in the fraternity house, Eisenhower refused to paddle the freshmen.

One reason the other SAE's tolerated Eisenhower's independence was his contribution to the fraternity. The small-town and rural Kansas youths who were his fraternity brothers had a terrible time in their English composition classes, and they were exceedingly grateful to Eisenhower for his help with their themes. His usual advice was to relax and write as if they were writing letters home. He became the treasurer of the fraternity, and when Mother Pasmore became too old for the job, he took over the chore of buying the food.

The SAE's helped Eisenhower too. As he expressed it, "Fraternity life helped me throw off any timidity I might have possessed, to learn social requirements, and to live in harmony with others." In his first semester the position of editor of the student paper, the *Kansas State Collegian*, was vacant. Knowing of Eisenhower's experience on the *Reflector* and his talents as a writer, his fraternity brothers urged him to apply for the job. They told him that they could use their influence to help him get it and that it paid fifty dollars per month, which equaled what he had made as a reporter for the *Reflector*. He applied and got the job.

The paper was "practically an adjunct of the School of Journalism," the school in which he had enrolled, Eisenhower later explained. He remained editor until his graduation. In addition, he took on the task of proofreading *The Industrialist*, the college's official faculty and alumni newspaper, for which he was paid on an hourly basis; and he established Kansas State's first humor magazine, *The Brown Bowl*. In his sophomore year he began writing feature articles for the *Kansas City Star*, the *Topeka Daily Capital*, and, most importantly, for the numerous farm magazines. His usual practice was to find an interesting photograph and then write a story to go with it. He earned fifty dollars per article. With the money he earned he paid his tuition, room and board, and fraternity dues; bought a set of golf clubs and new clothes; financed his dates; and still ended up with seventeen hundred dollars in savings when he graduated. He also gained added knowledge that would prove extremely valuable during his government career and his own college presidencies.

His curriculum, aside from journalism and the required biology course, was heavily weighted towards the social sciences and humanities. His most valuable course was speech, where he had an outstanding teacher, Howard H. T. Hill, known affectionately by his students as "Doc." When he first had to speak before the class, Eisenhower recalled, "not only did my knees shake, but I couldn't get my breath."

Hill worked with him patiently, making countless suggestions. Eisenhower discovered that "if I had something I really felt strongly about and wanted to convey to others, I would lose all nervousness and tear into the subject." He became so adept at public speaking that as an upperclassman he won the Kansas State extemporaneous speaking contest.[3]

Encouraged, he entered the Missouri Valley (now the Big Eight) oratorical contest, and he won that too. The *Columbia Missourian* recorded, "Mr. Eisenhower was especially to be commended for his delivery. His voice was deep and clear, his gestures unforced. With a sufficient amount of ardor, he presented his argument convincingly."[4] In later life his associates would marvel at his oratorical skill, whether he was speaking before a small, informal group or a large audience, whether from a text or simply ad-libbing.[5]

As editor of the *Collegian* and proofreader of the *Industrialist* Eisenhower was in frequent contact with the faculty and with the president, William M. Jardine. Jardine took to Eisenhower just as Harger had done and many others would in the future. A tall, balding agricultural scientist, Jardine was an ex-cowboy from Idaho. Rough-hewn in appearance and speech, he was direct and casual in manner. "For God's sake young man," he told a student visitor on a warm day, "get your coat off, you're in Kansas."[6]

Jardine brought Eisenhower into his family circle, frequently inviting him to his home for dinner. Their discussions, starting with this or that detail from one of Eisenhower's stories, would cover the spectrum, with the emphasis on national politics, Jardine's passionate interest. In a sense Jardine took the place of Harger in Eisenhower's life, and he had an even more profound effect on it.

Eisenhower's closest friend was a fraternity brother, Jack Eakin. The young men were inseparable, doing everything together—dates, golf games, classes, studies. Jack lived in Manhattan, so the two friends would frequently go to his home for a meal, as well as to make music. Eisenhower played the piano; Eakin the saxophone. One day in his sophomore year Eisenhower went to the Eakins' to practice. He already knew Mrs. Eakin, but he had not met the other members of the family—Mr. Eakin and Jack's brothers and sister. When the friends walked into the living room, Mr. Eakin was sitting in an easy chair, with his fifteen-year-old daughter, Helen, on his lap. Eisenhower scarcely paid any attention to the girl, who was attractive enough but five years younger than himself. He did shake hands heartily with her father.

LeRoy Eakin—"Daddy Roy" to his family, "L. R." to acquaintances— was an impressive man. Everything about him was big. Tall, well-built, with high cheek bones, a large head set off by a prominent nose, wide mouth, and conspicuous dimples, and nicely dressed, he had an engaging smile and a highly developed sense of humor. His warmth, sincerity, and fun-loving ways attracted people to him at once, as happened with Eisenhower. Eakin had a genius for business. Coming from Ohio with only a high school education, he had moved to Kansas before the turn of the century and opened a small retail store. He had expanded after making a trip to St. Louis, where he had bought every article in a fairly large department store that was having a "fire sale" of goods damaged by smoke. Eakin had hauled the articles back to Manhattan, cleaned them up, and sold them all at a substantial profit. That had given him his stake, which he had invested in some Kansas oil fields and real estate. He soon owned the major bank in town and added a wholesale business to his interests. By the time Eisenhower met him Eakin was a genuine millionaire, the only one in 1920 Manhattan and one of the few in Kansas.[7]

Eakin already knew something of Eisenhower, both from his son Jack and from President Jardine, who was one of Eakin's closest friends. He was much impressed by the young man. Eisenhower's appearance added to his reputation. He had let his hair grow longer, letting it come down to his ears, and had added a curl at the top; he even had a hint of sideburn. His face although fuller, was still dominated by his large mouth and full lips. He wore a stylish bow tie and a handsome tweed jacket.

Eakin quickly joined the ranks of those who wanted to help push Eisenhower's career along. In the spring of Eisenhower's junior year Eakin called him into his office at the bank. A bit apprehensive, Eisenhower went. Eakin asked him what his plans were, and Eisenhower replied that he wanted to go into either education or government work, with government somewhat in the lead. Eakin, always direct, replied, "Well, when you finish at Kansas State, how would you like to go to Harvard Law School? That would be the best preparation for government service."

Eisenhower shook his head. "I can't afford it," he replied. He added that he would probably take a job at Kansas State instead.

Eakin interrupted. "Begin to plan your clothes and other things because you're going to go to Harvard. I'll pay for it."

Again Eisenhower shook his head. "Mr. Eakin, it is kind of you to risk financing me, but you do not know that I would ever be able to pay you back."

Eakin gave him a sharp look and snapped, "Did I say anything about your repaying me?"

Still Eisenhower refused. No son of David and Ida Eisenhower could accept charity. Decades later he remembered, "It would have violated my Puritan sense of how one was supposed to behave." The incident strengthened the two men's feelings towards each other; for over the next half-century, in Eisenhower's words, "he meant the world to me." Despite the difference in age, they became the closest of friends.[8]

As a frequent visitor in the Eakin household, Eisenhower saw a lot of Helen. She was her father's darling. Like David Eisenhower, Eakin had a soft spot for girls, especially his own daughter. He did not much like music, but he would sit for hours and listen to his son Jack and Eisenhower play together only because Helen would sit on his lap to listen. He spoiled her shamelessly, giving her anything she wanted, from clothes to parties to a car.

In Eisenhower's senior year Helen entered Kansas State as a freshman. He suddenly began to pay more attention to her, as well he might, for she had blossomed into a great beauty. Her short, dark hair swirled in lovely curls on the top of her head, with an enticing bang down the middle of her forehead. Her face was perfectly symmetrical, soft but firm, with her father's high cheekbones. She had blue eyes and a classic nose and mouth. A bit slim, her clothes highlighted her handsome figure, which was rapidly changing from that of a girl into a woman's. She had long, beautiful fingers. With her father's—for that matter Ida Eisenhower's—gay disposition and fun-loving ways, she was at once charming, attractive, and appealing.

By this stage in his college career Eisenhower had already had a couple of love affairs. In his freshman year he had become infatuated with a "lovely girl, black hair, black sparkling eyes, straight as a ramrod, good dancer, not given to light talk." He asked her to go steady, but she preferred to play the field. That ended that relationship. The next year he found "a cute little girl, absolutely beautiful," and again thought he was in love. He gave her his SAE pin, which amounted to a sort of unofficial engagement. The affair lasted for a year.[9]

So he was unattached in his senior year, and now Helen seemed to him to be the most desirable creature in the world. They began dating. Helen liked golf, which had become a passion with Eisenhower. He would go to the Eakin house at 6:00 A.M., Helen would drive them to the golf course, and they would play nine holes before returning to the Eakins' for breakfast. For the next year they were "steadies," refusing to date anyone else.

Eisenhower's preoccupation with Helen did not curtail his campus activities. During Eisenhower's senior year an organizer for the Republican National Committee came to Kansas State. After talking with some members of the administration, he went to see Eisenhower, who by then had shed his youthful enthusiasm for Wilson in favor of the more traditional Kansas Republicanism. The organizer asked Eisenhower if he would form a college Republican club at Kansas State. Eisenhower agreed and put a notice in the *Collegian*, calling for an organizational meeting. The result was a near-disaster: only three other students showed up. Making matters worse, another journalism student, who wrote an occasional feature article for the Democratic *St. Louis Post Dispatch*, had decided to cover the meeting. Eisenhower learned that he intended to write a humorous piece on the four Republicans at Kansas State.

Eisenhower, who had been elected president of the club, spent the night on the telephone, calling every friend he had in the neighboring fraternities, as well as signing up all the SAE's he could find. In the *Collegian* the next morning he published a list of one hundred names, all charter members of the Kansas State Republican Club!

The organizer for the national committee, much impressed, suggested to Eisenhower that he take the examination required to apply for a post in the foreign service of the United States. Eisenhower filled out the forms, took the examination, and then forgot about the matter.[10]

In 1924, when Eisenhower graduated, Jardine offered, and Eisenhower accepted, a post on the Kansas State faculty to teach English and journalism. Helen wanted to take one of his classes, but he would not allow it. His refusal proved meaningless because two weeks into the semester he suffered an appendicitis attack and underwent surgery. Jardine wrote him a note: "What in the world has gone wrong with you? I was just twenty-six years of age when I had my appendix out and I have been glad ever since. No doubt the next thing I hear of you doing is accepting a college presidency somewhere."[11]

Eisenhower had scarcely left the hospital when he received a telegram from Secretary of State Charles Evans Hughes. He had finished first in the examination for the foreign service, and Hughes was offering him a post in the U.S. consulate in Edinburgh, Scotland.

Eisenhower was torn. He had just begun his career in education; if he stayed at Kansas State, he could earn a decent income as a faculty member while simultaneously pursuing his studies towards a Ph.D. in political science. But he had always leaned towards government service, and a position in such an exotic place as Scotland was tempting. He brooded over the problem and then decided to ask Jardine for his advice.

Jardine listened as Eisenhower outlined his alternatives. The president leaned back in his chair and said, "Milton, that's the sort of thing you have to figure out for yourself. But you're fired. There's no place at this institution for you for the next two years." As an expression of shock came over Eisenhower's face, Jardine continued, "If you want to come back then, I'll see what I can do for you. Now go away and make up your own mind!"[12]

Stunned, Eisenhower stared at the president. Somewhat naively, he had expected Jardine to plead with him to stay on at Kansas State, to speak eloquently of the rewards of a career in higher education, to appeal to Eisenhower's sense of loyalty to the college and the state of Kansas. Further, although Eisenhower had only the vaguest notion of a faculty member's rights, he suspected that even the president did not have the right to fire an instructor at the beginning of an academic year.

He continued to stare, speechless. A trace of a smile came over Jardine's lips. At once Eisenhower's grin appeared. He began to laugh. Rushing out of Jardine's office, he sent a telegram of acceptance to Secretary Hughes, called Ida and had her send his steamer trunk to Manhattan, and went to a travel agency to get railroad tickets to New York and a berth on the SS *United States*, which sailed later in the month from New York to Plymouth.[13]

The Eakins were still in Wisconsin, where the family went every summer to fish. Eisenhower called them with his exciting news. At Helen's insistence, the family abruptly ended their vacation to return to Manhattan. Helen wanted to make sure she had a chance to say farewell before Eisenhower left.

Although for Eisenhower the journey across the Atlantic was the height of adventure—after all, except for his stints with the Chautauqua, he had never been away from Kansas—once he arrived at the consulate in Edinburgh he found the work quite routine. His duties comprised handling applications from individuals and families who wished to emigrate to the United States, preparing studies of Scottish industry, and writing reports on the native economy. His more enduring rewards came from outside of the office. "My naiveté was monumental," Eisenhower later said. His two years in Scotland introduced him to a whole new world. He took Spanish lessons and other graduate courses at the University of Edinburgh and traveled throughout the United Kingdom on a motorcycle. Most significantly, he took a room at Ramsay Lodge, a university hostel beside the world-famous Edinburgh Castle. Fifty students lived there, most from the school of medicine. They came from England, Scotland, Wales, South Africa, Egypt, China, Canada, India, and Southeast Asia. Intelligent, hard-working, and friendly, they accepted the raw-boned American immediately. They joked, exchanged barbs, and drank together. They were serious about their studies, but after the day's assignment was completed they would invariably talk late into the night.[14]

The discussions provided an advanced education for Eisenhower, who later remarked that they contributed as much as his parents' attitudes had to his sense of objectivity. He had thought that he had learned how to think critically from Harger, but at Ramsay Lodge he found that his views on international relations were hopelessly unsophisticated and unblushingly, unthinkingly pro-American. The British Commonwealth students attacked the United States for failing to enter the League of Nations, for failing to cancel the British war debt, for its imperialism in Central America, and for a score of other crimes and shortcomings, real and imagined. Eisenhower defended his country and gave as good as he got, charging that Britain was the most imperialistic and greedy power in the world. His friends responded that His Majesty's Empire had maintained peace in the world and that if the empire broke up, wars would flare up everywhere.

These were not shouting matches but serious conversations among serious young men. From them, Eisenhower recalled, "I learned to compromise, to see the other fellow's point of view, to acknowledge that my country had made mistakes."

On Saturday nights the Ramsay Lodge students would go on a spree. A frequent practice was to move from tavern to tavern, having one drink in each, the object being to visit thirty or more establishments and still be able to walk home. Eisenhower, with no experience in drinking, would call a halt after the first stop or two.

When he left, in 1926, the students gave him a farewell dinner. They served Moselle wine, the only drink Eisenhower knew. Unknown to him, they had spiked the wine with brandy. He became hopelessly drunk, made an unintelligible speech, and passed out. When he woke the next morning he had a monstrous hangover. Ignorant of what was wrong, he moaned that someone should call a doctor. His friends roared with laughter. They filled him full of black coffee and aspirin and escorted him to the railroad station. Then, in the Scottish tradition, they stuffed him into the train, still moaning, through an open window and, with a cheer and waves of good-by, handed him a bottle of Moselle.[15]

Eisenhower's departure was brought about by the same man who had, in effect, sent him to Scotland—Jardine. In 1924 Jardine had written an article for a national magazine attacking the McNary-Haugen bill, an early attempt by America's farmers—already caught up in a depression— to establish the principle of parity by fixing agricultural prices within the United States while selling the surplus on the world market at depressed prices. The McNary-Haugen bill had widespread support in the farm states, but conservative President Calvin Coolidge adamantly opposed it. He liked Jardine's article and felt that having the president of a midwestern agricultural college in his Cabinet would strengthen his position. He invited Jardine to become his secretary of agriculture, and Jardine accepted.

Shortly after joining Coolidge's Cabinet, Jardine cabled Eisenhower, asking the young man to come to Washington to be his assistant. Once again Eisenhower was torn. He loved Scotland, and, despite the routine, he enjoyed his work at the consulate. He had almost decided to make a career in the foreign service and was already imagining that he might someday become an ambassador. He also appreciated the security he had in the foreign service and did not want to take a job as a political appointee, with the very real possibility that he would be out of work when the next administration came to Washington. He had become engaged to Helen, via correspondence. Perhaps thinking of his parents' experience, he did not want to begin married life with serious career uncertainties.[16]

Eisenhower wrote Jardine, expressing his hesitation. Jardine responded that there was an opening in the Department of Agriculture on the staff of the Office of Information, a civil-service post. He arranged for Eisenhower to take the regular Civil Service Commission examination. Eisenhower did so, again came out first, and early in 1926 got the appointment.

Aside from his friendship for Jardine and the potential benefits of being so close to a Cabinet secretary, an inducement for Eisenhower to move to Washington was Helen's presence there. Mr. Eakin had moved to the city, where he lived in a grand suite in the Mayflower Hotel. He had gone to Washington to be with Jardine, his close friend; while there, according to Kansas rumor, he paid Jardine's entertainment bills (Cabinet officers made only ten thousand dollars per year, not nearly enough for a man of modest means to meet his social obligations).[17]

With his Midas touch, one of Eakin's first decisions in Washington was to buy up farmland across the Potomac River from the Lincoln Memorial. He purchased two thousand acres, running out past Falls Church to Fairfax. When the Memorial Bridge was built shortly thereafter, the new highway went right through his properties. Helen, meanwhile, had entered The George Washington University, where she was majoring in French language and literature.

When Eisenhower arrived in Washington, he and Helen quickly confirmed face-to-face the engagement they had made by mail. They would have married right then, in the summer of 1926, but her parents insisted that she make a world tour with them before settling down. It was not that they objected to Eisenhower; indeed, Eakin had taken Eisenhower aside and told him, "If Helen is going to marry anyone—and I don't want to lose her—I'm glad it will be you."[18]

They were married on Columbus Day, 1927, in the presidential suite at the Mayflower. Helen wore a "gorgeous, white beaded dress." Earl Eisenhower was there: in Milton's words he "was tight but behaving himself." Older brother Dwight, by then a major in the Army and known to everyone by his nickname "Ike," was also present, along with his wife Mamie. Helen wanted a small wedding, so the guest list was kept to thirty-five. Ike wore his full-dress, white uniform and his saber. At Mamie's insistence, he gave Helen his saber to cut the wedding cake. The minister was the leader of the Washington Christian Church, to which the Eakins belonged. After their marriage the young couple joined the Episcopal Church. To this day Eisenhower attends Episcopal services every Sunday morning.

Milton and Helen went to New York City and Virginia Beach for their honeymoon, then set up housekeeping in an apartment at the Mayflower. Eisenhower would not allow Eakin to give him or his wife any money, but he did take advantage of "Daddy Roy" 's special wholesale privileges to buy furniture, and he did not object when Eakin gave Helen fur coats and jewelry. Altogether, for a twenty-six-year-old just beginning a civil-service career, Eisenhower lived well. By the age of twenty-six he had come a long way from Abilene.[19]

His work for Jardine quickly threw him into the higher reaches of government. After Eisenhower had worked for a short period at the Office of Information, Jardine arranged for his young protégé to become his assistant—he was the first civil-service assistant to a Cabinet officer. He controlled the Secretary's appointment calendar and dictated his correspondence (and proved adept at signing Jardine's name). Most important, he wrote Jardine's speeches, prepared his congressional testimony ("He was highly skilled but could butcher the king's English more than any other public figure who ever lived," Eisenhower later said of Jardine), and became Jardine's liaison with Congress, where the McNary-Haugen bill was still a burning issue. Twice the bill passed, and twice Coolidge vetoed it (without suggesting any alternative to help the farmers, as Jardine and Eisenhower had urged him to do); neither time could Congress override the veto. Before he was twenty-eight years old Eisenhower had obtained an intimate, practical knowledge of American government and its methods of operation.[20]

He was also learning a great deal about the United States. As secretary of agriculture, Jardine traveled constantly, usually taking his friend and assistant with him. Once they arrived in Butte, Montana, when the temperature was forty degrees below zero to attend the annual dinner of the National Wool Growers Association. Eisenhower, still shivering, found himself seated beside Jardine at the head table. To his surprise, the toastmaster asked him to say a few words before Jardine spoke.

"I don't make speeches," Eisenhower blurted out. "I only write them." Everyone laughed. Jardine rose and said, "Anything good in what I have to say is mine; anything else I attribute to Milton Eisenhower."[21]

In the spring of 1928 the position of director of information at the Department of Agriculture became available. It was a highly responsible post. The director supervised the publication of hundreds of farm bulletins, distributed by Congressmen to their constituents by the millions of copies. He controlled a large press service and operated a nationwide daily radio program that was carried on 134 stations around the country, as well as coordinated the information activities of the maze of bureaus that comprised one of the largest executive departments in the government. Despite Eisenhower's relative youth—he was still but twenty-eight years old—Jardine appointed Eisenhower to the position.

Eisenhower's was already a remarkable success story, almost too good to be true. He had moved from triumph to triumph in his studies, his work, his marriage, his social life. He had deeply impressed all the men he had worked for, winning their confidence and trust. He was on the go every minute of every day. He was completely self-confident without being cocky. Arthur S. Flemming, who met Eisenhower in 1927 and who would himself become secretary of the Department of Health, Education, and Welfare, recalled, "He had a very fine understanding of the issues of the day—and was very much involved with them. I was most impressed that a young man would already be working at such a high level."[22]

CHAPTER 4

"Love Life of the Bullfrog"

Washington Bureaucrat

From 1929 to 1942 Eisenhower worked his way up in the Department of Agriculture, serving under both Republicans and Democrats, while refusing to take a partisan stance himself, eventually establishing himself as the number-two man. During the New Deal the Department of Agriculture was one of the largest and most exciting of all the executive departments. Eisenhower developed an intimate relationship with its colorful secretary, Henry Wallace, and was almost as close to President Roosevelt.

He became an expert on the inner workings of the American government and highly skilled in the art of practical politics. As his responsibilities grew, so did his reputation. His home life was happy and serene, his marriage blessed by the birth of a son in 1930. Altogether, his years as a Washington bureaucrat were satisfying and rewarding.

Although Jardine had been one of Hoover's earliest and strongest backers, when Hoover entered the White House he asked Jardine to head up the new Federal Farm Board and appointed Arthur M. Hyde to the post of secretary of the Department of Agriculture. Protected by his civil-service status, Eisenhower avoided the political hatchet. Hyde was a former governor of Missouri, a successful automobile dealer, and an intensely partisan Republican. He knew a great deal more about politics than he did about farming or economics, an unfortunate circumstance for the American farmers, who remained mired in a severe depression.

Forced to address the farm problem, Hoover summoned a special session of Congress and asked it to create the Federal Farm Board (under Jardine). The board would help establish and finance farmer-owned and operated cooperatives which would acquire warehousing and marketing facilities, purchase and hold farm commodities until the price went up, and establish clearinghouses for the more orderly marketing of perishable commodities. Eisenhower remembered comparing the idea of buying and holding commodities when prices were low and selling them as prices went up, to the ever-normal granary operation of Egypt in Biblical times. Hoover's draft message proposing the creation of the Federal Farm Board also called for higher tariffs on industrial goods and, in certain instances, on agricultural products.

A few days after Hoover's inaugural Eisenhower accompanied Secretary Hyde to the White House to review the proposed program. They went to the Cabinet room, where each was given a draft of the message. Hyde was delighted. Eisenhower was not.

"I swallowed hard," he later recalled, "and said that in my judgment the statement was on shaky ground." He doubted that withholding products from market in the United States would have much effect on commodity prices, which were set on a world market. Raising the tariff on industrial goods, meanwhile, would simply reduce American imports, and consequently American exports, which were still largely farm surpluses. The net effect, he feared, would be to make a bad situation worse.

Hyde, unimpressed, dismissed Eisenhower's objections with a wave of his hand. At this point Hoover's assistant, George Akerson, came into the Cabinet room. He listened to Eisenhower's objections and Hyde's praise for the message, then took both their comments to Hoover. The president, unconvinced by Eisenhower's points, left the proposal unchanged, and Congress quiescently made it the law. Farm prices continued to fall and then plummeted after the stock market crash in the fall of 1929.[1]

Dutifully Eisenhower went on with his work. His job was to serve the president, despite his personal misgivings. He organized the "National Farm and Home Hour," a countrywide radio program, and was the editor of the *Yearbook of U.S. Agriculture*. In 1930 he coauthored *The U.S. Department of Agriculture: Its Structure and Functions*, a comprehensive survey that became the standard work on the subject. On a daily basis he oversaw all the informational activities of the huge department. In May of 1930 John R. Fleming, who would later become foreign editor of *U.S. News & World Report*, joined Eisenhower's staff. Years later Fleming stated that "Milton always did his homework. At budget meetings, I was struck by how well he knew information about all areas of the department budget. The budget people always listened when he spoke."[2]

Nevertheless, Eisenhower ran afoul of that bane of the Washington bureaucracy, the disloyal subordinate. An ambitious member of his staff sent voluminous documents to a Republican senator, charging that Eisenhower had manipulated information to help the Democrats. The senator complained to Hyde, who demanded an explanation. With some heat, Eisenhower flatly asserted, "I am as objective as humanly possible in my position and my work is non-partisan and impartial."

Hyde acknowledged the explanation, but in response to the senator he defended Eisenhower not on the grounds that he was objective. On the contrary, he argued that Eisenhower was as good and loyal a Republican as the senator himself. Eisenhower objected that he should not be defended on such grounds. Without Eisenhower's knowledge, Hyde took the issue to Akerson at the White House. Akerson called Eisenhower in, listened to his side of the story, and assured him that President Hoover would uphold a policy of nonpartisanship by career officers.[3]

But Eisenhower's involvement in the politics of the Hoover administration, and especially those of Secretary Hyde, was far from over. A short time later Senator Pat Harrison, Democrat from Mississippi, sarcastically charged on the Senate floor that the Department of Agriculture was wasting enormous sums of the taxpayers' money by publishing ridiculous farm bulletins. He waved above his head one issue which he said was entitled "Love Life of the Bullfrog." The story made the front pages across the country, and over the next week Eisenhower's office received a thousand requests for the bulletin.

Hyde, furious, ordered Eisenhower to attack Harrison personally. Eisenhower was caught in the middle of one of those ridiculous tempests that Washington and the national press so love. He knew that to directly attack a U.S. senator would destroy his position as a civil servant, so if Hyde persisted in his demand, he would have to resign. "The prospect did not at all appeal to me," he later wrote. "By then I had become completely absorbed in and fascinated by the functioning of the federal government." But if it was necessary, he was prepared to resign. He had had numerous offers for employment outside the government, including several to be editor of various national magazines, at a much higher salary than the government paid.

So Eisenhower ignored Hyde's directive. Instead he issued a factual press release that neither named the senator nor questioned his good faith. It simply explained that the Bureau of Fisheries of the Department of Commerce years ago had issued a technical bulletin on the production of frog legs and that the Department of Agriculture had never published anything about fish, frogs, or any other aquatic life.[4]

Once again there were headlines. The press repeated Harrison's charges, burying Eisenhower's explanation at the bottom of the story. That week the department received two thousand requests for "Love Life of the Bullfrog." Hyde was almost speechless with rage, but he did manage to let Eisenhower know how he felt. He summoned Eisenhower to his office and loudly declared that together they would go to Hoover himself for a "showdown."

Before going to the White House, Eisenhower spoke to Akerson by telephone. Akerson provided Hoover with this background, which made it easier for the president to remain calm while Hyde, red-faced and barely able to suppress his anger, demanded that Hoover set Eisenhower straight on the responsibilities of a highly placed officer in a Republican administration. Instead Hoover politely chastened Hyde, then turned to Eisenhower and reaffirmed his policy of nonpartisanship by career civil-service personnel. The president suggested that Eisenhower go on the "National Farm and Home Hour" and give the facts about the bullfrog story.

Eisenhower spoke for fifteen minutes over 134 radio stations. He explained that the Department of Agriculture knew nothing about frogs and had never published anything on the subject. For those who were interested, the Department of Commerce did have a bulletin on frogs; it was scientific in character and had nothing to do with the love life of frogs but was valuable to anyone who wanted to raise frogs for market. It could be purchased from the superintendent of documents for ten cents.

The newspapers repeated Harrison's charges and again only incidentally mentioned Eisenhower's rebuttal. That week Eisenhower's office received five thousand letters asking for "Love Life of the Bullfrog." Hyde was seething. He went on the radio himself and delivered a blistering attack on Harrison and all Democrats. To Hyde's chagrin and Eisenhower's secret pleasure, that week there were ten thousand requests for the bulletin.[5]

Finally Hyde decided to let go of the issue, the tempest died down, and Eisenhower remained in his post, still nonpartisan. He had learned invaluable lessons about newspaper coverage, public perceptions, and the futility of trying to correct a false story once it has gotten started. Throughout his later career he would warn that by vociferously denying an inaccurate statement an individual, or organization of individuals, may very well bring more attention to the statement than it otherwise would have received. The short-term consequences, however, were quite unpleasant. His last two years under Hyde were Eisenhower's only unhappy ones in Washington. The secretary continued to make caustic remarks about Eisenhower's lack of loyalty to the Republican party. Meanwhile, the Depression worsened, Hoover's popularity disappeared, and all of Washington sank into a profound gloom.

In his domestic life Eisenhower lived in a state of near-bliss. He and Helen adjusted to each other with only "mild difficulty." She missed some of the extravagances she had become accustomed to while living with her father, while he thought that in comparison to his mother, his wife had terribly expensive tastes. But he, too, liked and appreciated fine things. They bought only the best furniture, preferring to wait until they could afford a quality piece rather than buy a cheap one. Most items came from Carson, Pirie, Scott and Company, in Chicago, where Mr. Eakin could get them at a wholesale price. They moved from the Mayflower to a spacious apartment off Connecticut Avenue. Whereas they now had a fully equipped kitchen and a grand piano, they slept on a boxspring and mattress on the bedroom floor and ate at a card table surrounded by four camp chairs. In his retirement, Eisenhower gleefully remembered the night he and Helen entertained a vice-president of CBS and his wife at that table and chairs.[6]

Helen took charge of the family finances—once Eisenhower had decided that she had learned the value of a dollar—and of their social life. They mutually decided that he would never bring his office work or problems home, which was to be a haven from the problems of his career, a sort of sanctuary. Helen filled the apartment with books, music, a multitude of friends, bridge, and an occasional poker game. She was not a gossip and much preferred not knowing any details about her husband's work because in her ignorance she could not be "pumped" or manipulated by the wives of other government servants. The Eisenhowers continued this practice throughout their marriage.[7] In 1930 they had their first child, Milton Jr., nicknamed "Buddy." As a father, Eisenhower was at times preoccupied and often more than a trifle stern. Between his twelve to fourteen hour days at work and his active social life, he did not have as much time for his son as either would have liked.[8]

Eisenhower and Helen loved to spend time outdoors. One of their favorite activities was to launch their canoe on the Potomac north of Washington and then paddle downstream to the Lincoln Memorial. "We were good at timing," he later wrote. "The concert by the Washington Symphony Orchestra would start a few minutes after our arrival. We kidded: They had waited for us!"[9]

In the early thirties the Eisenhowers moved into their first house, at Twenty-fourth Street and Massachusetts Avenue. Dwight and Mamie lived within walking distance, in the Wyoming Apartments, just off Connecticut Avenue. Ike was then the principal assistant to Army Chief of Staff Douglas MacArthur. Being neighbors strengthened and deepened their already close relationship. They spent three or four evenings a week together. "We were not only intimate," Milton Eisenhower later said, "but we found that we liked to talk over our problems together." Ike added that "our thought processes dovetailed very closely."[10]

Milton was a bright star on the Washington scene, known everywhere as a "comer," while Ike, although holding a responsible position, was only a major in the Army. Around Washington the older brother, if he was known at all, was known as "Milton's brother."

Both brothers were delighted that their wives got along famously also. Helen and Mamie became, and remained, close friends. Once, in the twenties, when Ike and Mamie were about to leave Washington after a brief visit, Helen said to Milton, "You know we've so much enjoyed this visit from Ike and Mamie, I think I'll get her an orchid corsage for a going-away present. It'll probably be the only time in her life she'll ever have an orchid corsage." The line was much remembered and quoted in later years, when newspaper photographs frequently showed Mamie swathed in mink and orchids.[11]

In the thirties Milton was a great help to Ike, the newcomer to Washington. General John J. Pershing had selected Ike to write a guide to the American battlefields in Europe; Milton provided editorial assistance. The result impressed and pleased Pershing, which added to Ike's reputation in the Army, even though it did not win him a promotion.[12] Milton also took Ike along to parties and dinners, where he introduced him to high-ranking government officials and the Washington press corps. Years later a reporter remembered Milton's approaching him at one such function and saying, "Please don't go until you've met my brother; he's a major in the army and I know he's going places."[13]

The relationship was mutually beneficial. As MacArthur's assistant, Ike spent a good deal of his time on Capitol Hill, testifying before congressional committees. In their daily walk home together, or in their late-night discussions, Ike gave his younger brother additional insights into Congress and its members. They enjoyed arguing with each other over political theory, Milton inclining towards liberal idealism, Ike being more pragmatic. Both had a logical mind and were open to reason. As in the Rover Boys episode, Ike had an ability to cut through to the heart of the matter. He could support his position with facts and figures so well that occasionally his responses would leave Milton "embarrassed."[14]

Both had inherited that big grin, happy disposition, and fun-loving way. They played many practical jokes on each other, and on their wives. One favorite was to call the other's wife late in the afternoon. "Hello, Helen darling," Ike would say. "I'll be getting home late tonight."

Milton would make a similar call to Mamie, then chat with her about the affairs of the day in MacArthur's office and their plans for the evening. Their voices were so similar that neither wife ever suspected the hoax.[15]

The brothers had also developed a taste for good whiskey, almost impossible to get in the prohibition era. Milton solved the problem by making his own. He had two barrels, charred on the inside, filled with corn liquor, which he placed directly behind the coal furnace in the basement. Every time he went down to fix the furnace he would kick each of the barrels to stir the liquid. He let the whiskey sit for ten to twelve months, which was almost unheard of in those days, and thus earned a reputation for making the best homemade bourbon in Washington. Once again, their Abilene background served the Eisenhowers well.[16]

On March 4, 1933, Franklin Roosevelt was inaugurated as president of the United States. For Eisenhower, the pain of working for Hyde was finished, for Henry Wallace took over as secretary of agriculture. "A new style and vigorous action" replaced the old, tired, defeated administration. On his first day on the job Wallace called Eisenhower into his office, along with the other top officers, complimented them for their research and educational work, and asked for their cooperation in beginning a New Deal for American agriculture. "He made clear," Eisenhower wrote years later, "that it was essential to transform the department immediately into a vast action agency to restore parity of income to American farmers."[17]

Henry A. Wallace was perhaps the most flamboyant secretary the Department of Agriculture had ever had. He may also have been the best prepared for the job. His father, Henry C. Wallace, had held the post under presidents Harding and Coolidge, preceding Jardine. Natives of Iowa, for three generations the Wallaces had edited *Wallace's Farmer*, America's leading farm journal. A protégé of black scientist George Washington Carver, the elder Wallace was an outstanding plant geneticist who had started crossbreeding at the age of eight. Eventually he produced a high-yield strain of corn that made him famous and rich. In addition, he was a leader in the field of agricultural economics, the first to devise a corn-hog ratio chart that determined whether a farmer would make more money selling his corn or feeding it to the hogs. He also devised a system of predicting corn yields on the basis of rainfall and temperature records.[18]

To Eisenhower, the new secretary was "one of the most dedicated and intellectually honest men I have ever known. He was also an ideal administrator—one who, once policies and programs were formulated, delegated major administrative responsibilities and trusted those to whom delegations were made." Eventually, of course, Wallace's personal ambitions and lenient attitude towards the Soviet Union alienated him from most of the Democratic party. When Eisenhower worked for him, however, he was a solid New Dealer and a strong advocate of the then novel and exciting economic theory of deficit spending. (J. M. Keynes did not publish his *The General Theory of Employment, Interest and Money* until 1936.) He rejected Hoover's idea of fighting the Depression by balancing the federal budget. When Eisenhower remonstrated with his boss, saying he was appalled by the growing budget deficits, Wallace responded that a governmental budget need not be balanced in any particular year; the important consideration was that it be balanced over an economic cycle.[19]

The Department of Agriculture was one of the biggest spenders in the New Deal, due to the Agricultural Adjustment Act (AAA), legislation that took off from the old McNary-Haugen ideas and went beyond them. It was financed by processing taxes on certain commodities; it provided for government purchases of surpluses, which were sold abroad for whatever price they could command; it paid farmers to reduce production by allowing the land to lie fallow. The hope was that lowered production would lead to higher prices.

Eisenhower's firmly held conservative economic views put him in opposition to much of the AAA. He was not opposed to all of it, however, by any means. One of his aides later recalled, "Although Milton was a Republican, he felt things were in pretty bad shape. By 1932 he thought it was necessary to have a new administration. His sympathies were with the new administration. He was delighted with the appointment of Wallace."[20]

Nevertheless, Eisenhower was a Republican in a Democratic administration. Inevitably, Democratic partisans demanded that Wallace fire him. The man who led the demand was George Peek, the architect of McNary-Haugenism and leader of the discontented farmers. Ever the politician, Roosevelt made Peek the head of the AAA. Peek, who had an inflated sense of his own importance—he considered himself to be the real head of the Department of Agriculture—wanted his own way in administrative matters after his years of opposition to Republican presidents. He was contemptuous of Eisenhower, whom he denounced as a member of the "Jardine-Hoover clique," and even refused to speak to him when they passed in the halls. Again and again he demanded that Wallace fire Eisenhower.

Wallace refused. One of his aides, Russell Lord, later wrote that "it irked Peek when Wallace, in driving need of help, found Eisenhower so competent and conscientious as to merit promotion almost immediately to a sort of deputy undersecretariat." Wallace told Peek and others that

"Milton Eisenhower is the best young executive in the department." When Peek again angrily demanded that Eisenhower be replaced by a Democrat, Wallace responded, "Nothing doing."[21]

Wallace had support in his position. Charles Burton Robbins, an Iowa insurance executive and close friend of the Wallace family, had been an assistant secretary of war in the Hoover administration. Shortly after Wallace's appointment as secretary of agriculture had been announced, Robbins wrote him:

There is a young man in the office whom I wish particularly to commend to your attention. His name is Milton Eisenhower, who is head of the Bureau of Public Information, and is, of course, a civil-service employee. His brother, Dwight, is Major in the Regular Army and was in my office during my period of service. . . . I think the Eisenhower boys are topnotchers in every respect, and Dwight is considered one of the finest of the younger officers in the Army.

I am not asking you for anything in the way of particular promotion or anything of that sort for him, but if you are looking for a good man to do a good job I think you will find that Milton Eisenhower will fill the bill.[22]

Eventually it was Peek, not Eisenhower, who lost his job. Roosevelt took him out of the department and made him a special adviser on foreign trade. Shortly thereafter, Peek quit altogether, and in 1936 he campaigned for the Republican ticket.

A year earlier Eisenhower had told Wallace that if he caused the department any embarrassment, he was ready to resign. Again he had other offers, including one to be dean of the school of agriculture at a large land-grant university, at a salary a thousand dollars higher than he was receiving. He said he "was sorely tempted." Wallace waved his hand. "Milton," he said, "you will never be happy in such work," and turned to other business.[23]

Eisenhower and Wallace became close friends, even though they differed as much in style as in economic thought. Eisenhower was a dapper dresser, always well-groomed. Wallace wore loose-fitting, baggy clothes, and he had a shock of ill-kempt hair that was the delight of the cartoonists. Eisenhower moved smoothly through the Washington cocktail circuit; he knew everyone worth knowing, it seemed, and could talk comfortably to them all. Wallace knew hardly anyone and was ill-at-ease with almost everyone at formal social functions.[24]

Wallace was ill-at-ease with President Roosevelt as well, which worked to Eisenhower's advantage. Harold Ickes, Roosevelt's secretary of the interior, was a ferocious curmudgeon and an empire builder. He wanted Roosevelt to transfer the U.S. Forest Service from the Department of Agriculture to the Department of the Interior. Wallace fought him bitterly but feared he was losing. He called Eisenhower into his office. "Milton," he began, "I just can't seem to get the President to listen to what I say about Ickes' attempts to dismember the Department of Agriculture. When I go to his office he immediately begins telling me stories which fill the full period allotted to me. We never seem to get to the real issues."

Highly agitated, Wallace continued, "I'm very much afraid that I've offended President Roosevelt and made myself unwelcome. When I saw him this morning he began telling the same stories. Unfortunately, I lost my temper and told the President I had heard his blessed stories several times and now I wanted to take up with him a very serious matter. Well, as you can imagine, Milton, the President was startled. He glared at me for a moment and I braced myself for the explosion; then he broke into that hearty laughter of his. Finally he said, 'Okay, Henry, what's on your mind?' "

Wallace had then told the president that, far from considering transferring the Forest Service from Agriculture to Interior, he ought to be working to transfer the public lands and other parts of the Department of the Interior to Agriculture. As it was, the irrigation people at Interior were bringing new crops into production while Agriculture was paying farmers to reduce production. It made no sense.

"Well, what did the President say?" Eisenhower asked, barely suppressing a grin.

"He said he would think about it and launched into another story."[25]

Close to despair, Wallace asked Eisenhower to accompany him the next time he went to the White House. Eisenhower, flattered, readily agreed. Wallace was so impressed with the easy rapport that Eisenhower established with Roosevelt that thereafter he sent Eisenhower alone to talk to the president. The Forest Service stayed in Agriculture, and Eisenhower gained valuable experience in dealing with officials at the highest level.

Although never a close confidant of Roosevelt's, for the next ten years Eisenhower got along with the president exceptionally well. Their relationship had been cemented long before Dwight became Supreme Allied Commander. As Wallace knew too well, Roosevelt loved a good story, whether he was telling it or listening. Eisenhower shared that characteristic. Roosevelt especially liked a good punch line, at which he would throw back his head and roar with laughter. He delighted in Eisenhower's sense of humor and found that wide grin contagious. At the same time, both men were serious about their jobs and could come quickly to the heart of the matter when necessary. It became a regular practice for Roosevelt to put Eisenhower on his appointments schedule around the noon hour so that they could have lunch together—alone—in the Oval Office.

They had a vast amount of business to do. The New Deal was in full swing, with new legislation being passed at a breathtaking rate. The Department of Agriculture was at the center of the activity. In developing the numerous programs, Secretary Wallace received an endless stream of ideas from men like Professor Rexford G. Tugwell, of Columbia University, who had taken a post as undersecretary of agriculture. A charter member of Roosevelt's "brain trust," Tugwell was one of the original academic economists to go into government service. On many occasions Eisenhower helped Tugwell translate his ideas into legislative form and then helped lobby the bills through Congress. "Milton Eisenhower was very cooperative," Tugwell said later, "and very active."[26] Out of their efforts came the Farm Security Administration, the Rural Electrification Administration, and the Soil Conservation Service.[27]

As Eisenhower put it years later, "For a young man in his early thirties from rural Kansas, it was a heady experience." He continued to work at a furious pace, leaving most of the parental chores to Helen. "My interest in governmental affairs was consuming," he later confessed. "If not an academic-type scholar of our political system, I became at least, a serious student of it."[28]

With his easy access to the president, Eisenhower was the envy of nearly every civil servant—and many of the politicians—in Washington. His domestic life, too, continued to prosper. Buddy was growing into a strong, active, intelligent boy, while Helen thoroughly enjoyed the social life in Washington. They had moved to a remodeled, large regency house on Broad Street in Falls Church, Virginia, in a neighborhood Mr. Eakin was developing from the land he had bought before the bridge was built over the Potomac. Jack Eakin lived next door. The Eisenhowers entertained frequently. Ike and Mamie and the Eakins joined high-ranking government officials and Washington journalists at dinners and cocktail parties.

Eisenhower had established himself as one of the top bureaucrats in Washington. The next step was to become an administrator on his own.

CHAPTER 5

"The Greatest Possible Speed Is Imperative"

Washington Administrator

On a hot, sunny day in the spring of 1937, the New Deal triumphantly reelected, Henry Wallace suggested that he and Eisenhower take a walk to the Washington Monument and then go to lunch together. Wallace was a vegetarian and a firm believer in exercise. Eisenhower liked good red meat and, save for an early morning constitutional, never in his life saw any need for physical exercise. ("Poor Ike," Milton Eisenhower remarked in an interview when he was in his eighties, still fit and trim. "If he didn't exercise, he would bloat up like a dead fish. Me, I never had to lift a finger, and didn't, and don't.") When they arrived at the base of the monument, Wallace said on the spur of the moment, "Let's walk up."

Eisenhower had been to the top only once before, and on that occasion Helen had fainted halfway up. Just thinking of the climb made him weary. But the boss was the boss, so up he went, gasping for breath, his chest burning from too many cigarettes combined with the Washington humidity. When they returned to the South Building of the Department of Agriculture, Wallace insisted on walking up eight flights of stairs to the dining room, and the exhausted Eisenhower trailed sadly behind.

Finally seated, Wallace ordered his vegetables and then began discussing the contradictions in the programs of the Agriculture Department. The AAA was paying farmers to reduce their production of wheat, cotton, corn, and other commodities. The Soil Conservation Service was paying farmers to plant the same crops. The Farm Security Administration was lending and giving money to farm families to enlarge their holdings and raise more wheat, cotton, corn, and so on. The Soil Conservation Service and the Federal-State Agricultural Extension Service had agents giving contradictory advice to farmers. The Tennessee Valley Authority, under the Department of the Interior, was urging farmers in its area to plant more; the AAA was urging the same farmers to plant less. It was bureaucracy gone mad.

"I want you to set up an agency with the mission of overcoming these conflicts," Wallace told Eisenhower. "I've thought about this a great deal. I've discussed it with Paul Appleby and Rex Tugwell and they agree on what has to be done. You'll get our full support."

Still short of breath, Eisenhower swallowed hard. His face showed his concern. It was a charge to cleanse the stables, a Herculean task.

"I don't expect you to perform miracles," Wallace hastened to add. "This will be an extremely difficult task and you will surely make mistakes. But I hope you can make steady progress so that I can assure the President and the Congress that the problems and the conflicts are being resolved."[1]

Wallace said he wanted to call the new agency the Office of Land Use Planning. It would be a unit of the secretary's office. Wallace gave Eisenhower authority to draft the personnel he needed and promised to tell the agency heads to cooperate. He added that Eisenhower should also retain his present job as director of information.

Eisenhower was then thirty-seven years old. He had been in government service for thirteen years, all but two of them in Washington. He had won the respect of nearly all for whom he had worked. He had maintained his independence and established his position as a career civil servant who would be a yes man for no one. (Only a year before, in 1936, he had offered his resignation to Wallace when they had differed sharply over some international problems affecting agriculture. Wallace had replied that he liked having men about him who were not afraid to disagree, and refused the resignation.)

Based on his experience, Eisenhower had developed firm views on running an organization which were to guide him through the remainder of his career, a career in which he was the top man in a variety of different organizations and institutions. So when Wallace called on him, Eisenhower was prepared for a top-level, extremely difficult and sensitive administrative post. Eisenhower had become a stickler for organization but nevertheless believed that the organization chart was less important than the personnel in the slots. "The success of an enterprise depends primarily on the quality and the attitudes of the people in it," he later wrote. He wanted his staff members in close physical proximity to each other, in daily if not hourly contact.

His first assignment at the Office of Land Use Planning was very similar to the task he would face in his three university presidencies, namely, to shake up established, traditional ways of doing things. Confronting such a task, he was very much the practical politician, adopting what would become his trademark: an evolutionary rather than a revolutionary approach. When attempting to change people's thinking or organizational relationships, he declared, "one must be patient as well as persistent." Trying to do everything at once too often brought about chaos or caused staff members to dig in their heels or even sabotage the new program.[2]

Neither in his first executive assignment nor in any of those that followed was Eisenhower a leader who banged his fist on the desk—a demander, a shouter. He always preferred to use persuasion and reason, not his grant of authority, to lead. Sometimes it failed, because throughout his career as an executive he had to deal with strong-willed, independent men, but usually it worked. His charm, good sense, mastery of the issues, and patience were his greatest assets. Furthermore, when circumstances demanded, Eisenhower could be as tough as his toughest adversary. Many times his placid exterior belied a fierce determination.

Another of Eisenhower's lifelong principles was to involve others from the beginning, to give his subordinates a distinct sense that he needed and wanted their help. On his first day as head of the Office of Land Use Planning he called together the heads of all the relevant agencies, including the Agricultural Conservation Administration (which had replaced the AAA), the Farm Security Administration, the Soil Conservation Service, the Forest Service, and the Division of Soil Surveys. He explained his objectives and outlined how he hoped to proceed, with their help, to eliminate the contradictions in federal agricultural policy.

Predictably, and from the start, he raised deep suspicions and encountered entrenched opposition. The chief of the Agricultural Conservation Administration, by far the largest of the agencies, made it clear that if the conflicts were to be resolved the other agencies would have to make the changes, for he would not. The head of each of the other agencies was equally firm; what his organization was doing was absolutely crucial to stopping soil erosion, or protecting the national forests, or giving aid to poor farmers.[3] It was a response all too familiar to hundreds of reformers who have gone to Washington determined to clean up the mess in the nation's capital, only to be left frustrated and bemused, wondering what had happened.

Eisenhower decided to take another tack; this time he concentrated on the bottom of the organizational chart. He proposed to work with local agents of the various agencies, together with local advisory groups, to issue rules and regulations that would eliminate contradictions at the local level. He assembled a staff of twenty-five economists, survey experts, lawyers, and clerks; arranged for cooperation with the land-grant colleges and their agricultural extension services; and set to it. It took two years of time-consuming exhausting work, but eventually he enjoyed some moderate success, when all parties involved signed a nationwide agreement for local methods of cooperation between the agencies.[4]

Simultaneously Eisenhower attacked another problem that is also all too familiar to potential Washington reformers. Every agency in the Department of Agriculture had divided the nation into regions, and each had its own regional headquarters. The regions were arranged in a crazy-quilt pattern, boundaries overlapped without sense or design, and regional headquarters of the various agencies were seldom in the same city. Even in those few cases where they were located in the same city no two were in the same building.

Eisenhower told Wallace that he wanted to consolidate, to require all agencies to have identical regions with common regional and state headquarters and all personnel housed in the same buildings. The plan would obviously promote greater efficiency, save money, and put agents working on broadly similar problems in daily touch with each other. As a result, Eisenhower reasoned, related programs would be modified so as to complement, not compete against, each other. The difficulty was that the consolidation would also eliminate small federal establishments in hundreds of towns and cities, establishments dear to the hearts of the American politicians and their constituents.

Wallace saw the danger clearly but nevertheless approved enthusiastically. He did offer Eisenhower some advice: "I have two suggestions. First, you better get the approval of President Roosevelt, because that's where the political heat will be the hottest. Second, I think you ought to launch your program in the North Central states. That's my country. And if you make Milwaukee the headquarters for this region, you're going to have to move an office out of Des Moines, my hometown. Maybe if we demonstrate the importance of putting selfish interest aside for a nobler cause it will set a good example."

Eisenhower prepared two maps, one showing the existing situation, the other his proposed reorganization. He went to the Oval Office at noon, where over tea and sandwiches Roosevelt listened to his presentation. After the dishes had been cleared the president leaned back in his wheelchair and said, "You know that the political criticism will be substantial. And you can bet that some of the loudest critics will be the very same senators and congressmen who have been condemning the program conflicts you are trying to correct." Eisenhower nodded. Roosevelt continued, "I think what you want to do is right, Milton. So go ahead with your plan. I'll stand by you."[5]

With almost childlike enthusiasm, Eisenhower set to work. He began, as Wallace suggested, with the North Central states, where the reform went better than he had dared hope. Now more confident then ever that his plan would work, he turned his attention to the Southeast, where Atlanta would serve as the central headquarters. This required, among many other moves, transferring the regional office of the Soil Conservation Service from Spartanburg, South Carolina, to Atlanta.

Suddenly everything started to unravel. When that change was announced, Senator James Byrnes of South Carolina stormed into Roosevelt's office, protesting the move and presenting a petition signed by thousands of his unhappy constituents. Roosevelt sent for Eisenhower. This time there was no tea and sandwiches, and the president would not look him in the eye. Instead he looked at Byrnes's petition and said, "Milton, we're in trouble on that coordinating program of yours." Finally looking up at Eisenhower, Roosevelt said slowly, "I need Jimmy Byrnes."

"I'm sorry, Milton," the president continued, "but I have to ask you not to go ahead with the move of the Soil Conservation Office out of Spartanburg."

Eisenhower's heart sank. "If it were just this one move, Mr. President," he responded, "I could consider it a necessary compromise and move forward. But you know as well as I that this really means the end of the plan in all parts of the country. If we surrender to political pressure in a single city or region, the next move we try to make will bring even greater pressure to bear on this office."

"Yes, I understand that, and I still must ask you not to proceed with the move."

Roosevelt could have ended the meeting at that point—the presidential order had been given—but that was not his way. Roosevelt never wanted anyone to leave his office unhappy. Moreover, he liked and respected Eisenhower and wanted to make sure that he did not become too disillusioned. Hence, he launched into a long discourse on the far-flung duties and responsibilities of the president, all the problems he faced, the necessity for him to make an adjustment here, a compromise there, for the greater good. Byrnes was a leader among the southern Democrats. He had served fourteen years in the House, was in his second term as senator, and was frequently mentioned as a possible Democratic presidential or vice-presidential nominee. Roosevelt had to have his vote on matters far more important than a reorganization of the agencies of the Department of Agriculture. The dejected Eisenhower accepted the decision with the best grace possible. Nevertheless, it was a bitter pill to swallow.[6]

Eisenhower's home life helped ease the disappointments at the office. Buddy was doing well in school, and Helen seemed to be always on the go. In 1938 they had a daughter, Ruth. Like his father, Eisenhower had always wanted a daughter; like Mr. Eakin, he doted on her. Ike had gone off to the Philippines as MacArthur's assistant; Mamie and her son John stayed in Washington for a year so that John could finish junior high school. Milton and Helen had Mamie and John to their home on a regular basis, for dinner and for bridge. John and Buddy became close friends, almost like brothers.[7] For a month each summer the Eisenhowers and the Eakins would go to Wisconsin, where the men fished from dawn to dusk.

In October 1941, with the threat of America's entering World War II growing daily, Roosevelt established the Overseas Information Agency, under Robert Sherwood, and the Office of Facts and Figures, under Archibald MacLeish. Shortly after Japan's surprise attack on the U.S. naval base at Pearl Harbor, Roosevelt turned to Eisenhower for help. The president wanted a study made of all the war-related informational activities of the federal government. When Eisenhower had finished his study, Roosevelt said, he wanted him to recommend a system that would keep the American people informed about the war, give the Allies accurate information about the American war effort, influence neutral countries to enter the war on the Allied side, counteract the Axis propaganda, and, if possible, create anxiety among the people of Germany and Italy.

Eisenhower knew the field so well already that it took him only a month to complete the study. He recommended the creation of an Office of War Information (OWI), which would have both foreign and domestic branches and would have full authority to coordinate all informational activities from the War and Navy departments, the War Production Board, and the various executive departments. The head of the new agency should be directly responsible to the president. Eisenhower stressed in his report that propaganda, in the form of lies, half-truths, and cover-ups of military defeats, would destroy the credibility and thus the usefulness of the OWI. Eisenhower's approach was thus the direct opposite of that of the Creel Committee, which had handled propaganda for the United States in World War I. Eisenhower believed that because America sought no territorial gain and fought only for freedom in Europe and Asia, "our real strength lay in telling the truth, sticking to the facts, and presenting a full and accurate explanation of our war purposes."[8]

Roosevelt said he would study the report. Eisenhower flew off for a tour of Tennessee, where he was still trying to resolve the conflicts between the various agencies involved in agricultural programs. On March 10, 1942, while he was still in Tennessee, he received a message from the White House: the president wanted to see him urgently.

Eisenhower flew in from Tennessee and went directly to see the president. He was startled by Roosevelt's appearance. The man looked ten years older. His smiling, confident manner was gone; there were no opening jokes or even pleasantries. Hardly looking up from a document he was studying, Roosevelt said, "Milton, your war job, starting immediately, is to set up a War Relocation Authority [WRA] to move the Japanese-Americans off the Pacific coast. I have signed an executive order which will give you full authority to do what is essential. The Attorney General will give you the necessary legal assistance and the Secretary of War will help you with the physical arrangements. Harold [Budget Director Harold Smith] will fill you in on the details of the problem."

The president looked back at the paper he was reading. Eisenhower, realizing that the interview was over, turned to leave. "And, Milton," the president called out to him, "the greatest possible speed is imperative." Eisenhower took the opportunity to ask if he could take his staff from Agriculture with him to the new assignment. "Just let me know who you want with you on this job," Roosevelt replied, "and we will take care of it."[9]

Thus abruptly—and reluctantly—did Eisenhower find himself for ninety days in the middle of perhaps the most notorious and least admirable of incidents throughout America's participation in World War II. Thousands of Japanese-Americans, some of whom were aliens (Issei and Kibei) but most of whom were U.S. citizens (Nisei), were summarily uprooted from their Pacific Coast homes and relocated, without ever being charged with a crime, in what later critics have called concentration camps in the Western states. Their forced removal constituted one of the worst violations of civil rights in American history—what one historian termed "the major blot" on an otherwise improved record following the abolition of slavery.[10]

Eisenhower was not involved in the decision to establish the War Relocation Authority. That decision came directly from the Oval Office, where Franklin Roosevelt was unwilling to resist the escalating pressure to safeguard America from the potential threat of the "yellow peril." By the time he issued Executive Order 9066 on February 19, 1942, this pressure had become overwhelming for Roosevelt. It stemmed from many sources. Out-and-out racists—like General John L. De Witt, General Allen W. Gullion, and Colonel Karl Bendetsen in the military; Martin Dies,

John Rankin, and Tom Stewart in Congress; and journalists and radio broadcasters like Westbrook Pegler and John B. Hughes—playing on Americans' historic distrust of Orientals, as well as the desire to explain and revenge the nefarious and humiliating attack on Pearl Harbor, warned almost daily of the dangers of a Japanese-American fifth column operating on the West Coast. To them, there was no such thing as a loyal American of Japanese ancestry. Whether Issei or Nisei, according to De Witt, chief of the Western Defense Command and the Fourth Army, both headquartered in San Francisco, "the Japanese Race is an enemy race and . . . the racial strains are undiluted." Or, as Rankin put it, "Once a Jap, always a Jap. You cannot change him. You cannot make a silk purse out of a sow's ear."[11]

Racism was not the only motive. Economic groups, such as the Western Growers Protective Association, the Grower-Shipper Vegetable Association, the California Farm Bureau Federation, and virtually every Pacific Coast chamber of commerce seized upon the anti-Japanese prejudice as an opportunity to eliminate what they had long perceived as undesirable competition. But the most prevalent sentiment was simply fear. Caught off guard in 1941, Americans were not going to take any chances in 1942. Few were immune from the contagion. A week before Roosevelt's Executive Order the usually detached and liberal observer Walter Lippmann wrote, "The Pacific Coast is officially a combat zone: Some part of it may at any moment be a battlefield. And nobody ought to be on a battlefield who has no good reason for being there. There is plenty of room elsewhere for him to exercise his rights." Lippmann subscribed to the curious Catch-22 argument that the very fact that no evidence could be found of Japanese-American subversion implicitly proved the existence of a plot. Another leading exponent of this view was California's then attorney general Earl Warren, who later as Chief Justice of the Supreme Court earned a reputation as an avid champion of the oppressed. A declared candidate for his state's governorship, Warren believed in 1942 that an "Invisible Deadline for Sabotage" threatened California's, ergo America's, security. Testifying before a congressional hearing, the future interpreter of the Constitution asserted that the failure to uncover any "fifth column activities in this state . . . is the most ominous sign in our whole situation." He continued, "I believe that we are just being lulled into a false sense of security and that the only reason we haven't had disaster in California is because it has been timed for a different date. . . . Our day of reckoning is bound to come in that regard."[12]

Into this maelstrom of paranoia stepped forty-two-year-old Milton Eisenhower. He could not refuse the wartime assignment of his Commander in Chief, but he did not like it. Quickly briefed by Assistant Secretary of War John McCloy and Budget Director Smith, Eisenhower learned of the many abuses that had already taken place. When Roosevelt had first authorized the relocations, he had admonished its administrators to "be as reasonable as you can." Yet under the direction of military men like General De Witt, the initial program was anything but reasonable. Because of chaotic planning, for most of the Japanese-Americans only one week elapsed between their being notified of an evacuation date and their removal. Many were given as little as forty-eight hours to dispose of their property and possessions. As an inevitable result, the great majority suffered great and, often, irrevocable financial loss, not to mention the ignominy of being rounded up and shipped off like cattle. Placed in this no-win situation, Eisenhower hoped only to salvage as much as he could.[13]

Immediately after his briefing Eisenhower hopped a plane for the West Coast, where he met with De Witt, Bendetsen, and another future Supreme Court justice, Tom C. Clark, the coordinator of the Alien Enemy Control Program within the Western Defense Command. Realizing that voluntary evacuation was impossible, he resigned himself to collecting the Japanese-Americans in what he called "sand and cactus centers." In an effort to lessen the impact, he utilized one of his principal administrative tenets: he established an advisory council from among the Nisei leaders themselves. More concretely, he induced the officers of the Federal Reserve Bank in California to agree to do all they could to protect the physical assets of the evacuees. He also arranged for the WRA to provide legal advice, assist in the negotiation of leases, and serve as intermediaries in other financial transactions. Eisenhower could not undo the prior damage, but he did improve the situation significantly.[14]

Roosevelt had explained to Eisenhower that a major reason for his ordering the relocation of the Japanese-Americans was to protect them from the vigilante-type attacks that would undoubtedly arise as a result of the West Coast hysteria. Eisenhower still did not like the whole concept. On April 1 he wrote his last boss in the Agriculture Department, Secretary Claude Wickard, "I feel most deeply that when the war is over . . . we as Americans are going to regret the avoidable injustices that may have been done."[15] Nevertheless, he agreed that the president had a valid point. There had already been some killings. He decided, probably not without some rationalizing, that if he could expeditiously settle the Nisei in the interior states under satisfactory conditions, they would be able to wait out the hostilities safely and return home at the war's end. All things considered, Eisenhower convinced himself, they might be better off removed from California. In this way, necessity could be turned into virtue.

With this in mind, Eisenhower hopped another plane on April 7, this time for Salt Lake City. There he met with the governors or their representatives from ten western states—Utah, Arizona, Nevada, Montana, Idaho, Colorado, New Mexico, Wyoming, Washington, and Oregon. He reminded them that none of the Nisei had been found guilty of anything, that they had been evacuated for purely defensive reasons. Therefore, he reasoned, the best program would be one that resettled them as rapidly as possible and treated them as an imported labor force, not as prisoners.

Eisenhower proposed the setting up of fifty to seventy-five camps not unlike those of the Civilian Conservation Corps. Some of the Nisei would remain within the camps, performing reclamation projects or doing agricultural and manufacturing work. Others could find employment outside. And finally, some self-supporting communities similar to the subsistence homesteads of the New Deal could be established. Those who remained within the camps would receive the minimum wage paid American soldiers, twenty-one dollars a month (in fact, the maximum wage was eventually set at nineteen dollars). Those who found outside work could earn what the market would bear. To Eisenhower it seemed that such an arrangement would mutually benefit everyone.

Eisenhower asked the state leaders for their support and suggestions. Instead he received a stream of denunciations. The governors were no more willing to have Japanese running loose than were their Pacific Coast neighbors. Only Ralph Carr, of Colorado, ¬aised no objection, agreeing with Eisenhower that cooperation with the government's program was every citizen's responsibility. The rest insisted that the WRA was not going to turn their states into "California's dumping ground." What if some of the Nisei tried to buy land and settle permanently? As Governor Nels Smith of Wyoming put it, if any Japanese-Americans bought land in his state, "there would be Japs hanging from every pine tree." Furthermore, who was going to guarantee their safety outside of the centers? No, they chorused in unison. They would accept the evacuees only if they were kept under constant guard.[16]

Eisenhower had been naive to believe that the Western governors would be any less prejudiced against the Japanese-Americans than leaders of their home states. Later he would recall, "That meeting was probably the most frustrating experience I ever had." But he did not have time to dwell on the rejection. The longer it took to establish the relocation centers, the longer the evacuees would have to remain in the tar-paper makeshift quarters that had been hastily built for them on racetracks and fairgrounds along the coast. They lived with minimal privacy, their sanitary conditions were wretched, and the danger of hysterical neighbors' taking matters into their own hands was omnipresent. Thus once again Eisenhower tirelessly took to the air, heading for Washington, where he could assemble the chiefs of the National Park and Forest services, the Irrigation Service, and the Public Land Office. He obtained maps of all the publicly owned lands destined for development, and he looked particularly at those areas that would require vast amounts of work. Assistant Secretary McCloy promised to help in any way, and many of the agency chiefs loaned him top people from their staffs.

Encouraged by his new-found support, Eisenhower returned to the West. However, although he could now draw on detailed information and efficient assistants, finding suitable locations proved an almost impossible chore. He was restricted to selecting only federally owned land conducive to accommodating five thousand or more persons with only a relatively few guards, away from any strategic installations and certainly away from any concentrations of local population. Also, work had to be available. By the beginning of June he had found ten sites. The Army moved in and constructed barracklike buildings which could be subdivided into family dwellings. Eisenhower even managed to have some churches, schools, and recreation centers erected and to beautify the arid landscape with trees and shrubs. He called the sites evacuation centers, refusing to give in to the more common label of concentration camp. But no amount of buildings and trees could mask the high barbed wire fences that enclosed each one, or conceal the military police who patrolled day and night.[17]

In addition to setting up the most tolerable centers possible, Eisenhower simultaneously sought to find a means by which the thousands of Japanese-American college students who had been enrolled in West Coast institutions could somehow continue their education. Ironically, his most fervent allies were California educators themselves, most notably Robert Gordon Sproul, the prestigious president of the University of California, and Berkeley's provost, Monroe Deutsch. Squeezing hours on the telephone into his already cluttered schedule, Eisenhower canvassed the country for schools that would accept the Nisei as transfers. All declined. America's best-known universities, including Princeton, Massachusetts Institute of Technology, and Duke, were "not willing to receive American-born Japanese students even though they may be in good standing and not under suspicion." They claimed that war-oriented research was done on their campuses, that the military status of their geographical zone was uncertain, or that the students could not receive unquestionable security clearance. Thirty years later Eisenhower wrote, "I must confess that I am still distressed by the excuses I received from the educators I approached."

Just when the situation looked hopeless, Eisenhower enlisted the help of Clarence E. Pickett, executive secretary of the American Friends Service Committee. The Quaker leader traveled to hundreds of universities and colleges, pleading and cajoling until some finally relented to accept the Japanese-Americans. Necessary support also came from presidential assistant Harry Hopkins, who urged Roosevelt to "give Japanese-Americans a chance to leave reception centers and live normal lives." On May 18 the president approved the first significant relaxation of the policy of mass confinement. In dribs and drabs, ultimately some forty-three hundred Nisei students made the transition from the camps to college. One later wrote, "It was a thrill to become accustomed to feeling 'free.' . . . I think most of us realize our most important mission of being 'good-will ambassadors,' to show other Americans that we are also loyal Americans."[18]

The college-age Nisei represented but a small percentage of the total evacuees. Regardless of his initial rebuff, Eisenhower remained convinced that work within the centers could not sustain the tens of thousands of others. In June he received a break. Because farms in the intermountain states were going to ruin due to a lack of manpower, the governors suddenly reversed their positions and began requesting Japanese-American laborers. Eisenhower immediately drew up "seasonal leave" procedures, allowing males between twenty and fifty years old to leave the camps for temporary work but to return once their job was finished. Furthermore, he exacted a price: he required that state officials guarantee the workers' safety, mandate that they be paid the prevailing wage, and ensure that adequate housing and transportation be provided. When he heard reports of harassment, he threatened to rescind the leaves. The local farmers judiciously straightened matters out. By harvest time ten thousand Nisei—one out of every five male evacuees—were in the fields. Demand for their labor was so high that farmers even tried to entice them away from rival operations.[19]

Although deeply gratified by his victories, Eisenhower never became reconciled to his onerous assignment. On June 15 Secretary of the Interior Harold Ickes, who had criticized the administration of the relocation program at a Cabinet meeting ten days earlier, wrote Roosevelt, "I have it from several sources that Eisenhouer [*sic*] is sick of the job." That same day, in Washington to take care of one of the ever-pressing legal details, Eisenhower learned that he was being transferred to another agency. Three days later he wrote a lengthy memorandum to FDR. "Life in a relocation center cannot be pleasant. The evacuees are surrounded by barbed wire fences under the eyes of armed military police. They have suffered heavily in property losses; they have lost their businesses and their means of support." Then, as a legacy to his successor, Dillon Myer, he added,

The future of the program will doubtless be governed largely by the temper of American public opinion. . . . I cannot help expressing the

hope that the American people will grow toward a broader apprecia-
tion of the essential Americanism of a great majority of the evacuees
and of the difficult sacrifice they are making. Only when the prevailing
attitudes of unreasoning bitterness have been replaced by tolerance and
understanding will it be possible to carry forward a genuinely satisfac-
tory relocation program and to plan intelligently for the reassimilation
of the evacuees into American life when the war is over.[20]

Despite all his efforts on behalf of the Japanese-Americans, Eisenhower must live with the knowledge that he presided over a policy according to which the Nisei were, in his own words, "needlessly uprooted and sub- jected to indignities of historic proportions." He could have added, as one analyst did, that by yielding to the political pressure that no worker within the camp, professional or not, receive a wage greater than an Army private, and without the fringe benefits, he presided over a policy that created a "class of serfs in a free society." More fundamentally, his privately expressed misgivings notwithstanding, by acquiescing to and executing the program, he must, according to the legal standards set by the United States following the end of the war, share in the guilt. How- ever, as the most severe critic of the episode has written, "Eisenhower did at least try to ameliorate the conditions of the evacuation, and one shud- ders to think what it might have been like had not Eisenhower and the others at the top of the WRA bureaucracy been essentially on the liberal side of the American ideological spectrum." Michael Masaoka, national secretary of the Japanese American Citizen League and a member of Eisenhower's advisory committee, brought this point home dramatically when he presented the outgoing WRA head with a fifty-year-old bonsai, a magnificently sculptured dwarf pine tree. Masaoka explained that the gift symbolized his people's conviction that Eisenhower had done all he could in the face of nationwide hostility. Eisenhower treasures the bonsai as "the only pleasant memory I have of three agonizing months with the War Relocation Authority." But it cannot negate his involvement nor erase the pain. As he concluded in his memoirs, "I have brooded about this episode on and off for the past three decades, for it is illustrative of how an entire society can somehow plunge off course.... The evacua- tion of the Japanese-Americans need not have happened."[21]

Roosevelt's selection of Eisenhower as the first head of the WRA's deli- cate operation had manifestly signified the president's confidence in the forty-two-year-old's administrative—and political—abilities. Eisen- hower's performance had proven Roosevelt's judgment correct. Even when he was "sick of the job," he had energetically devoted himself to carrying out Roosevelt's program and had done everything that could have been expected of him, and more. On his part, Eisenhower had had another postgraduate course in responsible leadership. He had learned that the top executive must often make personally distasteful decisions, and live amidst criticism and controversy.

Eisenhower's new assignment furthered his education. Roosevelt chose him for another sensitive role, this time as Elmer Davis's associate director in the Office of War Information, which the president had established on June 13, 1942, along the lines recommended by Eisenhower back in 1941. Davis was a correspondent, columnist, and broadcaster with a national reputation but without any experience whatsoever in organization or administration. As he explained to the president, the only person he had ever had work for him was a part-time secretary. He took the position as head of the OWI only after Roosevelt promised to find him an associate who was "skilled in governmental organization and information matters." Eisenhower was a natural.

Over the next year Eisenhower worked smoothly with the white-haired, quick-tempered Davis. It was a demanding job, requiring a balancing act between the military's need for secrecy and the insistence of both of them that the public had a right to know all the facts at once. In addition, Eisenhower had to handle organizational and administrative matters. He attended presidential press conferences, arranged interviews, battled with the Joint Chiefs of Staff over what information could be released, and in general worked at a typically hectic Eisenhower pace.

At least he was living at home, in Falls Church, and was able to spend most nights in his own bed. Added to that satisfaction, his brother was living with him. General George C. Marshall, the Army Chief of Staff, had called Ike to Washington to be on the Operations Division of the War Department, where Ike worked long hours putting together a strategy for the war. Mamie had stayed at Ike's last post, in Texas, to settle household matters, and John was now a cadet at West Point (Milton had used his political connections to help obtain the appointment), so Ike had moved in with his younger brother.

Milton and Helen did everything to make him comfortable. They imposed upon their cook to get up at 6:30 A.M. to make Ike's breakfast so that he could be in his office by 7:30 A.M. Milton's day began shortly thereafter, so the cook had busy mornings. Ike usually came home late at night, having eaten his noon and evening meals at his desk. He liked to go to the children's bedroom—Buddy was then eleven, and Ruth three—wake them, and have a relaxing chat about their day. Buddy and Ruth "loved Uncle Ike and happily responded when he woke them," then fell back asleep a moment after he said good-night. Meanwhile Helen would prepare a snack, topped off by a pot of cocoa, which helped Ike get to sleep.

As Marshall's chief planner, Ike was sometimes summoned to the White House. One evening he came home grinning. He told Milton that he had seen the president that day; when he had entered the Oval Office Roosevelt had looked at him and then blurted out, "Well, General, your baby brother is causing me an awful lot of trouble and I've just had to spend an hour on him."

Startled, Ike replied, "Do you mean my brother Milton?"

"I do," said the President. "Four different government departments want him, and I have to decide which one will be lucky enough to get him."[22]

Mamie finally moved to Washington, but almost simultaneously Ike flew to London to take up his new assignment as commander of the American Army in Europe. Mamie spent her weekends at Falls Church. In November, thanks to his position at the OWI, Milton learned that Ike would command a surprise invasion of North Africa. On the night of the invasion, November 8, 1942, Mamie and several friends gathered at Falls Church for an evening of bridge. Milton left the radio on to catch the announcement of the invasion, which he knew was scheduled for nine o'clock.

"Milton, why do you keep that radio going?" Mamie asked with some irritation. "You're the one who always complains about the radio when we're playing cards!" Eisenhower mumbled that he was waiting for a presidential announcement of interest to the OWI.

At nine o'clock the announcement was made, followed by a personal statement from General Eisenhower himself. Mamie sat silent, tears in her eyes. Once she had composed herself she turned and said, "Milton, I am proud of you for not telling me."[23]

With the invasion, Ike suddenly became a world figure, a celebrity of the first rank. Never again would he be "Milton's brother"; from then on Milton was known as "Ike's brother." From that point in November 1942, as Ike took a place on the world stage that he would hold until his death, Milton had to put up with strangers who would recognize him in a restaurant or other public place—as they grew older the two brothers looked even more alike, especially when they grinned—come up to him, and say, "I'd like to shake your hand. I admire your brother so much." For a proud and sensitive man with a remarkable record of accomplishment of his own it was always a difficult situation. Milton handled such scenes with his usual grace, but inwardly he seethed.

Once, while fishing in Wisconsin with Mr. Eakin, "Daddy Roy" turned to him and said, "You know, Milton, when you married Helen, people referred to you as my son-in-law. Now they refer to me as your father-in-law, and I don't like it!" Milton said he sympathized, for the cross he had to bear in this regard was worse than Eakin's. Eakin snapped back, "Oh, no! Now they call me the father-in-law of Ike's brother!"[24]

Despite the irritation that Ike's fame sometimes caused him, Milton was terribly proud of his brother; despite the reversal of roles, as he became "Ike's brother," jealousy never came between them, just as it had not when Ike had played second fiddle. They had a deep love for one another, and each had the greatest respect for the other's abilities. They continually discussed each other's problems, solicited and accepted advice, and remained sensitive to the other's needs, hopes, aspirations, and disappointments. It was a beautiful relationship, and highly valuable—sometimes crucial—to each man.

Not surprisingly, given their respective positions, Milton's most difficult task during his stint at the OWI concerned the military decisions of brother Ike. In preparing for the North African invasion Ike had had to deal with the unpleasant circumstance that French soldiers, under the direction of Marshal Henri Pétain and his collaborationist Vichy government, were as likely to fight the Allied "invaders" as they were the Germans and Italians. The Americans had persuaded General Henri Giraud, a one-legged hero of World War I, to take control of the French in Africa and appeal to them to at least remain neutral. Unfortunately, the French were more interested in avoiding charges of treason to the Vichy government than they were in listening to a has-been general, so they met the Allies with stiff resistance.

Out of desperation Ike struck a deal with Admiral Jean Darlan, who had been captured in Algiers while visiting a sick son. As commander-in-chief of the Vichy armed forces and deputy head of the government, Darlan could deliver the neutrality that Giraud could not. In return for Darlan's cooperation, Ike made him the governor general of all French North Africa. The deal provoked a tremendous uproar in Britain and the United States. Here was America professing to be fighting for liberty, justice, and democracy. But in its initial war offensive the first major act of its commander was to enter into a partnership with a renowned fascist collaborator, a man who represented the very forces America was supposed to be fighting.

Much of the intense reaction resulted from naiveté. As historian Arthur Funk has pointed out, "Many Americans were still, in 1942, wallowing comfortably in a Wilsonian delusion that wars are fought to preserve the world for those on the side of right." Compounding the naiveté was a lack, or more accurately, a distortion, of information. The only communication cable connecting North Africa to Europe and the United States had been cut by a sunken ship, which prevented on-the-spot observers such as Drew Middleton from filing their dispatches. Hence the only reports of the situation that reached the democracies were through Radio Maroc, the station of the militant Free French. Since to the Free French, Darlan and the Vichy collaborationists were a worse enemy than the Nazis, the broadcasts painted the deal in the most perfidious terms. The accuracy of the broadcasts did not improve after Radio Maroc was taken over by Colonel "Wild Bill" Donovan's Office of Strategic Services. While Milton Eisenhower exaggerated when he characterized the OSS agents as simply "idealistic New Dealers," it certainly was true that the criticism of Dwight Eisenhower's arrangement with Darlan continued unabated, with little attempt to explain the rationale.[25]

Worse still were the reactions of Roosevelt and British Prime Minister Winston Churchill. These worthies acted as if they had never heard the name Darlan before and seemed astonished that General Eisenhower had taken such liberties in political matters. In truth, both had approved the Darlan deal weeks earlier, in principle if not in specific detail, when Darlan had first approached Roosevelt's representative in North Africa, Robert Murphy. The two heads of government had given Murphy and Eisenhower full authority to deal with anyone who could deliver the goods. And both Churchill and Roosevelt had insisted from the start that the invading force should do nothing to upset local government, which meant Vichy government. But neither man would come to Eisenhower's defense, which encouraged the press and radio to mount a campaign demanding that the deal be called off.

Ike realized how far out he had stuck his neck. Not at all naive, he understood that although he had made a military decision, he was being made a victim of political expediency. He had no power base of his own, he was unknown, he had won no great victories, he was expendable. At the first critical moment in his career his head was on the block.

Ike defended himself in a series of brilliantly written and argued messages to the Combined Chiefs of Staff, Roosevelt, and Churchill. (To Churchill he wrote: "Please be assured that I have too often listened to your sage advice to be completely handcuffed and blindfolded by all of the slickers with which this part of the world is so thickly populated.") Emphasizing the military necessity of dealing with Darlan, as Funk notes, he turned Clausewitz on his head by "insisting that military achievement be sought at the expense of diplomatic disaster." Another of Ike's justifications was to put the blame on his intelligence service, which had guaranteed that Giraud's appeal would be effective. To the Combined Chiefs of Staff he declared, "The actual state of existing sentiment here does not repeat does not agree even remotely with some of our prior calculations."[26]

The military case was indeed a strong one, but it would have been much stronger if Ike had immediately captured Tunisia and if the French fleet had rallied to the Allies. But the best Darlan could do was to get the French to stop fighting the Americans and to keep French ships out of Nazi hands. With German submarines sinking well over half of the Allied supply vessels, Eisenhower's forces remained too weak to take any dramatic initiatives. Ike had to map out his strategy carefully and bide his time.

At this point the politically sensitive Roosevelt must have been tempted to fire Eisenhower, repudiate the Darlan deal, put someone acceptable in Darlan's place, and make a fresh start. Churchill had fired a string of generals in Egypt and now looked like a genius for having done so, as General Bernard Montgomery had just won the Battle of El Alamein. But FDR had a sense of fair play, and he knew perfectly well that in dealing with Darlan, Ike had stayed well within his orders. He also knew that America's military effort needed both Darlan and Ike.

In addition, three men, representing three levels of the American government, came to Ike's defense: senior official and elder statesman Secretary of War Henry L. Stimson; Chief of Staff of the Army General George C. Marshall; and Milton Eisenhower. What these three men, so far apart in age and experience, had in common was the president's trust. FDR had a close relationship with all three men, and he believed what they told him. In Roosevelt's administration, as in most others, personal relationships were often crucial.

Secretary Stimson barged into the White House and flatly told Roosevelt that he, as president, absolutely had to speak out in Eisenhower's behalf. Marshall, too, insisted that Roosevelt had to defend Ike. Impressed by both their arguments, Roosevelt called in Milton and asked him to draft a presidential statement accepting the Darlan deal but emphasizing that it was temporary in nature and had been undertaken only for military expediency. Milton did as directed, brought back the draft for Roosevelt's approval, and then watched "with some pain as FDR added the work 'temporary' about six more times, which plus my four made ten times the word was used."[27]

Roosevelt sent Milton to North Africa to take over the operation of Radio Maroc (which he quickly did) and to use his skills and his OWI connections to bolster Ike's reputation. Milton met with Darlan, who complained to him, "I know I am but a lemon which you intend to use and then toss aside." Milton diplomatically pacified him and then turned to more pressing business. Ike's political adviser, Robert Murphy, recorded that Milton, furious that some newspaper and radio commentators were still calling his brother a fascist, told him that "unless drastic action were taken immediately, the General's career might be irreparably damaged. 'Heads must roll, Murphy!' he exclaimed. 'Heads must roll!' "[28]

No heads rolled, but the storm died down. Milton arranged for C. D. Jackson, of Time-Life, who later played an important role in Dwight's presidential administration, to manage Radio Maroc. Immediately the tenor of the broadcasts changed radically. Milton also demanded that the communication cable be promptly put in working order. As if overnight, the reports of Middleton and other sympathetic correspondents once again began to flow to the United States. And last, but certainly not least, on Christmas Eve 1942 Darlan was assassinated by unknown parties. With the root of the problem thus eliminated, Ike was finally absolved of the "guilt of association."[29]

Having completed the repairs in Africa, Milton returned to Washington to rectify the damage there. Henry Wallace, now Roosevelt's vice-president, noted in his diary that "Milton feels very strongly that his brother should not be called on to do both military and political work but he also feels that his brother ought to have sound political advice. In Milton's opinion, Murphy 'is bad either because of lack of ability or shorthandedness.' " Milton discussed the problem in private with both Roosevelt and Marshall. He also talked to reporters. One of them, the famous muckraking journalist I. F. Stone, wrote "Eisenhower's Friends Deny He's to Blame in North Africa Mess" for *PM* magazine. Stone included a photograph of Milton. For the duration of the war General Eisenhower received only laudatory coverage, in the view of the American public rivaling even Roosevelt as America's most respected and beloved figure.[30]

Milton, who was generally publicity-shy and especially so in his current position (most especially with regard to his personal involvement in smoothing over the Darlan crisis), was chagrined that he had received so much notoriety. He wrote Ike expressing his dismay at the Stone article and apologizing for any distress or embarrassment he might have caused his brother.

Ike responded from his headquarters in Algiers: "You should get one thing into your head, once and for all. . . . For many years I have respected your judgment, particularly in your branch of the public relations field, above that of any other person that I know. Do not ever, for one second, think that I would . . . give the slightest credence to reports that you had . . . done anything inimical to [my interests]. The *PM* article merely made me smile, and the only distress I ever had in connection with it was to learn that you had taken it so seriously."[31] The two brothers' relationship was stronger than ever.

CHAPTER 6

"Our Concern Is with the Education of Men and Women Determined to Be Free"

Return to Kansas State

Just before the end of 1938, while he was still working under Henry Wallace in the Department of Agriculture, representatives from Pennsylvania State College approached Eisenhower to offer him a deanship. Initially he found the notion appealing, recalling fondly the academic life that had ended so abruptly when Jardine had "forced" him to accept the foreign-service post in Scotland. But then he began to wonder whether he would be derelict in his patriotic duty if he quit government service as war clouds gathered over Europe. In addition, Eisenhower questioned whether he would find college administration as exciting and demanding as his present responsibilities. In typical fashion, he sought out the advice of Ike, then serving under MacArthur in the Philippines. Also typically, Ike responded within days with a three-page, single-spaced letter.

Ike began by analyzing the pragmatic considerations. He assumed that a college dean would be "practically impossible" to remove from office, so notwithstanding Milton's civil-service status, the offer provided added security. Moreover, the salary would undoubtedly be greater. Thus simply from the standpoint of Milton's obligations to Helen and the children, the Penn State job had definite advantages. But most of the letter covered more idealistic themes: By returning to academia Milton could do more as a "guide and inspiration to our youth" than he could as a government official, where "you are in danger of becoming only an extremely useful tool." Regarding the rigors of the position, Ike felt that Milton overworked himself in any case, whereas a good college dean's "value derives from character, knowledge and personality—not from ceaseless expenditure of nervous energy." Finally, and most important, Ike queried Milton about "freedom in self-expression." Removed from the legal and ethical constraints that prohibit a public servant from expressing himself on current issues, Milton could draw upon his tremendous "ability in composition, particularly in expository writing, and your wealth of experience," to become a national intellectual leader, a critical position at a time when fascism and war clouds consumed Europe and the Depression continued at home.[1]

Milton appreciated his brother's advice, but he decided to reject the offer. He felt that he still had vital work to do in the Department of Agriculture, and if the United States became involved in the war, Roosevelt might ask him to perform additional duties for his country. However, he never lost his interest in an academic position, nor did he forget Ike's well-taken points. By 1943, when he was approached once again, he was prepared to listen very carefully.

In May of 1943 Charles Harger, Eisenhower's old boss on the Abilene newspaper and the chairman of the board of regents in Kansas, came to Washington to call on Eisenhower. He reported that Dr. Francis David (commonly F. D.) Farrell, president of Kansas State College, was stepping down to return to teaching and that the regents were seriously considering asking Eisenhower to take his place. Might Eisenhower be interested in the position? The OWI's associate director replied that he would think about it, and two weeks later he flew to Kansas City to confer with the board of regents as a whole. Shortly thereafter the board made him a formal offer.

Eisenhower anguished over the decision for six weeks. He and Helen drew up long lists of pros and cons. Just as before, he wrote Ike, only by now his brother was one of the world's leading figures. Milton said he was inclined to accept but again added that he was afraid he would "feel that I was running away from a necessary and pretty arduous war post."[2]

Ike's response was quick and even more adamant than previously: Milton should take the job. "I regard the position described in your letter as one of public trust and offering opportunities for public service to challenge the talents of any man," he wrote. "Over a period of years it will allow you to be a real factor toward influencing a healthy development of young America." But for the troubled Milton Ike's final point was the most telling. He felt that no man in the country was in a better position than the General to advise him as to his patriotic duty. Ike was unequivocal. He emphasized that under no circumstances should Milton interpret his leaving the OWI in the midst of the war as some form of desertion. He assured him that final victory was not far off, and as a college president Milton would be performing the most critical task of all, training young people to meet the challenges of the postwar world. Ike was so convinced that Milton should accept the offer that he wrote their oldest brother, Arthur, to ensure that the family presented a united front. "The Presidency of a great college," Ike succinctly opined, "is a grand job for a man of Milton's talents and disposition."[3]

This time the pros outweighed the cons. Accepting Ike's view that he was burning himself out in Washington, Milton later confessed that he believed—in retrospect, mistakenly—that by taking the position at Kansas State he would be able to slow down and perhaps even do some writing and scholarly research of his own. However, his prime motivation stemmed from Ike's other argument. While working with both the WRA and the OWI he had witnessed all too closely the dangerous ideas that can be bred during wartime. He was appalled at how naive and narrow Americans could be and agreed with Ike that America's youth had to be better prepared to accept the burden of world leadership. This preparation would have to come from the educational system. Milton felt that the presidency of Kansas State would afford him the opportunity to work intimately with the future leaders of the United States, encouraging them "to think critically and objectively within a moral framework."[4] He accepted the challenge.

So on July 1, 1943, not yet forty-four years old, Eisenhower left Washington to return to Manhattan, Kansas, to begin a new career. He brought with him not only his finely honed administrative talents but also a carefully reasoned and highly developed philosophy of education. Many of his ideas were an amalgam of the countless theoretical discussions he had had with his former "patrons," Harger and Jardine. Both men had continually encouraged Eisenhower to pursue his own scholarly endeavors and, moreover, had impressed upon him the value of obtaining a truly comprehensive education. Of course, there was also the ever-present influence of Ike. The words of advice contained in Ike's letters were not prompted solely by his desire for Milton to accept a position in academia. On the contrary, they reflected the long conversations the two brothers had held together, beginning when they had lived as neighbors in Washington. Milton recalled that even in North Africa, when he would visit the General's residence, they would take time off from their pressing responsibilities to talk about the direction of the United States once the war was over. Both agreed that Americans had to learn to be citizens of the world, developing an understanding that transcended their parochial concerns. As Milton once told a *U.S. News & World Report* interviewer, "[I]n a democracy, we want educated people to have a true breadth of knowledge and understanding so that their judgments on all matters of citizen concern will be valid."[5]

Decades later, such concepts seem naively idealistic, the product of a homespun upbringing in Middle America. Yet they did not originate with the Eisenhower brothers. Each, but particularly Milton, had spent a great deal of time with educational leaders in the East. These influential figures knew that following the war hundreds of thousands of young Americans, many of them veterans, would be descending en masse on the nation's colleges and universities. In fact, around seven hundred thousand more students were enrolled in 1946 than in 1939, the most rapid growth in the history of higher education.[6] If there were to be no more depressions, if there were to be no more wars, these men and women would have to learn more than technical skills. Indeed, the Depression and World War II and then the specter of atomic devastation brought American academia to the threshold of revolution. A 1943 study aptly entitled *Education and the People's Peace* issued the call, "Now is the time for the American people to match the varied wealth of their great resources . . . with a moral and educational program of equal stature."[7] Three years later, as the cold war erupted, President Harry Truman appointed a Presidential Commission on Higher Education, urging that "we should now re-examine our system of higher education in terms of its objectives, methods, and facilities; and in the light of the social role it has to play." The commission, headed by George F. Zook, president of the American Council on Education (of which Eisenhower was a member), concluded, "In a real sense the future of our civilization depends on the direction education takes, not just in the distant future, but in the days immediately ahead."[8]

Milton Eisenhower entered the mainstream of such progressive thinking, which became the most discussed theme in academia over the next decade. Whereas his intimate relations with Harger, Jardine, and Ike produced within him a fervent devotion to the potential value of higher education, the many acquaintances he had established during his long stay in Washington and the experiences that he had shared with them suggested means by which this potential could reach fruition. Chief among the individuals who influenced Eisenhower's thought was James B. Conant. Conant, whom Milton introduced to Ike and who subsequently became President Eisenhower's high commissioner in West Germany, was one of America's leading scholars on education and served as Harvard's president from 1933 to 1953. He and Milton became good friends in the 1930s and 1940s, during which time Conant would bounce off Milton his theories on general education. The president of Harvard was so concerned that the prewar educational trends towards specialized study and overconcentration on the sciences were resulting in a generation of atomistic Americans, incapable of acquiring a holistic and humanistic understanding of the complex modern world, that in 1943, the year that Eisenhower went to

Kansas State, he appointed a faculty committee to study "the objectives of a general education in a free society." The resultant Harvard Report, published in the last year of World War II, became a landmark document in the country's shifting curricular emphasis towards the liberal arts. Articulating Conant's view, the "Red Book," as it was called, predicted that the widespread social dislocations of the 1930s and 1940s would usher in an era of mass democracy. It was therefore incumbent upon the colleges and universities to revitalize the liberal tradition in American education in order to infuse the democratic process with a responsible citizenry. Always attuned to the ideas surrounding him, Eisenhower took mental notes of his conversations with Conant; and it is to his lasting credit that he began to institute the essential recommendations of the Harvard Report a year before its publication.[9]

Eisenhower thus arrived at Kansas State with his mind set on liberalizing the curriculum. He knew he was in for a struggle. As the first native Kansan and first alumnus to be elected the college's president, he had not been away from his alma mater so long as to forget that Manhattan was far removed from Washington and the Ivy League. Little about Kansas State had changed since Eisenhower had graduated more than two decades earlier. For eighteen of these years its chief executive had been F. D. Farrell, a conservative by any definition of the term. The physical plant had grown only slightly because as a staunch opponent of deficit financing Farrell had refused all New Deal assistance. He did recognize the need to produce more well-rounded students, and during his tenure enrollments had increased in English, history, government, and foreign languages. Nevertheless, his view of liberal education was severely limited, and he unbendingly objected to establishing a program that would lead to a Bachelor of Arts degree. Kansas State should remain, in his words, "essentially a technological school." In the words of one of his faculty, "He wasn't exactly a hayseed farmer even though his sentiments were with that group . . . under Farrell what you might call the cultural types of education were pretty infinitesimal."[10]

To Farrell, as cited in one of his biennial reports, an instance of "liberalizing technological training" was the installation of a three-manual Austin pipe organ in the auditorium. His priorities are best summarized in his administration's description of Kansas State's purpose contained in the 1942/43 catalog. Only after listing "undergraduate and graduate instruction in agriculture, engineering and architecture, home economics, the sciences, and veterinary medicine" did it include "and to encourage sound thinking and good citizenship."[11]

Right from the beginning Eisenhower put the Kansas State community on notice that he was determined to initiate substantive changes. His inaugural address, broadcast nationally on September 30, 1943, reflected his conversations with Conant and others, as well as anticipated virtually every theme propounded in the more publicized Harvard Report. Never in the next quarter-century would he deviate from its essential thesis. The address (reproduced in appendix A) began by extolling the great advances in science and technology that had been made since he was a student, emphasizing the need for Kansas State to remain in the forefront of such research. But, Eisenhower added, "the fruits of science and technology cannot, in themselves, automatically instill into us the wisdom, the tolerance, the integrated reasoning required for the management of affairs in a complex and rapidly changing civilization." Highlighting the overarching concerns of many contemporary educators, he pointed to Germany, Italy, and Japan as countries where science had run amuck, where narrowly trained men with much practical knowledge had not been able to temper their judgments with the insights derived from a broad education.

Eisenhower then turned to the future, when the war was won and a massive number of armed service veterans would return home and enter college. He warned that "a heterogeneous lot of studies, in or outside a field of specialization, will not wholly satisfy the returning young people. For these war-experienced men and women will want also to understand many forces and values in their relation to one another, to the individual and to our free society. They will also want to know the relation of all these to the freedom they fought for."

Eisenhower explained that the liberal arts colleges would have to take the lead in providing general education. "But the technical schools and colleges have a responsibility, too." Indeed, "perhaps theirs is the greater responsibility. For in our technical colleges we specialize in scientific disciplines and we therefore face the danger of encouraging a man to become a specialist within one discipline, and a dogmatist in affairs within other disciplines."

In conclusion Eisenhower declared, "Our concern is that men shall conquer machines, that machines shall not conquer men. Our concern is that men and women trained in scientific methods shall also gain tolerance, and understanding, and wisdom. Our concern is with the education of men and women determined to be free."[12]

The audience in the old auditorium had come expecting much ceremony and little content. Nearly all its members were surprised. By no means were all pleased. Eisenhower was young, vibrant, usually smiling, personable, and eager to shake hands; and he made a good impression. Still, many older faculty members shook their heads. They did not much like this thrust towards general education, comprehensive curriculum, "sound judgment" ("whatever that might mean," they muttered among themselves). This brash young man had perhaps had too much contact with FDR and other Ivy League types back in Washington. He needed to be reminded that Kansas State's task was to produce more grain, not more intellectuals, better cows, not better humanists.[13]

Others reacted differently. One young man, Kenneth S. Davis, a journalist who would later become Eisenhower's assistant and chief speech writer at Kansas State; the author of *Soldier of Democracy*, the first biography of Ike; and eventually one of America's more successful freelance writers of history, recalls, "I sat up there in the balcony of that auditorium and I was just tremendously impressed." He had not yet met Eisenhower, but "that speech made me very eager to work with him. He was absolutely fantastic.... He had a kind of resonant singing voice." Like Eisenhower a product of Kansas, and even more of an idealist, Davis continued, "The only other voice as effective as that I've heard was Adlai Stevenson. Adlai could sing a speech out and make it very effective. And Milton could do this."[14]

So despite the sometimes muted, often vocal opposition of the senior faculty in agriculture, home economics, and engineering, Eisenhower pushed forward, his enthusiasm and determination undiminished. In February 1944 he declared that "the staff at Kansas State will see to it that the College is prepared to meet its responsibilites in the post-war period," and in his first biennial report he made clear what those responsibilities were. After avowing that every member of the college knew that military victory was the first goal, he continued: "Military victory alone will not achieve the great objectives for which this war is being fought. A way of life, here and throughout the world, is at stake." It was, he said, a way of life "which respects human dignity and retains basic social responsibility in the hands of the people themselves.... Military victory must be matched by a victory in our minds."[15]

Eisenhower had definite ideas on how to implement his ideas. He intended to institute comprehensive courses that would introduce students to the whole spectrum of human knowledge and culture, with a requirement that students take courses in each of four basic areas. The program, initially outlined in early 1944 and the first experiment of its kind, would inject liberal education into every technical curriculum. However, he did not yet know much about faculties: he did not know how fiercely a physics professor would resent teaching a course on man and the physical world in place of a straight physics course; how an historian would resent teaching a course on man and the social sciences rather than one on the French Revolution; how furious it would make an agronomist to have to teach about man and the biological world; or even how upsetting it would be to an English professor to have to teach about man and the humanities instead of about Shelley. But if Eisenhower did not know faculty types, he did know people, and he had learned at the Department of Agriculture that the way to bring about change within an institution was to involve the individuals who would do the changing. Also, he was not adverse to wielding all the power of his office when necessary.

One of his first acts was to call together the entire faculty and staff—about four hundred people—to ask their help in liberalizing the curriculum. As he confessed decades later, "At that time I was a little enamored of what's called comprehensive courses." He warned his audience that the engineering and agricultural students, "if you don't look out, will be ignorant of the social sciences, the humanities and the liberal arts."

Although asking for their help, Eisenhower was determined to have his way. His government experience had taught him that "there is nothing like letting those who are going to have to carry out programs participate in the development," as he put it, "so long as they make the right decision, and it is up to the central guy to see to it that they reach the right decision." As to his expectations, "I had had top jobs and when I said do it, it was done." He soon discovered that with faculty it did not work quite the way it did with career civil servants.[16]

Eisenhower appointed a general committee on postwar planning, of which he was chairman, and numerous subcommittees for each school, composed of the teaching faculty, to revise the curriculum. He had a weakness, common to Washington bureaucrats as well as to academics, for titles; some of the subcommittees had preposterous names, such as the Committee on Teaching Methods That Encourage Integrative Habits of Thinking. Eisenhower attended all meetings of the general committee and led discussions. "He knew what he wanted," one administrator recalled, "and he made sure that it happened." Although the engineering and agriculture faculty "fought and fought," Eisenhower, "a great believer in democracy, . . . wanted to achieve his ends so strongly that he was pretty tough . . . He guided things through with his personal imprint."[17]

According to historian James Carey, Eisenhower encountered "widespread opposition on the Kansas State campus." There was a general feeling that Eisenhower was meddling in areas he did not know anything about. He went "too far," a member of the animal husbandry faculty, Professor Rufus Cox, opined. Cox gave as an example replacing zoology, botany, and microbiology with a comprehensive course in biological science, which was "more or less watered down and didn't go deep enough into any one." As a result, Cox felt, upperclassmen in his advanced courses "simply didn't have enough background in zoology." The science and engineering professors likewise did not want their students wasting time on the humanities or social sciences. But Eisenhower had the zeal of a reformer. As far as Cox was concerned, "He took on almost a dictatorial attitude, crammed it down our throats." And the dean of home economics complained bitterly, "Milton Eisenhower used democratic means to achieve his dictatorial ends." Those who sympathized with Eisenhower interpreted the hostility from a different perspective. "He imposed this stuff," Ken Davis explained, "on a faculty that was incompetent to handle it and which resented having it imposed."[18]

In retrospect, Eisenhower will be among the first to admit that he probably moved too quickly. Moreover, his uncompromising attitude towards reform and personal involvement in the process must have seemed unduly authoritarian to many veterans of the Manhattan campus. While his predecessor, Farrell, had not been afraid of imposing his views, consistent with his conservatism, he had at least presented the appearance of decentralized power. The common adage was that Farrell had perceived the faculty as a "flock of sheep while using the dean as a crook to control that flock."[19] But Eisenhower appeared to go much farther. His activism, which included chairing the general committee on postwar planning, could easily give the impression that within a short span of time he had gathered all power into his own hands. Despite his smiling visage, the new president radiated authority and exercised it.

The faculty may have disagreed with Eisenhower's ideas and his approach, but most would grudgingly concede that he stirred up a sleepy campus and put a backwoods college in the forefront of educational initiative in the United States. Russell Thackrey, formerly head of the journalism department and for most of Eisenhower's tenure dean of administration, loves to recall his experience upon returning to Manhattan in 1944, on leave from the Navy. Attending a faculty party, he found, to his absolute amazement, that "everybody was furiously discussing curriculum." According to Thackrey, who had been a freshman in 1923 and an instructor in the 1930s, nothing even remotely similar had ever happened before.[20]

The faculty's resentment notwithstanding, of all his accomplishments at Kansas State, Eisenhower is most proud of his role in introducing general education. Even years later, when the cyclical nature of educational reform made the concept an object of ridicule, an obsolete theory outmoded in an age of computer technology and the race to the moon, he never abandoned his belief that well-rounded students represent the cornerstone of a thriving democracy. He and many of his supporters at Kansas State continue to be proud that their little school on the prairie instituted comprehensive courses before mighty Harvard recommended that all the nation's colleges and universities do so. Eisenhower was also proud that in 1946 Truman appointed him to his Presidential Commission on Higher Education, and it was not without a sense of personal satisfaction that he was able to report to his deans, some of whom remained skeptical of the liberal reform, that "the 30 members of the ... Commission agree unanimously that education for responsible, participating, effective citizenship is the most important single task facing all colleges and universities in this country; this goal has not been very successfully met in the past, but now it must be met or the entire free political system may disappear."[21] Eisenhower had no quarrel with the evaluation of his administration contained in the history of Kansas State: "Eisenhower's liberal views were in keeping with the broader interpretation of the Morrill land-grant wording which had provided for an education that was both liberal and practical," historian James Carey wrote in 1977. Eisenhower's legacy rested on "the broadening of the idea of what constituted an education."[22]

As mentioned previously and as Eisenhower himself later acknowledged, one of the reasons that he accepted the Kansas State job was his belief that as a college president he could lead a quiet, scholarly life with plenty of time for reading, reflecting, serious conversation, and some research of his own. In this regard he once again revealed Ike's influence, who told his son John that "I am happy that Milton has entered a career which will take him away from that Washington madhouse" and wrote to another friend that he had feared that "a continuation of the high pressure life Milton was leading in official Washington would have broken him down."[23] Those comments only indicate how little either of the Eisenhower brothers understood the unique role of the American college president.

One of the most apt descriptions of that role came from a man who was well acquainted with the pressures of high office, Rutherford B. Hayes. After leaving the White House, Hayes had served as a member of the Ohio State board of regents in the early 1890s, when the school was searching for a new president. He said, "We are looking for a man of fine appearance, of commanding presence, one who will impress the public; he must be a fine speaker at public assemblies; he must be a great scholar and a great teacher; he must be a preacher, also, as some think; he must be a man of winning manners; he must have tact so that he can get along with and govern the faculty; he must be popular with the students; he must also be a man of business training, a man of affairs, he must be a great administrator."[24]

Hayes's list, long as it was, was not complete. The president also has to be a fund-raiser and, if he is at a state-supported school, a lobbyist. Demands on the time of a college president are never-ending. "Don't overwork yourself," President Charles W. Eliot of Harvard wrote his friend Daniel Coit Gilman when Gilman was elected to the presidency of Johns Hopkins in 1876. As Frederick Rudolph remarks, "No successful university president, including Eliot, ever followed this advice."[25] Certainly Eisenhower did not.

As president of Kansas State, Eisenhower traveled incessantly. The itinerary for a typical trip, to southeastern Kansas from April 27 to May 9, 1944, had him speaking at the Iola Rotary Club (220 in the audience), the Fort Scott Rotary (400), the Pittsburgh Chamber of Commerce (100), a high school assembly in Parsons (500), a public gathering in the Parsons High School auditorium in the evening (600), the Lions Club in Independence (200), the chambers of commerce in Coffeyville (550) and Arkansas City (250), an open meeting in Winfield (1,300), the Kansas State alumni in Wichita (200), the Arts Institute in Wichita (200), the Rotary Club in Wichita (700), the high school in Whitewater (200), and the chambers of commerce in Marion (125) and Augusta (300).[26]

He worked six or seven days a week, twelve to fourteen hours a day. He spoke at some seventy-five high school commencements in five years. His hectic schedule, while contradicting one of his reasons for becoming a college president, reflected his view of the president's role. "The President," he believed, "personifies the whole institution; what he amounts to and what his reputation is has an enormous amount to do with the success of the institution." People who heard him speak would tell their legislators what a great guy Milton Eisenhower was (and often the legislator himself would be in the audience, or introducing Eisenhower). As a result, when he went before the legislature to ask for appropriations for Kansas State, it was, in his words, "a love fest [sic]." The legislature could not do enough for Kansas State.

In addition, talking to high school students was a way of attracting the best of them to Kansas State. Previously, the top students in Kansas had gone out of state to college or to the University of Kansas in Lawrence. After Eisenhower returned to Manhattan, Kansas State began getting its share of the brighter young men and women. Also, under Eisenhower enrollment in the School of Arts and Sciences came to exceed that of the School of Engineering, and it nearly doubled that of the School of Agriculture.[27]

Ken Davis, who accompanied Eisenhower on many of his trips, recalled that "he was very sensitive to pressures and very sensitive to people's reactions to him. . . . He could stand outside of himself and look at himself and see what kind of an effect he was producing on the audience." Often Eisenhower spoke extemporaneously, but when he prepared a speech,

Davis remembered, he worked hard on it. Davis knew—he wrote the first draft of many of them. Eisenhower, Davis said, would take an hour-long speech and cut it down to twenty minutes. "He'd underline words and he really concentrated on putting the thing over. . . . Milton was a great actor, like Roosevelt." Indeed, Davis thought Eisenhower an even better public speaker than Roosevelt.[28]

The relationship between Eisenhower and Davis requires some further elaboration, since it provides a view of Eisenhower through a different lens. When Eisenhower first came to Kansas State as president, he found Davis, an aspiring young novelist without a steady income, valuable for drafting occasional speeches or performing other part-time assignments. He was so impressed with the young man's ability that he persuaded Davis to write Ike's biography, for Eisenhower a sign of true confidence. The two men worked together closely on the project—Milton critiqued all the drafts—and in 1947, when he decided he needed a full-time assistant to help in writing speeches and articles, especially those concerning educational theory and philosophy, he asked Davis, who had taken a job in New York City. Davis had never adjusted to life in the big city, and he knew that a salary of four thousand dollars could go a lot farther in Manhattan (Kansas), so he did not need much prodding to return to his hometown.[29]

While both shared a profound love for their Kansas roots, the two were otherwise highly incompatible. Davis was an idealist, somewhat of a visionary, and above all an avid Democrat. Indeed, some years later he became such a devotee of Adlai Stevenson that following the 1956 presidential election he rejected all politics and opted for the seclusion of small-town America. Eisenhower respected Davis for his views but not for his methods. Whereas he always counseled moderation and evolution, Davis, in his opinion, was a "rebel." Eisenhower feared moving too fast; Davis felt that no movement was fast enough. A clash was inevitable.[30]

It was not long before Davis began to find fault with his boss. He was in total agreement with Eisenhower's educational philosophy and applauded the efforts to liberalize the curriculum. He also strongly supported the work Eisenhower did as chairman of the U.S. National Commission for UNESCO. As time went on, however, and he accompanied Eisenhower on what seemed like constant excursions away from the campus, he developed a more cynical view. Davis began to see in Milton what he would later label in an article about Ike "The Abilene Factor in Eisenhower." To Davis, that factor was ambition. "Milton was an Eisenhower," he believed, "and he was anxious to get ahead. He had that Abilene success anxiety." Most of the Kansas State community enjoyed the headlines Milton made during his travels; Davis felt that he "was using the college to promote Milton too much and was not there enough." No matter how often Eisenhower explained that his many speeches and public appearances were, in Davis's words, "to enhance the prestige of the college," the young idealist remained convinced that "it was really Milton's prestige that was being enhanced."[31]

Another of Davis's complaints was that Eisenhower did not fit his image of a college president. He remembered vividly his excitement upon listening to the 1943 inaugural address, thinking that his alma mater (Davis had graduated from Kansas State, and his father had been a professor there) would soon become a haven for intellectuals. He was disappointed. Not only did he consider Eisenhower too narrow, incapable of conceptualizing in the abstract, but he also felt that the college's top administrator was uncomfortable with those academics who did. To illustrate his point, Davis recalled the visit to campus of the philosopher and former president of Amherst Alexander Meiklejohn. Meiklejohn gave what Davis described as a "beautiful speech" on the value of freedom of expression, after which he attended a reception Davis held in his honor. According to Davis, the whole experience was for Eisenhower a "lousy time"; he was "utterly miserable that night." Davis undoubtedly exaggerated, but Eisenhower's own words describing Meiklejohn reveal that he was somewhat ill-at-ease with those less pragmatically oriented than himself. "Philosophers," Eisenhower wrote Davis following the reception, "love to define an ambiguous abstraction by a new abstraction, clear to the author but ambiguous to everyone else. I must confess I get a little tired of the sheer punning of words."[32]

The rift between the two eventually led to a chasm. The final break came when the young writer, eager to express his more esoteric ideas about education, began writing personal articles for local newspapers and magazines. Although Davis signed his own name, Eisenhower was concerned that his views might be construed as Eisenhower's. He told Davis, "You are just as free as any other citizen in any other position in this college to write your mind and you will never hear from me, but you can't be my assistant and have it assumed that these are my ideas that your are expressing." Davis took his cue and resigned. Unlike his relationships with other former assistants, Eisenhower has had very little to do with him since.[33]

Reflecting on the relationship more than a quarter of a century later, Davis conceded, "Now that I'm older, much older, I realize he really was a very good guy." He continued, "Milton's criticism of me was I was so rigid and critical and cantankerous and he was right. . . . Milton made me come alive."[34] Furthermore, it must be acknowledged that certain of his retrospective characterizations of Eisenhower, particularly his conviction regarding the "Abilene factor," did not coalesce until the 1950s, when

Davis became enamored of Stevenson and disillusioned with Ike. Nevertheless, his opinions cannot be discounted. Few others had the opportunity to work so intimately with Eisenhower in the realm of ideas.

Equally important, their estrangement points to another side of Eisenhower. Certainly a man in his position could not be expected to keep on a speech writer whose views "on social and political questions," to quote Eisenhower's later letters, "are [from his] far apart" and who "is too liberal for me."[35] His reaction to Davis, nevertheless, illustrates his great sensitivity to criticism. To Eisenhower, Davis was "brutally frank." Even early on in their association he objected to Davis's refusal to accept all his judgments in personal terms. For example, when, despite Eisenhower's recommendations, Davis left in the manuscript of *Soldier of Democracy* a less than favorable depiction of Ike's conduct during the Darlan affair and the contention that Abilene had a "right" and "wrong" side of the tracks, Milton requested that his name be omitted from the acknowledgments. (Eisenhower wrote Davis, "The value of your book is that it is an honest appraisal, containing both good and bad. Your book is important historiographically. I do disagree with your interpretation of North African developments, but I am wholly satisfied merely to have stated my own view to you.... I am a reviewer, not censor.")[36] Over time, as their conflicts became more severe, he came to dismiss Davis's assertions as those of a "brilliant nut, always ascribing nefarious thoughts to everyone." He has never forgiven him their differences.[37]

Regardless of their disagreements, whether personal or ideological, when Eisenhower and Davis collaborated, the product was often a masterpiece. Davis may have been, in his words, "rigid and critical and cantankerous," but he was also, in Eisenhower's words, "a beautiful writer." As noted, Eisenhower was an exceptional speaker. Melding his oratorical skills to Davis's literary ones, he could be spell-binding. A prime example is when the two teamed up on a speech dealing with a topic dear to both of them—Kansas and democracy. Eisenhower had recently returned from a six-week tour abroad, most of it at a UNESCO conference in Lebanon. Addressing the Native Sons and Daughters of Kansas in Topeka on January 28, 1948, he described the Middle Eastern country as "rising in snow-capped mountains out of the blue Mediterranean and bearing upon its shores and slopes myriad vestiges of ancient art, industry, and war." Already Davis's artistry with words is readily apparent. However, it is when the speech focused on its topic, "The Strength of Kansas," that the beauty of the word selection becomes most striking. Juxtaposing his description of Lebanon with his recollections of his drive home from the Kansas City airport, Eisenhower told his audience, "I was suddenly thrilled by the sight of Kansas mud in roadside ditches, by the sight of black earth reaching across the flat Kaw River bottoms to distant hills. I was thrilled too, by the friendly welcome of those hills around Manhattan. This was good earth—and I had seen so many deserts! These were honest, earthy, hopeful people—and I had seen so much synthetic brilliance overlaying a bleak despair."

The speech went on to explore the sources of Eisenhower's—and Davis's—excitement. He explained that Kansas's strength derived from so many sources: its wonderful mixture of peoples, its marvelously fertile soil, its tremendous vistas, its minerals, its educational system for all its inhabitants, its progressive character, its basic honesty. To Eisenhower, the sum of Kansas's assets was greater than any of its parts. As he put it, "We are balanced halfway between the America facing Europe and the America facing China; we are that happy mixture of town and country, agriculture and industry, which seems best suited to the maintenance of democratic attitudes."

As this last sentence evidences, while Davis may have crafted much of the prose, the speech was emphatically Eisenhower's. Not only, as always, did he edit the draft carefully, but it bore the indelible imprint of his ideas. Just as he demanded that the faculty of Kansas State devise a curriculum applicable to the postwar world, so he implored the people of Kansas to become the leaders of that world. "Kansas is now ready to serve," he proclaimed, "as the sane moderator of ideological extremes, the firm core of the American culture, the vital center of creative compromise. No other state is as well equipped to play these roles. No other challenge in a world of challenges is more thrilling."[38] There is perhaps no better statement of Eisenhower's ideals than "The Strength of Kansas." When not working at odds, he and Davis made quite a team.

One must not get the impression that Eisenhower became dependent on Davis. Relatively few of his speeches were formally prepared, and some believe that he was at his best when speaking extemporaneously.[39] Furthermore, Davis virtually never helped out on Eisenhower's articles. Eisenhower could not find the time to write as often as he had intended when he decided to enter academic life, but he did manage to publish an occasional piece. One such article brought national attention. Entitled "Wanted: A Program for Freedom," it appeared in the November 1946 issue of *Country Gentleman.* Not surprisingly, it reflected more of the Eisenhower philosophy; also not surprisingly, it was precisely and logically written. Its thesis was that big government, big labor, foreign problems, the atomic bomb, and other unwelcome features of the modern world were all here to stay. His style may not have had the flare of Davis's, but it was equally effective. For example, he was able to sum up his theme in three concise sentences: "Facts, pleasant or unpleasant, cannot be ignored, condemned, or wished away. They are the framework of successful planning. We must face all the relevant evidence, then understand it, and then devise a program of action."[40] To a large extent, Eisenhower had succinctly explained his own success as a government official and educational leader. One Midwestern woman thought the article an expression of the Communist philosophy. She was so upset that she wrote to every company that advertised in the magazine to demand that they never again advertise in *Country Gentleman*. Executives had to read the article to see what all the fuss was about. They were so impressed by it that the magazine received a flood of mail, requesting reprints. There were so many requests, in fact, that *Country Gentleman* issued the article in a small pamphlet entitled *One Nation: Indivisible*. There was national publicity, and tens of thousands of copies were circulated.[41]

For all his UNESCO work, traveling around Kansas, service on presidential commissions, and writing articles, Eisenhower did not neglect his faculty at Kansas State. Salaries, always the most important element in faculty morale, were abysmally low, averaging thirty-four hundred dollars for full and associate professors and twenty-four hundred dollars for professors at lower ranks. The Kansas legislature met only every other year, and during the war it would not raise salaries. Therefore not until 1947 could Eisenhower do anything about the situation. In the meantime the faculty work load had increased dramatically as a result of the influx of veterans. Classes began at 7:00 A.M. and went on until 10:00 P.M., and still the classrooms were overflowing. Professors, even the most senior ones, had an eighteen-hour load; yet the student-teacher ratio rose to twenty to one. All of this might have been accepted as necessary and a clear duty had not salaries been mired at Depression levels and had there not been an inflation rate of 20 percent in 1946 (still the highest one-year rise in prices in U.S. history).[42]

Hallam Davis, head of the English Department (who later, with Eisenhower's encouragement, built a first-class department at Kansas State), came to the president's office in the middle of the 1946/47 school year. "Milton," he is reputed to have declared, "we've just got to do something. The faculty is ready to mutiny."

Eisenhower reacted in characteristic fashion, as he would whenever faced with a crisis. He called a general faculty meeting and openly and bluntly explained the situation. He went through the budget in some detail, then told the faculty that because the legislature was not in session that year there was nothing he could do at that time about their salaries. He promised to make an all-out effort on behalf of the faculty when the legislature came back to Topeka; meanwhile, the only way he could raise

any salaries would be to reduce the size of the faculty by cutting enrollment. Obviously such cuts would severely affect the returning veterans;
and at the close of the war this was anathema to even the most destitute
faculty member.

"He just laid out what the situation was," one faculty member recalled.
"That was a great thing. Professors came up and said 'I wish we'd known
this before. It puts a different light on it.' And they basically said if it's a
choice between taking care of the veterans or not they'd be calm."[43]

In the next session of the legislature, Eisenhower was fully prepared to
make his case for his faculty. According to an associate, he had at an
earlier meeting of the regents "been chagrined by being unable to answer a
question or two." Thereafter "he prepared intensively for his budget hearings."[44] He also worked closely with Chancellor Deane W. Malott of the
University of Kansas, whose problems and goals were broadly similar to
Eisenhower's. Malott and Eisenhower were old friends—both had grown
up in Abilene, where Malott was the son of the town's principal banker.
(Two years later, when Ike became president of Columbia University,
Abilene could boast of having produced the heads of three major institutions. Malott soon went on to Cornell, where he became president; and
Milton Eisenhower went on to Penn State and then Johns Hopkins. Thus
Abilene, Kansas, provided the presidents of three great Eastern universities, which is surely some sort of record for such a small town, and no
small compliment to the Abilene public school system.) In addition,
Eisenhower was ready to collect on the investment he had made in all
those trips through Kansas, in all those speeches before businessmen's
clubs, high school commencements, and the like.

The result was a handsome increase in appropriations for Kansas State
and a much appreciated jump in salaries, to a level that made the college
competitive on a national scale. Over the next few years Eisenhower
raised salaries by some 75 percent. By the time he left, senior professors
averaged around six thousand dollars per year, and assistants and instructors made about two thousand dollars less. With conditions for recruitment thus improved, the size of the faculty and staff soared by over 70
percent.[45]

Eisenhower's efforts greatly enhanced his popularity throughout the
campus. The faculty enjoyed the salary increases and decreased teaching
load; the students benefitted from the reduced student-teacher ratio. Adding to his prestige was Eisenhower's reputation for fairness. No matter
how great the temptation, he refused any special privileges for himself. For
example, although it was not unusual for the temperature in central Kansas to reach 110 or even 115 degrees during the summer months, the college had no air conditioning. In 1947 the head of buildings and grounds

learned that he could acquire a secondhand unit incredibly cheap. He offered to install it in the president's office. "Milton wouldn't have it," one of his assistants recalled. "He said the rest of the faculty doesn't have one. Other department heads don't have one. We can't do this. It will be resented."[46]

Nor would Eisenhower allow his administrative heads to take advantage of their position. His dean of home economics was Margaret Justin, a silver-haired, sharp-nosed woman often described in Manhattan as an "old battle-ax" or, more politely, as "a very vigorous person." She was a formidable figure, a power on the campus. Every year after 1947 Eisenhower would raise salaries, allotting a lump sum to each unit and depending on the head of the unit to make appropriate adjustments in the salaries of the faculty members. Each year Dean Justin would take all the increase for Home Economics for herself. Like clockwork Eisenhower would call her into his office. "Dean Justin," he would say, "I expect at least a 6 percent increase for those who deserve it. I have to trust to your judgment since I don't know the individuals in Home Economics." He would then order her to bring in a new budget.[47]

Eisenhower's assistants were not blind to his weaknesses, although only Davis was openly critical. Many felt that he was too reluctant when it came to firing somebody. Thackrey explained that Eisenhower preferred "to go around people, to bypass them," rather than tell them they were ill-suited for a job and had to be replaced. This characteristic of Eisenhower's would appear again at both Penn State and Hopkins. Thackrey also felt that Eisenhower could be "taken in" by an impressive set of credentials and a good first impression by a fast-talking, well-groomed applicant. After hiring him, Eisenhower hated to admit that he had made a mistake and would keep him on long after he had revealed his incompetence.[48]

Donald Ford, a psychology Ph.D. who was a student at Kansas State and later worked for Eisenhower at Penn State, analyzed this reluctance from a different perspective. He remembered that Eisenhower once told him, "I have never regretted any appointment I've ever made. Nobody's perfect and everybody I've appointed has done some important and worthwhile things that I wanted them to do." Ford believes Eisenhower was completely sincere. "He's a builder and a creator and he wants to help people grow and develop."[49]

Eisenhower became president of Kansas State at precisely the time that the federal government began its extensive involvement in higher education. Previously the college's president had had to deal with only the state board of regents and the state legislature. The situation after the war, however, dictated that he also work with the federal government. Eisenhower obviously was in an ideal position, for few men in the country knew as many of the top-ranking Washington bureaucrats as he did. Nor were many as familiar with the ins and outs of the bureaucracy. Indeed, Eisenhower began using his connections and know-how for the good of Kansas State even before the war ended.

One such occasion arose immediately upon his arrival in Manhattan. Eisenhower decided that Russell I. Thackrey was the perfect candidate to be dean of administration.[50] Thackrey was a Kansas State graduate who had been on the faculty there, had worked for the Associated Press and at the University of Minnesota, and had then returned to Kansas State as head of the journalism department. He and Eisenhower had met as undergraduates and had maintained periodic contact ever since. In 1943 Thackrey had joined the Navy. On his way to his assignment at Quonset Point, Rhode Island, he had stopped in Washington, at Eisenhower's request. Eisenhower had confided to him that he was considering the regents' offer to become president of the college, and he wanted to get his opinion on certain matters.

Soon thereafter, after Eisenhower took the job, he asked Thackrey to join him. Thackrey said he was willing but did not want to leave the Navy. Eisenhower insisted. Thackrey had by then been assigned to the Writer's Unit, Aviation Training Division. He was certain that "the war effort would not suffer without me." Still, not unlike Eisenhower earlier, he had nagging doubts as to his duty. Finally he asked his commanding officer if he could be released from the service. His commander said no but suggested that Thackrey apply for a release; the commander would then recommend that his application be turned down. That way Thackrey would have indicated his interest in the post at Kansas State and could still be in the Navy. This would put him in a good position with Eisenhower once the war was over.

Thackrey did as advised. To his commander's amazement and consternation, his application was immediately approved. None of the officer's recommendations of this kind had ever been turned down before. Thackrey, however, received travel orders to Manhattan and terminal leave. Eisenhower, he later discovered, had written personal letters to both the secretary of the navy and the chief of naval operations, both of whom he knew, asking for Thackrey. Both officials had approved.[51]

Most of the agriculture faculty may have disapproved of Eisenhower's emphasis on general education, but most of them were delighted with his use of his connections in the Department of Agriculture to obtain research funds for Kansas State. They were even more pleased when Eisenhower convinced the state legislature to match the federal grants. They were a bit chagrined when he diverted large portions of the funds to the other departments, yet thanks to Eisenhower's efforts, there was enough for everyone. He set Kansas State on its way to becoming a prominent research institution. Under Eisenhower, Kansas State got an artificial insemination project, a pilot bakery in the milling department, a grain sorghum starch project, and a dehydration project for grains, eggs, potatoes, and alfalfa. Other significant work was started in botany, chemistry, entomology, horticulture, physics, poultry breeding, and animal husbandry.[52]

A major source of federal funds was the Veteran's Administration, which under the terms of the G.I. Bill of Rights paid veterans' tuition and living expenses. Kansas State's problem was that it had a ridiculously low tuition, not nearly high enough to cover the actual cost of instruction. Again Eisenhower's expertise proved invaluable. He persuaded the VA to adopt a policy whereby Kansas State would calculate the total amount of time spent by the faculty on teaching to arrive at the legitimate cost per credit hour for instruction. It then calculated the hours taken by veterans to arrive at the real cost of teaching G.I. Bill students. The VA then paid that cost rather than the much lower tuition.

Eisenhower also convinced the VA to give Kansas State surplus equipment, such as trailers, barracks, furniture, and office equipment. The regional office of the VA was in Wichita. Thackrey later recalled that once when the regional office held up a contract to the college, Eisenhower got on the telephone and said, "I'll give you to next Tuesday to get that contract back, or I'm going to Washington about it." The contract was in Manhattan in two days. Eisenhower had lived with red tape so long that he knew just how to cut through it.[53]

For the Eisenhower family the early years in Manhattan continued to be happy ones. Things were happening at Kansas State. Eisenhower was constantly on the go, as he liked to be, and he was getting a great deal of attention. He was frequently mentioned as a possible next governor or senator, talk which he did not necessarily discourage but which he had no intention of following up.

Despite his popularity and qualifications, Eisenhower's extreme sensitivity to criticism probably would have made him a poor candidate in an election. Throughout his long career in education he was time and again approached by politicians who wanted him to run for high office, in Pennsylvania and Maryland as well as in Kansas. He never did it. Eisenhower often said that he would have liked to be a U.S. senator, but only if he did not have to campaign or to deal with constituent problems—obviously impossible conditions. The rough-and-tumble of American politics, the bitter campaigns, and the scurrilous personal attacks added up to a price he was not willing to pay. In September 1949 *Collier's* ran a major article by Holmes Alexander predicting that Eisenhower was a shoo-in for senator from Kansas. Nothing came of it.[54]

While he never accepted the politicians' offers, he was certainly flattered by the confidence they had in him. And in Manhattan, where town and gown lived closely together, most of the town was flattered to have a national figure as president of Kansas State. This contributed to an extremely pleasant life, especially since Helen was delighted to be back home, among her childhood friends.

The family frequently drove to Abilene for Sunday dinner with Eisenhower's mother. Eisenhower's father had died in 1942. Ida, according to her youngest son, "lost her memory as soon as father died. It was a protective device and she lost it completely." Conversations, therefore, had to revolve around what was happening at the exact moment. Eisenhower enjoyed telling two stories about those Sunday dinners:

One day they got up from the dinner table, and Eisenhower said, "Mother, I bet you can't tell me what you just had for dinner."

Ida thought a moment, grinned with her eyes sparkling, and replied, "It was good, wasn't it?"

Another time Eisenhower said, "Mother, I bet you can't name your six sons in order."

"Why, I can too," she replied indignantly. "There's, there's. . . ." Then, laughing, "Why, Milton, you know them as well as I do."[55]

In September 1946 Ida Eisenhower died. Milton wrote a heartfelt eulogy: "The Eisenhower brothers have lost the focusing influence in their lives."[56]

Helen was the model college president's wife. She never complained about his long absences or his constant work. She was, Thackrey remembered, "a very remarkable, gracious woman. She was devoted to Milton. She carried on her life as wife of the president with grace and dignity, and without offending or alienating anybody."[57] The Eisenhowers gave numerous parties for the leading citizens, for the administration and faculty, and for visiting dignitaries. When they served liquor, which they usually did for visitors from Washington, they drew the shades—Kansas was dry.

Helen darned her husband's socks, packed his clothes for trips, and cared for their children. Ken Davis remembered Helen as "completely selfless. I've never known anyone so totally selfless in doing." She could never do enough for Eisenhower, and it appeared, at least to Davis, that "he was totally dependent on her."[58]

By modern standards, their relationship seems right out of a Victorian novel. But to Helen's best friend, a high school classmate, the wife of

Manhattan's leading banker, Thomas Griffith, Helen "was just an ideal wife. She waited on Milton from hand to foot." And she was happy in her role, "always laughing, always smiling, attending to all the details of home life, staying away from the details of Milton's career."[59] Clearly the Eisenhowers had managed to re-create the exceptionally warm environment in which both had been brought up.

Cooking was one of Helen's joys. She took pride in her collection of fifty cookbooks, and she became an avid canner of fruits and vegetables, often putting up over one hundred quarts in a season. Needlework was another hobby; at Kansas State she embroidered the college seal on a chair and covered eight others with various designs. She also enjoyed playing cards, especially bridge.

Her husband seemed much too busy to have any hobbies. He did anyway. Ike had taken up painting after being introduced to it by Winston Churchill; Milton, at Ike's urging, began "fooling around" with a set of watercolors that had originally belonged to his daughter Ruth. Soon he had over a hundred watercolors done and had moved on to oils. When Helen bought a camera for herself, he began reading on the subject of photography. Before long he had a movie-making outfit. Then when he bought Helen a Hammond organ, he started playing it.[60]

Midwestern life also agreed with the children. A photograph in the *Collier's* article shows the family striding across the Kansas State campus, Eisenhower with his arm around Ruth, only nine years of age and already attractive, self-possessed, and smiling. Buddy, then seventeen, has his mother's arm tucked under his. Tall, broad-shouldered, nicely dressed in jacket and tie, with a handsome head of hair and the good looks of all the Eisenhower men, he exuded confidence. His father worried because he was not a straight-A student at Manhattan High School, but he was certainly doing well enough. Thackrey thought that Eisenhower "did not quite realize the problems" that Buddy had in town because of his father's position, and others felt that Eisenhower did not have enough time for his children. Whenever Eisenhower seemed too busy, however, Helen made up for it. Buddy never suffered from lack of support or love.[61]

Eisenhower and his family were delighted with his decision to return to Kansas State. There was activity and a sense of mission and accomplishment as Eisenhower guided Kansas State into the twentieth century. There was also the pleasure and pride that went with being the most important family in town. The return to the prairie had been good for them.

CHAPTER 7

"Unsophisticated, Unspoiled, Eager to Learn"

The Students at Kansas State

Eisenhower was an ambitious man—for himself, for his college, and most of all for his students. From his first day at Kansas State until his last day at Johns Hopkins the students always came first. Throughout these three decades his goals for his students were the highest possible. Indeed, to take nothing away from his other achievements, Eisenhower's personal interactions with his students stand out as the most remarkable feature of his presidencies.

"I set out really to try to build," he said unabashedly, when he was eighty-one years old, of his earliest days at Kansas State, "to create a new American, an American who was not only competent in whatever his or her specialty might be but who had the ability and the educational background and the desire to formulate sound and creative judgments on world affairs and take part in this new world in which the United States had to be the leader."[1]

General education and comprehensive courses were, as noted, a central feature of his program for reaching that goal, and he took great pride in what he accomplished in broadening the curriculum at Kansas State. But there is much more involved in the college experience for young people than the four or five hours they spend in the classroom each day. Eisenhower was keenly aware that his opportunity to influence the development of the American youth extended far beyond the curriculum.

Eisenhower believed, in large part because of his own experience as a young man at Ramsay Lodge in Scotland, that a crucial, albeit intangible, factor in a broad education was the exchange among fellow students of different backgrounds. Kansas State had traditionally been almost exclusively for in-state students, "a homogeneous bunch," in Eisenhower's words. He described them as "freshly scrubbed young men and women who came from the rural sections of Kansas—unsophisticated, unspoiled, eager to learn. They had come to the college for a definite purpose; they worked hard; they studied; there was never a disciplinary problem; they were clean; nice kids to know, not much difference between them."[2] It was the last point that bothered Eisenhower: he wanted his students to be exposed to different ideas, different outlooks, different cultures. Only in this way could they truly become world leaders. Eisenhower believed that parochialism bred misunderstanding. Of course the G.I.'s helped greatly, bringing to the campus the perspective of their extensive travels and wartime experiences. In addition, through his many speeches and other activities, Eisenhower attracted a growing number of out-of-state students.

His most satisfying and innovative effort, however, was to bring foreign students to Manhattan. Again, he was in the vanguard of what would become a trend among American institutions of higher learning. In the decades following World War II what began as a trickle of foreign students studying in the United States turned into a flood. Eisenhower, perhaps recalling his difficulties trying to place the Nisei students while at the WRA, started "recruiting" in August of 1945, immediately after the Japanese surrender. He wrote newly appointed Secretary of State James Byrnes inviting students from other countries to enroll at Kansas State and offering to create programs that would provide them with special help in the English language. He made a special effort to make sure that Japanese-American students were included among those welcome at the college. (During the war Governor Payne Ratner of Kansas had expressed strong anti-Japanese sentiments, and Nisei students had been prohibited from matriculating at any Kansas state school.) As a result, by the end of the year, Eisenhower was able to open the doors to the Nisei as well as hundreds of foreign students from around the world. The day-to-day contact between the foreigners and the in-state students played an incalculable role in the education of both groups. The foreign presence also led to a highly successful mock U.N. General Assembly debate each year and a vigorous UNESCO chapter on the Kansas State campus.[3]

For Eisenhower, encouraging cultural dialogues was but one step in promoting a well-rounded educational environment. He also wanted to create an informal relationship between his faculty and student body outside the classroom and to get to know the students better himself. To this end he instituted a program of student encampments. A week or so before the beginning of the fall semester, the orientation period at most campuses, the president of the student government association would select twenty students and Eisenhower would select fifteen faculty members and two or three administrators to accompany Eisenhower to the Four-H Rock Springs camp and conference center, a 348-acre site a few miles outside Manhattan. There they prepared their own meals, washed their own dishes, and "brought up any problem under the sun that affected students and faculty, and the relationship between administration and faculty and students."[4]

The program gave the Kansas State faculty and staff a closeness to the student leaders and student problems not present on most other campuses. The encampment was not meant to be an arena for major policy decisions, although it was within this setting that Eisenhower decided that the time had come to abolish Kansas State's long-established tradition of no smoking on campus. Rather, Eisenhower conceived of these retreats as vehicles for breaking down the long-standing gulf between students and the administration. Of course, only a relatively few student leaders attended, but for them it was a unique experience. Many would spread the word to their peers that the Kansas State president and faculty were really okay and, more important, concerned for their welfare.

Donald Ford, an alumnus of the encampment program, recalled that "it was a kind of primitive place, little cabins with several bunks and a central mess hall, a little lake and so on. And, you know, you get the dean of engineering washing dishes in the mess hall after supper with a bunch of kids and they would come to find out he was a person and not an ogre, and he would come to find out they were people worth listening to and nice people, and you develop some camaraderie. And it would carry over, and you did get quite a different kind of climate, a greater sense of community, in the institution."[5]

Eisenhower developed a particular affection for Ford. The following year, after Ford had successfully campaigned for the student body presidency, Eisenhower called him into his office to tell him confidentially that he had hoped Ford would accept the responsibility for running and that he had hoped even more that he would win. That revelation naturally endeared Eisenhower to Ford, and they have remained friends for over thirty years. Ford never forgot his early experiences at Kansas State. He remarked in 1980, "My first impression of Eisenhower was that he couldn't be the president because he behaved like an ordinary mortal and treated people like equals." Mortal yes, but hardly ordinary. In Ford's words, he learned to hold Eisenhower "in some bit of awe because his mind was so clear and so quick. He just absorbed facts like a sponge."

Eisenhower appointed Ford to a number of committees, including one concerned with the plans for building a student union. He also designated him director of the temporary union, which was an old barracks where the student government association showed free movies on weekends. On Sunday mornings, after church, Ford would take that week's movie and give Eisenhower, Helen, Buddy, and Ruth a private showing. All had a wonderful time, and for Ford the experience was most rewarding.[6]

Eisenhower's personal contact with the students extended beyond the elite. On his walks around campus he would often stop to chat with small groups or individuals. He advertised that his office door was open to anyone with a problem, especially any student. "It was easy to get in to see Milton," Thackrey recalled. Ken Davis, who was frequently in the office when students came in, said that "most of them swore by him—they loved him."

Eisenhower met with the student body as a whole on a regular basis. He would have an assembly at the beginning of each semester, and "the whole damn student body would be there, which doesn't happen very often anywhere." In Davis's opinion, "He gave wonderful speeches that the kids used to love."[7]

One assembly that was long remembered by those present came in April 1945. FDR had just died, suddenly and without warning. Eisenhower, who was deeply affected by the death of the president, with whom he had had such frequent and friendly contact, called a special convocation to pay tribute to FDR, "which he did in a moving and obviously sincere talk." All who attended, even the arch anti-New Dealers, were noticeably impressed. And a number of the students came away feeling proud that their president had known the legendary national leader.[8]

When Ike wrote Helen from Algiers in October of 1943 to thank her for the recording of Milton's inaugural address and to praise the speech, he added, "I wish he would have referred to one other responsibility of the educator. It is the necessity of teaching and inculcating good, old-fashioned patriotism—just that sense of loyalty and obligation to the community that is necessary to the preservation of all the privileges and rights that the community guarantees."[9]

Milton, whose beliefs, as usual, coincided with his brother's, had already conceived of a means to put Ike's ideas into practice. Shortly after creating the Kansas State College Endowment Association in early 1944, he persuaded Hal W. Ludnow, of the class of 1917, who was president of the William Volker Charities Fund of Kansas City, Missouri, to contribute two hundred thousand dollars to finance an institute of citizenship at Kansas State. Eisenhower used the money to hire a small faculty for a Department of Citizenship. In keeping with his emphasis on general education, it was an interdisciplinary program. Initially chaired by Robert

Walker, a University of Chicago Ph.D. in political science, it included professors from philosophy, economics, education, and the hard sciences. The institute offered such courses as Freedom and Responsibility and covered the general fields of law and justice, war and peace, government in economic affairs, and education in a democratic society. "It was tremendously exciting," Ken Davis remembered. "They [the faculty] were really bright boys, full of enthusiasm." Certain of the regular faculty, however, were not so enthusiastic. Just as they had opposed comprehensive courses, they opposed the multidisciplinary approach. As a result, the institute's faculty "got caught in a crossfire, and it was causing a lot of row with people in the traditional disciplines."

The opposition stemmed in part from Eisenhower's paying the institute's faculty more than his regular faculty and trying to protect them from the criticism. As Davis put it, "Milton was their bulwark against the technicians." When the funding from the Volker Fund ran out, and after Eisenhower left Kansas State, the institute collapsed. It did, nevertheless, leave a legacy. Its more popular courses became absorbed within appropriate departments of the School of Arts and Sciences. Moreover, according to Thackrey, its "real effect in the long run was that it developed a substantial program in the areas of political science, theory, etc., which had been completely nonexistent before."[10]

Thinking back to his days at Kansas State decades later, Eisenhower—like so many college presidents—could tick off each building erected on the campus during his tenure in office, the number of new faculty he had brought in, the new programs he had initiated, the raises he had managed for his faculty, and other tangible achievements. But the achievement that made him most proud was a quiet one, not measurable in bricks and mortar and little noticed at the time, which was the way he wanted it and, he was convinced, the only way he could bring it about. It was the breaking down of the systematic policy of racial segregation in Manhattan and at Kansas State.

In taking steps to alter traditional racist attitudes, Eisenhower chose the evolutionary path, which clearly suited his personality and ideology. Moreover, to a certain extent it reflected his own gradual development in the area of race relations. It was not that Eisenhower himself was prejudiced; the River Brethren philosophy of both his parents preached tolerance for all peoples. Rather, born in the nineteenth century into a nation almost totally dominated by white Anglo-Saxon Protestants and having spent the bulk of his life in homogeneous rural Kansas and the Capitol

Hill bureaucracy, Eisenhower's experience with minorities, save for the Japanese-Americans, was severely limited.

To give an example, in February 1946 a committee of students and faculty recommended that an all-faith memorial chapel be constructed on campus to commemorate the alumni who had lost their lives during World War II. Since the College Endowment Association had already raised sufficient funds for the project, Eisenhower eagerly began to formulate the plans. When it was brought to his attention that the small number of Jews on campus might want to use the chapel also, he dutifully solicited the advice of two rabbis as to whether they would oppose Christ's being represented in the stained-glass windows. He may have misunderstood them, but he received the impression that there would be no problem provided Christ was portrayed only as a shepherd. Therefore he was both surprised and distressed when the Jewish community strenuously, and quite naturally, objected to the windows after they were put into place. Eisenhower would never make such a mistake again.[11]

It was not necessary for Eisenhower to be intimately familiar with the attitudes of black people to realize the extent of the prejudice against them. Ken Davis, a native of Manhattan, recalled that during his childhood "there wasn't even a place in town where a black could get a haircut." The cafes and soda fountains on the edge of the Kansas State campus would not serve blacks, nor were the 150 or so black students welcome in the student cafeteria. They could not play on Kansas State's athletic teams nor live in the dormitories. Black students were "excused" from the requirement to achieve minimum competence in swimming, which was a polite way of prohibiting them from using the college swimming pool. They had their own section in church. This had been the only Kansas Eisenhower had ever known.[12] But he knew that World War II had brought a new era, and he was determined to bring about change. If the college were to instill the values he deemed essential for moral leadership, Eisenhower reasoned, discrimination could not be tolerated.

When he was a student at Kansas State, Eisenhower, like most of the white population, had been virtually oblivious to the plight of the blacks. As president twenty years later, however, he received a steady stream of complaints. He had thought that extreme racial prejudice existed only in the Deep South. Now he learned that it was just as bad in midwestern Manhattan. "Appalled and angered," he was tempted to issue a series of sweeping edicts that would put an end to all segregation at Kansas State immediately and forever. But such an action would go against the value of moderation that he stood for so strongly, as well as contradict the lessons he had learned while in Washington, particularly those learned while working with the WRA. Eisenhower was absolutely convinced that if he tried to overcome decades of segregation by executive fiat, he would be defeating his own purpose. Rather than produce acceptance of the blacks, a command by the Kansas State president would, he believed, "lead to discord, force people into fixed ideological positions from which they could not retreat, and possibly even lead to campus disruptions that might injure the educational enterprise." Resistance would be greater than ever.[13]

There were some liberal activists, such as Davis, who urged him to go ahead and issue the decrees. In their opinion, an injustice was being committed every hour that the situation was allowed to continue, and on a campus headed by a man with the reputation for speaking out on the responsibilities and glories of American citizenship. How could Eisenhower be true to his own ideals, Davis argued, if he hesitated to right such a blatant wrong? It was his duty to act decisively and immediately. Decades later Davis remained critical. He bluntly asserted, "Milton compromised where he didn't have to compromise."[14]

Eisenhower listened to Davis attentively and sympathized with his impatience. Nevertheless, he would not budge from his conviction that evolution was better than revolution, and after all, he was the man in charge. Moreover, he still points proudly to the record to show that while he may have worked more quietly than Davis would have preferred, and sacrificed the headlines that a frontal assault on segregation would have evoked, in no instance did he "compromise." In retrospect, whether or not Davis was correct is a moot question. Eisenhower did it his way, and he was effective.

Eisenhower's strategy was to apply the same techniques that he had used previously when faced with difficult problems. He began by summoning to his office the president of the student council, whom he knew well from the fall encampment and other meetings. Quickly coming to the point he asked, "Do you folks care if the black students swim with the whites?" Somewhat startled, the unsuspecting student sat silent for a moment. Then he replied, as if with a shrug, that he did not think the student body cared very much one way or another. A more positive response would have been better, but Eisenhower was satisfied. As long as the students remained neutral, he could effect his plan. He then suggested that the student president discuss the matter privately with the one black member of the council. If the two agreed that a resolution would pass, they would propose to the entire council that it, not Eisenhower, recommend that the pool be opened to all students. Within a short time the council approved the recommendation. In the meantime Eisenhower called the director of athletics to tell him to let the black students swim. When the director objected, the Kansas State president let him know in no uncertain terms that his opinion was not being solicited. The blacks started swimming. Later Eisenhower commented that had his strategy not succeeded, he would have, as a last resort, "directed that the pool be open to all students. Believe me, I'm glad it did not come to that. It could have frozen many minds."[15]

The movement to end discrimination at Kansas State was under way. On the surface, Eisenhower's efforts to obtain for blacks permission to swim in the campus pool seem relatively insignificant when compared with later freedom marches or voting-rights campaigns. But he had to begin somewhere, and he fully realized that the initial step was always the most difficult. Equally important from Eisenhower's perspective, he had demonstrated that desegregation could be achieved without evoking conflict and animosity. Almost immediately he demonstrated it again. Acting on another Eisenhower suggestion, the student council, this time with the athletic director's full cooperation, voted to include blacks in the college's intramural athletic program. Their participation caused scarcely a ripple. Then in 1946 Kansas State received federal funding to build inexpensive housing for G.I. Bill students. After construction of the first units had begun, Eisenhower approached the white student leaders for a third time. "Now," he asked, "do you care whether the black students are housed here too?" They discussed it among themselves and returned to the president with the proposal that he set aside thirty rooms for the blacks "and let us work out whether we want to mix up together, and we think the blacks will like it too." Eisenhower asked the blacks what they thought of the proposal; they replied that they were delighted. Thus, practically unnoticed, Manhattan soon had the first integrated housing project in its history. Shortly thereafter the two races were rooming together.[16]

On occasion Eisenhower had to intercede more directly. Early in his administration the blacks charged that two professors were discriminating in their classrooms. When Eisenhower confronted them with the allegations, they vigorously denied them. Staring them right in the face, Eisenhower said that was good, for as long as he was president racist practices would not be tolerated. He never received another complaint about a professor.[17]

The School of Veterinary Medicine posed a special problem. In 1947 Eisenhower wrote Dean R. R. Dykstra to find out how many black students were currently enrolled. Dykstra answered that there were only two. Eisenhower wanted to know why there were so few. The dean explained that the admissions procedure was extremely difficult, regardless of the applicant's color. He had even had to turn down a white young man who had been recommended personally by the governor. Eisenhower would never suggest that Dykstra establish a quota system for blacks, but he did inquire whether those blacks already accepted were eligible for the junior chapter of the American Veterinary Medicine Association. He learned that only Cornell University allowed blacks to join. Eisenhower matter-of-factly told Dykstra that from then on it would be only Cornell and Kansas State. His new policy was that any honor society that excluded minorities would automatically forfeit its charter. This was the only "edict" concerning civil rights that Eisenhower ever issued at Kansas State.[18]

By this time the desegregation movement had gained momentum throughout Manhattan. The wife of a faculty member began a campaign to halt the practice of segregated seating at the local motion picture theater. The manager contacted Dean Thackrey to suggest that he or Eisenhower persuade the woman to drop the campaign on the grounds that "everybody was better off" if the blacks sat in the rear of the theater by themselves. Surely, he felt, the college would not benefit from publicity of this sort. Thackrey talked to Eisenhower and then told the manager emphatically that Kansas State had an official policy of nondiscrimination and that the wife of a faculty member—or a faculty member for that matter—was perfectly free to engage in any lawful off-campus activity. Thackrey added that as citizens, the president of Kansas State and his dean of administration intended to encourage the faculty wife in her campaign. Furthermore, they would personally sit wherever a seat was available whenever they went to the movies. Subsequently the manager lifted all seating restrictions.[19]

Having successfully integrated the newly built student housing units, Eisenhower thought it logical to do the same with the existing dormitories. However, because Kansas State did not yet have a student union, the first floor of the girls' dormitory was the social center of the campus, which meant that it was the scene of all the big dances. If the dorm were integrated, the dances would inevitably become racially mixed. Eisenhower had no doubt that when parents learned that their white daughters were dancing with blacks the uproar would be even more substantial than if they were just living under the same roof. He sought the support of the girls themselves. Meeting with them both individually and in groups, he found that the overwhelming majority were not at all opposed to integrating the dorm nor to socializing with the blacks. Assuming that if the students did not make a ruckus most of the parents would at least go along, Eisenhower announced that race would no longer determine living arrangements. Some of the parents did object, and one even wrote that if racial purity were not restored to the dorms, he would withdraw his daughter from the school. Eisenhower promptly replied in his best diplomatic language that he hoped the student would not be deprived of her opportunity to attend Kansas State and that he deeply regretted that the parent was upset. Nevertheless, he would not change his decision, nor would he make any exceptions. The girl completed her four years. In fact, to the best of Eisenhower's recollection, no student ever left Kansas State over the issue of race.[20]

Circumstances demanded that Eisenhower not limit his focus to the Manhattan campus. Historically only white students had been able to take part in Missouri Valley Conference athletics, of which Kansas State was a member. But once the swimming pool had been integrated, and then the intramural program, no reason remained for preventing blacks from participating on the intercollegiate teams. In fact, in 1949 Eisenhower persuaded the athletic director to give scholarships to blacks. The presidents of the University of Oklahoma and the University of Missouri protested. They notified Eisenhower that whatever the Kansas State policy was concerning its own students was its business, but they were not going to let their athletes compete on the same field with blacks. Eisenhower said that he would instruct the athletic director to schedule contests outside the conference. The two presidents proffered a compromise: they would have no objections to blacks playing in games played in Manhattan, on the condition that when Kansas State visited their respective institutions the blacks would not travel with the team. Eisenhower would make no promises, and when Kansas State went to play at Oklahoma and Missouri, there were blacks in the starting line-up. As Eisenhower put it, "They played and that was the end of it."[21]

When asked about Eisenhower's desegregation program, Donald Ford recalled an incident in 1948 at the Casino, a small cafe just off campus. A black student walked in and sat down at an adjoining table. Ford remembered that one of his friends commented that "it took a Milton Eisenhower to be able to bring that about." What the student meant, Ford explained, was that had someone who was not as trusted, who was not as respected, or who, and at this point the tone of Ford's voice changed, was not as careful as Eisenhower tried to do what he had done, that black student probably would have had to buy his coffee elsewhere. Now, however, students and townspeople could hardly remember when segregation was commonly practiced. Ken Davis asserted that Eisenhower compromised when he did not have to. In Donald Ford's opinion, "He did that [desegregated Kansas State] so smoothly that most people didn't even know it was happening."[22]

The year of the Casino incident, Ike took over as president of Columbia University. Milton wrote to him about the widespread discrimination against Jews and Negroes in New York colleges and universities. Milton noted that he knew about the situation because of his membership on

President Truman's Commission on Higher Education and because his assistant, Ken Davis, had made a study of it. Columbia, the evidence showed, seemed to be "one of the worst offenders in this business of discrimination."

Milton then gave Ike some brotherly advice. "At Kansas State I have moved very gradually against discriminatory practices and now, at the end of five years, I have got rid of most of them. A few still exist. I suppose this is the only sensible way to deal with the problem, as I'm sure you'll discover when you get to Columbia. But at the same time I think that steady, positive progress against unAmerican practices is imperative."[23]

Because of the tactics he used, Eisenhower's initiatives to desegregate Kansas State attracted no national attention. Not a single story appeared in a newspaper outside of Manhattan. Eisenhower personally, nevertheless, had firmly established himself as a national figure. This was partly due to his brother's prominence. But more significantly, Eisenhower was constantly engaged in activities that made him newsworthy. For example, the year after he became Kansas State's president, he was elected to the executive committee of the Association of Land Grant Colleges and Universities. By 1946 he was the committee's chairman. (Eisenhower became president of the association in 1951.) It has previously been noted that in the immediate postwar years he served as the chairman of the U.S. National Commission for UNESCO and was a delegate to the UNESCO conferences. And, of course, President Truman selected him to be a member of his Commission on Higher Education. But Truman requested even more of Eisenhower, and Eisenhower always saw it as his duty to accept. While he was carrying out these other responsibilities, he found the time to represent the public on a three-man fact-finding board to mediate the General Motors strike, to serve on the Famine Emergency Relief Commission, and to advise the Department of Agriculture on its reorganization. Truman found Eisenhower so valuable that he said to him, "President Roosevelt once told me he complained to General Eisenhower about you. Four different agencies were asking for your services. General Eisenhower remarked that he could use you too, but that would be nepotism!"[24]

Truman was not the only one who coveted the Kansas State president. In 1948 a New York group led by Amory Houghton and Frank Weil asked Eisenhower to become head of the Boy Scouts of America, enticing him with an excellent financial package which included a custom-built home. Politely, Eisenhower refused—twice. He explained to Ike, "Helen and I much prefer not to live in New York, and I don't want to move out of the field of higher education in which I've made something of a mark during the past five years."[25]

Around the same time, he received an offer that had neither of the disadvantages of the Boy Scout job. The University of Tennessee trustees said they would pay him twenty thousand dollars a year, provide him with a generous expense account, and throw in a house and a car if he would become their president. Once more his answer was no. Again confiding in Ike, he wrote, "I do not feel that I would be happy or effective in a southern state." He then added, "I am sufficiently contented with my work here at Kansas State that only an outstanding post elsewhere would cause me to change."

As the letter continued, however, it became apparent that Milton was not as contented as he initially professed. He still had unfulfilled ambitions, and while not actively on the job market, he was looking around for "an outstanding post." He told Ike (he wanted to be so sure that the letter remained confidential that he typed it "on my own battered typewriter at home") that friends had recommended him for the presidency of Penn State and were "simply awaiting the opportunity" to do the same at the University of Michigan. As yet, neither institution had made any direct inquiries. Milton conceded, nevertheless, that he would seriously consider an offer from either one of them. He was particularly interested in Penn State. State College was only a few hours' drive from Washington, and Helen had expressed a desire to be closer to her aging parents at the Mayflower Hotel. Milton liked the location also. He was getting tired of the seemingly endless train rides from Manhattan to the White House, and he had no reason to expect that his services would be required in Washington any less frequently in the future. Nor would he want them to be, both because he never lost his enthusiasm for government work and because many of his closest friends still lived in the capital. The letter concluded with the plaintive postscript, "And I must say that I get lonesome out here, too."[26]

Eisenhower could not be certain that he would be offered either opportunity. What is important, however, is that by 1948 he was ready to make a move. It was not just that he wanted to return to the east, nor had he become disenchanted with Kansas State. Rather, he felt that his work there had reached a plateau, and he had become restless. He had already achieved most of what he had wanted to achieve. As Eisenhower himself later said, "I didn't want to start coasting. I wanted to keep up the same kind of vigorous work." Jeff Peterson, one of the assistant deans, put it another way: "The bloom was over at Kansas State. He had gotten his program through."[27]

Eisenhower remained in Manhattan for two more years. He probably would have left sooner had Penn State's board of trustees had a different chairman. Ralph Hetzel, the college's president, had died in 1947. Under the Penn State constitution, the chairman of the board of trustees serves as acting president until a proper search is conducted and a successor elected. In this instance, however, the chairman, Judge James Milholland, wanted the position for himself. He went so far as to move himself and his family into the president's house and authorize the funds for it to be refurnished. In late 1949, when his candidacy finally came up for a vote at a board meeting, Milholland lost.

The trustees lost no time in calling Eisenhower and asking him if he would meet with their committee in Chicago. Not surprisingly, he agreed. At the meeting he asked the obvious questions: What were the faculty salary levels? How was their morale? How would they rate the quality of the students? The trustees replied with the obvious answers. They told him that the college was in top shape, that it was well on its way to becoming a first-class institution, and Eisenhower would have all the support he needed to ensure that it got there. What they did not tell him was that he would immediately become the rival of the chairman of the board. Had Eisenhower known, he later remarked, he probably would have declined. Furthermore, the trustees' allegiance to Penn State, he soon found out, jaded their objectivity. "They always tell you that everything is hunky-dory," Eisenhower recalled. In truth, at least in his opinion, "the place was still kind of a rural institution. It had no sparkle, it was way under-financed, its salaries were terrible, and the quality of its students was not what it should have been."[28]

It appears odd that a man of Eisenhower's experience would accept a position without checking the facts more carefully. But by this time his desire to move, and to move back to the East, had increased greatly. Moreover, despite its drawbacks, Penn State did offer many advantages. Donald Ford, who by coincidence followed Eisenhower from Manhattan to State College in order to take a Ph.D. in clinical psychology, succinctly compared the two land-grant colleges, both located away from any urban centers, both with reputations based on agriculture and engineering, both overshadowed by more prestigious universities in the state. Ford remembered that when he first arrived at Penn State, "it really had the impact of coming to a university in contrast to the sense of being in a college when I was at Kansas State. The environment was really richer and there were more good people on the faculty. So Milton had a base to start building from that was a notch up from where he started at Kansas State."[29]

In June 1950 Eisenhower presided over his last commencement at Kansas State. As he stood on the podium, looking out at the audience and then canvassing the campus, he reflected on his years there. They had been good years, and rewarding ones. Kansas State had changed radically in his seven years as president. Under his guidance new buildings had been built, the student body had greatly expanded, and the size and quality of the faculty had kept pace. Glancing over the list of graduates, both black and white, many from the School of Arts and Sciences, many with advanced degrees, Eisenhower smiled. These students had taken up a collection among themselves to have his portrait painted, and they had dedicated their class yearbook to him. Yes, Eisenhower was proud of what he had accomplished, and he felt confident that his successor, James A. McCain, the former president of Montana State University, would carry on in his tradition. Eisenhower had, to use the words he himself had used in his letter to Ike three years earlier, "made something of a mark" in the field of higher education.

Nevertheless, there were some who were not sorry to see him leave, primarily disgruntled members of the faculty; they had never accepted the philosophy behind his innovations nor forgiven him for what they considered his heavy-handed tactics. Eisenhower had not appreciated how deep their resentment was. When he returned to Manhattan for his son's graduation in 1951 he expected to receive an honorary degree. No such degree was awarded. More fundamentally, within a short time the institute for citizenship had been dissolved, and the comprehensive courses replaced by more traditional offerings.

Yet in the long run, even if some of his reforms were transitory, even if he failed to institutionalize some of his programs, Eisenhower achieved his overriding objectives. The most enduring changes came, as Kansas State's official historian, James Carey, has written, because Eisenhower "had stirred many of the faculty and some of the students to ask such questions as: What constitutes an educated person in the twentieth century? What is a liberal education? What is a reasonable interpretation of the role of the land-grant institution in the mid-twentieth century?" Summarizing Eisenhower's contribution, Carey concluded, "Until World War II, Kansas State had remained encased in its vocational or technical school philosophy. Eisenhower succeeded in shaking the college free from the harder aspects of that shell. . . . Under his leadership the goal of the college had broadened to include development of the ability to solve theoretical as well as practical problems. It had become important to consider how to live as well as how to make a living."[30] Over time Eisenhower's most adamant opponents came to recognize what he had done. He did eventually receive an honorary doctorate. And today in the center of the campus stands a grand building devoted to history and the liberal arts. Its name is Eisenhower Hall.

CHAPTER 8

"To Change the Character of the Institution"

Penn State

E isenhower had scarcely set foot on the Penn State campus before he became acutely aware that most of the students and faculty did not share the exalted opinion of the college presented to him by the board of trustees. While in Manhattan Eisenhower thought that he had learned all there was to know about running the "other" school in a state, about how to overcome a "cow college" reputation. On the East Coast, he came to realize, the problem of self-image was exponentially more serious. No matter how hard his predecessors had worked to improve Penn State's quality, the pervasive sentiment still persisted that anybody who was anybody went to Princeton, Yale, Harvard, or, perhaps worse, the University of Pennsylvania. Many students' attitudes reflected their belief that they were mired in State College because they could not gain admission elsewhere. Most faculty saw Penn State as a stepping stone to someplace better. It seemed that the great majority of the campus's population suffered collectively from what Donald Ford called "a real inferiority complex."[1]

Eisenhower was astonished by this condition; he had not been prepared for it. In Kansas, where agriculture and the technical sciences remained a way of life, he had had to struggle to liberalize the curriculum. But in the East the emphasis was on the great urban centers, the professions, and the postwar industrial boom. Its youth wanted to leave the farm, to move to the cities and then to the suburbs, to establish themselves firmly within the growing middle class. The Washingtonians Eisenhower had known epitomized this ideal, and many of his acquaintances in education—including Ike at Columbia—were connected with the prestigious institutions that represented what the East stood for. Eisenhower had had very little involvement with the eastern non-elite, with those who considered themselves outside of the contemporary, upwardly mobile mainstream. These were the people he found at Penn State.

The president before Eisenhower, Ralph Dorn Hetzel, had inadvertently contributed to Penn State's negative self-image. It is ironic that Hetzel should be so criticized, for in guiding the college from 1926 until his death in 1947 he significantly improved the quality of Penn State in virtually every dimension. Indeed, as Wayland Fuller Dunaway wrote in the school's official history the year preceding Hetzel's death, "As a wise and tactful leader, strongly entrenched in the esteem of the trustees, the faculty, the students, the alumni, and the general public, he has measured up magnificently to the duties and responsibilities of his office. . . . Under his leadership the college has reached the high-water mark in its history."[2]

The difficulty stemmed from Hetzel's conception of that "high-water mark." He supported expansion of the student body and faculty, research, curricula, and financial resources so long as the expansion did not compromise what he defined as the integrity of the college as the *state* school. In other words, according to Hetzel, such activities as educating foreign or out-of-state students or providing services for the federal government should be left to the private colleges and universities. "He proclaimed the doctrine," Dunaway wrote, "that since the college was a public institution, it was under obligation to be responsive to the needs of the people of Pennsylvania and to adjust its policy to this end; its primary mission had always been, and would continue to be, to serve the citizens of the Commonwealth."[3]

In short, Hetzel imposed limits on Penn State's development. On the one hand, it expanded dramatically, until by the 1940s it was the fourteenth largest degree-granting institution of higher learning in the United States, and it had the seventh largest undergraduate enrollment among the fifty-two land-grant colleges and universities. It was three times the size of Kansas State.[4] On the other hand, it never received the notoriety nor earned the reputation that these credentials warrant. Hetzel's notion of a good public-information office, as explained by Judge Roy Wilkinson, the college's legal counsel, "was one that kept your name out of the paper." Not only did he not publicize Penn State's accomplishments but he discouraged members of his staff or faculty from participating in national organizations. If they did, he warned, "all we'll do is to tell 'em how we do it and then it won't be a secret anymore." Due to the premium he placed on Penn State's charter, Hetzel considered it anathema to solicit private funds. Besides, he once commented, "our endowment is the legislature, so it compares favorably with Harvard's."[5]

Although in many ways commendable, Hetzel's conservatism did little to build up the confidence of Penn State's community, particularly that of the faculty. Most of them respected Hetzel, but prestige is a cherished commodity among faculty members, and the Penn State faculty wanted to put State College, Pennsylvania, on the map. With the nation's estimation of higher education growing every day, and the availability of individual grants increasing concomitantly, they took issue with Hetzel's low-profile approach and envied their counterparts who received more publicity, and funding. The Penn State faculty considered their president out of step with the times. His personal habits only reinforced their opinion. An introvert, he painted his office dark, dark red and worked by a desk lamp wearing an old-fashioned green visor as an eyeshade. He was hardly ever seen on campus, except for ceremonial occasions, almost never took vacations, made few official trips, and generally shunned invitations to speak publicly. If there were those at Kansas State who criticized Eisenhower for promoting himself too much, many more at Penn State criticized Hetzel for not promoting himself enough.[6]

Campus morale sank even lower following Hetzel's death in 1947. As noted, Penn State's constitution mandated that Judge James Milholland, the chairman of the board of trustees, take over the executive functions as acting president. Milholland loved the college, having graduated in the class of 1911 and maintained strong ties ever since. He found the prospect of becoming its eleventh president absolutely delightful. Nevertheless, save for his own education and involvement with the trustees, Milholland had no administrative nor academic background. As Wilmer Kenworthy, who served as an assistant to every Penn State president from Hetzel through Eisenhower's successor, Eric Walker, analyzed, Milholland "ran the presidency like a judge." He would only pass on recommendations brought before him, considering it improper for the chief executive to take the initiative. Furthermore, he affirmed that all decisions affecting the college belonged within the exclusive province of the administration. His much publicized rejoinder to the faculty's request to have a representative on the board—"Do the workers at a pickle factory help make the decisions?"—typified his outlook. The professors had enough problems with their self-esteem without being compared to pickle makers.[7]

In sum, therefore, while Penn State had a lot going for it in 1950—its size, its able albeit dissatisfied faculty, its beautiful setting, its devoted alumni—it was far from the utopia described to Eisenhower by the trustees. Relations among the administration, faculty, and student body needed much improvement. As will become clear, unlike in Manhattan, town and gown were at odds. And most of all, Penn State needed a new spirit; it needed to believe in itself. It needed a dynamic leader, someone who would take charge, someone who envisaged a great national university, not a provincial college. Eisenhower suited this need. He was a well-known public figure, he had an indefatigable drive, he had experience, and he had ambition. Asked to write an article for the *New York Times* the week of Eisenhower's Penn State inauguration, Ken Davis captured the essence of his former boss's leadership skills: Eisenhower, he wrote, "doesn't just occupy an administrative office: he absorbs it. He doesn't just exercise the powers of office: he makes them arms of his personality."[8]

As he had done during his previous presidency, Eisenhower immediately set out to awaken Penn State from what he considered its narrow, lethargic attitude. "He had the view of a university that was like his view of community," Donald Ford recalled. "You know, you get all these interests and you mix them up together and that's where you get real movement. He tried to create an atmosphere of 'C'mon gang, there are exciting things to do, let's go, let's build something. We're worthwhile people. You're worthwhile people. We're doing good things. Let's do better things.' " To the cynical, such cheerleading may appear absurd for an institution approaching its hundredth birthday. But it worked. As Ford pointed out, Eisenhower was more than a cheerleader. "He had this ability to look at a program or unit or institution and immediately begin clicking off in his head some things that could be done of a practical nature to begin to solve the problem, create momentum, and move the thing."[9] Another student, Samuel Vaughan, now Doubleday publisher, added, "He brought a small town, farm country touch which was congenial in those parts, but he also brought the air of a man who has been at work in Washington and other places, a sophistication which was uncommon in central Pennsylvania."[10]

His goal was, in Wilkinson's words, "to change the character of the institution."[11] Eisenhower intended to transform Penn State from a leading agricultural and scientific college into a distinguished international university and to bring to it the glamor and reputation for excellence that that term connotes. To do so, Eisenhower had first of all to sell Penn State's potential to its own faculty, its student body, the legislature, and the people of the state. This would be difficult. Despite all its educational achievements, Penn State was still thought of as a cow college, a carryover from its origins as The Farmers' High School of Pennsylvania in 1855. What little prestige it had resulted from its highly touted football teams. The University of Pennsylvania, a private school, was generally regarded as *the* state university, as illustrated by its popular nickname, "Penn." In addition, the tradition of a great land-grant institution, so thoroughly established in the Midwest and the West, did not exist in the Northeast.

Penn State also suffered from its location. The lovely campus, set in the beautiful Nittany Valley, nestled between the Seven Mountains and Bald Eagle Mountain, twelve hundred feet above sea level, is located in almost the exact geographical center of Pennsylvania. At first glance that seemed an advantage, but in fact the campus was, as the phrase popularized by Penn State's eighth president, Edwin Sparks, had it, "equally inaccessible from all parts of the state." It was—and is—difficult to get to from Pennsylvania's major centers of population, isolated and easily forgotten or, worse, never noticed in the first place.[12]

Penn State's inaccessibility made it a task for visitors to reach it; it was also a task for Penn State people to go anywhere. Yet Eisenhower had learned at Kansas State the value of getting out to the people, of making himself visible. Diametrically opposed to Hetzel, he felt that public relations was one of the most important aspects of the president's job, at least in a state institution, and he accepted every speaking invitation that came to him and even went out of his way to solicit engagements.

In the 1950s the airplane had not yet replaced the automobile as the common mode of travel, and many Pennsylvania towns were little more than back-road hamlets. So the college purchased a Cadillac, and Eisenhower found a young driver, Samuel ("Sammy") Blazer. Together, they covered sixty thousand miles during Eisenhower's first year alone. "I am telling you," Eisenhower reminisced years later, "I've been to every industrial organization in the cities and towns of Pennsylvania, every agricultural organization, cultural organizations, political organizations, everything, and everywhere I went I explained the college to them. I said we need help, we need your understanding, here are some things you can do for us." Agricultural groups received his remarks enthusiastically. Businessmen and professionals often needed more convincing. To such audiences, Eisenhower would carefully point out how much Penn State could do for them.[13]

Typically Eisenhower would underscore the inherent partnership between the nation's educational and vocational sectors. For example, in one speech quoted in the college newspaper he explained: "Of paramount importance is the fact that, in our democratic society, business and education are reciprocals. It is impossible to explain the growth, or to insure the survival of either without reference to the other." After presenting his thesis, Eisenhower would shift from the general to the particular. Referring to Penn State, he said on this occasion, "My own institution has complex and cherished relations with nearly every type of industrial and business enterprise in Pennsylvania. Thus, on a project basis we do nearly a million dollars worth of natural-science research each year for hundreds of enterprises. We train men and women for every type of industrial enterprise."[14]

In almost every instance Eisenhower's words struck a responsive chord. Sammy Blazer recalled that after the meetings, when he would be waiting outside to begin the long ride home, people would come out saying, "What a job that guy did" or "What a wonderful speech that was." Blazer would pass this along to Eisenhower, who would reply with a smile, "Well, we really had them fooled today" or something to that effect. He was visibly pleased; it was as if the favorable crowd reaction gave him added energy. "Everybody liked him," Blazer remembered not completely objectively. "He enjoyed having people with him."[15]

From the beginning, Eisenhower developed a warm relationship with Blazer. On one of his first tours of the campus the president stopped off at the college garage, walked over to Blazer, stuck out his hand, and said, "I am Milton Eisenhower and we'll be seeing a lot of each other, I am sure." They did indeed. They were on the road together two or three days a week almost every week of the year. "I just kept thinking that he was going to slow down," Blazer recollected with a laugh, "or he was going to quit traveling, or something, but it just kept snowballing. And then it got to be enjoyable, and he kind of got to look forward to it." Blazer added that no matter what time they got home, whether at five o'clock in the afternoon or two o'clock in the morning, Helen would be waiting up, a snack already prepared.

Eisenhower would ride in the front seat. As if it were a ritual, he would turn on the radio for the hourly news, and he listened to all the baseball games. Often, especially when it was late at night, the two men would talk about their families—Blazer also had two children. Eisenhower's son Buddy was a graduate student at Penn State and had a job as a disc jockey; it amused Blazer that "he didn't use the name Eisenhower; he called himself Bud Stover." Eisenhower treated Blazer more as a friend than as an employee. They shared each other's concerns. For example, Blazer remembered how distressed Eisenhower was when a horse fell on Ruth's leg. Conversely, the driver always felt that his boss was genuinely interested in the Blazer family's affairs. When there was a lull in the conversation, Eisenhower liked to work crossword puzzles; Blazer remarked that "I never saw a guy do one [puzzle] as fast as he could." But soon they were back talking.

As a part of making himself more visible and in order to indulge his own interests, Eisenhower instructed Blazer to pick up any student hitchhiker. He also attended nearly every athletic event on campus. "It got to the point," Blazer said, "that when the students would come into the gym they would automatically look up to the section reserved for Milton to see him. That was part of going to the event." On one particular winter day when Eisenhower and Blazer were coming home from a trip Eisenhower urged Blazer several times to hurry up. Finally Blazer asked him what the rush was. Eisenhower told him that Penn State was up for the national championship in wrestling and he did not want to miss that night's meet. The last ten miles into State College was all mountain road "and really tough." There did not seem to be any way the Cadillac could make it up through the snow. Blazer started to pull over, deciding it would be best to wait for the snowplows. Undeterred, Eisenhower suggested, "How about you driving off the highway, get the right wheels on the gravel, and I'll get out and push." They did just that, and when the meet started the students saw their president in his customary seat.[16]

Eisenhower cultivated his relations with the students as carefully as he did his relations with alumni, business, professional, and agricultural organizations. The student body at Penn State was much larger than that at Kansas State; but it was more select because Penn State was not required to take all high school graduates. To contrast the two groups, Eisenhower commented, "Instead of homogeneity in the student body [at Penn State], I saw every aspect of economic activity represented—sons of miners, industrial millionaires, farmers, teachers; some came from small communities, others from great cities."[17] The Penn State students may have been different from those in Manhattan, but they came to view Eisenhower with the same affection.

The closeness between Eisenhower and the Penn State students began even before he took up his official duties. In February 1950, shortly after he had accepted the presidency, to become effective on July 1, a group of Penn State coeds sent him a message by short-wave radio: "Come have a milkshake with us, figuratively of course." From Manhattan Eisenhower radioed back, "Of course I will have a milkshake with you, but why figuratively?" Within the month he made an orientation visit to State College, where a thousand students were waiting for him. He took a representative group of the girls to a local ice cream shop, where he treated them to milkshakes. He chatted easily with them, shook hands all around, smiled at everyone, asked questions about student life, answered questions about his own career and philosophy, and generally made a good impression. The school newspaper photographed the event for the next day's front page.[18]

As it had at Kansas State, his inaugural, held in October 1950, generated national publicity for the college. Finally Penn State was achieving recognition. An added attraction was the presence of General Eisenhower, at the time president of Columbia University. Once again Milton extolled the virtues of a liberal education, emphasizing that one of the great glories of America's colleges and universities was that they provided a background sufficiently broad that any boy could grow up to be president of the United States. At that instant a photographer caught Ike, who had turned down probable nominations from both parties in 1948, looking lost in thought. Since the presidential campaign was not far off, the photo appeared throughout the country with an appropriate caption.

The students were grateful to have as their president the brother of America's greatest war hero. They were also grateful when Eisenhower demonstrated that he refused to put on any airs. A few days after the inauguration, the lead story in the campus newspaper began, "Having heard of Milton Eisenhower's record of always having a ready ear and an open door for students at Kansas State, two liberal arts juniors decided to see for themselves." The story related how following the ceremonies a pair of coeds had walked over to the president's house and knocked on the door. Ruth opened it, introduced herself, then called Helen, who told the students to make themselves comfortable until her husband could come down—he was upstairs dressing. First Milton, then Ike, and finally Earl and Edgar came down to talk to both of them. The story quickly made the rounds; Eisenhower's "open door to all students" policy was thus quickly established.[19]

In record-breaking time the students responded to Eisenhower's warmth by bestowing on him the title "Prexy." Less than a year after Eisenhower took office, during the Honors Day program student body president Robert Davis announced, "It has become quite obvious that the door to the president's office swings on well-oiled hinges. It is open and accessible to all students—as much as possible during the day and often many hours at night. The time is ripe for us to say we're glad you're here." He then pointed out that Hetzel had been known to generations of students as "Prexy" and that he had liked that name better than any honorary degree he had ever received. Eisenhower, too, was delighted to be called "Prexy," so much so that for one of the few times in his life he was left speechless. He had recovered by the next day, and in a letter to the students he wrote, "I would rather merit the esteem and affection of students than to receive any other honor that might be bestowed upon me." From that day on, whenever Eisenhower walked across the campus nearly every student would greet him as "Prexy." For Eisenhower, "the friendliness of the students was a joy."[20]

Being called "Prexy" brought Eisenhower great pleasure. What brought him greater pleasure, however, was his success at building a sense of community among the students, the faculty, and the administration. Never an advocate of trial and error, he began by establishing a student encampment program just like the one that had worked so well at Kansas State, only on a grander scale. In the mountain range south of Penn State, at Mont Alto, a forestry school had been converted into an extension campus, complete with a good dormitory and swimming pool. Eisenhower thought it a perfect setting for the encampment. Every fall, for the better part of a week, he would gather together a hundred or more student leaders, from every part of the campus, along with a dozen or more members of the faculty and an equal number of administrators, and bring them all to Mont Alto. Just as in Manhattan, the more the participants worked, played, cooked, and did the dishes together, the more comfortable they felt discussing their problems. Sometimes these "gripe sessions" resulted in corrective policies. Other times the administration decided that the plaintiff was wrong, or that the funds necessary for a suggested reform were not available. On all occasions complaints were listened to and explanations given. Not everyone got his or her way, but they were generally satisfied that they had received a fair hearing. Eisenhower later judged the student encampment, and the spirit that it represented, one of his most important contributions to Penn State. "I think every university should have such a program," he said during his retirement. "Many of the harmful confrontations of the 1960s could have been avoided if there had been an intimate relationship between students, faculty, and administration." Probably the encampments would not have prevented the confrontations of the 1960s; nevertheless, to quote Wilmer Kenworthy, they "humanized" the administration.[21]

During the school year Eisenhower and his assistants consulted on a regular basis with a smaller group of students, the dozen or so who made up Lion's Paw, a quasi-honorary fraternity that included the editor of the student newspaper, the editor of the humor magazine, the head of the athletic group, the president of the student council, and other student leaders. The sole purpose of Lion's Paw was to work with the president, to bring him ideas from the students and to take back to them the information gained in the meetings. Eisenhower liked to meet informally with Lion's Paw at a small cabin on a stream in the nearby mountains that for years had served as the president's weekend place. (But not for the Eisenhowers because Helen hated the place. She complained that it was always dark and damp and that she spent two hours getting it open, half an hour there, and then two hours cleaning it up. She would not let the university send any staff to the place to do the work for her. Consequently, the family seldom used the cabin.) The members of Lion's Paw relished the cabin and their meetings there with Eisenhower. "In conversations," he remembered, "no holds were barred. It was always a sort of cleansing experience. Some of the former members I hear from to this day; now that they are lawyers, or congressmen, or ministers, or educators. The Lion's Paw young men and I developed an abiding friendship."[22]

The students appreciated Eisenhower's friendship. More important, they appreciated his encouragement and the confidence he placed in them. The year before he arrived at Penn State the graduating class had bequeathed the seed money to establish a campus radio station. By the time Eisenhower took over a dispute had broken out between the students and the speech department as to who would be in charge. Characteristically, Eisenhower summoned both student and faculty representatives to his office so that both cases could be presented. Samuel Vaughan, who attended the meeting, recalled that the students assumed that Eisenhower would side with the speech department. After all, they thought, as president he would have to live with the faculty long after the students had graduated. Some might have remembered Hetzel, who believed that "students come and go and therefore if you deal with them, you're dealing with a will-o'-the-wisp."[23] Most probably remembered Milholland, who was usually "blunt" and "curt" with them.[24] To Vaughan's and the others' surprise, nevertheless, after listening to the arguments, Eisenhower ruled in favor of the students. Perhaps Eisenhower spoke to the speech department faculty beforehand. He did not like to go into meetings uncertain of the outcome, and he always prepared meticulously. And he must have taken special pride when his son Bud became one of the station's leading disc jockeys.[25]

Forging close relations with the board of trustees required a different kind of effort. Ironically under the circumstances, the trouble did not come from board chairman Milholland, whose personal disappointment over not being elected president could easily have precipitated an awkward situation. On the contrary, Eisenhower and Milholland worked well together and even became good friends. Usually the difficulties that did arise stemmed from the attempt of one trustee or another to advance his particular interest. For example, Eisenhower remembered all too well Walter W. Patchell, vice-president of the Pennsylvania Railroad, who "was always criticizing. He was angry that we were bringing coal into Penn State by truck rather than over the railroad. He was always grumpy and critical." Then there was Milton Fritsche, vice-president of Horn and Hardart, who demanded that the board investigate the food services on campus. Penn State did its own baking, and not surprisingly Fritsche argued that it was much more economical to buy from vendors. In the end,

Eisenhower had to call in a professional consulting company from Boston. After three days of monitoring the food service, the firm reported that it was extremely cost-efficient.[26]

It seemed to Eisenhower that he was continually being placed in the position of having to defend his policies against what he considered selfish interests, and he resented it. Judge Wilkinson related an anecdote that illustrated this. Eisenhower's daughter Ruth was married in October 1961, by which time Eisenhower had left Penn State. Considering that the former president of the United States would be attending, the reception instantly became a high-society event.

In looking over the guest list, Wilkinson suddenly realized that the only Penn State trustee invited was Roger "Cappy" Rowland. Many members of the board were distinguished, including bandleader Fred Waring. Yet Eisenhower had invited the one man who appeared, at least superficially, to be the most out of place at such a gathering. Eisenhower characterized Rowland as "rough-and-tumble," and Wilkinson described him as a "ward politician type, cigars and lots of unattractive four-letter words, and so on." Rowland had been a flyer in World War I, a close friend of ace Eddie Rickenbacker, and had gone on to become a successful Pennsylvania manufacturer. Eisenhower always was meticulous in preparing for such occasions, and Wilkinson wondered why he would have invited the incongruous back-slapping Rowland.[27]

The judge could not resist asking Eisenhower. Eisenhower replied that Rowland was "one of the best" on the board, that he had been one of the president's most loyal supporters. Then he almost whispered, "And Roy, he is the only trustee at Penn State who never asked anything improper for himself." Wilkinson smiled knowingly. At the reception he pulled Rowland aside and said, "You know why you were invited? Because you were the only trustee who never asked Milton to do anything improper." Rowland did not blink an eye. He shot back, "Well, what kind of a son of a bitch do you think I am?"[28]

Of course Eisenhower would never describe the other trustees as sons of bitches; but he did describe every board meeting as "hard work." In fact, Eisenhower believed that the primary reason he managed to establish good relations and win support for his policies is that prior to each meeting he went to their drinking parties at the Nittany Lion Inn. Eisenhower himself was a light drinker, rarely indulging in a second bourbon. He understood, however, that he could often accomplish more over cocktails than he could around the board table. In most instances he was able to settle disputes before they had the opportunity to erupt, so by the time the trustees met formally the major decisions had already been made.[29]

On other occasions highballs and casual conversation were not enough. One explosive bone of contention arose over an issue about which trustees and presidents collide on many American campuses— athletics. At Penn State football was king. In fact, it was the one area in which the college had earned a national reputation, the one area in which Penn Staters felt they were second to none. Along with money and prestige, football nevertheless brought problems. For one thing, it bred elitism. The program was so geared towards intercollegiate competition that little attention was paid to the ordinary student who wanted to play intramurals. Second, the football coach received virtually unlimited funding, which severely cut back on the resources available for other sports. And finally, Eisenhower considered the almost complete independence of the football program totally unacceptable.

To a large extent these conditions resulted from the fact that the alumni, not the administration, ran Penn State football. They handled the scheduling and the recruiting. The most formidable force was Lester "Pete" Mauthe, who served as a trustee from 1938 until his death in 1967. Mauthe, star of the undefeated 1912 team, the first Penn State player to be elected to the Collegiate Football Hall of Fame (1957), was a living legend, considered at the time the greatest fullback in Penn State's illustrious gridiron history. By hard work he had risen through the ranks to become president of the Youngstown Sheet and Tube Company, and he applied the same effort to the football program.[30] There was nothing he or his supporters would not do to ensure that Penn State's team continued as a powerhouse. Wilkinson recalled the countless times the college ran afoul of the National Collegiate Athletic Association because some high school football star had been offered an automobile or some other illegal inducement to come to State College. The admissions committee even kept the athletes' academic records in a separate category.[31]

For the first few years of his administration Eisenhower accepted this arrangement, feeling that he did not have enough allies on the board to confront Mauthe head-on. In 1953, however, the athletic director, who was really Mauthe's agent, retired, and Eisenhower persuaded Ernest B. McCoy to take his place. McCoy had been an assistant to Fritz Crisler at Michigan and had been highly recruited by colleges and universities throughout the country. In order to get him, Eisenhower had willingly promised that there would be no interference from either the trustees or the alumni in running the program. At the next board meeting the president revealed his coup, announcing, "We're going to put all athletics under Ernie McCoy and therefore I'll have to ask Mr. Mauthe to no longer participate in scheduling or anything else."[32]

One would have thought that Eisenhower had unilaterally decided to terminate Penn State football. Mauthe threatened to walk out, and a heated argument ensued. Seeing that he was getting nowhere, Eisenhower agreed to carry the matter over until the next monthly meeting. "If he had locked horns right then," Wilkinson said, "he'd have lost." But Eisenhower was not about to lose. With a granitelike expression on his face, he told the assembled trustees, "I'm going to bring it up at the next meeting, and I expect you to approve it."[33]

Eisenhower had forced a showdown. Not for a moment, however, did he fear that he might not emerge on top. He had expressed his views on the issue so unequivocally that no board member could doubt that Eisenhower would resign if the vote went against him. Eisenhower was fully aware that he was much too important to Penn State for any trustee to risk letting this happen. His record was his trump card. And sure enough, when the board met for a second time they passed on Eisenhower's recommendation unanimously. McCoy was confirmed as the new athletic director and given complete control of the program. After the meeting ended, Mauthe came up to Eisenhower and extended his hand. All he could say was, "Of course, you are right."[34]

As it turned out, under McCoy Penn State put together one of the outstanding athletic programs in the nation, in intramurals as well as in intercollegiate competition. In addition to football, the college excelled in wrestling, gymnastics, basketball—fourteen sports in all. McCoy expanded the golf course to thirty-six holes and added an ice rink and other much-needed and welcome facilities; and he put the recruiting of athletes on a systematic, aboveboard basis. Wilkinson later remarked, with a sigh of relief, "Ever since then we have been as clean as a whistle in all our athletic programs." Penn State likes to boast that it graduates a higher percentage of its athletes than any other school.[35]

And the football program became, if anything, stronger. For a head coach McCoy selected Charles "Rip" Engle, from Brown University, who brought with him his young assistant, Joseph Paterno. Engle coached until 1965, when Paterno succeeded him. Both men were tremendously successful. The Penn State team is nationally ranked virtually every year, and it maintains this tradition without sacrificing its academic or ethical integrity.

Eisenhower had succeeded again, and he had succeeded because he knew how to get things done. In assessing Eisenhower's method for winning over the opposition, Donald Ford stressed his persuasive abilities. Eisenhower believed, according to Ford, that "you just gotta get the right conditions and you'll get it out of them." Sam Vaughan proffered a slightly different perspective: "I always had the impression that Milton knew how to bide his time, prepare the way, and act forcefully."[36]

The same year that Eisenhower took on the traditions of the Penn State football program, he began a campaign that struck even deeper at the college's historic roots. This time, however, he was destined to lose. The controversy, which had been brewing since his arrival on campus, involved a matter that most people—at least those who did not attend the school or live in State College—might have considered quite trivial. As part of his objective of enhancing Penn State's reputation and uplifting the self-esteem of its students and faculty Eisenhower rapidly set in motion the process to change its name. In his opinion, to call Penn State a college was not just a misnomer but a qualitative insult. He wanted Penn State to be called a university, to denote that as an institution it had moved beyond an undergraduate orientation to offer strong graduate and research programs. He believed that the school had undergone this transformation even before he became president, and it was his fundamental goal to build upon this foundation.

He soon discovered that any effort to change the name to Penn State University would require a tangled legal morass. Since its original incorporation as The Farmer's High School in 1855, the school had straddled the line between public and private ownership. Technically it had been founded as a private institution, but from the beginning certain state officials, including the governor and the state secretary of agriculture, had served as ex officio trustees. The other board members were appointed by the governor, elected by delegates from the agricultural and industrial societies, or chosen by the alumni. Penn State College was chartered as a corporation, with legal title to its own property, and its own board had the power to set fees and standards, select administrators, buy and sell real estate, and otherwise run its affairs. Nevertheless, it was the land-grant institution in the Commonwealth, dependent upon the public legislature for its appropriations. To complicate matters further, its logical name, from Eisenhower's perspective, had already been preempted by the totally private University of Pennsylvania.[37]

Under the careful supervision of legal counsel Roy Wilkinson, who as a devoted Penn Stater threw all his support behind the project, Eisenhower proceeded step by step. The laws of Pennsylvania clearly state that one corporation cannot choose a name deceptively similar to that of another corporation. Thus before they approached any public officials, Eisenhower and Wilkinson went together to see Penn's administrators and trustees. Had the Penn authorities objected strenuously to the proposed name change, they probably could have put an end to the idea right then and there. But no one at Penn voiced any opposition, so Eisenhower and Wilkinson went on to the next hurdle. They made successive trips to Harrisburg, where they met with the state director of education, the secretary

of the Commonwealth, the head of the other concerned agencies, and finally the governor. In all cases they argued that Penn State deserved to be
called a university. In all cases they proved convincing. The groundwork
having thus been firmly established, it was merely a formality when
Wilkinson petitioned the Centre County Court nearly two years later. In
November 1953 Eisenhower became the president of the Pennsylvania
State University.[38]

At first few took notice of what Eisenhower and Wilkinson were doing.
After all, since Penn State had been granting advanced degrees for many
years and had long been divided administratively into schools of business, agriculture, liberal arts, engineering, forestry, science, architecture,
and so on, the change in name had little immediate impact on the day-to-
day life. Not one new program was added because of it. However, as
Eisenhower had correctly predicted, in the long run it had a major significance. Superior high school students began to request Penn State's cata-
logues with increased frequency. Faculty recruiting became easier among
status-hungry academics, including European scholars, who had traditionally displayed contempt for any "college." Most important, the sense
of pride that Eisenhower had found so lacking at Penn State surfaced
throughout the campus. No longer was its reputation predicated on the
record of its football team.. Eisenhower had indeed changed the character
of the institution.

Still, there were those who disapproved. A minority of the faculty,
alumni, and town residents resented that a man who arrived in State College only a short time before had taken it upon himself to initiate such a
change, and without consulting them. This minority became dispropor-
tionally influential when Eisenhower started the next stage of his reform
the following year. When the school had officially opened its doors in
1859, the town had been called appropriately Farm School, Pennsylvania. Over the years as the school's name changed so did the town's, until
in 1874 it settled on State College. Now, Eisenhower thought, "it was absolutely silly" to have Penn State University located in State College.
State University had an awkward ring to it, so Eisenhower came up with
Nittany, after the surrounding mountains and valley. However, a small
town already bore that name, forcing Eisenhower to settle on the slightly
longer Mt. Nittany. Without thinking much of it, he proposed the new
name to the town as a whole.[39]

Eisenhower later commented that "it never occurred to me that there
would be any opposition." He had seriously miscalculated. State College
had a population of only about fifteen thousand, and about half of that
consisted of faculty and their families. Thus any minority could make a
lot of noise. That is precisely what those who had opposed the school's

name change did. As far as they were concerned, the upstart Eisenhower had once again thrown down the gauntlet. They had been unprepared the first time, but now they were going to get back at the president by insisting that the town remain State College. As Judge Wilkinson put it, they perceived their resistance as "a punch in the nose for Milton Eisenhower."[40]

Joining these forces were the townspeople who had no institutional connection with the school, who had never gotten along with it, and who now saw the administration as trying to impose the school's new name on them. Eisenhower should have realized that he was exacerbating the already strained relations between town and gown. The state of that relationship had been emphatically brought to his attention not long before, when he had dutifully attended the scheduled town meeting. At that time town representatives had demanded that Penn State pay the entire cost for the local police force, arguing, as Eisenhower paraphrased the mayor's words, "We wouldn't have a police problem in this town if it weren't for the university and all its students." The mayor had then applied the same logic regarding the responsibility for the fire department, as if only colleges or universities (in this case the precise name did not matter) caused fires.[41]

According to Wilkinson's memory of the incident, "Milton would have nothing to do with this." It had not taken long for him to learn of the ways in which the local merchants sought to "gouge" the students by, for example, trying to pressure the school into remaining in session until two days before Christmas so that students would have to do their holiday shopping in State College. He also knew that without Penn State–related business State College would become a virtual ghost town. It had been nothing but pasture until the opening of the Farmer's High School. Nevertheless, in the interest of better harmony, he had agreed that the university would assume a greater share of the financial burden for public services. But he had extended the stick as well as the carrot. "We can hurt you if you want us to," he had warned. "We can put in a bookstore and the students will never buy a book in town. We can put in a drug store and they will never buy any drugs from you. We are a private institution, we can put in anything. We can buy up the apartment buildings and run them ourselves, and they will be taken off the tax rolls. So you can't hurt us, but we can hurt you. If that's the way you want it, okay, that's the way we'll do it."[42]

The town representatives had accepted defeat, but not graciously. So when Eisenhower called together the mayor and the chamber of commerce to tell them of his plan to change the town's name to Mt. Nittany, he reopened a festering wound. No matter how hard he tried to convince them that to continue to use State College would be "misleading, incongruous, and confusing," he bitterly recalled, "it didn't do a damn bit of good." When the proposition was put to a town vote it was turned down, two to one.[43]

Obviously Eisenhower had failed, and he took it as a stinging rebuke. If he could have analyzed the defeat from a less personalized perspective, however, he would have realized that the issue involved more than Milton Eisenhower. The conflict between town and gown had begun before Eisenhower came to State College, and it continued after he left. Moreover, he was severely handicapped by Pennsylvania law, which stipulated that a town's name had to be changed to another name. In other words, Eisenhower could not ask the townspeople to vote first on whether they wanted the name changed and then on their preferred alternative. They had to vote on the specific proposal that the name be changed from State College to Mt. Nittany. Thus, those who agreed with Eisenhower regarding the inappropriateness of State College but did not like Mt. Nittany voted negative. In Wilkinson's view, "If we could have changed the name of the town in two steps, it could have been done easily.... We couldn't get an absolute number that agreed that you want to change the name to Mt. Nittany. No matter, the Lord himself supporting it, it could never be accomplished that way."[44]

Yet Eisenhower interpreted the vote as a personal criticism, and he did not like it. But he did not permit himself to get openly angry. Instead, he calmly applied to the United States Postal Service for the university's own post office. To the confusion of all outsiders, Penn State University, located in State College, Pennsylvania, now receives correspondence addressed to University Park.

Eisenhower's defeat on this particular issue did not obscure the significance of what he had accomplished. The switch from "college" to "university" signified a coming of age for the institution. Along with the visibility Eisenhower provided the school through his travels, and the outstanding students and faculty he attracted to University Park, it helped to bring Penn State the national and international recognition it had earned. Neither the town's mayor, the chamber of commerce, nor anyone else could take that away from the university's president.

CHAPTER 9

"Days of Tension and Hysteria"

Deans, Faculty—and Civil Liberties at Penn State

E isenhower was not content merely to designate Penn State as a university, so he moved quickly to turn the various "schools" into "colleges." In many cases thie entailed basic reorganization. For example, although personally always partial to the liberal arts, Eisenhower considered it essential to establish a College of Business Administration as a new, independent unit. He discussed his plan with Ike, who said that while he was taking Columbia's dean of business administration, Philip Young, to Washington with him as director of personnel for the president, Young's assistant, Ossian MacKenzie, might be induced to come to Penn State. Milton talked with MacKenzie, liked him, and offered him the position of dean of business administration. The new dean, Eisenhower promised, would have the full support of the president. He was as good as his word. As Donald Ford remarked, "Milton picked people and then he let them do their job, trusting that the people he picked would do it the way he wanted it done."[1]

MacKenzie also lived up to his word. With Eisenhower's backing, he drew major portions of his faculty from the College of Liberal Arts, particularly from the economics department. However, whereas economics had been mainly theoretical in orientation, concentrating on macro- and micro-economics, MacKenzie structured the College of Business Administration in a more practical direction. But neither Eisenhower nor MacKenzie wanted to make the program purely a nuts-and-bolts affair. Although they appreciated that the surge in enrollment was due primarily to the students' ambition to become leaders of business, they insisted that education not be measured just in terms of dollars and cents. To ensure that the college offered a broad academic perspective, MacKenzie instituted a Ph.D. program and required that his faculty engage in innovative research. Moreover, in keeping with Eisenhower's philosophy, he established as the college's objective "to produce competent business leaders who are keenly aware of the great social responsibilities that rest upon them in the nation's economic system." By the time Eisenhower left Penn State, MacKenzie had attracted some of the top people in the country to his faculty.[2]

Penn State recruited good people in all fields, such as C. Raymond Carpenter in psychology. He had been working in the field of educational television, a field in which Eisenhower had a deep and influential interest. Indeed, Eisenhower had chaired a national commission that had met at Penn State and urged the Federal Communications Commission to set aside frequencies for educational use, a recommendation eventually leading to the creation of the Public Broadcasting System. At Penn State Carpenter did path-breaking research on the educational effectiveness of closed-circuit television.

One of Carpenter's graduate students in psychology was Donald Ford, later dean of the College of Human Development, the only man to whom Eisenhower ever awarded three degrees—an A.B. at Kansas State and the M.A. and Ph.D. at Penn State. When Ford received his doctorate, he received simultaneously—and was about to accept—an offer to join the faculty of the University of Arizona. Eisenhower asked him to stay at Penn State to help Robert Bernreuter, whom Eisenhower had hired to direct a new, large-scale counseling unit. Eisenhower was very persuasive, Ford recalled, both personally and by "creating conditions at Penn State for young people to grow in."

The counseling unit was a typical Eisenhower innovation. With the influx of students after World War II, Penn State had been sending its freshmen to other colleges—Slippery Rock, Erie, Philadelphia, and six other two-year college campuses. By 1950 new dormitories had been constructed at State College. More freshmen were admitted, and many of those who had been "farmed out" returned. Then, according to Ford, "all hell broke loose among the faculty, who were saying, 'My God, we're getting all these dummies in the university, we have got to raise standards.'" As one might expect, as standards increased, so did the rate of student failures. Eisenhower and some others, however, took the view that the student failures often stemmed more from the difficulty of adjusting to campus life than from academic ineptitude, that "there were a lot of reasons why kids were flunking besides being dumb."

Hence, Penn State's president, working individually with key members of the faculty, suggested establishing a counseling unit to work with the students that were doing poorly to see whether their difficulties could not be straightened out. After much study and debate, the faculty senate agreed that the idea was worth a try, and in 1954 the counseling unit came into existence. Eisenhower put Bernreuter in charge, with Ford as his chief assistant. Their attitude was the same as Eisenhower's: in Ford's words, "You don't just dump 'em if they are having trouble, but you try to help." It soon became the largest counseling program in the nation, and it worked. Years later Ford proudly reflected, "We saved a lot of souls." That was literally true; after the program went into effect, not only did Penn State's flunk-out rate drop markedly but it had the lowest percentage of suicides of any major university in the country.[3]

Bernreuter and Ford discovered that "one of the reasons why kids fail is that they get started in the wrong field 'cause the old man or the old lady says that's what we want you to do." So they proposed to Eisenhower that the freshmen's parents be invited to campus for an orientation along with their children. Eisenhower supported the program immediately. Parents would become familiar with what their children would encounter, and moreover, the school would benefit from the added public relations. The program succeeded on both scores. The parents gained a better understanding of student life, and, Ford described, "they would go through an experience where they were treated individually and intensively and with great consideration. And they could go away singing praises of the place, and they would tell their neighbors about it, and they would do all kinds of things for the university." The parent orientation helped substantially to dispel the notion that Penn State had gotten so big that a freshman would just be lost in the crowd. It also emphasized that Penn State was a place where the students were taught to develop their individual interests and that to a large extent their development depended as much on parental encouragement as on faculty supervision.[4]

Eisenhower had intended to follow the lead of many other institutions by merging the College of Liberal Arts with the College of Science. However, this was one reform he did not make. One simple reason was that he ran out of time. As he later explained, "I had so much to do in my six years at Penn State that I never initiated the move." Yet given Eisenhower's energy and list of accomplishments, time probably was not the sole factor. Indeed, a more fundamental factor was his well-developed leadership style and his views on organization management. From his early years in government bureaucracy, Eisenhower had learned that any organization is only as good as the individuals involved in it. The dean of the College of Sciences was Dr. George Heller, an excellent

administrator and an enthusiastic supporter of research and development. Heller opposed combining his college with the College of Liberal
Arts, and he was doing such a good job that Eisenhower did not want to
interfere. He would never depart from his belief that the secret to any
successful organization was that it be staffed by outstanding people; no
organization chart could compensate for inferior personnel. In this case
Eisenhower thought it better to sacrifice the chart than to run the risk of
Heller's resignation.[5]

Similarly, Eisenhower understood that no two administrators were the
same, and in selecting his associates he had to consider a broad range of
individual attributes. Heller, for example, possessed a great sense of
humor, which he used to create a relaxed and informal environment.
And he spent money lavishly; certainly he was the first administrator at
Penn State to own two Cadillacs and a Rolls Royce. By contrast, when
the long-time dean of Engineering, Harry P. Hammond, retired, Eisenhower convinced the almost spartan Eric Walker to resign from his position with the Defense Department in Washington, where he was in
charge of research, and come to State College. Whereas Heller liked to
joke around with his faculty and students, Walker, in Eisenhower's opinion, "was a stern, sometimes hard-acting man, quick in his judgments,
usually right, but in being right he often made others angry." However,
he possessed a quality that Eisenhower considered vitally important: he
inspired those who worked with him.

Once again Eisenhower's instincts proved correct. Walker and his
students built the first two computers at Penn State, putting Penn State
in the nation's forefront in another significant field. Not long thereafter,
Eisenhower asked Walker if there was anything the College of Engineering really needed, especially anything that might produce pioneering
research. From his years at the Pentagon Walker had learned never to be
bashful regarding such an offer, so he requested the funds for a nuclear
reactor. Thus Penn State became a leader in atomic research, the first
U.S. university to have a reactor capable of criticality. Shortly before his
own resignation, Eisenhower appointed Walker as vice-president for
research, the school's initial vice-president, making it clear that he was
Eisenhower's personal choice to succeed to the presidency. In this way
Walker became the first in a line of former Eisenhower subordinates who
went on to be distinguished college or university presidents themselves.[6]

As both Heller and Walker illustrate, one of Eisenhower's basic criteria
for selecting his deans was that the candidate be research-oriented (Heller
later became General Electric's vice-president for research). They also
had to be superior administrators. In academics, this meant primarily
that they be able to work with the most troublesome group on any cam-

pus, the faculty. Eisenhower's tenure at Kansas State, as well as his travels throughout the country, had made him all too familiar with the particularist interests of faculties. Generally they are composed of "other-minded" and independent individuals who are extremely hard to please. Universal harmony is practically impossible to achieve. The faculty at Penn State was no exception.

Eisenhower's deans were invaluable to him in instilling loyalty and a sense of teamwork among the faculty. Equally important was his provost, Larry Dennis. Indeed, Dennis was the only person Eisenhower had brought with him from Kansas State, where he had been on the faculty before joining a newspaper in Des Moines, Iowa. Himself a great conciliator, Eisenhower had immediately recognized Dennis's facility for getting a group to make a decision. "He was a genius at collaboration." Thus, after persuading Dennis that his normal attire of a red shirt, orange slacks, and a green coat were inappropriate for an eastern institution, he offered him a job as his personal assistant at Penn State. He subsequently promoted him to the position of provost, putting him to work on those areas that had traditionally caused the most faculty unrest. More times than not, Dennis managed to find a satisfactory solution before the problem ever reached the president's desk.[7]

Eisenhower made his associates' work easier by personally involving himself in faculty affairs. As noted, before Eisenhower came to Penn State the faculty had frequently criticized the administration, and not just on superficial matters such as the way the president's assistant dressed or Milholland's unfortunate phrase comparing the faculty to workers in a pickle factory. Eisenhower knew that the quickest way for a president to win over a faculty is to raise salaries. Here Eisenhower's travels and public-relations work paid large dividends. Legislative appropriations went up rapidly—from $10 million to $25 million within five years—and Eisenhower put much of the money into salaries. The general salary levels of the faculty increased about 75 percent in the five-year period, ranking Penn State near the top nationally. Eisenhower became especially popular with the junior faculty because he put a premium on narrowing the spread between salaries of instructors and assistant professors on the one hand and between full and associate professors on the other.[8]

Eisenhower also pleased many of the faculty by a stand he took on a perennial problem area, promotion. About midway through his presidency he set the council of administration to work studying and drawing up a statement of policies for promotion. Although he was a great booster of research and the graduate program at Penn State, Eisenhower was disturbed by the result, which emphasized research and publication as the criteria for faculty promotions to the virtual exclusion of all other standards. He did not want the faculty ever to forget its responsibility to teach. He therefore sent the members of the council a memorandum citing an article by Dean Donald Morrison, of Dartmouth College, that had appeared in the *Dartmouth Alumni Magazine* entitled "Dartmouth's Faculty Policies."

Eisenhower quoted liberally from the article, excerpting such statements as, "Recommendations for promotion should be limited to men who are demonstrably superior as teachers or scholars. A bibliography is not a prerequisite for promotion. But if an individual has little or no interest in research or publication he should not be recommended for promotion *unless* he is, in the judgment of the department, a really distinguished teacher. In short, Dartmouth can always use outstanding teachers who may not be researchers, but she has few places for men who are not strong teachers" (emphasis in the original).

In his covering memorandum Eisenhower commented, "With nearly 10,000 undergraduate students at Penn State, we constitute an undergraduate institution nearly four times larger than Dartmouth. I am sure we are no less concerned about the quality of our teaching." One cannot determine the impact of Eisenhower's intervention, but a strict publish-or-perish policy did not prevail at Penn State.[9]

Eisenhower made more friends among the younger faculty by his creation of an ad hoc group he called the Faculty Advisory Council. A faculty senate had long existed, but the administration dominated most of its deliberations. As Wilkinson explained, most junior members of the faculty "didn't trust it very much. They still don't, because you were kind of an establishment person if you tend to get into it."

The newly created Faculty Advisory Council had no authority nor official status, but Eisenhower met with it once a week. He told the members, who were selected solely by their colleagues and who came primarily from the junior ranks, "You are here to work with me on anything you want to bring up." He encouraged the council to study administrative policies, the budget, "everything that's going on, and then you call me in and we'll sit down and talk. There is the room. I'll be in there or not, as you wish."

Wilkinson thought the council "very, very useful," and Eisenhower said that "a president's calling in faculty for help in administration was an unheard-of thing, but I did it because it helped."[10] It helped most of all in giving Eisenhower an open line of communication with his faculty. At Kansas State he had felt, as do many college presidents, too isolated. The close contacts he had established with students and administrators had not extended to many of the faculty. The Faculty Advisory Council at Penn State made it possible for him to hear and deal with most grumblings and discontents before they exploded into crisis issues, if, of course, Dennis or someone else had not intervened previously.

The one glaring exception was the MacRae case, a situation that, in Wilkinson's words, "could have torn this place apart." A good bit of background is required for it to be fully appreciated and understood.

The MacRae case was a civil-liberties case that arose in the late summer of 1952, a most awkward moment for Eisenhower, whose brother was just then running for the presidency of the United States at a time when McCarthyism was at its height in America. Although Milton always sought to separate his affairs from his brother's, he was acutely aware that the press kept close tabs on any potential controversy at Penn State. The MacRae case had all the classic ingredients: a state loyalty oath, an active and suspicious American Legion, a bitterly divided faculty, and a high-minded, idealistic Penn State staff member. Civil liberties at Penn State had already caused some headlines, since the college (not yet a university) had just emerged—not at all unscathed—from a case that had been settled on the eve of Eisenhower's arrival at State College in 1950. The sequel, in 1952, however, caught Eisenhower in the middle.

The first case had concerned Lee Lorch, a mathematics professor whose contract had not been renewed at least partly because he had rented his house, in a segregated development in New York, to a black family. Eisenhower was never personally involved in the Lorch case, but because it had emotionally and intellectually divided the campus and produced an angry attack on Penn State in a *New York Times* editorial, it had compounded the distrust that already existed between the faculty and the administration.[11]

Within this context, Eisenhower had acted, even before tackling the system of faculty promotion, to establish a tenure policy at Penn State. Within months of his inauguration he had created a faculty committee on tenure and indicated that he personally preferred that it use the 1940 statement of principles of the American Association of University Professors as a guide.[12] The committee made its report along the lines Eisenhower suggested, and he presented it to the board of trustees with his full support. On December 4, 1950, the board approved the proposal, and Penn State had the first official tenure policy in its history. The policy granted un-tenured faculty the same rights of academic freedom that tenured faculty enjoyed and set up a faculty-administration committee to hear appeals from teachers in disputed dismissals.[13] In Judge Wilkinson's view, the policy was perhaps too generous, certainly "much more generous than we otherwise would have had" had it not been for the Lorch case. Eisenhower, however, considered it congruent with his own beliefs and felt that it went a long way towards elevating faculty morale and ameliorating the distrust of the administration.[14]

But in the climate of the times even a liberal tenure policy proved insufficient. In 1950, the year Eisenhower took over at Penn State, something near to hysteria swept across the United States. On January 21 of that year a jury found Alger Hiss guilty of perjury, and ten days later President Truman announced that the United States was developing a hydrogen bomb and Russia was expected to have one of its own in two years. Early the next month the British government announced that Dr. Klaus Fuchs, a high-level American atomic scientist, had confessed to spying for the Soviet Union; on February 22 Senator Joseph R. McCarthy announced at a Lincoln's Day speech in Wheeling, West Virginia, that he had the names of 205 "card-carrying Communists" who were working in the State Department, shaping the foreign policy of the United States. Then in June the North Korean army crossed the border into South Korea. By year's end Congress had passed the McCarran Internal Security Act, which required Communists to register as agents of a foreign government and prohibited the employment of Communists in national-defense work. Suspicion replaced trust at the foundation of all too many relationships.

Fanning the hysteria, McCarthy was hurling accusations the way politicians had historically hurled compliments, charging, among other things, that the American churches and educational system had been infiltrated by Communists. Loyalty oaths, a formal affirmation of one's loyalty to the nation, became a national rage. The American Legion, along with other patriotic organizations, helped McCarthy search out hidden Communists, fellow travelers, and other liberal activists.

Professors became especially tempting targets. They were visible, they supposedly held the future in their hands, they were public employees, they were vulnerable. The Penn State faculty was not immune. When charges were made, Eisenhower and Wilkinson would meet with the accused. Their approach was, as Wilkinson remembered, "If you're falsely accused, the university pays for your defense." Eisenhower insisted on that. But the legal counsel would then add, "The minute we find that you are associated with the Communist party, you're on your own and you're done." As a result, no Penn State professor ever took the Fifth Amendment when asked if he or she were a member of the Communist party, "because they knew we would defend them."

There were some on the faculty who had had, or did have, Communist affiliations. Penn State's position was never to defend an individual's right to remain at the University despite such a record. But it did try to provide the accused with every opportunity to prove the allegations false. Wilkinson recalled one case in which a faculty member "who had a solid, solid relationship with the Communist party" reportedly denied his connections. Wilkinson checked and checked again, and each time the results showed the charges to be "very authentic." So he talked the matter over with Eisenhower, then went back to the accused party and said, "O.K., you're entitled to your day in court, but I cannot sweep this stuff under the table." The professor asked if he could have a day to think about Wilkinson's suggestion that he request a tenure hearing. The next morning he resigned. As had been his policy when working with the WRA, Eisenhower would not refuse to perform what he felt was his duty, in spite of his personal views, but he would attempt to make an intolerable situation somewhat less intolerable.[15]

The MacRae case illustrated, however, that Eisenhower's style of seeking compromise, easing personal distress, and avoiding volatile incidents did not always succeed. The controversy really began on January 15, 1951, when Senator Albert R. Pechan, Pennsylvania's legislative chairman for the American Legion, introduced in the state legislature Senate bill 27, requiring every employee of the Commonwealth or any of its political subdivisions to file a written statement under oath that he or she was not, according to the bill's definition, a subversive. By the time Senate bill 27 became the Pennsylvania Loyalty Act on December 22 of that year, it had been amended nine times, had increased from two to seventeen sections, and had been broadened to encompass more than just public employees. The Pechan Act, as it was commonly called, led to what one University of Pennsylvania law professor described as "a bitter, prolonged, and widely publicized debate" that "generally took the form of support of or opposition to a loyalty oath." Eisenhower sought vainly to keep the debate out of Penn State, but the university became one of the focal points, and Eisenhower found himself a central participant.[16]

Prior to passing Pechan's proposal, the Senate added that public funds would be withheld from any state-aided institution of learning unless that institution required its employees to take a loyalty oath. Therefore, when in April the bill came up for discussion in the House, the Committee on State Government invited the presidents of Penn State, Penn, Temple University, and the University of Pittsburgh to Harrisburg to testify at the hearings. Eisenhower consulted his closest advisers and, confident that he was thoroughly briefed on the issues, prepared a statement opposing a mandatory loyalty oath for university faculty and staff on the grounds that such a procedure would "depart from sound American principles." Prophetically warning that "some loyal citizens would refuse to sign on philosophical grounds while subversives would sign without compunction," Eisenhower declared that as the president of Penn State he would "very much prefer to trust the heads of the various state agencies and the trustees and administrators of our schools and universities to eliminate subversives from their ranks, if any are actually there."[17]

In short, Eisenhower took the lead in arguing that the principal state-assisted universities in Pennsylvania could best achieve the legislature's objective of keeping subversives out of their institutions by developing their own internal procedures. Already there had been problems in the University of California system, where the board of regents had instituted a blanket loyalty oath, whereas Maryland's Ober law, which delegated responsibility to the individual institutions, had caused hardly a ripple. Although Pechan himself remained unconvinced, later remarking to reporters that "I don't know why anyone should object to an oath of loyalty. I get a thrill when I take my oath," the other legislators found Eisenhower's argument telling. The House dropped the compulsory oath for university faculty and staff. Instead, on final passage Section 13 of the act mandated that in order to receive public funds, each of the presidents would have to file with the governor "a written report setting forth what procedures the institution had adopted to determine whether it has reason to believe that any subversive persons are in its employ and what steps, if any, have been taken or are being taken to terminate such employment." Just as important, the president had to "unequivocally set forth that the institution has no reason to believe that any subversive persons are in its employ."[18]

Thus, subject to the governor's approval, the law left it up to each school to prescribe its own policing procedures. Yet before Eisenhower could set up any machinery to work on the problem, in fact before the Pechan Act became law, Eisenhower's ability to mind his own shop was called into question. In the summer of 1951 the Twenty-third District of the Pennsylvania American Legion demanded that the Commonwealth investigate Penn State, charging that the school had become a locus for "un-American influences and activities." Feeling compelled to reply, Eisenhower issued a two-page press release on July 26 refuting the allegations and adding that neither the American Legion nor any of its members had ever presented any evidence suggesting, let alone proving, the presence of subversives on campus. Then, taking a more positive tack, he declared that the Penn State community consisted of "loyal Americans, devoted to the principles of democracy, abhorrent of totalitarian practice and philosophy, and highly competent teachers and research workers." He asserted that they deserved the citizens' respect and appreciation, not their approbation. "These days of tension and hysteria," Eisenhower warned, "require each individual and every loyal American organization to be restrained and accurate in action and judgment, for if we are not careful we shall through mistaken zeal and unwarranted public condemnation seriously injure loyal people, loyal institutions, and the very values we all seek to protect." But even as he issued the release, Eisenhower recalled his unhappy experience at the Department of Agriculture, when he had become embroiled in the "Love Life of a Bullfrog" controversy. He feared that just as before, the charges would not go away. And in the end, people would be seriously injured.[19]

When, shortly after the 1951/52 winter recess, work began on developing the procedures necessary to meet the Pechan Act's guidelines, Eisenhower hoped that the eventual result would meet three essential conditions. First, of course, the plan should be just and satisfy the majority of the community. Second, nothing should be "imposed" on the faculty, but as a group it should arrive at a mutually acceptable proposal. And finally, the procedures should be uniform for all four of the Pennsylvania universities. To achieve these ends, he predictably opened his doors to all interested members of the faculty, met with both the Faculty Advisory Council and the senate, and held a series of conferences with the presidents of Penn, Pitt, and Temple. However, it is always difficult to reach a consensus when the issue involves civil rights, and during the McCarthy era it was virtually impossible.[20]

Divisions surfaced from the start. There were those on the faculty, such as R. Wallace Brewster, chairman of the political science department, who suggested that each department head certify as to the loyalty of those in the department. Brewster conceded that a few instances might arise when the chairman would feel that he had too little information on which to base a judgment or would have reservations regarding an individual. In these cases, the administration could investigate the few individuals in question. This method, notwithstanding such atypical circumstances, would obviate having to investigate the entire faculty and staff, and it would eliminate the need for a loyalty oath. No one proposed a mandatory oath, but there were some who thought a voluntary one could be instituted. To Brewster, the adjective "voluntary" seemed meaningless; anyone who refused would immediately come under suspicion. This could easily put Penn State in the position of having to refute individual allegations and, in doing so, being forced to reveal information acquired through otherwise private investigations. If the school refused to disclose the information, it would become suspect also.[21]

It took but two days for Eisenhower to reply. He agreed with most of Brewster's analysis, except for the aspect regarding the voluntary oath. If it were unfair to require an oath, he suggested, would it not be equally unfair to deny those individuals the opportunity to take an oath if they wanted to? The issue, after all, was freedom of choice. Eisenhower requested that Brewster respond to this "bothersome point."[22]

Eisenhower's letter to Brewster had been short and to the point.

Brewster's reply covered three pages. The political science chairman believed that even if the unavailability of an oath occasioned some negative reaction from those who were anxious to take it, "the adverse results arising from the use even of a voluntary oath would be greater than the adverse results of not having any oath at all." In stronger terms than previously, he reiterated his conviction that the use of a voluntary oath would present "the district Legion, etc., with a made-to-order challenge to liquidate the 'subversive' core of non-signers." Indeed, he projected a scenario in which the legionnaires would sit around the post collecting the names of non-signers, who would then become "Legion-bait." This situation would create an impossible predicament for the university administration, for the Legion's hostility would require the investigation of all non-signers, who Brewster assumed would far outnumber the signers. Should the other universities decide to institute a voluntary oath, or the governor require that they do so, Penn State would have no choice but to go along. However, if Eisenhower had gone on record as opposing the procedure, the State College community would know that *"our administration had at least tried to stand on principle"* (emphasis in the original).[23]

Brewster concluded his letter by commenting to Eisenhower that he had "the utmost faith in your desire to protect [the faculty] as fully as possible against this threat to academic freedom."[24] Six months later he became one of the president's most severe critics. As events unfolded that spring, the administrations of Penn, Pitt, and Temple decided on just the sort of procedure Brewster desired. Without requiring an oath or an investigation, the department chairman and other supervisory officials would certify that they had no reason to believe that anyone under their supervision was a subversive person as defined by the Pechan Act. The respective presidents, as called for by law, could then unequivocally state to the governor that his institution had no reason to believe that any subversive person was in its employ. According to a University of Pennsylvania *Law Review* study, such certification was "a sensible method of complying with the Act and at the same time not infringing academic freedom." Having carefully studied the legislative history of the controversial Section 13 of the law, the author concluded that the section did not contemplate that an institution adopt a loyalty oath or any analogous procedure that "might be as offensive to reasonable faculty sensibilities as an oath." In fact, "avoidance of the furor and harm that such a requirement would cause was the purpose of amending the Bill after the April discussions in Harrisburg."[25]

On the afternoon of May 16 Eisenhower attended meetings of both the faculty senate and the department heads and deans. He indicated that personally he found the procedures adopted by the other three universities acceptable. However, he had been advised by Counsel Wilkinson that since he, as president of Penn State, had taken the lead in opposing the original provisions of Section 13, the school had a "higher degree of responsibility" than the other institutions. Wilkinson was convinced that under the circumstances Penn State must have "something in the files on everybody," a written document enabling Eisenhower to certify unequivocally the loyalty of his employees on a more solid basis than "simply going home and signing your name." More important to Eisenhower, he told the faculty, most of the department heads had expressed their reluctance to certify unilaterally their personnel; indeed, some said they would refuse to do so. "Some felt," Eisenhower later wrote Brewster, "that they could not conscientiously give me a certificate for all individuals, and others felt that they should not be called upon to do for others what others could do for themselves."[26]

On May 2, because of such factors and because Wilkinson's legal position was now that some form of written certification from each university employee was not only preferable but mandatory in order that the governor approve Penn State's procedure—a position that proved incorrect in view of the governor's acceptance of the other school's methods—Eisenhower and his staff drafted a twenty-one-page "Tentative Procedures Designed to Enable the Pennsylvania State College to Comply with the Terms of Section 13 of the Pennsylvania Loyalty Act." At the May 16 meeting the president clearly indicated that the proposal was for discussion only and that no one should interpret the procedures outlined as final. In fact, the May 2 document had already undergone revision. The proposal epitomized Eisenhower's reliance on the art of compromise. As in the Penn, Pitt, and Temple plans, the responsibility for certification would rest with the supervisory officials. However, the Penn State procedure shifted the burden of evidence to the individual faculty or staff member. In other words, rather than a department head's merely certifying that he or she had no reason to believe that an employee was subversive, the employee had to furnish written proof that he or she was loyal. Acceptable proofs included security clearance from the federal government, evidence of a loyalty oath previously taken for the federal or state government, or the satisfactory completion of a questionnaire specifically designed by the college for those without other documents. The procedure did not deny an individual the opportunity to substitute a voluntary oath, but it did stipulate explicitly that "failure to request or execute such an oath by others is not evidence of disloyalty." By this method Eisenhower hoped to satisfy reluctant department heads, the governor, and the American Legion.

The major innovation was the questionnaire, and it seemed innocuous enough. While serving the same function as a loyalty oath, it avoided, at least in the eyes of most of the community, the distasteful connotations of one. Essentially it asked the respondent (1) whether he or she advocated the overthrow of either the federal or state government by force or violence; (2) whether he or she was a member of any political party, club, society, or organization that advocated such a violent overthrow and, if so, to explain; and (3) whether there was any reason why the president of Penn State could not certify unequivocally to the governor that the individual was not or would not become a subversive and, if there were, to explain. The May 2 draft had permitted the respondent, in lieu of answering question (2), to list all the parties, clubs, societies, and organizations of which he or she was a member, a provision deleted by May 10. If, owing to the responses, a department head could not certify an employee, that employee's name would be referred to a Loyalty Review Board. Only then would there be an investigation. Once the investigation was completed, the board would certify to the president—and the wording is important—either "(a) that to the best of its knowledge and belief the employee in question is not a subversive..." or "(b) that a *fair preponderance* of evidence shows the individual to be a subversive" (emphasis added). In the event of the latter, the employee could request a hearing before the review board, which would judge each case individually. If the review board determined that a fair preponderance of the evidence showed the employee to be a subversive, employment would be terminated within sixty days. The board's decision would be final.[27]

Penn State's faculty approved the tentative procedures partly because the proposal contained a minimum of objectionable features and partly because at least some of its members received the impression that the governor definitely would require some form of written certification from each employee. The regulations became official on May 20. However, by June 30 the administration had "slightly revised" the phrasing, as Eisenhower had indicated it might. The adverb *slightly* is hardly appropriate. The college's legal staff had been concerned that as the outline provided, an individual under suspicion could appear before the review board and refuse to answer any questions. Lacking the "fair preponderance" of evidence necessary to prove the employee a subversive, the review board would therefore have no alternative but to recommend certification. This concern greatly distressed Eisenhower, for ultimately he would be the one to report unequivocally to the governor that he had no reason to suspect his personnel. It was Eisenhower's duty to make the report; it was his reputation that was at stake. Thus the most significant revision stated that the board should refuse certification not only if a fair preponderance of the evidence proved the suspect a subversive but also if it lacked sufficient evidence essential to prove loyalty.[28]

The administration sent the revised statement of procedures to the office of services for duplication on July 2. Unfortunately, not until August 1 was the duplication finished, and, as Eisenhower himself noted on September 9, some faculty and staff members did not receive their copy until August 22. The reasons for the delay seem inexplicable, especially since only six days after the distribution had finally been completed Eisenhower wrote Wendell Scott MacRae that under the adopted procedures, "I have no alternative but to discharge you immediately as an employee of the Pennsylvania State College."[29]

Eisenhower did not like the idea of compulsory certification, but unless he challenged the state law, which he never considered doing, he had no choice other than to construct a procedure. After weighing all the factors, he and his staff felt that they had developed a process that, albeit cumbersome, presented so many alternatives that no one was likely to refuse to comply. The faculty's representatives had not objected, and none of the individual faculty members felt that their rights were being sufficiently trampled upon to cause them to balk. Of the some thirty-eight hundred Penn State employees, including politically sensitive professors such as Brewster, only one failed to abide by the school's procedures. Indeed, it is somewhat ironic that the one person who would stand on principle, who would create such a furor, was a "big, bumbling, homespun-looking guy," the fifty-two-year-old publications production manager in the Department of Public Information, one of those campus functionaries who rarely venture out from their secluded back offices. Wendell MacRae was the son of a Presbyterian minister, a former marine, the father of two, a fraternity man, a Republican, a member of the American Legion and the Red Cross. As one Penn State official put it, he was "in no way the picture of a militant activist or SOB troublemaker."[30]

Nevertheless, when Louis H. Bell, director of public information, opened MacRae's interoffice envelope, he found the loyalty oath and questionnaire forms unsigned and uncompleted. Enclosed was a memorandum, dated May 23, stating that MacRae "respectfully declined to take a political oath or to answer questions that are essentially political, as conditions of holding a job with the Pennsylvania State College. To fail to resist such efforts at thought control is to court further and worse legislative encroachments on intellectual freedom." MacRae reminded Bell that the United States had been founded by those willing to oppose "oppressive and tyrannical" legislation. As a native-born beneficiary of their struggle for freedom, therefore, he felt obligated to "resist any un-American legislation such as the Pennsylvania Loyalty Act which on the pretense of bolstering national security encroaches on fundamental liberties." Referring to Eisenhower's press release the previous year replying to the American Legion, he cited the president's defense of Penn State against "the scurrilous attacks of publicity-seeking patrioteers." MacRae saw no reason why that defense no longer remained valid.

MacRae suggested that Bell certify him on the basis of his three-year record as an employee of Penn State, his service to the community, and his standing as a U.S. citizen, far better guideposts to his loyalty than any "tongue-in-cheek answers I might make to an absurd and insulting questionnaire."[31] While this method would have satisfied the requirements at Penn, Pitt, and Temple, the Penn State procedure called for individual certification *in writing*. Helpless to do otherwise, Bell could only inform the Loyalty Review Board that MacRae had not presented him with the information necessary for certification. On June 25 the board chairman, A. O. Morse, the outgoing provost and a veteran of the Lorch case, informed MacRae that he had not been certified and that if he did not request a hearing within thirty days, he would receive his sixty-day notice. The day before his grace period elapsed, MacRae requested the hearing.[32]

It took another month for the hearing to be held, and it lasted precisely one hour. Representing the review board, which was made up of members of the faculty and the technical, service, and clerical staffs, as well as Chairman Morse, was Penn State legal counsel Roy Wilkinson. Although he had been coached, MacRae chose not to have counsel present, since he had been told by Morse that the procedure would be informal. Therefore, he was caught off guard and protested when Wilkinson began the proceedings by delineating the formal format that would be followed. The misunderstanding made little difference. When Wilkinson began by asking whether MacRae had ever advocated the overthrow of either the state or federal government the former marine simply declined to answer, stating that he had refused to answer the question previously and that was the reason for the hearing. Indeed, each time the board's counsel tried to get MacRae to respond verbally to essentially the same questions posed on the questionnaire MacRae repeated his refusal.

In keeping with his understanding that the hearing was being held so that he could offer evidence in his behalf, MacRae had wanted first to present his case and then respond to the board's questions. Nevertheless, he courteously waited while Wilkinson completed his examination and read into the record copies of all the previous correspondence. Once given the opportunity, however, MacRae challenged the legal basis of the inquiry. Comparing the hearing to the trial in *Alice in Wonderland*, since the college had released a statement more than a month before stating that the

"Trustees and Administration . . . declare categorically that to the best of their knowledge there are no subversive persons on the payroll of the institution," he insisted that the procedures adopted by Penn State went well beyond the authority delegated to it by the Pechan Act. For the board to question his loyalty, he maintained, it should present evidence of his subversive activities. MacRae contended that because no such evidence had come forth, he should not be put in the position of having to defend himself.

Regardless of this argument, MacRae did defend himself. Now reading from a sworn statement, he listed more than twenty-five noncommercial organizations of which he had been a member, ranging from the schools he had attended to the Republican party. He paused to point out that in accepting his commission in the Marine Corps he had taken an oath to support and defend the Constitution. As a matter of fact, he suggested to his examiners that in currently "taking a stand for Constitutional law" by refusing to comply with the certification procedures, "I feel that I am fulfilling an obligation under that oath." MacRae's statement closed with a quote from Richard W. Slocum, the keynote speaker at Penn State's summer commencement exercises. "We must feel strength through freedom instead of fear through repression," Slocum had told his Penn State audience some two weeks earlier. "The burden of protecting and improving what we have and resisting the erosion of our freedom, particularly as established in the First Amendment, rests on citizens like yourselves."

Having concluded his statement, MacRae then called Bell and his neighbor Victor Held as personal witnesses. Each testified that he had absolutely no grounds to consider MacRae a subversive, and Bell added that were it up to him as an individual, he would certify his subordinate without question. With their testimony the hearing concluded.[33] The next morning Morse wrote MacRae a one-sentence letter which read, "You are hereby advised that the Loyalty Review Board of the Pennsylvania State College finds that it lacks sufficient evidence essential to certify to the President of The Pennsylvania State College that you are not subversive as the term 'subversive' is defined in the Pennsylvania Loyalty Act."[34]

Immediately MacRae wrote Eisenhower, appending a copy of his statement to the board and protesting the verdict as "blind adherence to procedure that has no basis in law or equity" and appealing to him as "the ultimate certifying authority to accept my statement and the evidence of my loyalty accompanying it as adequate to permit you to certify me." He also offered to meet with the president at any convenient time. Wilkinson, however, advised against such a meeting and in fact counseled Eisenhower not to even discuss the case. The review board's decision was final. Therefore, Eisenhower simply wrote MacRae that he had no alternative but to dismiss him, enclosing a check to cover his salary for twenty-eight days in August and sixty additional ones.[35]

Morse, Wilkinson, and Eisenhower felt bound by the procedures they had written. There is no evidence that any of them ever questioned MacRae's loyalty. But Eisenhower had personally signed the letter to the governor stipulating the precise procedures required of each Penn State employee to obtain certification, procedures MacRae refused to follow. Had the list of organizations of which he was a member still been an acceptable alternative to question (2) of the questionnaire, MacRae still could not have been certified, because he would not sign the questionnaire. Similarly, even though he had taken a previous oath for the Marine Corps, he would not take a loyalty oath under the threat of losing his job. The question still remains, however, why MacRae's signed statement for the hearing, including the list of organizations and quoting the Marine Corps oath, along with the witnesses, did not constitute sufficient evidence for the board. The answer must rest with the technicality that he would not answer the questions posed by Wilkinson. Had Eisenhower overruled the board's "final" decision, he would have nullified the entire certification procedure. Since the law required certification by September 1, the governor would have had to withhold public funds from Penn State. MacRae correctly perceived this logic when he wrote to Eisenhower that "the verdict of the Board was preordained" and that "the hearing was not an alternative method to obtain certification."[36]

Too many at the college, however, did not see the issue in the same light, and within days of the decision the whole campus was in an uproar. Individual professors such as Brewster wrote to Eisenhower that the procedure had permitted the serious violation of MacRae's rights. In Brewster's opinion, most of the community was incredulous that Eisenhower had let such a travesty of justice happen, and he warned that "the deep respect, trust and downright affection which you have built up in the past two years will be severely affected—if this decision stands."[37]

Professor of American literature William Werner used his "Bookworm" column in the local newspaper to solicit support from the public, and Werner and four other members of the faculty formed a MacRae Defense Committee to challenge both the decision and the administration's conduct throughout the controversy. It wrote lengthy letters to Eisenhower and faculty colleagues, not only defending MacRae's innocence but also maintaining that the administration had not been forthright in initially proposing the certification procedure and had not adequately consulted the faculty regarding the final revisions. The committee circulated a petition resolving that Eisenhower restore the "fair preponderance of evidence" clause to the procedure, affirm the principle that the Loyalty Review Board constituted an alternative method of certification, and reopen the case of Wendell Scott MacRae.[38]

Eisenhower responded as best he could. He addressed a public letter to the faculty and staff in which he reviewed the steps leading up to the adopted procedures and defended the administration's practices. He also responded personally to those like Brewster who exhibited individual concern. The situation did not improve; in fact, one recent Penn State appointee, upon learning of the MacRae case, resigned due to "conscientious objections." Wilkinson recalled that even Philip Klein, the distinguished historian, who normally stayed out of campus politics, called him to say, "I would as leave teach ethics in a whorehouse as history at an institution that would fire MacRae because he's a Communist. No matter what you say or how you slice it, it's ridiculous." Eisenhower changed his position. Writing Brewster on September 22 that he regretted "more than I can possibly express that some members of the faculty are now questioning my integrity," he lamented, "In nearly thirty years of public life this is the first time such a thing has occurred to me. It makes me feel more like a politician than an educational administrator." Eisenhower informed Brewster that he had decided to set up a faculty committee to review the whole situation. Reflecting the sentiment of a beleaguered leader, he remarked, "I have never assumed that my judgment is infallible."[39]

Eisenhower's decision to establish the special committee, essentially a decision to rely once again on the technique of involving those most affected by an issue, broke the logjam. Headed by professor of fuel technology Charles R. Kinney, the seven-member Special Committee to Study Loyalty Procedures proposed modifications in the certification procedure, including the restoration of the "fair and preponderance" clause, and recommended that the president reopen the MacRae case. Submitting its initial report on October 28, its original proposal was that a five-person board be established to conduct a new investigation if MacRae reapplied for his job. By this time, of course, with MacRae no longer in the school's employ, Eisenhower had submitted his certification report to the governor and satisfied the Pechan Act's provision for public funds. After further discussions with the administration and the Faculty Advisory Council, however, the special committee decided that there were few, if any, in State College who could judge MacRae impartially. The committee and the Faculty Advisory Council thus agreed unanimously to select an eminent individual from outside the community to serve as an independent investigating authority. Several days later Earl G. Harrison, a Philadelphia attorney and former dean of the University of Pennsylvania Law School, accepted the position.[40]

On November 17 MacRae applied for reinstatement, and the next day he met with Harrison in State College. The former dean also held conversations with Eisenhower, Morse, the chairman of the Faculty Advisory Council, Werner's MacRae Defense Committee, and public information director Louis Bell. By November 28 he had submitted his report. It emphasized that no one, not even anonymously, had ever charged MacRae with disloyalty; that his record showed "not a scintilla of evidence of anything approaching subversiveness or disloyalty"; that because of the Lorch case MacRae had been investigated "unusually" thoroughly when he first came to Penn State; and that his past associations, especially the Marine Corps, illustrate that there is "absolutely no question" about his loyalty. Moreover, while not examining MacRae as Wilkinson did at the hearing, or requesting that he sign a questionnaire, Harrison elicited the answers to the questions in two lengthy theoretical discussions with MacRae. He concluded that MacRae "unequivocally" believed in the constitutional form of state and federal government and that he "does not advocate, and has not advocated," the use of force or violence to bring about change. Harrison did ask him directly whether he knew of any reason why he should not be certified as a non-subversive, to which MacRae answered simply "No." Thus Harrison could reach but one judgment: "It is crystal clear to me there is no longer any reason to hesitate to certify Mr. MacRae," he reported to Eisenhower. "I unqualifiedly certify that Wendell Scott MacRae is not a subversive person as that term is defined in the Pennsylvania Loyalty Act or under any other reasonable definition."[41]

Certainly MacRae had been more responsive to Harrison than he had been to the Loyalty Review Board. Perhaps it was because he thought that he had made his point earlier, or perhaps it was because of the manner in which he was examined. MacRae later released a statement to the effect that had he been permitted to present his case at the beginning of the hearing, as he had requested, and then been examined on the evidence he had presented, he would have presented the board with the same information. As it was, the board had asked no questions following his testimony or that of his witnesses. In any event, since Harrison was now duly constituted as the certifying officer, Eisenhower had no difficulty reinstating MacRae. He went back to work on December 6. Everyone seemed satisfied, and in Wilkinson's words, "We moved on."[42]

Penn State did move on, yet so did McCarthy, Pechan, and those like them who created the atmosphere that made the MacRae case possible. Three years later it was Eisenhower himself who was victimized by the senator from Wisconsin. McCarthy charged that Ike's younger brother was the "unofficial president of the United States" and "one of the most left-wingers you can find."[43] But that too blew over. Eisenhower was not a villain in the 1950s, nor was Wilkinson or any member of the Loyalty

Review Board. If there was a villain, it was the American people who, through fear and ignorance, permitted the situation to persist. In April 1953 Eisenhower announced that employees could be certified without taking a loyalty oath or completing a questionnaire. However, not until 1975 did Pennsylvania's attorney general, Robert Kane, declare the Pechan Act unconstitutional, and it is fitting that in State College it was Wendell Scott MacRae who delivered the eulogy. "This absurd law," he wrote to the editor of the *Centre Daily Times*, "seeking to pry into personal political beliefs, was pushed through a reluctant legislature in the early '50s by drumbeating, bandplaying veterans' organizations with intent to eliminate alleged faculty 'pinkos' from state-aided educational payrolls. . . . its demise has gone unmourned by press or self-conscious patriots. It flushed out no communists. It afflicted the loyal and comforted the disloyal, if any. It cheapened the time-honored ritual of swearing in public servants and military defenders of the Republic."[44]

CHAPTER 10

"How Much I Have Valued Your Counsel"

A Brother in the White House

T he most influential person in the new government is not, offici- ally, in the government at all," *Reader's Digest* reported in June 1953. "He is not and never has been in politics. He is 'Prexy' Milton Eisenhower, Ike's younger brother." The brothers, the *Digest* wrote, "think alike and their thinking has led them to like conclusions and convictions." As a mat- ter of fact, the article stated, Ike's middle-of-the-road philosophy had been worked out between Ike and Milton back in the thirties "in bat- ting ideas back and forth." Ike especially relied on Milton for help in his dealings with the federal bureaucracy, because "few men know more than Milton Eisenhower knows about the vast mechanism of our federal government."[1]

Even though this biography does not purport to cover Eisenhower's governmental activities once he had left the Washington bureaucracy, no study of Milton would be complete without some discussion of his service to Dwight.[2] The presence of a brother in the White House, especially one who depended upon him for advice on the entire spectrum of problems a president has to face, put Eisenhower in a delicate position. Eager to help but sensitive to criticism, willing to assist his brother and his country wherever he could but keenly aware of his responsibility to his university, delighted by his brother's success and worldwide prominence but insis- tent on being his own man and standing on his own feet, Eisenhower han- dled the situation with tact and a finely tuned sense of the appropriate. He defined his own role, and in the process he created a unique position for himself as an adviser to and the confidant of the president. For eight years Milton Eisenhower navigated the rapids of being a full-time university president and a nearly full-time adviser to the president of the United States.

Eisenhower told *Newsweek* magazine in 1977, "I don't think it made any difference in my own life that my brother was President. I had my own career."[3] He exaggerated. Obviously being the brother of the president, the brother of probably the best-known and best-respected man in the United States, made *some* difference. Nevertheless, his seemingly inexhaustible energy, combined with an acute sense of responsibility and propriety, kept that difference to a minimum.

"There was absolutely no doubt all the time Milton was here at Penn State," Judge Wilkinson declared, "that the university came first." To illustrate the point, Wilkinson recalled an incident in October 1953. The administration of Dwight Eisenhower was but nine months old, and the Republicans in Pennsylvania decided to hold an extravaganza for him in Hershey, calling it "The President's First Birthday Party." It was a fundraiser, a hundred-dollars-a-plate affair, a sizeable sum of money in those days. It was to be for "everybody who was anybody," with Penn State trustee Fred Waring's orchestra doing the entertaining, Sam Snead and other famous golfers demonstrating their craft, Ringling Brothers and Barnum and Bailey's Circus providing the tents, and all the Eisenhower brothers invited as special guests.

Milton flatly refused to go. Wilkinson, astonished, said, "Well, for heaven's sake, this is a birthday party for your brother." Milton replied, "Who are you kidding? This is a fund-raising party for the Republican party, and I won't be there." Wilkinson protested that not just Waring but all the members of the Penn State board would be present. Milton remained adamant. "I'm not going to do it," he said. "This is a good time for me to establish right now that I will work with my brother in the operation of the country, but not in the operation of the Republican party. That wouldn't be good for the university."[4]

Another anecdote illustrates more poignantly Eisenhower's commitment to Penn State. On June 7, 1956, Eisenhower was participating in an all-day meeting of the board. At 10:00 A.M. a secretary handed Wilkinson a note saying that press secretary James Hagerty was on the phone from the White House. He handed the note over to Eisenhower, who wrote at the bottom of it, "Tell him I'll call back at noon." When the meeting broke for lunch, Eisenhower asked Wilkinson to come back to his office with him while he made the call. He listened as Eisenhower talked to Hagerty.

The news was bad. The president had been stricken with an ileitis attack and would have to undergo a serious emergency operation. He wanted his brother with him, and, Hagerty reported, the White House had already sent a plane to fly Milton immediately from State College to Washington.

Eisenhower thanked Hagerty but said that the plane—and his brother—would have to wait. He explained that he had to continue the board meeting that afternoon and that the next day he was required to preside over the graduation ceremonies. Only then would it be possible for him to leave for the capital.

Hagerty could not believe what he was hearing. Quickly he passed the phone to Dr. Howard Snyder, an army general, Ike's longtime personal physician, and a friend of the family. Bluntly, Snyder said, "Milton, if you wait 'till tomorrow, your brother may not be here." Still Eisenhower resisted. Snyder went one step farther: "You've got to come, and you've got to come this afternoon," he said loud enough for Wilkinson to hear. "We're having trouble getting your brother to go to the hospital until he talks to you." Frowning, Eisenhower replied that he would call back and hung up.

Turning to Wilkinson, Eisenhower explained the situation and asked, "What can we do?" Wilkinson, who had overheard virtually the entire conversation, was as incredulous as Hagerty. "What can we do?" he snorted rhetorically. "Why, we'll get along without you, that's what we can do." Not yet convinced, Eisenhower asked, "Who will give the degrees?" After all, there was no one at Penn State empowered to assume his functions. Wilkinson nevertheless persisted that someone could cover for him and that his place was beside the president, his brother, in this moment of crisis. Eisenhower finally gave in. It would have been his last commencement as president of Penn State, and it would be the only one he ever missed.[5]

From beginning to end, Eisenhower involved himself deeply in his brother's political life. It was inevitable that this would be so, given their intimate relationship, Milton's years of experience in Washington, and Ike's high regard for Milton's ideas, knowledge, and counsel. Indeed, Ike often said that had Milton not been his brother, he would have appointed him to a high Cabinet post either in Agriculture or at State.

Yet both brothers knew that in addition to avoiding the charge of nepotism, being outside the government allowed Milton to range more freely than otherwise would have been possible. He gave advice on everything. Nevertheless, despite his virtually unlimited access to the president, Milton insisted, successfully, on remaining in the background. Unlike Colonel Edward House or Harry Hopkins, he made few enemies. He had spent much too much time in Washington not to realize the fundamental error of using his position to circumvent the established lines in the bureaucracy. When he wished to suggest some action, he went *through* the appropriate Cabinet department, not around or over it.

Milton Eisenhower himself described what he *did* do in a letter written to a friend in 1976. "Since I was President Eisenhower's most intimate confidante [sic]," he explained years after his brother's death,

> I know that comments I made and questions I asked were helpful to him as he worked toward the best solution to knotty problems. . . . I tried never to urge a particular decision. That approach is not particularly enlightening and can, in fact, result in the other person's firming up in his mind a contrary view. Intelligent decisions require a balanced view of all the facts, a calm consideration of the alternatives, the priority to be assigned to a possible action in view of total needs, and so on; in all our intimate visits my brother had a logical method of achieving the balanced view and I know I was helpful in this regard.

Eisenhower saw his role as transcending that of an adviser per se. "When I say to you that my brother and I discussed over a period of eight years nearly every major decision he made," the letter continued," I must be sure you have this in mind: Most persons in positions of leadership like to think out loud with someone he deems to be intelligent, well informed, conscious of all the nuances from fiscal policy to political possibility, can be trusted absolutely never to divulge a secret, and whom he admires; it is that kind of person who should be the President's principal confidante [sic]."[6]

Milton's role as confidant actually predated his brother's election. Even during the period before Ike agreed to accept the Republican nomination Milton was a key figure in providing him with a necessary picture of what was happening domestically on the political front. Ike was then in Europe, serving as the head of the newly formed North Atlantic Treaty Organization (NATO) forces. Milton wrote him long letters, which he personally typed, outlining the development of the movement to draft Eisenhower. And no one knew the situation better. East Coast Republicans determined to make Ike the party nominee—men like Hugh Scott, Lucius Clay, Thomas Dewey, Henry Cabot Lodge, Jr., William Robinson, Nelson Rockefeller, C. D. Jackson, Arthur Summerfield, Paul Hoffman, Herbert Brownell, and many other prominent figures—bombarded Milton through letters, telegrams, long-distance calls, and personal visits to State College. They implored him to use his influence to persuade Ike to accept a nomination.

That was not Milton's style. He did not want to be a king maker, nor did he really want his brother to subject himself—and his hard-earned reputation—to the rough-and-tumble of American politics. As accurately as he could, he summarized his discussions with the Republican leaders, all the time emphasizing how he discouraged any political talk mentioning General Eisenhower. On one occasion he wrote, "When I see how terribly bitter the intellectual divisions in this country are becoming, when I read the most obscene sort of literature that passes as political forecasts, when I realize how very dirty the coming Presidential campaign is going to be, I just pray that you will in no way be identified with it."[7]

Nevertheless, like Ike, Milton feared that the Republicans might nominate Senator Robert Taft, which would possibly lead to another Republican defeat, an outcome both brothers felt might signal the end of the two-party system in America. Indeed, there had not been a Republican president in two decades. On the other hand, if Taft won the election, that could be even worse than another Democratic victory. Taft represented to a large extent the midwestern isolationist wing of the Republican party, and one of the Eisenhowers' strongest convictions was that the United States could not turn its back on the rest of the world. All the Republicans talking to Milton harped on the same point: only Ike could save the Republican party, the country, and the noncommunist world. Thus Milton said in an October 20, 1951, letter, "The possibility that the American people must choose between Taft and Truman is so terrifying that I think any personal sacrifice on the part of any honest American citizen is wholly justified."

"Sooner or later," Milton lamented, "no matter how violently you may wish, on a purely personal basis, to remain aloof from partisan politics, you are going to have to decide what, if any, public responsibility you have in the situation. . . . I hope you don't mind my saying that I am terribly sorry for you. I know you would like to keep out of all this. I know that instinctively you'd like to issue a blast and put a stop to it once and for all. But that deep-seated sense of duty which was drilled into you must be causing you to suffer much anguish."[8]

In 1948, when he had been the popular candidate of both parties, Ike had categorically taken himself out of the race. Now, convinced that if Taft were elected he would renege on America's commitment to NATO and otherwise withdraw from the collective security of the free world, the General decided to run as a Republican. Milton became his brother's most enthusiastic supporter, passing on the views of the flow of visitors to his office, providing advice about delegates in the pre-convention fight with Taft, laying the groundwork for Ike's return from Europe. He would lament how Truman "rigged" the Wage Stabilization Board following the seizure of the steel mills to favor the unions, or relate the "ugly rumor" that the Democrats were spending Department of Agriculture money to "impress upon farmers how much the present administration has done for them since 1933." Devotedly, Milton threw himself into the campaign, but he never did like it. One letter concluded, "How glad I am that I'm not a candidate for anything."[9]

In June 1952 Ike came back to the United States to begin his full-time campaign. Milton agreed to help him in every way he could, but first he offered the Penn State board of trustees his resignation in the event that the members felt that his participation in the campaign would in any way injure or compromise the university. He also offered to take a leave of absence if the trustees preferred. The trustees responded that so long as he kept up his university duties, he was as free as any other citizen to participate in political life.[10]

During the ensuing months Milton divided his time between Penn State and the Eisenhower whistle-stop tour of the country. Despite his proven speaking ability, Milton did not take to the stump for his brother, preferring, as usual, to remain out of sight. Initially, he prepared speeches primarily on agricultural subjects, but soon he became one of Ike's principal speech writers. Ike would normally give him the draft of a speech written by someone on the staff. Milton would go over it, rearrange it, tighten it, and send it back. Then it would be Ike's turn to use the blue pencil. This practice continued and even expanded after Ike moved into the White House. Throughout Ike's tenure as president special messengers moved seemingly incessantly back and forth between the Oval Office and Milton's office carrying drafts of speeches for Milton to work on. When Ike wrote his White House memoirs, *Mandate for Change* and *Waging Peace*, he insisted that Milton read the entire manuscripts before he would allow them to be published.

In a letter of February 2, 1953, marked "Personal and Secret," Ike told Milton that he could not expect to be thanked for each and every act of assistance because "in the first place, I would never be able to express adequately the degree of dependence that I feel on your wisdom and judgment and devotion—in the second place, I am selfish enough to expect your help to be almost a continuous thing." Ike added that "in the case of the speech which I am to give within a couple of hours, you have transformed it from something that I almost hated into a document that may be of real value."[11]

Milton's role as a principal speech writer for the president, although obviously important, was but an adjunct to his other duties. Ike also assigned him more formal responsibilities: along with Nelson Rockefeller and Arthur Flemming, he was on the three-man Presidential Advisory Committee on Government Organization (PACGO), and he served as the president's personal representative to Latin America, which involved lengthy trips to Central and South America. Such vital assignments notwithstanding, his major contribution undoubtedly was as presidential confidant. The White House was virtually Milton's weekend home for eight years. While he was living in State College, either Sammy Blazer would drive him down on Fridays or he would fly by small plane. (After he discovered that Ike was paying a guest fee for his room in the White House, Milton insisted on spending his nights in Washington at his father-in-law's apartment in the Mayflower Hotel.)

At breakfast, over cocktails before dinner, or late at night the two Eisenhower brothers would discuss the problems of the world. The press, always fascinated by those who are close to the seat of power and have the president's ear, wrote extensively about Milton, usually comparing him to House or Hopkins. He resented such comparisons. Milton insisted that in contrast to House or Hopkins, he had no political ambitions of his own, never sought power for himself, and insofar as possible kept in the background. But no one who is close to the president can remain anonymous, whatever his desires, and so it was with Milton.

Eisenhower succeeded better at refusing to solicit special requests of the president than he did at maintaining his "passion for anonymity." Not even close friends could induce him to exercise what he considered inappropriate influence with his brother. For example, on one occasion Nelson Rockefeller, feeling frustrated that his views were not reaching the Oval Office, asked Milton if he might serve as his conduit. Milton respected Rockefeller's opinions and thought it important that his brother hear them; nevertheless, he realized that if he himself brought them up, he would essentially be Rockefeller's advocate. "I am not going to mention this to him [Ike]," he replied. "I never initiate a subject, but I express an opinion on anything he asks me about." All Milton would do was make sure that Rockefeller got on the president's appointment calendar.[12]

As one of Milton's Penn State assistants put it, because of his long association with Coolidge, Hoover, Roosevelt, and Truman, he had a "very high regard for the office of the Presidency." No one who knew him well would ever ask him to intervene with his brother or, most certainly, to ferret out secrets. Ike had Milton install a direct telephone line from the White House to Penn State: "We all got out of the room when it rang," said the aide. There was even a hot line to Milton's bedroom.[13]

In a penetrating article entitled "When He Talks, Ike Listens" in the September 1955 *Saturday Evening Post*, Demaree Bess sought to analyze Milton's role. Within a few weeks the president was to suffer his first heart attack, which in retrospect increased the significance of the analysis. Milton, Bess wrote, "has become perhaps the most helpful member of the multitude, official and personal, around his brother." The reason seemed clear: Milton "has no vested interest. He is not subservient. He owes nothing to any one element of the national society, and thus can talk without partisanship or localities—without, to use one of the President's words, parochialism. . . . His discussions with the President have one quality the President considers priceless—inviolate privacy."[14]

Invariably, all presidential advisers are suspected of being potential, if not actual, Rasputins. Milton was no exception, especially during the second term, when Ike's questionable health prompted wide speculation as to who in fact was running the government. Even the normally friendly *New York Times Magazine* wrote in 1959: "There are various estimates of Milton Eisenhower. Outside the White House, there are those who regard him as a favored courtier, really the power behind the throne. Others, still outside the White House, regard him as a master of intrigue, lurking behind the stage with a stiletto ready to sink into a person or a policy. There are those who believe he exerts a dangerous Left-Wing influence on the President."[15]

That last point became a popular theme among conservative critics of Ike, who claimed that his administration was too liberal precisely as a result of Milton's influence. The critics, such as Senator McCarthy, usually cited Milton's years of service to the New Deal as proof of his supposedly leftwing views. Paradoxically, analogous criticism came from the other side of the aisle. In looking for a political broadside during the 1956 campaign, Democratic candidate Adlai Stevenson charged that Milton was using his influence with Ike to bolster rightwing dictators in South America, especially Juan Perón in Argentina. Much like the earlier cited incident concerning McCarthy's allegations, Stevenson's charges brought out the big brother in Ike and led to one of his legendary outbursts of temper. Departing from his usual practice of avoiding direct reference to personalities, he issued his own blast at Stevenson, who had not gotten his facts right.[16]

During the week, when he was away from Washington, Milton wrote frequent, lengthy letters to the White House, all marked "Personal and Confidential," all typed by himself at the typewriter he kept by his desk. He would place his letters in two envelopes, the outside one addressed to Ike's private secretary, Mrs. Ann Whitman, to ensure that they went directly to the president and not by way of some staff assistant. The details of this correspondence are beyond the scope of this study. The collection of hundreds of letters, now in the Eisenhower Library, in Abilene, Kansas, is available to scholars. Suffice it to say that the subjects ranged from stag dinner invitations to international crises, with an omnipresent emphasis on educating the population.[17]

No topic fell outside Milton's purview, and when he felt it necessary, he could be quite blunt. In those rare instances when he disagreed with what his brother was doing, he did not hesitate to tell him so. For example, Ike had difficulty in dealing with the Republican leadership in Congress, an issue on which one might have expected Milton to remain silent. On the contrary, he wrote early in the administration that "I doubt you can succeed quickly enough in having a program adopted and public support retained by the cooperative method you have been employing." Both brothers fervently believed in the conciliatory approach, but in this case, when conciliation repeatedly failed to achieve cooperation, Milton advised that "the remedy lies in your more obviously taking the lead on all major issues and then in insisting that Republican leaders fall in line." In short, the president must become a stronger leader. "The people want a sense of direction," he counseled, "and they want it from you." Ike was similar to Milton in that he was highly sensitive to criticism. But when Milton criticized, astute observers such as Bess realized, the president listened.[18]

Milton, of course, was not the president's only brother (however, Ike frequently remarked that "Milton is the smartest of all of us"), and the others, being Eisenhowers, were men of firm convictions and were not reluctant to express them. Milton at times had to assume the additional responsibility of riding herd over the brood, despite his standing in age. Edgar was probably the farthest to the right politically—he once said that everything that had been done since 1933 was unconstitutional—and he was definitely the one most likely to speak out regarding his complaints. In November 1955 Edgar warned Milton that "I am about to make a public blast against the government subsidies to the farmers, but before doing so, I thought that you might give me some moral or economic reason why we should subsidize the farmer." He pointed out that farm subsidies were "originally a war measure, but as far as I am able to learn, we are not now at war, and therefore, the war powers are not enough excuse for this kind of action." He concluded, "The probabilities are that you and Dwight are going to hate me—but by Gad, here she goes!"[19]

Milton replied immediately, urging Edgar to "not give way to your emotions." After conceding that such a complicated subject as the nation's farm program required a book, not a letter, and inviting Edgar to come to Pennsylvania to spend some hours discussing it, he proceeded to present a succinct four-paragraph history of U.S. agricultural policy since the turn of the century. His major intent, however, was, not to convince

Edgar that he was wrong, but to plead with his older brother to "restrain yourself" because it would "not be fair to Ike" to give the press such a ready-made headline. Milton explained the obvious—that the publicity value of such a statement from Edgar depended entirely upon his being the president's brother. Anything Edgar said would be newsworthy, Milton wrote, not because you "personally said it," but because you "happen to be a brother of the President."

It must be noted that Milton's actions in this instance, which were taken to try to protect Ike from the embarrassment of having to answer the criticisms of his own brother, reflected another aspect of Milton, his sense of propriety. In the same way that he felt it inappropriate to use his personal relationship with the president to obtain undue influence within the administration, he felt it inappropriate to use the family relationship to obtain undue influence with either the press or the public. At no time during his brother's eight years as president did Milton ever compromise his position as a confidential adviser by taking advantage of his notoriety to promote a certain viewpoint. In fact, he carefully refrained from making any statements that could potentially have had a political impact, even though such statements would certainly have been congruent with his own position as president of a prominent institution of higher education. Milton admitted to Edgar that at times his silence had "been difficult for me," because prior to Ike's election he often had spoken out on issues. Were he now to use his name to attract a public forum, however, he would be humiliating himself and failing to serve the president of the United States. In fact, in 1957 Edgar did publicly criticize the Eisenhower administration's position on federal support for higher education. "I am mad as hell!" Milton stormed to White House appointments secretary Bernard Shanley. He did not feel that Edgar's broadside would hurt the administration. "Ike can take care of himself," he explained. "What my brother doesn't seem to realize (meaning Edgar) is that he would have no press at all if it weren't for his brother Ike," Shanley quoted Milton as saying. "I am mad because it cheapens the whole family name."[20]

Similarly, Milton would accept nothing for himself because his brother was president, at least nothing in the way of financial reward or personal power. However, he did not forget his responsibilities to Penn State, and he had no intention of depriving the school of the benefit his connection with Ike could bring. This is not to say that he sought benefits in terms of government grants, contracts, or similar "favors." Rather, he realized that where the president goes so goes the press, and such favorable publicity was important when it came time to solicit funds from the state legislature or to attract alumni support. Not surprisingly, therefore, Ike became a frequent visitor to State College.

A highlight was Penn State's hundredth anniversary, when Milton induced the president to give the commencement speech. Ceremonies were to take place in the stadium, with an expected audience of thirty thousand. Milton fondly recalled breakfast with his brother that morning. The local meteorologist called to report a 50 percent chance of rain. If the ceremonies were moved inside, only six thousand guests could be seated. Milton, of course, hoped for as big a crowd as possible, anticipating the next day's headlines throughout the country. But he felt it only right to defer to the guest of honor. Ike grinned, waved his hand, and said, "You decide. I haven't worried about the weather since June 6, 1944!"

Milton took the risk and ordered that the program remain outside. A drizzle was falling as the brothers walked onto the speaker's platform, but the Eisenhower luck held. The rain stopped, the sun emerged, and the occasion was a huge success. Across the nation newspapers featured photographs of the president addressing throngs of Penn Staters, with Milton smiling in the background.[21]

In the fall of 1955 President Eisenhower suffered a serious heart attack. For the next several months it appeared certain that he would not be a candidate for reelection. Leading Republicans, well aware of both the magic of the name Eisenhower and Milton's abilities, began a "Milton for President" boom. It is no exaggeration to say that Milton hated such talk. In words much more personal than those that he had used to advise Edgar, he commented years later, "It was clear to me that if I let my name be bandied about, it would be primarily because I was a brother. That would have humiliated me. . . . I really would have suffered. . . . I confess that I have always been quite sensitive, and offering myself to the people, begging them to support me, would be foreign to my nature."[22]

Unlike in the situation with Edgar, however, Milton could not avoid public attention simply by keeping his opinions to himself. As Ike recuperated in Denver, and Milton frequently traveled there on weekends for private discussions, press speculation about his possible candidacy continued to escalate. Milton's embarrassment grew apace with the speculation until finally he saw no alternative but to stay away from his brother completely. A public statement denying his interest in the nomination would violate the lesson of the "Love Life of the Bullfrog" controversy. Perhaps more important, he wrote Ike, it "would smack of effrontery."[23]

In order to console his younger brother, Ike wrote back light-heartedly two days later, "Don't you know that long before I became President, you were my favorite candidate for that office?"[24] Ike's expression was only half in jest. In 1951, when he was being courted for the presidency, he had entered in his private diary, "Incidentally, my real choice for President, by virtue of character, understanding, administrative ability, and personality, is my youngest brother, Milton."[25] Once elected, Ike often repeated this. His May 14, 1953, diary entry read, "I have no hesitancy in saying I believe him [Milton] to be the most knowledgeable and widely informed of all the people with whom I deal.... So far as I am concerned, he is at this moment the most highly qualified man in the United States to be president. This most emphatically makes no exception of me."[26] And to boyhood friend "Swede" Hazlett he added, "As I have more than once told you, the man who, from the standpoint of knowledge of human and governmental affairs, persuasiveness in speech and dedication to our country, would make the best President I can think of is my younger brother Milton."[27]

It was not just in private that Ike made such comments. In late 1952, after he had been elected but before his inauguration, Ike listened to Milton deliver an address to a dinner party in New York. When it came his turn to speak the president-elect recalled, "When I was elected president of Columbia University, there were some people who, knowing my brother, Milton, thought the trustees had elected the wrong Eisenhower." He continued, "If the people of the country hear a few more speeches like the one they've just heard tonight by Milton, they will begin to think the same thing about this latest job I've been elected to."[28]

In the context of the mounting speculation, Milton found little consolation, or merriment, in his brother's opinion as to who would make a better president. Indeed, Ike's well-known estimation of Milton's abilities made things worse. His view of Milton, combined with the fact that the two Eisenhowers thought, sounded, and even looked so much alike, down to the famous grin, presented journalists with a golden opportunity to project the possibility of Milton's candidacy. Hy Gardner reported in his syndicated column that "Me for Milt" buttons and bumper stickers "are popping up around the country."[29] In November 1955 Vance Packard wrote a major—and extremely favorable—article on Milton for *American Magazine*.[30] That same month *American Press*, a nationwide Sunday supplement for small-town newspapers, underscored that Milton was the third choice (behind the more political-minded Richard Nixon and Earl Warren) of 891 weekly newspaper editors.[31]

Influential White House correspondents joined the bandwagon. Roscoe Drummond wrote that three Republican governors—McKeldin of Maryland, Kohler of Wisconsin, and Russell of Nevada—had spoken out for Milton, and he quoted Oregon senator Mark Hatfield as declaring, "Milton represents the more enlightened wing of our party and he probably has more profound knowledge of government than Ike." Drummond also cited a politician who told him, "I don't pretend to know what influ-

ences other voters, but I know what would influence me. I ask myself:
Who is President Eisenhower's closest, most trusted, most influential adviser, and I know the name is Milton Eisenhower. If Milton Eisenhower
were President, who would be his closest, most trusted, most influential
adviser? The answer is that it would be Dwight D. Eisenhower. I would
like that very much. I think many other voters might, too."[32]

As the boom became serious, serious opposition arose. "Politicus," in
American Mercury, viewed a Milton Eisenhower candidacy with great
alarm. Milton, according to the ultra-rightist publication, "is a Left-
winger who makes even Mr. Truman look like a conservative." "Politicus" sensed a conspiracy. "There are many in Washington," the author
claimed, "who will tell you that Milton has been *the* Eisenhower all along.
According to this theory, he has been the scheming brain who has put
brother Dwight where he is, and has guided him unobtrusively throughout his White House years." While admitting that "there are no indica-
tions that Milton was ever a conscious Marxist," the *Mercury* was disturbed because "the man who buttonholes you in a club or social function
these days and confides that 'Milton is the man' is apt to be your banker,
or a stellar corporation lawyer, or one of the trained seals of the Luce
publications. It is the same crowd that put over Willkie."[33]

Charges that Milton was an "internationalist," a "liberal Republican,"
or, worst of all, a "New Dealer" brought forth defenders. Chief among
them was Drummond, who used his widely read column in the *New York
Herald Tribune* to assert on January 20, 1956, that "if Milton Eisenhower
is a dangerous radical, then the country better get Ike out of the White
House," since the two men thought alike.[34] Moreover, in an article that
appeared in *Collier's* the same day, Drummond reported that Milton had
no "trigger-happy interest in politics," concluding that his "overriding
purpose is to do all he can all the time . . . to assist his brother and relieve
the President wherever he can, so that Dwight Eisenhower will have the
best chance of living a long and rewarding life—either inside or outside
the Presidency." "Fortunately," Drummond wrote, "it comes natural to
him to conduct himself prudently and work without any desire to be in
the front window."

Analyzing the prospects for a Milton Eisenhower candidacy, Drummond considered it highly unlikely, although not impossible, that the
president's younger brother could win the nomination. A more realistic
appraisal would put Milton in second place on the Republican ticket.
"You can sense something of the appeal, in prestige and political
'oomph,'" Drummond wrote, "of a ticket which read: Earl Warren and
Milton Eisenhower . . . or Richard Nixon and Milton Eisenhower." Nev-

ertheless, he interjected, "there are some influential Republicans who would like to see these tickets reversed."[35]

Any pleasure Milton might have gotten from the flattering comments of journalists such as Drummond was more than offset by the knowledge of the circumstances under which they were made. Moreover, under *no* circumstances would he consider running, as either president or vice-president, and it upset him profoundly that party leaders kept insisting that only a Republican with the name Eisenhower could be elected. This was also a major reason for his resenting the pressure mounting on Ike to declare that he would be a candidate for reelection. Therefore, with the president's concurrence and approval, he wrote a series of letters to prominent Republicans suggesting that Ike would refuse to run again and that they "should not constantly be telling the nation (or themselves) that only one man can win. They simply must think in terms of possible alternatives, and if none seems now to exist, new ones must be developed." He concluded on the ominous, and in retrospect prophetic note, "To be candid about it, I am greatly concerned for fear that the Eisenhower Administration principles and programs are not yet sufficiently established within the party to be its integrating, driving force when the President is no longer at the helm."[36]

Of course, the primary factor in ending the speculation concerning a "surrogate" Eisenhower candidacy was Ike's remarkable recovery, and the extent to which the "Milton for Presidency" boom would have gained momentum must remain forever moot. Except perhaps for Milton himself, the Eisenhower probably most pleased with this development was not Ike but Edgar, who told a reporter at the time, "I've had all the damn presidents in my family I want to. I've been bothered to death and I want to live a peaceful life for the years I have left."[37]

Had it been left up to Milton, there would have been no Eisenhower candidacy at all in 1956. On January 16 of the election year the president convened a dozen of his closest associates for an intimate meeting in the family-area study upstairs in the White House. All knew that the result would determine whether Ike would accept the Republican nomination for a second time. Milton intended to be the impartial moderator, having obtained promises beforehand from two of the participants that they would be sure to bring up all the negative considerations bearing on the decision. To his dismay, however, not one person in the room voiced a single reason why Ike should not run.

With the decision thus all but made, the president asked Milton to summarize the discussion. Milton had always tried to remain on the periphery of such forums, leaving the momentous political matters up to the politicians. Except for rare occasions, he proffered political advice only in private. This was one of those occasions. Speaking more as Ike's brother than as an adviser, and having already made known his views on the efficacy of the Republican party, he took the opportunity to state what the others would not. He reminded everyone that the president was sixty-six years old and that, if elected, he would become the oldest man to serve in the White House. He had already had one near-fatal heart attack, and there was no guarantee that he could survive the campaign, let alone another full term. In Milton's eyes, the assemblage was urging his brother to risk not only his reputation, as noted in chapter 1, but also his life.[38]

Even as he spoke, Milton knew that Ike would never place such personal considerations over what he believed to be his responsibility. He was an inveterate "sucker for duty."[39] In February he announced that he would run, and the electorate responded by returning him to office by an overwhelming majority. Milton put his misgivings aside, and he supported the president as enthusiastically and effectively as he had during the first term. He made another extensive trip to Latin America and subsequently played a leading role in persuading Ike to push legislation through Congress that led, under John Kennedy, to the Alliance for Progress. He accompanied Richard Nixon to Moscow on the visit that included the famous "kitchen debate" with Khrushchev. He continued to rewrite speeches for the president and to discuss with him on a confidential and absolutely private basis the problems of the day.

Ike himself summarized Milton's contribution best when, two days before his death, he motioned for Milton to lean close to him in his hospital bed. Ike did not have much strength left, certainly not enough to share with his brother all his thoughts. He only whispered, "I want you to know how much you have always meant to me, how much I have valued your counsel." Of all the tributes Milton has received, he treasures this one sentence the most.[40]

CHAPTER 11

"Milton Eisenhower Is Not a Loner"

Helen's Death and the Decision to Leave Penn State

O ur married life was truly ideal," Eisenhower wrote years later of his relationship with Helen. She made their home "a haven from the problems of my career, a sort of sanctuary. It was a place with books, music, a multitude of friends, bridge, occasional poker games, plays, operas, and so on. Never did we permit anything to take the place of or interfere with our first love, namely, our home and our children."[1]

Throughout his life Eisenhower enjoyed exemplary relationships with the people about him. Although the list of his intimates was indeed long, he undoubtedly reserved the top spots for his parents, his brother Ike, his children, and his wife Helen. Eisenhower unabashedly believed that his marriage was made in heaven, and few who knew the couple at Penn State had any reason to disagree. In addition to attending to her husband's every domestic need, Helen threw herself tirelessly into the job of being the wife of the president of the university. As soon as Eisenhower decided to accept the position at Penn State, Helen began to prepare herself for her new assignment. She studied the histories of Pennsylvania and Penn State and even read historical novels about the region. Once she arrived in State College, she immediately set to work on an embroidery of the school seal for the Eisenhower home. She became a familiar sight on campus, where she could often be found at the local chapter of her undergraduate sorority, Pi Beta Phi, or rushing about organizing a fund-raiser for her favorite project, the construction of an all-faith chapel. Each afternoon that she was home she opened her house to faculty women and co-eds, and it seemed that everyone took the opportunity at least once to come by and chat informally over tea and refreshments. "She would never make a speech," Eisenhower recalled, "but she loved to visit, answering questions and drawing information from others."[2]

If any of her visitors hoped to use these occasions to pry loose administration secrets, they were invariably disappointed. Helen continued her practice, begun at Kansas State, of never talking shop with her husband and thus was never placed in a compromising position. Moreover, albeit with limited success, she sought to provide Eisenhower with a sanctuary from his presidential duties, not to remind him of them. When he did bring his work home with him, a frequent occurrence, she wanted to enable him to devote his full attention to it. As she remarked during her first official interview, "I gave up long ago trying to make him take it easy. When he has a pressing problem he isn't happy until he has solved it, so all I can do is try to protect him from interruptions when he is working and relieve him of as much family responsibility as possible."[3]

In fact, particularly after Ike became president and Eisenhower began traveling to Washington nearly every weekend, Helen's time alone with her husband became increasingly rare. She would keep busy working on the chapel project or tending to her much beloved rose garden, although all the time looking forward to the few hours they would have together. On his part, Eisenhower could hardly wait to return home on a Sunday night to tell Helen about the goings on at the White House. Again Eisenhower would shield her from any confidential matters of state, but she loved to hear about the interesting dinner conversation he had had with Winston Churchill, or what Richard Nixon had predicted about the next election, or what John Foster Dulles felt about the upcoming Geneva summit. Perhaps best of all, Eisenhower brought with him the latest news from Mamie, Helen's close friend now for three decades.[4]

Sometimes Helen was able to participate in Eisenhower's service to his brother. The crowning moment came in 1953 when she accompanied her husband on his goodwill and fact-finding tour of Latin America. Since Eisenhower was the special ambassador and personal representative of the president, Helen was the official hostess, and she sat on the right of the president of each nation the entourage visited. The five weeks of constant travel, replete with formal dinners, was demanding. Nevertheless, Eisenhower could not remember a single instance when Helen was not smiling or otherwise being the very model of a gracious hostess. "And they loved her," he wrote, "wherever we went."[5]

Helen's attitude throughout the exhaustive mission was especially remarkable in that the year before a biopsy had revealed a cancerous tumor. At first the doctors optimistically believed that they had caught the cancer in time. But it had metastasized, and in 1954 a second tumor was discovered. Radiation treatments were the only hope, so first every day, then every other day, and finally once a week Sammy Blazer would drive her to the hospital. A quarter of a century later Blazer could still vividly recollect the look on her face when she would come out of the hospital. He could see the tears running down her cheeks. He was constantly amazed that by the time she reached the car she would again be smiling. But even Helen could not hide the pain, and she would stretch out on the back seat to ease the discomfort. "Sammy," she would say, "you try to get home as fast as you can. I'll watch for the police." All the way home she would stare intently out the back window.[6]

At the end of the 1955 academic year the doctors told Eisenhower that Helen could die at any time. He tried to act normally, while staying as close to her as possible. If Helen knew or suspected that she had only a few months left, she did not let on. Then in July she suffered an attack of viral pneumonia. Buddy, who had recently graduated from Penn State with an M.A. in business administration, was at home awaiting assignment in the Army. Ruth, who had just completed her junior year of high school in State College, was due back in a few weeks from summer camp in Vermont. The pneumonia was getting better; there seemed no reason to cut Ruth's vacation short. But on July 20, while Helen was having lunch in her bedroom, a sudden blood clot moved into her heart. She died at 2:45 P.M. She was not quite fifty years old.

Services took place at the local St. Andrew's Episcopal Church, and Helen was buried in Centre County Memorial Park. Ike canceled his scheduled address to the annual conference of governors to be there, along with Mamie, their son John, and his wife Barbara. Eisenhower received hundreds of condolences from literally all over the world. One of the most moving came from Ken Davis. "She was a gallant person," Davis wrote, "fine, brave, generous, utterly selfless in her devotion to others. And the pang of grief Flo and I felt at the news of her death, the sense of loss we continue to feel, must be a very pale thing compared to your own."[7]

The two men had had their differences. Yet Eisenhower recognized the feeling expressed in his former assistant's letter. "Your letter touched me deeply," he responded. "Helen was uniquely unselfish and selfless. My grief is indescribably severe. It is even greater, in its way, than was the strain for the final four months when I knew, but Helen did not, that she could not live. Thank God, she did not suffer pain or mental anguish. Indeed, her last three months were among the happiest we ever had. We gaily had all meals together. . . . I'm sure the only way I can be worthy of her is to carry on as she would want me to. At the moment, I'm desperately tired. Hoping for sleep, but not getting much. I *am* sustained by the devotion of my two children—so like Helen—and my faith in the basic Christian thesis."[8]

A beautiful portrait of Helen now hangs in the all-faith chapel, which Judge Milholland announced in December 1955, in the midst of its construction, would from then on be called the Helen Eakin Eisenhower Chapel. In choosing the name, Milholland explained, the trustees "gave thoughtful consideration to many excellent possibilities, but invariably came back to the name of a person whose life exemplified the ideals and objectives of the chapel in the highest degree and who fostered the project with equivalent zeal." Milholland might have added that more than half the funds donated for the chapel's completion were contributed in Helen's honor.[9]

But Eisenhower found it difficult to carry on. Ken Davis remarked, "Milton wasn't very good at being alone." And Sammy Blazer added, "Once Helen passed away I didn't think that he would be around long, 'cause it was a big lonely house." Perhaps it was Judge Wilkinson, Eisenhower's closest friend in State College, who put it best. "I've been very close with some very important people, most of whom were loners," Wilkinson commented. "Milton Eisenhower is not a loner."[10]

The morning after Helen's death, Ruth came to the breakfast table, sat in Helen's chair, smiled, and said, "Good morning, Father." Over the course of the next year she was a great help to Eisenhower. They even took a ninety-day whirlwind tour of Europe together. But in 1956 she graduated from high school and prepared to go off to college at Swarthmore. With Buddy in the Army, Eisenhower felt lost. His only satisfaction came through helping Ike. "In this period I lost interest in Penn State," he later confessed. "I found that the faculty and students annoyed me and I cared little about University progress." He concluded, "I had to leave the University for its sake."[11]

Ike knew about Milton's unhappiness. After conferring with Secretary of State Dulles, he changed his well-known position and offered Milton the post of ambassador to the United Nations or, if he preferred, an appointment as ambassador-at-large. Milton, however, still thought it utterly improper for the president's brother to hold any high office. Under no circumstances would he create the impression of a family dynasty.[12] He wanted to continue to serve in an unofficial, informal capacity. He did, however, like the idea of moving to Washington permanently, in order to be closer to the White House. But first he would have to free himself from his responsibilities in Pennsylvania.

These included not only his Penn State duties but also a call from the state Republican party. Philadelphia's reform mayor, Democrat Joseph S. Clark, had announced his intention to challenge Senator James Duff in the 1956 election. Moderate Republicans wanted Milton Eisenhower to replace the conservative Duff on the ticket. The common wisdom was that Duff did not have a chance against Clark. Eisenhower, the political handicappers felt, would win easily.

Wilkinson, a longtime leader of the Pennsylvania Republicans, requested his friend's permission to state that the Penn State president would consider running if Duff agreed to withdraw. Eisenhower immediately turned him down. He replied that only after Duff withdrew would he give even the slightest thought to his own candidacy. Reminding Wilkinson that Duff had been an early and strong supporter of Ike, he lectured, "It would be completely inappropriate to cause trouble for my brother. How could he pick between Duff and me? How could I put him in that position?" Neither question, of course, needed an answer. Eisenhower did confess to Wilkinson that "that's the one office I'd take, the United States Senate. I think I could be a good United States senator." But Duff wanted to run, so Eisenhower's personal interests became academic. Furthermore, he had never felt comfortable within the rough-and-tumble milieu of campaign politics, and still reeling from the loss of Helen, the prospect of a knockdown fight with Clark in the general election was out of the question. As had been the case in Kansas, and would be the case again in Maryland, Eisenhower rejected the opportunity to win almost certain election to public office.[13]

One consideration that did not influence Eisenhower's decision was a desire to remain at Penn State. In fact, about the only thing during this time of which he was certain was that he wanted to leave State College, to get away from the big lonely house with its many reminders of Helen. Ruth's presence had enabled him to go through the motions of president for a year, but with her imminent departure, he realized that he could no longer continue. In May 1956 Eisenhower submitted his letter of resignation. The trustees refused to accept it, offering instead an extended leave of absence and a substantial raise in salary. Eisenhower thanked the board for its vote of confidence but said that his decision was irrevocable. He would put off his resignation until the trustees met again the next month. At that time, regardless of what they did, he would resubmit the letter and insist that they accept it, effective no later than December 31 of that year.[14]

Eisenhower's letter barely exceeded one page. Stating simply that "I am taking this action for personal reasons," he wrote that his years at Penn State had been "rewarding" ones, and "I have treasured my personal relations with the Trustees, faculty, students, alumni, and friends of the University." Progress during the past six years had been "remarkable," he continued, and "Penn State, now an excellent university, is on the verge of becoming one of the most distinguished state institutions in the nation." To achieve this objective, he counseled, what was needed was even more broadening of the technical curricula, even more salary increases for all university personnel, and even more expansion of the physical facilities and financial resources. Eisenhower expressed his fullest confidence that these needs would be met. "Under different personal circumstances, I would have been proud to be identified with Penn State's future. It is, I assure you, with a feeling of utmost regret that I have had to decide to deny myself that association."[15]

Although, as acting president George H. Deike later told reporters, "there is nothing this Board would not do to keep the services of Dr. Eisenhower," this time it reluctantly accepted the resignation.[16] However, the question of who would be the next president remained. The always forthright Cappy Rowland threw the gauntlet down to Eisenhower. Eisenhower responded calmly that the outgoing president should never express an opinion on his successor. Not so calmly, Rowland replied, "That's a lot of you know what. Now who ought to be president of this institution? You know better than anybody else. I'm not going to go through another three years looking for a president like we did when we got you. Who should it be?"

Eisenhower said only, "Well, if I were choosing, and I'm not, it would be Eric Walker." Ralph Hetzel, son of former president Hetzel, shouted that he was unalterably opposed to Walker and demanded that the board set up a search committee to look for an alternative selection. Now it was Rowland who was calm. He looked Hetzel in the face and said, "O.K., we'll wait until the next board meeting—and then we'll elect Walker." It was done, and proved to be a remarkably successful appointment. Walker served for fifteen years, continuing and expanding on the base Eisenhower had built.[17]

Milton Eisenhower's six years at Penn State had been years of growth—in the physical plant, the faculty, the student body, the graduate school, and most of all in prestige. There were new buildings all over campus, capped by the Hetzel Union Building and the Helen Eakin Eisenhower Memorial Chapel. Enrollment had risen from twelve thousand to fifteen thousand. Faculty salaries were up nearly 50 percent overall, and in some cases 75 percent. Schools such as Liberal Arts and Engineering had become colleges, and new units had been added—the College of Business Administration, the School of Forestry in the College of Agriculture, the School of Journalism, and the School of the Arts in the College of Liberal Arts, the Department of Veterinary Science and the Department of Agricultural Engineering in the College of Agriculture. The graduate school, although one of the youngest in the country, had become one of the largest, with a regular-session enrollment of fifteen hundred and a summer enrollment of three thousand. The library budget was up 50 percent, and the library staff increased by 26 percent. These were all statistics Eisenhower could, and did, point to with pride.[18]

Some of the money came from private funds, raised by Eisenhower in his innumerable trips around the state. Most of it came from the state legislature, whose budget sessions with Eisenhower continued to be a "love fest." "Dr. Milton had a keen understanding of the political process," explained Keith Spalding, a *New York Herald Tribune* editor who had become Eisenhower's assistant at Penn State. "He never inflated a budget to ask for more than he needed. He always went into legislative hearings with an absolutely defensible budget. This was a great change in style for Pennsylvania politics and Penn State."[19]

The happy result was that in six years Eisenhower doubled Penn State's appropriation, from about $10 million to about $20 million, and he did this during a period when the national rate of inflation averaged only 1¼ percent a year. Perhaps the finest tribute to his administrative ability and the respect that he had earned for Penn State came following his last appearance before the state legislature. Astonishingly, the politicians sitting in Harrisburg granted Penn State $1 million *more* than Eisenhower requested. He could have received no greater compliment, nor could he have bequeathed to his successor a more appreciated legacy.[20]

Decades later an interviewer asked the historian Phil Klein, for many years one of the most prominent members of the Penn State faculty, to assess Eisenhower's impact on the school's development. "We got to be accepted as a university and Milton Eisenhower had a lot to do with it," Klein asserted. "It went much deeper than changing the name.... Dr. Eisenhower brought in an academic atmosphere and a hell of a lot more. His predecessor had looked at Penn State as a factory and did not have Eisenhower's broad look. Dr. Eisenhower took what had been an engineering and agricultural college and gave it a national image and made Penn State significant in a large way." Responding to the same question, Robert Bernreuter, who set up the counseling center and performed many other valuable services for Eisenhower and the university, added, "When Dr. Eisenhower came here, we sort of considered Penn State as number two or three among the colleges in Pennsylvania. But when he left, we thought of it as number one."[21]

In 1955 representatives of the Middle States Association of Colleges and Secondary Schools visited State College to conduct an extensive evaluation of Penn State. They could not have agreed with Klein and

Bernreuter more. In fact, the association's official report, which listed the scores of improvements accomplished during Eisenhower's tenure, concluded, "All in all, Pennsylvania State University seems to have a magnificent potential, second to none among America's state institutions."[22]

To Eisenhower, however, while the potential was there and the future was clearly bright, Penn State was a long way from meeting his expectations. From the day he accepted the appointment at Kansas State, in 1943, his first concern remained always with the undergraduate students. Penn State now had more undergraduates than ever before in its history, undergraduates with a greater variety of career choices open to them, a better faculty to learn from, a more conducive atmosphere to work in. Nevertheless, in his view these same undergraduates still cared too much for drinking, too little for studying. Therefore, his farewell speech did not dwell upon the past but looked toward the future. "I leave Penn State with a great sense of dissatisfaction about raising the student standards," he uncharacteristically declared. "Although these standards have been upped, we still haven't established a real academic atmosphere." In part he blamed himself, but he also blamed the faculty, the students themselves, and the students' parents. In doing so he challenged them all to guide Penn State far beyond the level at which he was leaving it.[23] Nineteen fifty-six marked the end of Eisenhower's fourteenth year as the president of an institution of higher education. Few were more keenly aware of what higher education truly was.

In all likelihood Eisenhower never would have been completely satisfied. Still, he had thoroughly enjoyed his first five years in State College, and he probably would have remained there had Helen lived. "Oh, I know he would have stayed at Penn State until after Ike was out of office," Judge Wilkinson declared. "And I am almost sure that he had played a part in [Ike's] decision to buy the Gettysburg place. Now I was privy to some of those conversations where Ike wanted some place close enough to Washington, and not too far and not too close for people to get to him and to be near to Milton, and everything was just right, but they wouldn't be close enough to smell what each was having for dinner, and all that kind of stuff. Yes, I think if Helen had not died, and he had stayed on, in that case he would have gone on to the Senate eventually."[24]

Wilkinson, now a justice on the Commonwealth Court of Pennsylvania, remains one of Eisenhower's closest associates and friends, and his summary of Eisenhower's qualities warrants quoting in full. "It is trite to say that his great facility was to find an accord," Wilkinson said of Eisenhower.

To get people who are in disagreement and get them to agree. That is a great quality that is very hard to find. But there is another quality that is somewhat unusual, in my experience, and maybe I've just had bad luck. But one quality is that people forget that you've done things for them. The water that's by the mill doesn't run the wheel. And you carry your own bag to the station. Milton doesn't do that. Milton picks up his tab. You do something for Milton, and you want some help, it doesn't matter how many years ago, he'll remember that when the chips were down you stepped in for him and he'll step in for you. He won't do anything improper, but nobody would ask him to do anything improper.[25]

Eisenhower got a great deal out of Penn State, and he gave a great deal in return. There was little or no resentment over his decision to leave. The trustees, the faculty, the students, and the people of Pennsylvania universally understood. Indeed, the trustees tried to make him president emeritus of the university. He refused the honor at the time, pointing out that he was only fifty-seven years old. Two decades later, in 1975, Eisenhower was awarded the distinction of being an honorary alumnus of Penn State. In 1976 the board conferred on him the title of president emeritus. And in 1977 the university auditorium was named the Milton S. Eisenhower Auditorium. The mark he and Helen made on Penn State is a permanent one.

CHAPTER 12

"There Is Nothing Else Like It Anyplace"

The Johns Hopkins University

Not long after Helen's death, word began to spread around the country that Eisenhower might consider leaving State College. Slowly offers started to drift in, many from private businesses and of a "name your salary" nature. These Eisenhower turned down out of hand. If he were to leave academic life, it would be only to work for his brother in a full-time, albeit still informal capacity. Furthermore, after Ike made the decision to run again and the polls showed him a virtually certain winner, Milton became increasingly suspicious that many of the business concerns were as excited over the prospect of having four years of ready access to the president as they were over having a man of his abilities in their employ. Eisenhower had much too much pride and integrity to put himself or his relationship with Ike up for sale in such a manner.

There was one possibility, however, that Eisenhower did not rule out. Dr. Lowell Jacob Reed had retired as president of The Johns Hopkins University, and the trustees had begun the search for his replacement. For Eisenhower, the job had a strong appeal. Although one of the youngest private universities on the East Coast and among the smallest, Hopkins had earned an extremely distinguished reputation. Its graduate and medical schools were exceptionally notable, both for their innovative programs and the pioneering research of their faculties, and on the undergraduate level it attracted some of the most serious students from around the country. Judging from the composition of the board of trustees, which was made up almost exclusively of prominent Baltimore citizens,

Eisenhower concluded that Hopkins had traditionally enjoyed enthusiastic local support. But most important of all, were he to be offered the presidency, he could remain within higher education and yet be less than an hour's drive from the White House.

Despite his record of accomplishments, it surprised Eisenhower when Thomas Nichols of the Hopkins board approached him in late 1955 to discuss whether he might be interested in the job. After all, Eisenhower had not had any experience in running a private institution. Moreover, Hopkins was a scholar's school, and it always had been taken for granted that the president must himself be a renowned scholar. Before becoming president, Reed had been an eminent biostatistician at the Hopkins School of Hygiene and Public Health prior to becoming dean of the school and vice-president of the university and the hospital. Eisenhower held close to a score of honorary doctorates, including one awarded him by Hopkins in 1952, but as a student he had never advanced beyond the B.A. And what of his age? Eisenhower was almost fifty-six years old; he assumed that Hopkins would be looking for a younger man.[1]

Nichols, nevertheless, made it unmistakably clear that the board wanted Eisenhower. Although tempted, Eisenhower refused. He had not yet decided that he would definitely leave Penn State, and if he did, he explained, he planned to work with his brother. He suggested several alternatives, including his friend Franklin Murphy, at the time president of the University of Kansas (who shortly would move to the University of California at Los Angeles). Nichols persisted. He owned his own plane, and he began making the trip from Baltimore to State College as if it were around the corner. Eisenhower softened, and in the spring of 1956 he agreed to come to Nichols's estate in Greenspring Valley, where he met with a committee of five from the board plus Barry Wood, vice-president of the university's three medical institutions. Eisenhower was as impressed with them as they were with him. When the committee told him that the trustees would "proudly and gladly" grant him whatever time he thought appropriate to help out the president, he knew that they would offer him the position. And he was almost as certain that he would take it.[2]

However, nothing was official. Indeed, this was the way Eisenhower wanted it. Not until May did he first submit his resignation to the Penn State trustees, and even then he did not want it known that he was seriously considering moving to Johns Hopkins. On the one hand, he did not want to "hurt the feelings of good people at Penn State" by possibly creating the impression that he was leaving in order to accept another position. In fact, because he felt that he could no longer apply himself to a job in which Helen had played such an integral part, he had decided to leave Penn

State months before his meeting with the Hopkins committee of five. Furthermore, it was up to Hopkins's full board, not Nichols or the committee of five, to make him a formal offer, and if there were widespread speculation about what he called the "Hopkins connection," it could be embarrassing to him, to Penn State, and to Johns Hopkins.[3]

So technically Eisenhower was correct when he wrote in his letter of resignation to the Penn State board that he had not decided what his future responsibilities would be and that for the time being he would merely continue to serve Ike. But there was no question in his mind that he would shortly be going to Hopkins. In fact, when on May 14, 1956—before his Penn State resignation had even been accepted—he wrote Ike, who knew about his meetings with Nichols and the others, to caution him against saying anything at his press conference that might imply that he had accepted another position, he left no doubt that he had already reached an understanding with Hopkins. He went so far as to suggest that Ike "say something to the effect that you and I have always been agreed that I could be of greatest service to the government during your administration by maintaining my independence and responding to requests for voluntary assistance to the best of my ability. Even a tiny pat on the back for free services rendered or to be rendered will, I know, be of help to me *at Hopkins*" (emphasis added).[4]

As noted, the Penn State board finally accepted Eisenhower's resignation in June. Although he agreed to remain long enough to help his successor prepare the next biennial budget, with the academic year completed, he was essentially free to turn his attention to government service. Consequently, the next month he accompanied his brother to Panama for a meeting of the presidents of the member nations of the Organization of American States. It was an historic occasion, the first gathering of all the presidents since the days of Simón Bolívar. Ike felt it appropriate that Milton, as his chief adviser on Latin America and a personal acquaintance of many of the leaders, come along. He also wanted his brother to be the one to represent him at some of the meetings should his recent ileitis operation cause him excessive discomfort or fatigue.

There were many meetings, exhausting ones. On the afternoon of July 23, for diversion, Ike persuaded Milton to come with him to the Canal Zone, where the President wanted to inspect the new central communications system. Neither knew that that very afternoon the Hopkins board of trustees was holding a meeting of its own and for the first time Eisenhower's name was brought up for a formal vote. While the two brothers were touring the complex facility, a corporal at the switchboard ran up to them with some surprise and said that there was a long-distance call for Milton. On the other end of the line was Hopkins board chairman Carlyle

Barton. He told Milton that he had just been unanimously elected president of the university, and over fifty newspapermen and photographers had gathered outside the board room in anticipation of an announcement. Barton asked Eisenhower point-blank whether he would accept the offer.

Eisenhower later recalled that "it just flashed through my mind, look that [Hopkins] is only an hour's drive from Washington, with a White House telephone in my office, and in my home, easy to get back and forth to work. Even after work at night I can help in Washington and still carry on my own profession. So I just said, 'I accept.' And I turned to Ike and said, 'That's a crazy way to accept a presidency of a university.'" In retrospect, however, his acceptance was not all that "crazy." For all intents and purposes, Eisenhower had accepted the position three months earlier.[5]

The next day news of Eisenhower's appointment received front-page coverage throughout the United States, Europe, and Latin America.[6] When Barton made the announcement, he stressed the new president's "broad experience outside the classroom and laboratory" and his ability to "relate the classroom to world affairs, the laboratory to human progress, the scholar's study to the conference table." The *New York Times* added that "the appointment was not expected to impede Dr. Eisenhower in his role of unofficial adviser and frequent handyman for the White House."[7] Good wishes from educators, business leaders, experts in international relations, and all segments of the Baltimore community flooded the university's public-relations office, and students from Kansas State and Penn State sent messages of congratulations to their counterparts at Hopkins. No one was more pleased than Eisenhower himself. His third university presidency seemed to provide him with everything he wanted. "I look forward to coming to Baltimore," he commented, "and intend to spend the years left to me in being part of this great institution." He would.[8]

Eisenhower fully expected to find Hopkins much different from his two previous schools. Nevertheless, he quickly learned upon his arrival in early October that state and private universities invariably have one thing in common: their trustees, when looking for a president, always overstate the strengths of their institutions and ignore or minimize the weaknesses. "The trustees had indicated that the salary level was adequate," Eisenhower remembered. "It was pitiful. They said all private universities have financial troubles, but we're just as good as any of them. They had had a deficit in thirty-two of the preceding forty-two years." Indeed, Eisenhower remarked, Hopkins's fiscal situation was so bad that "the annual budget was called deficits. They had lived with it so long that they just reversed the whole process of a budget. They did not inform me about the wall that existed between the faculty and the administration. Nor did I know of the philosophy of the institution."[9]

The trustees also did not tell Eisenhower that although Hopkins had an international reputation it was ingrown at heart. His predecessor had retired after a thirty-eight-year association with the university, and the dean of the Homewood (arts and sciences) schools, G. Wilson Shaffer, had taken his A.B. and Ph.D. degrees at Hopkins in the twenties and had been there ever since. Deans G. Heberton Evans and Richard T. Cox also had both earned their degrees from, and done their teaching at, Hopkins, as had Abel Wolman, chairman of Chemical Engineering, Sanitary Engineering and Water Resources, and Robert H. Roy, the dean of Engineering. "A whole horde of people who had lived with Hopkins all the way ran the place," Dean Shaffer recalled. They tended to be fierce defenders of tradition, cautious about changes.

The most cherished tradition was smallness. "When I was an undergraduate," Shaffer explained, "I don't think I was ever in a class of over thirty-five, and most of them under twenty around the table. And some of them would be graduate students and some would be undergraduate students. And I knew as many graduate students as I knew undergraduate students. And it was real, in some ways maybe an emotional scene, for us. That this is Johns Hopkins. There is nothing else like it anyplace."[10]

Nor had Eisenhower been told that for years this tradition of smallness had been the cause of a fierce debate. Administrators and professors who had not spent their entire career at Hopkins, who had come from Harvard, Yale, or Berkeley, tended to equate size with health and urged the university to expand not just its facilities but its faculty and student body. They had been supported by Isaiah Bowman, the president from 1935 to 1948. Shaffer and the other old-timers were unalterably opposed to such growth. Shaffer recalled one incident in which Bowman proposed that the number of undergraduates be increased from about nine hundred to seventeen hundred. The dean countered with a ceiling of twelve hundred. After a long argument, Bowman finally threw up his hands and asked, " 'Wilson, what is the difference between seventeen and twelve?' I said, 'Well, roughly five, but that's not what I am talking about. I am talking about the character of the institution. In my opinion, one of the strongest things that Johns Hopkins has is that it is the only one of the top universities where the undergraduate population does not overpower the graduate [at this time the graduate program included about seven hundred students]. And if we lose that, we have lost almost everything we have.' I remember him saying, 'Wilson, if you go to fifteen hundred, I'll give you a box of cigars.' I said, 'I don't smoke cigars.' "[11]

Bowman's successor, Detlev Bronk, had also advocated growth, and Reed had not been president long enough to have a significant impact on the debate. Thus Shaffer and the others were quite concerned that Eisenhower, who was not an academic, who had had no previous association with Hopkins, and who, after all, had earned a reputation during his previous presidencies by expanding and changing the character of his institutions, would fail to recognize their arguments. They were therefore extremely relieved and pleased when the new president stated right from the beginning his intention to maintain the university as it had always been—a uniquely intimate university with a balanced undergraduate and graduate program. By doing so, Eisenhower overcame his first hurdle.[12]

While Eisenhower was all in favor of maintaining the integrity of Hopkins's traditions, he could not accept its longstanding policy of deficit financing. Not only did the policy completely violate his most ingrained principles but it had brought the university to the edge of financial ruin. Hopkins had been severely affected by the pre–World War II depression, and it had never fully recovered. Bowman had managed to maintain the school's excellent academic standing, but at the expense of other essentials. For example, only one new building had been constructed between 1929 and 1946. Bronk seems to have devoted as much time to his many extracurricular activities as he did to his Hopkins responsibilities, and Reed, who at age sixty-eight had accepted the presidency only on a temporary basis, had been unable to stem the tide. As a result, Eisenhower found the entire economic infrastructure, in his words, "badly neglected."[13] Salaries were no longer competitive, physical facilities were inadequate, library acquisitions had fallen woefully behind, many faculty posts were vacant. In short, by the time Eisenhower arrived, "the continuing financial drain had taken a heavy toll," one trustee wrote. "Johns Hopkins was caught in a downward spiral."[14]

The dilemma that confronted Eisenhower was how to reverse the downward spiral without compromising the integrity of the university. On the one hand, his solution was quite simple: He had quickly to raise sufficient money to cover the Hopkins deficit. No one, he realized, would want to put money into a failing institution. But on the other hand, he knew that in order to attract the large sums necessary to set Hopkins on a sound economic footing, he had to offer a worthwhile product. To Eisenhower, that product could only be the school itself, with its traditions, its uniqueness, its potential, its standards.

On February 22, 1957, Washington's Birthday and the eightieth commemoration of the university's founding, Eisenhower delivered his formal inaugural address. In it he revealed his formula for the future. "Our strength cannot be in numbers," he began. "It must be in excellence. Here must be a community of scholars who, in an environment of courageous freedom, are constantly pushing back the dark walls of the unknown. Here must be students ... who, inspired by association with eminent minds, strive to become extraordinary humanists, extraordinary scientists, extraordinary engineers and social scientists: leaders in whatever they do. It is in character for Johns Hopkins to fulfill this role." To do this, he continued, "we must enlarge and strengthen the faculty ... raise the compensation of faculty members ... strengthen the adviser program ... improve physical facilities ... enter new fields of scholarship ... and attract superior students." And all this had to be done within the context of fiscal responsibility. Eleven years later board chairman Charles Garland quoted from this address to summarize Eisenhower's tenure: "What was then a catalog of challenges has become an unprecedented record of accomplishments.... Not since its first decade has Johns Hopkins experienced such progress. Not since those early years had the promise of [founding president Daniel Coit] Gilman been so close to fulfillment."[15]

As an octogenarian Eisenhower recalled, "When I got to Hopkins, there was only six hundred thousand dollars left to pay the deficit or the place would have folded. The miracle to me was that the institution had retained eminent people in the midst of all the trouble." A primary reason for the miracle was the quality and dedication of the board of trustees. Not one of the forty (in 1956 there were two vacancies) Hopkins board members would not do virtually anything to help out Eisenhower or the university. Eisenhower was particularly fond of Tom Nichols, who had played such a prominent role in recruiting him in the first place. Nichols's generosity had long been a matter of record: he was responsible for establishing a number of four-year scholarships. Nichols had promised Eisenhower a new house in Baltimore. However, he soon discovered that the budget had no room for such a project and that the seventy-five thousand dollars obtained from the sale of the old president's house had already been spent on prior deficits. Undaunted, Nichols quietly donated a quarter of a million dollars of his own money. As a result, Eisenhower moved into a handsome new residence, tucked snugly away adjacent to the Hopkins Club, removed from the flow of traffic yet easily accessible from all parts of the campus.[16]

The trustees, of course, did a lot more than build houses for Hopkins's president. Eisenhower had the greatest respect for them all, and he frequently declared that they made up not only the best board he had ever worked with but the best in the country, a model for all others. The trustees were equally positive about Eisenhower. Their meetings were invariably excellent. Eisenhower always prepared carefully for them, made up the agenda, and stuck to it. He kept the members informed on all important issues, sought their advice, and acted on their suggestions. And while he did not want them merely to rubber-stamp his views, he insisted on a harmonious relationship. Just as during the controversy at Penn State over control of the athletic program, he told one assistant that any time the board failed to support him he would resign, because "that would mean they have the wrong guy in the job."

Eisenhower's presentations at the board meetings, according to the same assistant, would flow together incredibly gracefully. "I would just devour it. If Henry Fonda had gotten up and done it, he would have gotten the Academy Award." But Eisenhower was not acting. He believed strongly that the trustees must feel that they were active partners in running the university. Everything was "we," never "I." Eisenhower created a climate guided by the principle that "when things go wrong, we're all in it together; when they go right, we'll all share the credit."[17]

This climate of cooperation was not based on illusion. Eisenhower and the board established a clear-cut division of labor. In short, the trustees "knew what they were supposed to do, and they knew what they were not to do." What they were not to do was meddle in the prerogatives of the president. For example, some universities had trustee committees on student or faculty affairs. Eisenhower insisted that the Hopkins board not become involved in such matters. If it did, he explained, students and faculty members would soon be circumventing his office and going directly to the board; in this manner his authority would be undermined.

Conversely, the university's constitution stipulated that the board was legally responsible for overseeing the school's investments and allocating monies from the endowment. Therefore, Eisenhower suggested that the trustees have not only a budget committee but also a general research committee. Working in tandem under the supervision of the executive committee that had traditionally handled Hopkins's finances, these committees enabled the board to set priorities for future development. It could thereby assure that it applied its fund-raising efforts judiciously and coherently and that the money raised was spent for the most constructive purposes. Of course, the board always consulted Eisenhower and his staff, but nevertheless it had an equal voice in shaping Hopkins's direction.[18]

The working relationship Eisenhower developed with the trustees was facilitated by concomitant personal friendships. In addition to Nichols, he became extremely close to men like Dr. Edwin Jarrett, J. H. Fitzgerald Dunning, Alonzo Decker, Jr., Theodore Wolfe, Stuart Janney, and Benjamin Griswold. They were all stalwarts of the Baltimore community, financial titans, and the ease with which Eisenhower could approach them added immeasurably to the success of his projects. The construction of a centralized library serves as an apt illustration. One of the first complaints Eisenhower received upon coming to Hopkins was that the library system, separated by disciplines and scattered in various buildings across campus, was both inconvenient and inefficient. For two years he worked with a faculty committee to devise a solution. Finally they decided that the only suitable location for a library to house Hopkins's entire holdings was just to the south of Homewood House, directly across the quadrangle from Gilman Hall.

The reason it had taken so long to settle on a site was that, in keeping with Hopkins's tradition of smallness, neither Eisenhower nor the faculty members wanted to ruin the aesthetic and architectural balance of the campus by erecting a multistory building that would stick out like a sore thumb. In fact, only after the committee had been assured that most of the building could be constructed underground did it agree to the location. The drawback to this plan was that it would cost $5 million, an extravagant sum of money in the 1950s. Eisenhower did not want to go ahead without assurance in advance that he could raise the funds. He called Ben Griswold, a partner in Alex. Brown & Sons, the oldest investment house in the country. The company had a long association with Hopkins, having helped to establish the Baltimore & Ohio Railroad, the first railroad in the United States and the source of the university's original endowment. Candidly he told Griswold that he would not even consider a campaign to raise the money until he could demonstrate a local commitment. He wanted an initial pledge of $1 million before he would even look outside of Baltimore. Griswold commented that the board had approved a new library, and he asked whether Eisenhower felt that the proposed one was worth the money. Eisenhower replied that he would not have called if he did not think so. Griswold said that was all he had to hear. "And he got on the telephone and personally went around and in no time at all he came in with a million bucks."[19]

Griswold was far from unique. Ted Wolfe was another of Baltimore's most prominent civic leaders. Eisenhower hardly made a move without first discussing it with Wolfe and enlisting his support. Rarely was Wolfe unable to use his connections within the community to further Hopkins's interests. Then there was Dr. Ed Jarrett, who persuaded his patient U.S. Navy captain Newton H. White, Jr., to donate $250,000 for scholarships. When Captain White died, his widow mentioned to Jarrett that she wanted to do something special for Hopkins in her husband's memory. Jarrett immediately consulted with Eisenhower, and together they went to Mrs. White with a list of possibilities. She expressed an interest in building an athletic and recreation center, so "Milton pulled out all the stops, presenting her with a good written text on why it was needed. He made a beautiful case." Today, on the northern edge of the Homewood campus, stands the modern, spacious Newton H. White, Jr., Athletic Center.[20]

While each of the trustees contributed unhesitantly of his time and money, throughout Eisenhower's administration the dominant force on the board, and Eisenhower's closest friend, was Charles "Chuck" Garland. Like Griswold, Garland was a partner at Alex. Brown & Sons. A graduate of Yale and a world-class tennis player (he was once a member of the American Davis Cup team), he was nine months older than Eisenhower. Although he had no direct connection with Hopkins—even his children attended other schools—like many Baltimore residents, he had a great love for and an abiding interest in the university. Eisenhower estimated that he gave one-fourth of his time to Hopkins and "without one cent of compensation, not even accepting expenses."

Eisenhower described Garland as a man "about my size, with a rosy complexion, a ready but restrained smile, a built-in radar system (sensitivity) which enabled him to relate to all others, businessmen, faculty, students, alumni, fellow trustees. . . . He and his wife Aurelia were the perfect leaders of the Baltimore social set, but Mr. Garland was as at home with the house painter as he was with the wealthy owner of a major business. . . . It has been my good fortune to be associated with many great men, wonderful men and women, leaders and followers, but none surpassed Charles Garland in ability and in my affection."[21]

Garland became chairman of the Hopkins board the year after Eisenhower's arrival, when Carlyle Barton, then seventy-one years old, decided that the demanding job required a younger man. One would be hard put to find a better relationship between a president and a board chairman than the one that sprang up immediately between Eisenhower and Garland. Aurelia Garland often acted as Eisenhower's hostess at social occasions, and the three went to church together regularly on Sundays. Frequently Eisenhower and Garland would return to the president's house for breakfast, after which they would go over university affairs. It may be an exaggeration to say, as one former trustee did, that "Milton and Charles Garland ran the university, with Milton running the campus and Garland running the finances," but there is no doubt that a lot of Hopkins business was conducted in this informal Sunday morning setting.[22] "Chuck and I would agree on things that had to be done right away,"

Henry Wallace *(left)* and Milton worked well together in the Department of Agriculture. *(Courtesy of Dwight D. Eisenhower Library, Abilene, Kansas)*

Milton's last assignment for President Roosevelt was as deputy director of the Office of War Information. *(Courtesy of Dwight D. Eisenhower Library, Abilene, Kansas)*

The Eisenhower brothers liked to hold reunions at a Wisconsin fishing retreat. *Left to right*: Arthur, Milton, Earl (who had just sat on a fishing hook), Dwight, and Edgar. *(Courtesy of Dwight D. Eisenhower Library, Abilene, Kansas)*

Milton treats a group of Penn State coeds to milk shakes before becoming president in 1950. *(Courtesy of Pennsylvania State University Archives)*

As president of Columbia University, Ike attended Milton's Penn State inauguration. *(Courtesy of Pennsylvania State University Archives)*

Penn State students greeted Milton affectionately as "Prexy." *(Courtesy of Pennsylvania State University Archives)*

After an awkard beginning, Milton and Penn State board chairman Judge James Milholland became close friends. *(Courtesy of Pennsylvania State University Archives)*

Milton often settled student problems in his Penn State office. *(Courtesy of Dwight D. Eisenhower Library, Abilene, Kansas)*

Milton with daughter Ruth in Copenhagen in 1955. The two traveled together throughout Europe for three months following Helen's death. *(Courtesy of Dwight D. Eisenhower Library, Abilene, Kansas)*

At Johns Hopkins Milton was only a short drive from the White House. Here President Eisenhower greets Milton on his return from Central America in August 1958. *(Courtesy of Milton S. Eisenhower)*

184

Nikita Khrushchev toasts Milton and Vice-President Richard Nixon on their official trip to Moscow in July 1959. *(Courtesy of Dwight D. Eisenhower Library, Abilene, Kansas)*

In 1961 Ross Jones became one of Milton's most valuable assistants at Johns Hopkins. He is now the university's vice-president for university affairs. *(Courtesy of Ross Jones)*

In his office at Home-
wood House Milton
sought the reactions of
his staff to his proposals.
*(Courtesy of Wilbert E.
Locklin)*

President Lyndon B. Johnson made Johns Hopkins his first campaign stop in
1964. Ronald Wolk is fourth from the left. *(Courtesy of Ronald Wolk)*

In 1966 Springfield College elected Milton's assistant Wilbert E. Locklin its ninth president. Locklin conferred his first honorary degree on Milton S. Eisenhower. *(Courtesy of Wilbert E. Locklin)*

Brooks Robinson and the entire Baltimore Orioles team helped their favorite fan celebrate his seventy-fifth birthday with more than five hundred friends at Memorial Stadium in Baltimore in 1974. *(Courtesy of Dwight D. Eisenhower Library, Abilene, Kansas)*

Eisenhower recalled, "that couldn't wait for a meeting, and when I would come into the next meeting and report on what we had agreed and that we had done it, they always passed a resolution." As for the views of the two men, Eisenhower could not remember a single instance when they disagreed. Not only did they not disagree, he remarked, but "we often didn't even have to finish a sentence we were speaking but the other one would know precisely what you wanted to do."[23]

Eisenhower received all he could have hoped for from the board, and much more. But Garland and the other trustees, at Eisenhower's insistence, entrusted Hopkins's day-to-day operations to Homewood House, to the office of the president. A university president's responsibilities are seemingly endless, but none are more important, or take up more of his time, than managing the budget. Eisenhower had a lot of help, but in terms of the budget, as all his assistants testified, he was truly a magician. It was his bread and butter. He had been dealing with budgets since his days in the Washington bureaucracy, and although he had spent a decade involved in the New Deal, he always felt that putting an end to the sentiment that deficits were fashionable was one of his greatest contributions to the institution. "It took me twelve months to balance the budget," he recalled all too vividly, "and I never again had a deficit."[24]

Eisenhower attacked the budget from both directions. He began by eliminating any expenditures he deemed not absolutely necessary. "Milton knew what it was like to be poor and not to waste," one of his assistants explained. "Milton could never buy a throwaway razor. To him, that kind of thing was obscene. This was the sense of responsibility that Milton so brilliantly instilled in all of us."[25] But Milton had always been a builder, and his objectives for Hopkins went far beyond simply cutting back. Therefore, at the same time that he trimmed off the budgetary fat, he devoted at least as much effort to raising, as he would put it, "big money." However, since previously virtually all of his fund-raising had been before the state legislatures, he had had practically no experience in attracting private support. Fortunately, he had the assistance of Wilbert E. Locklin, "a great guy who did a really top job, who knows more about fund-raising than anyone I ever talked to."[26]

Locklin, although only thirty-six years old when Eisenhower came to Hopkins, was another of the old-timers. A 1942 Hopkins graduate, he was the assistant to the president when Eisenhower took office. He told Eisenhower that of the eight presidents in Hopkins's history, he had worked for four. Eisenhower's reaction was, "My, they don't last very long, do they?" Eisenhower had brought along with him his administrative assistant at Penn State, Keith Spalding. Spalding had much in common with Eisenhower: he was from Kansas and had been a journalist before entering the field of education. Eisenhower brought him to Hopkins with the title "Assistant to the President." Since that had been Locklin's title, and since formerly the Hopkins president had had but one official "assistant," Locklin had his name taken out of the catalog so that only Spalding would have that title. Naturally, he worried about his future. It took him about a year to feel comfortable with Eisenhower, with whom he was at first "nervous and in awe."

Locklin likes to recall the "breakthrough," which came in 1957. The occasion was a speech Eisenhower was to deliver at Shriver Hall. Locklin was to pick the president up at his home and drive him to Shriver Hall. Normally this was Spalding's job, but he was too busy that day. Spalding warned Locklin not to try to make small talk, that Eisenhower would not be talkative because he would be thinking about what he planned to say. Locklin followed the advice. Neither he nor Eisenhower spoke a word on the way to Shriver Hall. During the drive back, however, after the speech had "just knocked them on their ear" and the president "was on the greatest high imaginable," Eisenhower opened up completely. Locklin found him so friendly and so easy to talk to that, in contrast to his feeling on the trip to Shriver Hall, he now regretted that the distance between campus and Eisenhower's home was so short. By the time the evening, which included a nightcap at the president's residence, was over, it was Locklin who was on the high. As soon as he got home he exclaimed to his wife, "Hey, my name's going back in the catalog. I've made it."[27]

Locklin certainly had made it. Until leaving Hopkins to become a college president himself, he was Eisenhower's key assistant in the area of fund-raising. They made a formidable team. In Locklin's opinion, when it came to soliciting gifts from private individuals, whether alumni or just prominent citizens, Eisenhower knew no peer. He simply resumed where he had left off at Kansas State and Penn State, making more than a hundred appearances a year at small and large gatherings. "Any college president will tell you the greatest evening is not to entertain the alumni or some other such group," Locklin commented from personal experience. "You always have to be on your toes for a zinging question; the undershirts are damp at the armpits." Yet Eisenhower seemed to relish each appearance. To Locklin, he was "the personification of the university president," handling every occasion with ease, tact, and dignity.[28] Not surprisingly, in the ten years after his coming to Hopkins the endowment doubled, and the annual private-gift income increased from an average of less than $3 million to more than $7 million. During that time Hopkins raised well over $100 million in private gifts, and in one three-year period alone the total was $36 million.[29]

When it came to obtaining grants, however, Eisenhower had a great deal to learn. Yet neither he nor Hopkins suffered from his inexperience. Like the good executive that he was, he immediately looked to his staff for help, and he could have found no better assistant than Locklin. Locklin not only had an expert's knowledge of the Ford, Kresge, Rockefeller, and other foundations but he had developed personal relationships with many of their top specialists. When Hopkins was considering an expensive new program Locklin would go to the right foundation and speak to the right people. Then he would report to Eisenhower, and together they would rework the grant proposal to coincide with the information Locklin had gathered. They were remarkably successful. Eisenhower paid Locklin his ultimate compliment: he was "truly an educated man."[30]

It did not take long for Eisenhower to catch on. In Locklin's words, "Milton is what is known in the theater as a 'quick study.' " In this case Eisenhower studied exceptionally hard. He had Locklin take trips to the headquarters of the Internal Revenue Service, on New York's Lexington Avenue, in order to read every grant that foundations had been given. The grant proposals, on file at the I.R.S., often went into more detail than the foundations' annual reports. Eisenhower would carefully review the material Locklin brought back, looking for whatever in the proposal was distinctive or "trendy." He and Locklin would thus be able to design a "marketable concept" with which to approach the foundation. Armed with this concept, Eisenhower would submit Hopkins's proposal personally. Locklin commented that "I've never known a person who could be more persuasive. He saw to it that he had a marketable inventory, which was of his own creation and design, in concert with others, and then there was no one who could market it any better than he could. I don't care if you never met the guy, you couldn't spend fifteen minutes with him without being impressed and without being anxious to buy whatever it was that he was trying to sell."[31]

What Eisenhower sold was The Johns Hopkins University. Again and again he underscored Hopkins's uniqueness, mastering the art of demonstrating the university's worthiness. He did this during his personal presentations and, just as important, in the formal proposals themselves. He went over each page of the hundreds of proposals, editing the wording, correcting facts, scratching out paragraphs, rearranging others, and adding new ones.[32] He "loved to fool around with the documents themselves," one aide commented, "to polish and repolish."[33]

Yet Eisenhower realized that in the final analysis the foundations would judge Hopkins not on its uniqueness but on its record. He perceived each grant that the university received as a test for the future. "You don't raise money by rattling a tin cup," he told his assistants. "You raise money by proving that you are using the money well. Everybody bets on a winning horse."[34] The Eisenhower administration turned Hopkins into a winner, and the foundations bet. Ford granted it $6 million with the stipulation that the university match it two to one. Hopkins raised the $12 million in a little more than a year, well under the allotted time. Based on this performance, Eisenhower and Locklin went to Ford again, again received a grant, and again matched it easily. It was this type of track record that Eisenhower could proudly, and confidently, present to the foundations.[35]

Perhaps their greatest success had to do with Hopkins's School for Advanced International Studies (SAIS), located in Washington, D.C. SAIS had been founded in order to train knowledgeable foreign-service officers, and its faculty included prominent policymakers such as Christian Herter and Paul Nitze. Eisenhower grew attached to it from the start. He had a deep interest in and great concern for the future of U.S. foreign policy: and he had many friends among the SAIS faculty and shared their conviction that the school should emphasize a practical curriculum.

Compared with other Hopkins programs, however, especially the medical institutions, SAIS had been badly neglected, set aside as a kind of lonely orphan in the nation's capital. When Eisenhower arrived, he remarked years later, "[SAIS] was held together with chewing gum and thread," occupying two separate run-down houses on Florida Avenue. It had an inadequate library and insufficient faculty. Eisenhower sent Locklin to Washington, where he spent three weeks studying precisely what SAIS needed. After he returned to Baltimore, the two men collaborated on a hundred-page report stating the purpose of the school. It emphasized the reasons why the United States needed a school to prepare people for the foreign service and to educate businessmen engaged in international commerce. Eisenhower took the document to the Ford Foundation in New York. Ford gave $3 million, with the proviso that only $1.5 million could be spent on a building because the foundation normally did not make a grant for a building.

Next Eisenhower went to the Rockefeller Foundation, where future secretary of state Dean Rusk was president. Rusk knew Eisenhower well. As Eisenhower recalled the conversation, Rusk told him bluntly, "You've got to get a good man to head SAIS, and I won't give you a nickel until you do." Eisenhower said he was trying to get Francis O. Wilcox, then an assistant secretary of state. Equally bluntly, Rusk asked Eisenhower what salary he had offered. Twenty thousand, Eisenhower replied. Rusk said that if he made it twenty-five thousand, Wilcox would take the job. And he did. Eisenhower immediately called Rusk to tell him that he had his new dean. Rusk said that now Rockefeller would be pleased to support SAIS.

In addition, Rusk suggested that Eisenhower go to the Kellogg Foundation for even more money. Eisenhower instructed Locklin to sound out Kellogg. Locklin listened politely but thought to himself, "He doesn't know what he's talking about." He confided to Spalding that he knew all about Kellogg and the foundation never gave money for such purposes. Spalding advised him to go ahead and make the proposal. Kellogg would turn him down, but he would have done his job and satisfied the boss. So Locklin called Kellogg's chief, Emery Morris. To his surprise, Morris was exceptionally cordial, inviting him out to the Battle Creek headquarters and offering to pick him up personally at the airport. Locklin could not believe it. Nevertheless, over an elaborate lunch he described to Morris the site on Massachusetts Avenue, across the street from the Brookings Institution, where SAIS hoped to construct a new building. According to Locklin, "All of a sudden Morris says, 'You know, it's funny. A short time ago I was discussing how Kellogg should get involved in international affairs with my old friend Dean Rusk.' " He advised Locklin to have Eisenhower submit a formal proposal. Six weeks later SAIS had another $250,000.[36]

In the end, Eisenhower raised $4,247,000 from six different foundations for SAIS. "We had a great esprit de corps," Locklin maintained. "We believed there was nothing we couldn't do together."[37] The statistics bear him out. During Eisenhower's tenure the Ford Foundation alone granted Hopkins some $45 million. By the time he retired for the first time, in 1967, private-gift money was running at a rate of more than $10 million annually, and the budget had tripled. Faculty salaries had risen until they ranked in the top ten in the country, and the university's investment in plant facilities had increased from $9 million to $80 million. The faculty had grown steadily, doctoral production was up by nearly 40 percent, and new educational and research programs had been initiated in every division of the university. All this was done, as Eisenhower had pledged in his inaugural address, in accordance with the strictest fiscal responsibility. Every year since 1956 the Hopkins budget had shown a financial reserve on hand.[38]

CHAPTER 13

"The Whole Thing Is One Massive Personal Equation"

Assistants and Faculty at Johns Hopkins

I always wanted an assistant who was so damned good that you couldn't expect him to stay in a subordinate position for more than five years at the most," Eisenhower said.[1] At Hopkins he got what he wanted. He hired good men, trained them carefully, and beamed with approval as they moved on to greater challenges.

He also worked them terribly hard, making near-impossible demands on their time and energy. "Milton had a way of burning out his assistants," Ross Jones commented from experience, "because he expected you to live his life completely."[2] But none complained. Eisenhower became for each assistant a model to be emulated, almost an idol. "Any one of us would do anything for him," Locklin declared years later, after he had changed hats and become a college president himself. "We recognized that any real skill that we have, we owe to him."[3]

That Eisenhower would have placed such a high premium on his choice of assistants, and required so much of them, is highly consistent with his own background. Throughout his life he retained the lessons learned during his days as a young Washington bureaucrat. Having been a valued assistant of such men as Jardine and Wallace, and having followed so closely Ike's experience with Fox Connor, MacArthur, and Marshall, he knew well how rewarding this type of association could be, for both the assistant and the man in charge. A trusted assistant gains intimate knowledge of the ins and outs of the administrative process. The more knowledge he acquires, the more responsibility he can assume. As a consequence, he can relieve his superior of countless minor details. To Eisenhower this relief was imperative. He wanted assistants with ambition, ability, and drive equal to his own who sought to shoulder increased burdens, who did what Eisenhower desired before being asked and then did a little bit more. Therefore as president, he could devote his full energies to the larger, more important issues and problems with which he had to deal, and for which he had great appetite.

Thus beginning with Ken Davis at Kansas State, and continuing over the years, Eisenhower made it a practice to work closely with his assistant or assistants. The more they did, the more he could do. His assistants became extensions of his mind and thereby extensions of the office of the president. Moreover, he mastered the art of delegation. Just as Jardine and Wallace had relied on his help, so Eisenhower progressively relied on his subordinates to help draft speeches and presentations, to organize his considerable work load, to manage his hectic schedule, and to shield him from petty distractions. He also found them an essential sounding board for ideas and proposals that were still in the nascent stages. Each assistant's education increased in direct proportion to the confidence placed in him. Eisenhower left his mark on them all.

"I wanted an assistant to know everything I knew, I did, everything I thought," Eisenhower said in describing Spalding's functions and why he brought him from Penn State. "I hoped he would think the way I thought. I wanted his office so located that he knew everybody that went in and knew what I talked about when we were in there." Spalding, thirty-six years old in 1957, from Wichita and the University of Kansas, "was perfect." When they went on trips Spalding made the hotel reservations, got the tickets, took care of the baggage. When there was a reception for the freshman class, a meeting with alumni, or a gathering of the board Spalding "made sure that all the arrangements were precisely as they ought to be before I got there." Spalding also dictated much of Eisenhower's correspondence.

In this role, Spalding "couldn't have been better." But Eisenhower understood that his assistant needed the opportunity to grow. He increased Spalding's responsibilities, and in 1959 he changed his title from assistant to the president to secretary of the university. "He should have been called the vice-president. He was my main man with the board of trustees." He drew up the agenda for board meetings, helped set up the board's subcommittees, and took charge of making sure the board's decisions were implemented.

Thanks in part to a strong recommendation from Eisenhower, in 1963 the trustees of Franklin and Marshall College, in Lancaster, Pennsylvania, elected Spalding their president. "And he walked into one of the toughest positions I've ever heard of," Eisenhower said, "because F&M had an old, old board which had gotten into the habit of running the college, and the president was just kind of their servant to carry out the orders of the board." Having been Eisenhower's assistant, Spalding quickly realized that a successful president could not tolerate such a situation, and he was well prepared to remedy it. He arranged for some new members to be appointed to the board, handling it with the tact, diplomacy, skill, and firmness that he had observed Eisenhower use at Penn State and Hopkins. The result, in Eisenhower's judgment, was highly beneficial to Franklin and Marshall. "Keith has done a great job there," Eisenhower proudly remarked.[4]

Spalding helped recruit his own successor, Ross Jones. Like Ken Davis at Kansas State and like Spalding himself, Jones had a journalism background. (Eisenhower always had a soft spot for reporters.) A 1953 graduate of Hopkins, Jones had earned an M.S. in journalism at Columbia in 1958. He had written for the Associated Press in New York and then returned to Columbia as an information officer. In June 1961, when talk of Spalding's leaving Hopkins began, Eisenhower started, sensitively and sensibly, to shift his assistant's responsibilities. But he needed someone to shift the responsibilities to. After discussing the matter with Spalding, provost P. Stewart Macaulay, and placement director J. Lyon Rogers, Eisenhower learned of Jones's qualifications. He was impressed. Spalding asked Jones to come to Baltimore for an interview. "Milton and I hit it off beautifully," Jones recalled. "There was a certain chemistry between us."[5] For his part, Eisenhower said of the thirty-year-old Jones, "I was lucky to get a chap of his caliber."[6]

Spalding brought Jones along, telling him that Eisenhower would expect him to know everything the president was doing. They shared Spalding's Homewood House office, adjacent to Eisenhower's—visitors had to go through it to get to the president—so Jones could receive on-the-spot training in Eisenhower's methods. He learned how to monitor all Eisenhower's phone calls—"surreptitiously, with a hand over the receiver."[7] Another of Eisenhower's secrets was to keep his door slightly ajar whenever he held a conference in his office. Spalding taught Jones how to listen inconspicuously from the doorway, even pointing out the squeaky floor board that had to be avoided lest the noise cause the conferees to look up. This procedure enabled Jones to take notes on the discussions and, often, to be able to begin following through on decisions almost before the meeting had ended. Eisenhower characterized Jones as "tireless, well-informed, open and honest with everybody."[8] Jones interpreted even his early trips with Eisenhower "as part of the tutorial."[9]

Within a short time Jones became "absolutely superb at his job," another assistant, Ron Wolk, declared. "He just anticipated everything that Eisenhower needed—he knew exactly how to manage the traffic, when to tell someone that he could go in to see Milton; and when Ross would say, 'Hey, don't go now, he's in a bad mood,' no one went."[10] Eisenhower was not an easy person to work for. He expected everybody to be busy at their desk when he arrived at Homewood House, which was usually at twenty past eight in the morning. And when he left in the evening, at five o'clock sharp, he wanted his desk clean. If any of the day's business remained unfinished, he would either take it home himself or give it to one of his assistants. They all put in inordinately long days, sometimes seven days a week. Their morale never suffered, however, because in keeping with his concept of teamwork, Eisenhower never demanded more of his staff than he demanded of himself. When not scheduled to attend a meeting or some other function, he normally spent the evening laboriously memorizing statistics and details for his next speech or presentation. It was all his younger assistants could do to keep up with him. "You never dared tell Eisenhower you did not have time to do something," Locklin said with a smile that reflected his view that Eisenhower was not a tyrant but a mentor. He instilled devotion to the job, not fear of the consequences. "When Milton asked to see one of us," Locklin continued, "the reaction was never, 'What have I done now?' Instead, we would look forward to it."[11]

The first lesson learned by all of Eisenhower's assistants was that he religiously adhered to his two fundamental axioms of executive leadership: (1) the delegation of responsibility among a loyal and efficient staff is the *sine qua non* for success; and (2) the final decision cannot be delegated. According to Ron Wolk, when the time came for Eisenhower to decide on an important matter, "he would close his door and stay by himself for however long it took. He had an immense ability to focus and concentrate." Only after he had made up his mind would he open his office door, announce the decision, and permit the staff to express disagreement. Nine times out of ten any arguments were futile. "Milton Eisenhower," Wolk maintained, "wasn't an easy man to change."[12]

Ron Wolk's association with Eisenhower began somewhat differently than the other assistants'. Once his brother no longer occupied the White House, Eisenhower could comfortably begin a project he had long contemplated—a book about Latin America based on his observations and experiences as special ambassador. He quickly wrote the first draft. To polish the rough edges, however, he decided to hire someone with finely honed editorial skills and, just as important, capable of saving him time. He asked Spalding if he knew of anyone who might be able to help. Spalding recommended the twenty-nine-year-old Wolk, who had joined the staff of the prize-winning *Johns Hopkins Magazine* in 1958 and had been named its editor one year later. Following a single interview, Eisenhower decided that Wolk was exactly what he wanted. The drawback was that his advance left a mere thirty-five hundred dollars to pay an editor's salary. Wolk recalled that at the time he was making fifty-two hundred dollars annually. Nevertheless, he swallowed hard and accepted the offer on the spot. Few at Hopkins would have passed up an opportunity to work directly for the revered president. By the next day another journalist had officially entered Eisenhower's fold.

Still, Wolk was somewhat uncomfortable about having agreed to edit the manuscript sight unseen. His initial reading put his mind at ease. In his opinion, the draft was already very impressive. "Eisenhower was a remarkable, incredible writer," he remarked retrospectively, "in the sense that he could put down and pound out the material, mostly from memory, because his diaries and those sorts of things were mostly incomplete. He just poured these things out, and he handed me a manuscript which was 60 percent to being a publishable book." Yet the remaining 40 percent represented a lot of hard work ahead. Wolk recognized that the problems were not so much in the writing style as in the organization. He tried to tell Eisenhower what he thought had to be done. Eisenhower did not want to listen. In fact, Wolk received what he considered to be a crash course in what to expect if you told Eisenhower something he did not like to hear. "He changed the subject. We talked about something else, and suddenly I knew it was time to leave. He had a way, some mannerism, that let you know the meeting was over."

Wolk had three more appointments with Eisenhower, "and each time I tried to get at the real heart of the problem, and he would put me off, he detoured me, he distracted me." Finally one day Eisenhower, without any expression on his face—"and I could tell it was painful, he was annoyed with me"—simply told Wolk that it was time to get to work.[13]

All that summer, Wolk and Eisenhower worked together at the president's dining room table. Their efforts did not go unrewarded. Doubleday published *The Wine Is Bitter* in 1963 to rave reviews. The *Political Science Quarterly* found it "fascinating and important," while in the *American Political Science Review* Louis Kahle praised Eisenhower for his "quite objective and non-partisan" analysis.[14] The *Virginia Quarterly Review* pointed out that one thing that emerged clearly was "the ability of Dr. Eisenhower to learn the most fundamental facts about Latin America even though these facts clash rather harshly with many of the ideas which he had before starting his study of the region." This reviewer, Rutgers's distinguished expert on Latin America, Robert Alexander, called it the "most authoritative" recent book on the subject, adding, "It is obvious . . . that those steps taken in the last two years of the Eisenhower Administration to move towards some sensible and understanding United States policy towards the rest of the hemisphere owed a great deal to the observation, comprehension, and insistence of the President's brother."[15]

The Wine Is Bitter received top notices in popular magazines as well, including *Time, Newsweek,* and *Saturday Review.*[16] Best of all, the *New York Times Book Review* gave it front-page coverage. Ted Szulc, of the *New York Times* Latin American staff, described it as a "startlingly blunt and almost painfully honest book, immensely thoughtful."[17] Even normally anti-Republican publications liked it. Writing for the *New Republic,* Samuel Shapiro commented, "Eisenhower's liberal views on tariffs, foreign aid, social reform, and the need to cooperate with government-run enterprises are all the more impressive because he arrived at them reluctantly."[18] Similarly, Dan Kurzman, of *The Progressive,* wrote that the study provides keen insights into "one of the most important chapters in the history of American foreign relations."[19] With such praise from these diverse sources, it is small wonder that the book made the best-seller list (Eisenhower contributed all his royalties to the Hopkins Scholarship Fund). It also helped solidify Eisenhower's claim that he was the real author of the Alliance for Progress, for which John Kennedy took the credit but which Eisenhower insisted got started during his brother's administration, at his urging.[20]

When Eisenhower and Wolk finished their work on *The Wine Is Bitter,* Wolk accepted a job in Washington. He was on the verge of moving there when Spalding called to say that Eisenhower wanted to see him. Wolk went over to Homewood House, where Eisenhower asked him if he would like to become his assistant. For the second time, Wolk accepted Eisenhower's offer of a job on the spot.

The position had materialized because Spalding was about to leave for Franklin and Marshall, and even though Jones had been hired to assume his duties incrementally, all agreed, and the tandem of Spalding and Jones had demonstrated, that the position properly called for two men. "That was true," Wolk admitted, "because Keith really used to sleep in the office. He was a real workaholic." Hence Eisenhower decided that Spalding's responsibilities would be officially divided between two assistants. Jones took over the office management as university secretary, and Wolk became responsible for special projects.

Wolk's first assignment was to draft a speech for Eisenhower to deliver at Kansas State. Eisenhower told him what he wanted, but Wolk could not get it right. He found editing someone else's draft manuscript and writing someone else's draft speech from scratch entirely different. Eisenhower gave him the same advice he had gotten from Secretary Jardine in the Department of Agriculture in the twenties. Wolk clearly recalled Eisenhower relating Jardine's words: "Look, Milton," the Agricultural secretary had said, "don't write the speech for me, write the speech for yourself." Wolk did as advised; Eisenhower read the result, made a few changes, and it was done. The audience loved it. Wolk had no further trouble. Eisenhower continued to draft most of his speeches himself, but it was reassuring to have a man with Wolk's ability to fall back on.[21]

Wolk resembled Ken Davis in the services he provided for Eisenhower and in his politics. He was a liberal Democrat, and in much the same way Davis had, he often tried to pull his boss a bit to the left. Shortly after he began to work in Homewood House some students came to see him. They complained that Baltimore landlords were discriminating against foreign students and blacks, and they wanted Hopkins to refuse to list their apartments on the university-approved housing list. Wolk agreed, but Eisenhower did not. And when Eisenhower disagreed he could be bitter. "We have no business whatsoever telling them who they can rent their places to," Eisenhower stormed. In his view, the housing list had been instituted as a convenience for the students, not the landlords. And it clearly indicated those districts open to minorities. If Hopkins attempted to force integration, it would only lead to confrontation, embarrassment, and probably the refusal of most landlords to list their units. Wolk, furious, said he would not argue the point, but he demanded to be relieved of all responsibility involving housing and even threatened to resign if necessary. As he recalled the incident, Eisenhower "never said a word. He acknowledged my position." Ross Jones took on the assignment.[22]

Shortly thereafter, the students brought their case to Eisenhower himself. The president repeated his argument that while they had a legitimate complaint, their proposal that the university refuse to list restricted dwellings would only make matters worse. This virtual ultimatum would not change any attitudes, he counseled, and without the listings, minorities would not know what housing was open to them and inevitably would knock at an increasing number of wrong doors. He urged the students to accept the list as an expedient compromise. They would not. At Jones's prodding, Eisenhower reluctantly gave in. Yet he did not change his own position. Rather, he decided that since the list was provided for the students' benefit, they had a right to attach any conditions to it, even if the conditions were detrimental to their own interests. Jones sent a letter to all landlords announcing the policy that unless they were willing to rent to all students, Hopkins would not carry their listings. But Eisenhower bristled. The president of Johns Hopkins never liked to admit he was wrong. In this case, he never doubted that he was right.[23]

The solution to the controversy, however unsatisfactory to Eisenhower, did remove a potential source of conflict with Wolk. Soon they had both put the incident behind them. It would have been business as usual but for the intervention of politics once again. This time Wolk found himself in full support of his boss. In the fall of 1963, because of his position as a leading Eisenhower Republican and at the request of his brother, Eisenhower accepted the chairmanship of the Citizens Committee's Critical Issues Council. The Citizens Committee, comprised of leading Republicans, had established the council in order to prepare for the forthcoming national election by producing position papers on the vital issues. Eisenhower's associates included politicians, economists, military officers, publishers, bankers, agricultural specialists, lawyers, and other educators—twenty-four in all—with names like Gerald Ford, Admiral Arleigh Burke, Claire Booth Luce, and Melvin Laird. Wolk and Jones accompanied Eisenhower to the meetings. "It was the first time I ever found myself in the company of the movers and shakers," Wolk remembered. The council studied a broad spectrum of subjects ranging from national security to fiscal policy to conservation of resources. Wolk, however, was just as interested in the conduct of the participants. Compared with Eisenhower, the other council members seemed to be "such dunderheads. They were so impressed with their own importance. None of them had done their homework, and they were just sloshing about. Milton was just heads and shoulders above everybody, so much more the professional."[24]

Barry Goldwater had been opposed to the council from its beginning. He went so far as to appeal to Edgar Eisenhower to try to influence his "baby" brother to moderate its recommendations, particularly regarding civil rights. Milton could not be persuaded. Moreover, Goldwater's position convinced him even further that the Arizona senator should not be the Republicans' standard-bearer. For months he had been urging Governor William Scranton of Pennsylvania to seek the nomination, but to no avail. Then at the last minute Scranton changed his mind and asked Eisenhower to give the nominating speech at San Francisco's Cow Palace. Wolk helped draft the speech, as did Malcolm Moos, a former Hopkins professor and speech-writer for Ike. (Moos also became a university president.) They were almost finished when several Scranton lieutenants decided to look it over. They edited it beyond recognition. Wolk showed Eisenhower the revised draft while returning to the hotel in the chauffeured limousine. Outraged that they had tampered with his words, Eisenhower threw the new version against the windshield. That night he and Wolk started all over again. Over champagne and macadamia nuts, and with Eisenhower pecking away at the typewriter in his inimitable two-finger style, they finished only a few hours before the nominating speeches were to begin.

Had Scranton committed earlier, the moderate Republicans possibly could have headed off the Goldwater landslide. As it was, the last-ditch effort in San Francisco proved futile. Nevertheless, it did permit Eisenhower to express in clear and forceful terms the "progressive conservative" philosophy that he, and his brother, held so dear. The speech was the high point in Eisenhower's political career. Before the balloting took place, Scranton phoned to assure him that "regardless of the outcome, your nominating speech was the best I ever heard." Walter Cronkite called it a "masterpiece," and Chet Huntley and David Brinkley pointed out that the Nielson ratings placed Eisenhower's appearance second only to Goldwater's acceptance speech. As for Wolk, the entire experience, from the Critical Issues Council to the convention, brought him closer to Eisenhower than ever. He gained an increased respect for Eisenhower as a man and a new respect for Eisenhower as a politician. Other liberals agreed. Indeed, for several weeks following the speech there was some speculation in Washington that Eisenhower might be an excellent vice-presidential candidate—on the Democratic ticket.[25]

Wolk, in Eisenhower's view, "is one of those individuals who will die on the vine if he doesn't have new challenges." Eisenhower had "hated like sin" to have to ask him to pass up his opportunity in Washington and stay on at Homewood House, but with Spalding leaving, he felt he had to do it. When it came to Johns Hopkins, Eisenhower could be very selfish.[26] Shortly after Eisenhower retired in 1967, however, Wolk accepted the post of assistant to Clark Kerr, who had, amidst the student protests, given up the presidency of the University of California to undertake a massive study of American higher education for the Carnegie Foundation. The Kerr-Wolk association did not work out. As Wolk commented, "Milton spoiled me. I never again found anyone I could respect or work with like Milton. Everyone else was a second-rater compared to Milton Eisenhower."

Wolk insisted that he was not an Eisenhower-worshipper, "but, by God, as a professional he was just outstanding."[27] The specific trouble in working for Kerr was that Wolk could never get to see him, quite a shock after his experience of unlimited access to Eisenhower. Wolk resigned. He was without a job.

Just at that point, in July 1968, President Lyndon Johnson made Eisenhower the chairman of the President's Commission on the Causes and

Prevention of Violence. Wolk called Eisenhower to ask if he had a position for him. As had become their custom, Eisenhower immediately offered him a job and Wolk accepted. He became the special assistant to the chairman, doing his usual efficient job. "Milton saved me," Wolk said. Eisenhower thought it was the other way around.[28]

As will be discussed in the penultimate chapter, Eisenhower's involvement with the commission proved to be one of the most important events of his later life. The final report, not completed until the first Nixon administration in 1969, received broad public and political acclaim. More important, its wide coverage in the media brought potential remedies for the violence in the United States to the attention of a nation sickened by the Vietnam War and racial unrest. Although Eisenhower threw himself totally into the commission's study, initially he had not wanted the chairmanship. And Wolk wondered if he could handle it. After all, the politics of a presidential commission, especially one concerned with so emotional an issue as national violence, could be a lot more sensitive than even those of a university faculty. However, Wolk never regretted his decision to take the job. In his judgment, in his capacity as commission chairman Eisenhower demonstrated, perhaps even more than he had as president of Hopkins, that as a conciliator he was "just magnificent. My respect for him just kept climbing the longer I got to know him. He just took that commission and welded it together."[29]

The year the commission issued its report Wolk was elected vice-president of Brown University, in Providence, Rhode Island. "He could have stayed there forever," Eisenhower said, "but he wasn't a man to stay in one place forever."[30] In 1978 Wolk left Brown to resume his writing career and to serve as president of Editorial Projects for Education, in Washington, publishers of *The Chronicle of Higher Education*. Wolk also began a parallel publication, *The Chronicle of Preparatory Education*. He may someday return to a university setting. One thing is certain: like Eisenhower, he will always be an educator.

Locklin left Hopkins a few years after Spalding because he, too, was elected president of a college. Springfield, in the foothills of Massachusetts's Berkshire Mountains, was a YMCA college. Locklin broadened and expanded the program. In Eisenhower's words, "It's amazing what that guy has done. He's changed it into a reasonable liberal arts institution, well financed, every bill paid, never has a deficit, built lots of buildings, improved the faculty, and not eliminated the old thing, but the YMCA part became of minor importance."[31] As a matter of fact, Springfield College, without the prestige of Hopkins or the Eisenhower name, has become one of the most successful institutions in the nation at obtaining grants. No longer is it known only for public health and physical education. It is an excellent, all-round college. And Locklin is the senior tenured college or university president throughout New England.[32]

Locklin credits his success—and, by extension, Springfield's—to Eisenhower. To go one step further, he notes with pride that each assistant trained by Eisenhower who has gone on to be a president himself has succeeded. Locklin described Eisenhower as "a master teacher." He stressed that his association with Eisenhower "is the greatest thing that ever happened to me. . . . Keith and I have often remarked that when we do well it is because we remember what Dr. Milton taught us, and when we fail it is because we have forgotten what he taught us." In sum, "I am indebted to no one other than my wife and children more than Milton Eisenhower."[33]

Locklin remains overwhelmed by Eisenhower's mental powers. "His mind is so full of ideas that they just tumble all over each other to burst out." Eisenhower, according to Locklin, does the Sunday *New York Times* crossword puzzle in half an hour, in ink. "He lacks imprecision." Yet he never made people feel ill at ease in his presence. On the contrary, "You watch this gentleman, and the grace and ease and skill with which he moves among people—he is a great conciliator." This was the crucial lesson of administration that Eisenhower taught all his protégés: "The whole thing is one massive personal equation."[34]

The last word on Eisenhower by one of his assistants belongs to Ross Jones. Before retiring, Eisenhower had recommended Jones for several college presidencies. "And Steve Muller [Eisenhower's eventual successor] came to me and said, 'Please don't do that for at least a year, for I consider Ross to be the one indispensable man that I've got to lean on.' " Jones stayed on as vice-president, providing the necessary link between the Eisenhower and Muller regimes. He remains at Hopkins today. Eisenhower still feels that he would make a great president of a liberal arts college. "But," Eisenhower remarked from years of experience, "fortune does not always act with judgment."[35]

No one worked more closely with Eisenhower, and for a longer time, than Jones. While he agreed with all the other assistants in praising his superior, he, too, was not blindly idolatrous. In his view, the flaws in Eisenhower's administration stemmed from two aspects of his personality. First, perhaps to compensate for never having completed his own graduate studies, Eisenhower had an almost deferential demeanor towards those who held the Ph.D. Obviously, such an attitude occasionally made it difficult for him to deal with some of the more overbearing members of the Hopkins faculty. (Ron Wolk concurred: "Milton came in with a great respect for the faculty," he commented. "He envied them in a way. They had Ph.D.'s, and they were scholars. . . . Usually he left the academic decisionmaking to the people who were qualified to do it.") It also colored his relations with his counterparts at other institutions. "I do know," Jones asserted, "that he felt it fairly uncomfortable to deal with a fair number of his fellow presidents who were much more scholarly." Like all successful men, Eisenhower had "a healthy ego."[36]

The other chink in Eisenhower's armor, according to Jones, was that he did not like unpleasantness of any kind. Now, this was not necessarily a fault. On many occasions Jones watched Eisenhower lose his temper, especially regarding budgetary matters. But almost never would he take his ire out on others—at least in public. However, Eisenhower's sensitivity to individual feelings did make him vulnerable to the same criticism recognized by Russell Thackrey back at Kansas State. He would never fire anyone, no matter how poor he considered the person's performance. Rather, he would attempt to administer circuitously, working around the inefficient staff member, isolating him or her as much as possible from particular responsibilities. Hence to some extent Eisenhower sacrificed efficiency to harmony. Conversely, Jones was quick to add, Eisenhower mitigated the adverse effects of this technique: "I think he got the best out of the people who were here."[37]

Jones's summarizing opinion of Eisenhower probably best reflects the views of all his assistants. He regretted that too few Milton Eisenhowers ever devoted so much of their lives to higher education and lamented that such people are even less likely to do so in the future. If you asked someone to list the qualities necessary for a good university president, Jones concluded, "Eisenhower had them all. And he had that added benefit to Hopkins...of giving himself entirely to the university, because as a widower whose children were grown, he did not have family responsibilities to hold him back, and he just transformed himself into the institution."[38] No one would disagree with Jones, except perhaps to interject that at Kansas State and Penn State Eisenhower seldom held back.

The sense of loyalty and devotion, perhaps even the sense of family, that Eisenhower instilled among the members of his administrative staff did not extend uniformly to all the faculty. This was in part due to traditional faculty attitudes, attitudes which, if anything, were amplified at Johns Hopkins. The Hopkins faculty, both on the Homewood campus and at the medical school, consisted largely of internationally known scholars. Many were as eccentric as they were brilliant, as spoiled as they were hard-working, as petty as they were famous. As a group the faculty had long been accustomed to the benign neglect, if not the deferential treatment, of Eisenhower's predecessors. Most of the professors, especially the senior ones, firmly believed that they knew best what made for a superior academic program. Eisenhower's own views, as noted above, generally coincided with their expectations. As a consequence, he tended to reinforce their preconception that the president should not meddle in the faculty's domain. When he came to Hopkins relations were, to use Eisenhower's mild description, "somewhat distant."[39]

This distance was most pronounced on the Homewood campus. There the faculty tended to subordinate their undergraduate responsibilities to their personal research and graduate students. A normal teaching load consisted of one undergraduate course and one graduate seminar each semester, with the emphasis decidedly on the seminar. Eisenhower, congruent with his long-established policy of placing a premium on undergraduate education, attempted to persuade the professors to divide their time more equally. He tried to induce them to offer more introductory courses in the liberal arts, thereby encouraging premed students or those concentrating on the hard sciences to acquire a broader background in the humanities and social sciences. Often he received little support for his efforts.

Eisenhower considered his lack of success in reorienting the priorities of the Homewood faculty the greatest single failure of his Hopkins administration. In one sense, he cannot be faulted. It is, after all, up to each department to establish its own curriculum. Nevertheless, Eisenhower's propensity to tread softly when it came to faculty relations certainly limited his ability to influence departmental policies. Had he exerted the leverage available to him, which included budgetary controls, approval of additional positions, restrictions on leaves of absence, and the like, he undoubtedly could have demanded more responsiveness to his wishes. But Eisenhower thought that a scholar should be accommodated. Instead of cracking down on the prima donnas, he pampered them. In Eisenhower's view, he simply created a climate that would ensure that Hopkins continue to attract a faculty of world-class caliber who would bring prestige—and support—to the university through their distinguished research. From another perspective, he was overly indulgent, placing the faculty on so high a pedestal that he forfeited his own jurisdictional prerogatives.[40]

"Milton was always partial to the East Baltimore campus." This opinion, held by Ron Wolk, seems inconsistent with Eisenhower's abiding devotion to the liberal arts. Yet it is explicable by the fact that, unlike its counterpart in Homewood, the School of Medicine faculty enjoyed teaching and paid as much attention to their students (whose number, of course, did not include undergraduates) as they did to their research.

Moreover, the M.D.'s appeared less concerned than the Ph.D.'s that Eisenhower did not hold an advanced degree. They deemed his breadth of knowledge and expertise in financial management to be excellent qualifications for the Hopkins presidency. The prominent professors at the School of Medicine "really respected Milton and courted him," Wolk continued.[41]

Not surprisingly, Eisenhower responded enthusiastically to their attitude, which resembled adulation. He also found the M.D.'s esprit de corps and loyalty towards the university most satisfying. "There are some things that unite the medical faculty much more than you find in Arts and Sciences," he explained, "because it is a mission-orientated school. And the desire to do the greatest job that you can in the world in protecting human life, which brings the specialists together, is a highly unifying influence. There is a cohesion that develops." For someone who had stressed teamwork throughout his entire life, this comradeship, this dedication to the whole, brought incalculable satisfaction.[42]

This is not to say the Eisenhower did not encounter any problems when dealing with the East Baltimore campus. The School of Medicine faculty was not immune to political infighting, especially when it came to filling a senior position. A post at Johns Hopkins was a much sought-after appointment, and physicians can be as fiercely loyal to their network of associates or friends throughout the country as they are to their institution. Eisenhower sometimes felt that every faculty member advocated a different candidate; rarely did the final selection meet with unanimous approval. Eisenhower recalled several occasions when following his announcement of an appointment, "we got inundated by angry protests from the losers."[43]

Or when School of Medicine professors feared that a reform threatened their professional autonomy, such as when the obstetric and gynecology departments were consolidated, they could not easily be pacified. Fortunately Eisenhower could invariably count on support from the executive vice-president of the three medical institutions—the School of Medicine, the hospital, and the School of Hygiene and Public Health—Dr. W. Barry Wood, Jr. Wood was an eminent internist and microbiologist, but to the Hopkins president he was much more. "He was one of the great statesmen of American medicine," Eisenhower unreservedly asserted. "He was the sort of man that when you had a very difficult problem in the governing board, we'd talk a lot, and then when Barry Wood was ready to speak we'd all listen. And no one would want to talk after that."[44]

It must not be forgotton that Wood had joined with the board of trustees committee of five in convincing Eisenhower to come to Hopkins in the first place, and Eisenhower characterized their association as "one of the happiest things that ever happened to me." He was a good friend and top administrator. Largely due to his help, Eisenhower thoroughly enjoyed his initial foray into the world of medicine. However, a year later the honeymoon almost came to an abrupt end. In 1957 Wood requested what Eisenhower thought to be a routine appointment. Hardly had the two men sat down when Wood broke the news. "Milton," he said, "I just hate this administrative work. I've got to get back to doing research and teaching. So I am going back to Washington University [in St. Louis] as head of the department of medicine."

Eisenhower thought his heart skipped a beat. But he regained his composure quickly enough to reply, "Barry, if there were a position here that appealed to you, that was open, in the School of Medicine, is your commitment to Washington so firm that you can't get out?"

Wood assured him that it was not. Eisenhower immediately called the School of Medicine's advisory board together, explained the situation, said that he had heard that the position of head of microbiology was open, and indicated that he hoped the board would select Wood to fill it. It did. Still, because of his responsibilities, Wood earned more than most department chairmen, and it was unlikely that he would accept a sizeable cut in pay. Eisenhower came up with a plan to take care of the difference. He appointed Wood as his personal adviser at the School of Medicine, which meant that in addition to his regular chairman's salary, he would receive compensation from the president's administrative budget.

The formula worked. Wood unhesitatingly agreed to stay on, leaving Eisenhower with but one remaining problem. Who would become the new coordinator of the medical institutions? He asked Wood if he had any suggestions. Again Wood did not hesitate. He could think of no better replacement than Eisenhower himself. "That's the craziest idea I ever heard of," Eisenhower responded with equal speed. To effectively coordinate three medical institutions, including a hospital, required far more expertise than he possibly could have acquired in so short a time.

"Look," Eisenhower remembered Wood arguing, "even though you have been here only one year, all the members of the faculty in the School of Medicine have great confidence in you as an administrator and a man in policy and human relations and decisionmaking. And they know that you respect them and their judgments as professionals. And this might be better than having a medical man as head, who might want to substitute his judgment for theirs. So just try for a little while."

Eisenhower, full of trepidation, ultimately agreed. Working closely with the entire Hopkins medical community, he acted upon the recommendations of the Bard Committee in 1949 and breathed life into the

Medical Planning and Development Committee, made up of the dean of
the School of Medicine, Thomas Turner; the dean of Hygiene and Public
Health, Ernest Stebbins; the director of the hospital, Russell Nelson; and
himself—the chairman. "We met very often," Eisenhower recalled, "and I
never gave it up. I did it for the next ten years. It was all exciting to me, it
was all new. And I had more damned fun."[45]

More significant than the fun was the progress over which Eisenhower
presided. In the words of university historian Robert Sharkey, under
Eisenhower, "a truly extraordinary degree of cooperation and coordination was becoming manifest among the Schools of Medicine, Hygiene
and Public Health, and The Johns Hopkins Hospital."[46] Eisenhower left
most of the curricular and academic policy decisions to the experts,
although he did have a major input into an innovative program inaugurated in 1958 to shorten the length and cut the cost of a medical
education. By the mid-1950s, training qualified doctors had become so
time-consuming and expensive that applications to medical schools
across the nation had actually declined. The program designed at
Hopkins permitted a select group of students to begin their medical
studies after their sophomore or junior year, provided that they continue
to take some subjects in the humanities and social sciences. Eisenhower
felt that the program yielded the added benefit of breaking up "the first
two years of medical school, the dreariest, dullest ones." It was much appreciated by the medical students, who could liven up their medical
school routine with exciting courses in the history of warfare or English
literature, saving money in the process. Just as important in Eisenhower's
opinion, students who might otherwise spend their last years as undergraduates concentrating exclusively on premed courses were encouraged
to take advantage of the liberal arts electives.[47]

Eisenhower's primary contribution to the East Baltimore campus,
however, involved streamlining the administrative machinery and improving cost-efficiency. At the same time, he set about rejuvenating the
physical plants of all three institutions to accommodate the levels of
achievement to which the medical community aspired. Added to the
School of Medicine and the hospital were the Lowell J. Reed Residence
Hall, the W. Barry Wood Basic Science Building, the Biophysics Building, the Children's Medical and Surgical Center, and the Thomas B.
Turner Auditorium, to list just some of the new construction. Three
wings were built onto the main building of the School of Hygiene and
Public Health. All of Hopkins took particular pride in the affiliated John
F. Kennedy Institute for the Habilitation of the Mentally and Physically
Handicapped Child.[48]

Eisenhower developed strong emotional attachments to virtually all the M.D.'s. His experiences contradicted the conventional generalization that doctors are too narrow, that they are overly preoccupied with diseases and clinical analyses. When confronted with this view he fumed. "That is the greatest misunderstanding in the world," he retorted with some heat. "It still amazes me that some of the most active civil and political figures that we have in Baltimore are Hopkins doctors. Some of them can write beautifully, and some of them are enormously knowledgeable in literature." He mentioned specifically Wood, Thomas Turner, and psychiatrist Jerome Frank, and speculated that "there is something about the practice of medicine . . . that causes them to keep on studying, and reading, and listening. You could go over there to East Baltimore and pick almost any good doctor you wanted to, and he could talk about a half-dozen subjects." This was precisely the type of doctor Eisenhower wanted the Hopkins medical institutions to produce.[49]

Despite all the rewards Eisenhower obtained from his involvement with the medical institutions, his passion for the liberal arts never waned. And it was not long before he was calling many of the members of the Homewood faculty by their first name, had made a number of close friends from among them, and had become a frequent guest at their social gatherings. Eisenhower's conciliatory and amiable nature in all probability would have enabled him to gain the faculty's acceptance under any circumstances. However, he also benefited from an additional "asset." Eisenhower quickly earned the friendship and respect of Dr. G. Wilson Shaffer, a professor of psychology, the popular dean of the Homewood schools from 1942 to 1967. Shaffer spent his entire career at Hopkins and was the man responsible for holding the Homewood campus together. Eisenhower described him as "one of the biggest procrastinators I know, but also one of the most effective educational leaders I ever met." He was Eisenhower's primary liaison with the faculty, an indispensable ally.[50]

To illustrate Shaffer's effectiveness, Eisenhower related how the two of them had teamed up to bring some order to the degree-granting system for undergraduates. "I was astounded when I came here and found that there were no requirements for a bachelor's degree," he recalled. "To put it simply, a student received a degree when the faculty made up its mind that he was entitled to it." In Eisenhower's opinion, such discretionary latitude existed because the Homewood faculty, with its unique emphasis on the graduate program, thought it quite reasonable to apply similar standards to undergraduates. In order to confirm his intuitive suspicions, Eisenhower requested that the registrar supply him with the transcripts of some one hundred students selected at random from graduates over the past five years. To his unmitigated horror, he discovered that Hopkins undergraduate courses carried no specific credits. So he decided to make some calculations of his own. He assigned hourly credits for a course on the basis of class meetings—he gave the student 3 credits for an English class that met three times a week, 5 credits for a chemistry course that met every day. On this basis, he determined that one student had received his B.A. with 95 credits, while another had taken 185 hours before getting his degree. Both students had a cumulative B average.[51]

This absurd—and patently unfair—system could only have been maintained at Hopkins, where undergraduate education was viewed not as an end in itself but primarily as preparation for subsequent studies. The absence of any coherent faculty organization likewise reflected this casual attitude towards the underclassmen. There was a humanities group, a social-sciences group, a physical-sciences group, and so on, but there was no coordinated hierarchy. At the conclusion of the sophomore year, students had to apply to one of the groups to continue their studies. Concurrently, an academic committee without any direct connection to the groups decided at the end of each term whether a student could stay in school. The ensuing difficulty, as Shaffer explained, was that "we had a large number of students, the academic committee had said they could stay in college, but when they applied to groups, no group would take them. So when Eisenhower came here there was kind of a terrible situation where you would have a boy who the committee had said is in college, but no group would take him."[52]

Eisenhower appointed an ad hoc faculty committee that recommended what he considered to be a "very fine undergraduate program." It established regular credits for courses, required 120 credits for graduation, and allowed students who did not have a major field of study to take a general B.A. degree. Eisenhower heartily approved the committee's proposals and confidently put them before the entire faculty, meeting as the General Assembly. He could not believe that such rational measures would arouse opposition. The Hopkins faculty, however, was not ready to accept such sweeping changes in the traditional methods of doing things. The old-timers resisted, the newcomers were afraid to buck the system, and the General Assembly voted down the proposal, four to one.

Dismayed, Eisenhower turned to Shaffer, his "educational troubleshooter." Eisenhower had already learned that whenever he had a problem that "no one else could handle, I could turn to Wilson. And since we thought alike, and got along well, he would work it out." Shaffer applied his keen understanding of the faculty's idiosyncrasies to meet the challenge. "And despite his procrastination, he worked hard. He worked with every department on campus in developing ideas." He met with the faculty members individually, over lunch, over coffee, after class. After a month or so, Shaffer reported to Eisenhower that he had managed to effect enough compromises to make everyone happy. Eisenhower called another meeting of the General Assembly to present the new proposal, which in truth was nearly identical to the one previously turned down. "We got unanimous approval. So that war was over."[53]

In fact, Eisenhower and Shaffer had just won a major battle. Shortly thereafter, the president called another meeting of the General Assembly. In one of his more lengthy presentations, he proposed the creation of a new faculty council, arguing that "Hopkins needs much more critical thought about the whole program than the General Assembly can give it." The faculty would elect its own representatives to the council, and Eisenhower would serve as ex officio chairman. "I may try to persuade," he explained, "but I will not vote." After an extended debate the faculty accepted the proposal. With the establishment of the Academic Council, it was not long before undergraduate education at Hopkins began to receive the careful consideration it deserved. Eisenhower was never completely satisfied; yet, in his words, "The work that council has done has been phenomenal, considering the chaos that existed before." And in 1966, epitomizing the new emphasis on cohesion and integration, Homewood's faculties of philosophy and engineering science merged to form the new Faculty of Arts and Sciences.[54]

A plethora of academic programs began or were expanded under Eisenhower's administration. Among his proudest accomplishments were the creation of independent departments of social relations and the history of science; the reorientation of the School of Engineering, as represented by its new name, the School of Engineering Science; the consolidation of the departments of aeronautics, civil engineering, and mechanical engineering into a single Department of Mechanics; the institution of a Masters of Liberal Arts program in the Evening (formerly McCoy) College; the establishment of the Humanities Center; and the enlargement of both the School of Advanced International Studies and its Bologna Center in Italy. Perhaps Eisenhower's favorite, however, from both a personal and professional standpoint, was the addition of the Eisenhower Project. In 1963 David Donald, Frederic Lane, and Charles Barker, of the Department of History approached Eisenhower informally with the suggestion that Hopkins acquire the rights to edit and publish his brother's papers. Acting as spokesman, Donald, the Harry C. Black Professor of American History, argued that although he knew of Eisenhower's reluctance to take advantage of his family connections, Hopkins did not own any collections of presidential papers. Appealing to Eisenhower's sense of history and to his civic-mindedness, Donald stated the obvious: Ike's correspondence and official papers would be of enormous value to both historians and government officials. Appealing to his family pride, he added that every president's reputation declines during his first years out of office and invariably the publication of the papers reverses this trend.

Quite naturally, Eisenhower was excited over the prospect of Hopkins's publishing his brother's wartime and presidential documents. He arranged for the historians and the former president to hold a morning-long meeting. Ike, who had already begun the second volume of his memoirs, readily agreed.[55] Delighted, Barker, the department chairman, induced Alfred D. Chandler, Jr., a renowned business and administrative historian, to come to Hopkins from the Massachusetts Institute of Technology to be the editor. Chandler, who had previously worked on the Theodore Roosevelt papers, could not resist the challenge. No one had yet attempted to publish the collected papers of a modern (post–World War II) president. More specifically, the problems inherent in running such a massive bureaucracy as Eisenhower's wartime headquarters, SHAEF, sparked Chandler's scholarly interests. Milton Eisenhower raised the necessary funds and provided Chandler with all possible assistance, including making certain that the editor had unlimited access to Ike himself.[56] Seven years later, in 1970, the Johns Hopkins Press published the first five volumes of *The Papers of Dwight D. Eisenhower: The War Years* to uniformly excellent reviews throughout the world. In 1978 four additional volumes, covering the first months of the occupation of Germany and Eisenhower's subsequent stint as Army Chief of Staff, were published, with Louis Galambos replacing Chandler as editor. It will take another decade or more to complete the whole project. And as Donald predicted, already the series has greatly enhanced Ike's reputation.

Eisenhower succeeded in developing a good rapport with the Homewood faculty because he applied the same leadership methods that he had been using his entire adult life: he was always careful to involve them in the administrative process, and he dealt with each member on a personal basis. Years into his retirement he still enjoyed recounting his countless pleasurable experiences with so many of them. For hours he could go on about such professors as Barker, Lane, Chandler, and Sidney Painter of the History Department, Maurice "Maury" Mandelbaum of Philosophy, Charles Singleton of Romance Languages (who also headed the Humanities Center), or art historian Phoebe Stanton, to mention just a few. Then there were deans like G. Heberton Evans, Robert H. Roy, and of course

Shaffer. To the academic world these were all distinguished scholars. To Eisenhower they were distinguished scholars and wonderful individuals. He even enjoyed the company of Donald, the brilliant Civil War expert who so often criticized Hopkins before moving to Harvard. Donald was usually fidgety, sometimes arrogant, always working, a man who demanded a total commitment from his graduate students and drove them as hard as he did himself. "A lot of folks didn't like David Donald," Eisenhower said, "but I did." He also appreciated the contributions Donald made to Hopkins, including a federally sponsored program that brought high school teachers from the South to Baltimore each year to study with him.[57]

The list of outstanding members of the Homewood faculty was endless, but ironically, of all of them the one probably best known to the public at large was Owen Lattimore, a lecturer from 1938 to 1963 who specialized in the history of the Far East. Lattimore became a headline figure in the early fifties due to Senator McCarthy's sensational accusation that he was the top Soviet agent in the United States. According to McCarthy, Lattimore was the man most responsible for the "loss of China" to the Communists. This was a gross exaggeration of Lattimore's relatively minor role as a part-time Office of Strategic Services agent during World War II and later consultant to the State Department on Far Eastern affairs, but it put Lattimore in a vulnerable position. Hopkins gave him time off at full pay to defend himself against the charges.

When Eisenhower arrived in Baltimore in 1956, Lattimore visited him almost immediately. Eisenhower recalled the meeting vividly. "You understand that I have tenure," Lattimore told the new president. Eisenhower acknowledged the fact. "I have a feeling you are against me," Lattimore continued, in all likelihood referring to the fact that both McCarthy and Dwight Eisenhower were of the same party.

"I don't know why you should have such a feeling," Eisenhower responded. "I have never seen you before, I have done nothing to affect your work, and as long as you live by the rules I shall never do anything but treat you with the same respect as any other faculty member."

Without a word, Lattimore walked out of the office. He continued on at Hopkins, and as McCarthyism became but a painful memory, his notoriety faded. In fact, Eisenhower believed that others on the faculty tended to ignore Lattimore, which, after his having been a cause célèbre, was a blow to his ego. Moreover, he was bypassed for promotion, which left him with an inferior salary. Finally in 1963 Lattimore accepted an offer from Leeds University in England. Eisenhower did not have any regrets.[58]

Lattimore's case was almost unique. Most of the others on the Homewood faculty came to like and respect their president. Eisenhower boasts that a physics professor once told him that he had managed in a few short years to tear down the wall that for decades had separated the faculty from the administration. Eisenhower treated the faculty as individuals, raised their salaries, built new buildings, supported their research, and expressed a genuine interest in their work. Shaffer went so far as to comment that Eisenhower proved to the whole Hopkins community that "you don't have to be a scholar to be scholarly." Indeed, in the opinion of Shaffer, dean of the Homewood schools for a quarter-century, "Eisenhower was the best president Hopkins ever had."[59]

Shaffer spoke for the majority. When Eisenhower announced his imminent retirement in 1966, he received numerous tributes and accolades. Perhaps his most cherished came from George Boas, because Boas was Eisenhower's friend and because Boas epitomized the Hopkins tradition for excellence. He had been at Homewood since 1921, and as a renowned professor of the history of philosophy he was a scholar's scholar. "I was very sorry to read in the [Baltimore] *Sun* on my return from Iowa City recently that you were planning to retire from the presidency of Johns Hopkins," Boas wrote in April.

I have served under six presidents and can honestly say that you have done more for the University than any of your predecessors. It has been a great satisfaction for one who has seen so many of the ups and downs of Hopkins to feel that the institution was in safe hands and prospering. I hope it has been an equal satisfaction to you. You will be swamped with letters of regret, I know, and you must feel no need to acknowledge this one. But I couldn't bring myself to read the news of your resignation and take no notice of it.[60]

Eisenhower was satisfied, albeit never completely. He took pride in the expansion of programs and buildings; in the sense of community and cohesion he fostered; in the administrative reforms; in the recruitment of several hundred new faculty members, the creation of thirteen endowed chairs, and the high rate of faculty retention; and in the tremendous output of scholarship the faculty produced.[61] Yet his relations with the Homewood faculty never quite reached the level that they did with the medical institutions, not to mention with his assistants. Moreover, he remained disappointed that he could not get more of the faculty to apply their undeniable talents enthusiastically to the undergraduate program. "You know," he remarked while trying to recall all the distinguished scholars whom he had gotten to know so well, "I am inclined to think that most of the great ones love to teach."[62]

CHAPTER 14

"When the Light Is On"
The Students at Johns Hopkins

F ew biographies of a university president include a chapter on the president's relations with his student body. In the majority of cases, the biographer would be hard-pressed to stretch a description of the president's relations with the student body over several pages. Eisenhower is exceptional in this regard, and at Hopkins the fondness and concern for students that he had shown at Kansas State and Penn State flourished into a patriarchal relationship. No student was unaware of the tradition that when the light over Eisenhower's library door was on, the president welcomed student visitors. Not all accepted the invitation, but many did. A number came back for a second time and a third, until they and Eisenhower had developed a friendship that defied the age differential. These young men appreciated his vast experience, his patient style of conversation, his self-assurance. Most important, they liked him.

The trustees, his assistants, and the faculty at Hopkins all had profound respect and affection for Eisenhower, and he for them, but it was from his relations with his student friends that he derived his greatest satisfaction. It would be impossible, and irrelevant, to try to determine who got more out of them, Eisenhower or the students. It is safe to say that in his final retirement, when a large number of his contemporaries had passed away, the vast majority of his intimate friends were former students, fifty years his junior.

For his part, Eisenhower had no doubt that he was the prime beneficiary. "It is not unusual for an older person to be interested in young people who are intelligent, thoughtful, and likeable," he wrote a student friend in 1975, "but it is not so common for young persons to be interested in ones my age."[1] He frequently remarked that his association with younger men kept his own mind fresh and active. On one occasion he said of a contemporary, "He's a nice guy, but Christ, he hasn't had a new idea in twenty-five years."[2] Even in his eighties, Eisenhower remains active, both physically and intellectually, which is due, in no small part, to the remarkable rapport he maintains with young people.

"Originally they were not friendly," Eisenhower said of the Hopkins students. "As I walked across campus," he remembered, "I felt an iceberg must be close by." This was to be expected. None of the former presidents and few of the faculty had ever actively sought to talk to undergraduates.[3] The students came from every state of the union and from many foreign countries. Among the academic elite, at least 80 percent of them selected Hopkins with the intention of going into graduate work or professional work in law or medicine; many began doing original research in their junior or senior year.

"Hopkins had a trait," Russell Passarella (who entered in 1966) explained, "that people either very much enjoy or hate. From the day that you walk onto that campus you are treated like a graduate student. Nobody holds your hand, nobody tells you that you have to do this. When I was there they never took attendance. . . . It was 100 percent honor system. They treated you like an adult the day you walked onto the campus." Eisenhower, too, encouraged independence. Nevertheless, Passarella added, "if someone felt lost and was having trouble, he might very well go to Milton to talk about it."[4]

Eisenhower initially tried to melt the iceberg by instituting a program similar to that which he had used at Kansas State and Penn State, a student encampment held at a rural retreat for three days prior to the opening of each academic year. Twenty members of the faculty and thirty or more students would attend. As at its predecessors, students and faculty divided into study groups to discuss problems uppermost in their minds and formulated suggestions for consideration by the student council, faculty governing groups, and the administration. Later Eisenhower hosted these conferences at Evergreen House, a mid-nineteenth-century Italianate mansion on North Charles Street. (The Garretts, founders of the Baltimore & Ohio Railroad, had bequeathed Evergreen House to Hopkins, after which it had been turned into a beautiful cultural center.) Then in 1967 Eisenhower inaugurated a series of monthly coffee hours in the Garrett Room of the Milton S. Eisenhower Library, where a regular exchange of information and views could take place between faculty, administration, and students.[5]

Eisenhower attempted to reach all the students, not just the leaders. Freshman Orientation Week became a major event. Eisenhower started the week off with what Neil Grauer described as a "warm, forceful pep talk" to the incoming class gathered at Shriver Hall. Grauer, a 1965 freshman, recalled "hearing some world-weary upperclassman say it was the 'standard Uncle Miltie speech,' but I was not that cynical and was mighty impressed."[6] Following the convocation, Eisenhower held a reception at the president's house. It was a lovely lawn party with food and drinks served in the living room and in the garden in back. Practically the entire class attended.

Eisenhower had a formal receiving line and, in the view of a former participant, he "made an effort literally to say hello and talk to every freshman that came in."[7] "He had a way of looking at you very intently when you were speaking," another commented, "sometimes with a skeptical eye." He wanted to know where the student came from, what his parents did, what his plans and hopes were.[8]

After the ritual of shaking hands had ended, Eisenhower would go out on the lawn to chat informally with small groups. For as long as three hours he would mingle, constantly talking. "He had in effect a moving press conference with these kids," Ron Wolk remarked.[9] Other administration people were there, along with deans and faculty members, but Eisenhower was the magnet. "I've always loved to watch him work his charm on a gathering," Grauer said. "He is incredibly adept at putting people at ease. You might say that he worked the student crowds like a seasoned campaigner."[10]

The conversations usually concerned politics, especially in the mid-sixties, when so many young people expressed strong feelings about such issues as the civil-rights movement and the war in Vietnam. "I, along with many of my friends, considered ourselves leftwing Democrats, if not socialists, during those years," George Gorse (a freshman in 1968) remarked. As was not unusual for that era, Gorse's relations with his parents were strained, the immediate issues being hair style and attitudes towards the war. ("To my folks, I looked like a tramp, and my political ideas about the war were even quarantined from my brothers and sisters. They told me not to talk about it in the house!") Eisenhower, however, enjoyed the interchange of ideas between two individuals, so long as each showed respect for the other's views. To Gorse's surprise, at their first meeting Eisenhower looked right past the long hair and sloppy clothes and was "a very patient and tolerant listener and counselor towards many of my wild ideas."

Eisenhower further surprised students when he frankly expressed his own views. Like most of the freshmen, Gorse assumed that Eisenhower was a conservative Republican. He prepared himself for a conventional, probably stuffy sermon. Again Eisenhower did not fit the mold. "I immediately found out that he was really a liberal on human rights and civil-liberties issues, while a conservative on fiscal affairs."

"I remembered that he had grave misgivings about the Vietnam War," Gorse went on, "and he was sympathetic towards students who were demonstrating against the war. He was also a fervent supporter of the civil-rights movement, and he spoke many times about the need to educate blacks to get them out of the ghetto. He sounded like a liberal to me, and I was amazed that his words were coming out of an Eisenhower!"[11]

Students who held similar discussions with Eisenhower described Gorse's experience as typical. Russell Passarella said that Eisenhower "was against the Vietnam War from the first day I talked to him," at the freshman reception in September 1966. Nevertheless, Eisenhower told Passarella, he refused to oppose the war in public because he feared that his views would be taken not as "Milton Eisenhower's views but President Eisenhower's brother's views." Eisenhower also indicated that he had no problems with student protests against the war or for civil rights as long as the protests took the form of civil disobedience. But, he emphasized repeatedly to Passarella, "he had no tolerance for the ones who would say 'Now give me amnesty because I am morally right.' Where he really drew the line and lost all sympathy for them was when they said 'I am morally right so don't punish me even if I did something wrong yesterday.'" Eisenhower made it clear, too, that he was against violence under absolutely any circumstances, that he did not mind a student sitting on a lawn but he would not tolerate his disrupting someone else. "In a way he was a classic liberal," Passarella said.[12]

Given Eisenhower's sympathy, tolerance, and openness, students quite naturally turned to him in times of trouble, which in the sixties came all too frequently. Whenever there was a crisis, whether over some act of discrimination against blacks in Baltimore, a drug bust, an escalation of the war in Vietnam, or a political assassination, Eisenhower's home became his young friends' equivalent of a local pub. They felt a need to talk to him, to get his advice, to hear his ideas.

In Baltimore, the most severe crisis developed in the wake of Martin Luther King's murder, when the city erupted in a three-day riot. "We went over to Eisenhower's house," Gorse recollected (Eisenhower had retired by then and lived off campus; students still came to him often),

and I remember how distressed he was. He told us how the assassination, the riots, and the violence were going to put back race relations in our country perhaps a decade. He admired Dr. King and his courage, particularly his convictions about nonviolent political change. And he continuously counseled us to follow the nonviolent road, particularly when the antiwar demonstrations were getting to be uglier and uglier. Confrontation and violence, he said, were always going to be counterproductive. I am not sure that we always believed him.

I remember one story from that visit. Eisenhower told us that his housekeeper and cook, Margie, had broken down, sobbing, when she saw him that evening while Baltimore burned. Margie was black, and I don't think there was ever a person that Eisenhower felt more for. [Margie had lived in Eisenhower's home and done his cooking since his first year at Penn State.] Not in a paternalistic way, but in a human-to-human relationship. Margie actually tried to apologize for the riot, and the actions of her people, as well as pouring out her own grief about Dr. King's death. Eisenhower referred to Margie that day, and his own attempt to console her, as an example of the dangers and emotions of the moment. . . . He counseled us not to lapse back into hatred and violence. I was very touched by the story.[13]

Crisis situations, by definition, are rare. Student visits to Eisenhower's house were not. For example, intuitively attracted to incoming freshmen, he would invite them over on the slightest pretext, for a talk or for dinner or even as overnight guests. Grauer was a fledgling artist (he later became a reporter and cartoonist for the *Baltimore News American*). In the receiving line at the 1965 freshman reception he shook hands with Eisenhower and casually said, "I've drawn a caricature of your brother and I'll draw one of you." Eisenhower grinned and replied, "I'd love to see it." Grauer did the sketch and dropped it off at Homewood House, thinking that would be the end of it.[14]

A few days later he received a letter from Eisenhower: "Goodness," the president wrote, "I do hope I don't appear to be as grim as you have pictured me. We must get better acquainted; perhaps then you will add a trace of a smile to the caricature." He extended an invitation to "stop by my office . . . and set a time when we can get together at my residence."[15] Grauer did, and a warm friendship ensued, one that blossomed as the years went by. Grauer and his roommates would have dinner at Eisenhower's home two or three times a year and entertain him at their apartment an equal number of times.

If Grauer's experience was not universal, neither was it exceptional. On an impulse, Thomas Harris sent Eisenhower a Christmas card one year; two days later he had a letter from Eisenhower inviting him over to the house for cocktails. Harris went. He found Eisenhower's interest in him flattering, Eisenhower's talk about the latest books of Maury Mandelbaum and Alfred D. Chandler fascinating, and Eisenhower's authoritative discussion of several recent School of Medicine publications most impressive.[16] Another student, William Knowles, could not believe that after he first met the president, Eisenhower immediately invited him over for a game of pool.[17] (He had a regulation-size pool table of which he was very proud and on which he played extremely well.) Illustrative of the countless notes Eisenhower wrote (he was old-fashioned about invitations, much preferring letters to phone calls) was a 1965 letter to student Eugene Zeltmann: "I am going to have a cook-out for a few of my student friends at my residence on Tuesday evening, May 18, at 6 p.m. I would be pleased if you could join us. It will be very informal, so sport clothes—even shorts, if it's a hot evening—will be in order. Please let me know if you can come."[18]

Eisenhower would also answer the door himself, a custom much appreciated by his young visitors. He was very dignified in his looks, usually dressed in an impeccable suit and always wearing large glasses, dark plastic on top, rimless on the bottom. The lenses were glittering and thick, magnifying his large brown eyes and emphasizing his academic demeanor. Yet his warm welcome, his unpretentious attitude, and of course that famous Eisenhower grin usually made even the most ill-at-ease student feel at home.[19] And Eisenhower's relaxed manner belied his rather formal appearance. Ross Jones remarked, "Milton's tastes often were simple. . . . For example, he loves chili, and will sit in the back room with somebody and have a bowl of chili, or a hamburger."[20] On these occasions Eisenhower served a more elegant fare, but his style remained simple.

"I learned very quickly not to be shy or nervous around him," one student remarked.[21] As a result, discussions would range from topic to topic. "Spending evenings with Dr. Eisenhower was something of a lesson in American history," Jonathan Krant said. "As an impressionable college student I was a rapt audience at the backgammon table, ball game, or dinner table—listening to the impressions of a cub reporter for the Abilene newspaper back when William Jennings Bryan came stumping through, to the polemics of a Republican anti-inflationist, to a keen observer of Latin American politics."[22] Students soon discovered that Eisenhower loved a good story or joke. Over dinner, however, he generally preferred more serious talk, perhaps because he treasured these opportunities to explore the minds of his youthful friends. Indeed, in Grauer's opinion, "Eisenhower was not one for idle chat. He liked conversation with substance."[23]

Donald Spear of Pennsylvania, John Barksdale of Texas, and Jack Watkins of New England, all freshmen in 1962, became frequent dinner guests. Barksdale was class president that year, which was Eisenhower's excuse for inviting him and his roommates the first time. During their sophomore year, when they no longer had to live in the dorm, the three found an apartment together about a mile from campus. As part of their furnishings, they built bookshelves by stacking plain red bricks and placing boards across them. Construction was booming at Homewood, so they obtained the bricks and boards from the workers on campus. They were proud of their ingenuity.

Eisenhower became one of their favorite guests. One evening when he was over, they told him of their source and joked that they intended to finish their interior decorating by taking some of the lounge chairs from the just-completed Milton S. Eisenhower Library. Eisenhower became terribly upset. He related an incident when he was at Penn State during which some students had stolen something and were caught. Eisenhower had talked with them. He explained that he felt as if they had stolen the items from him personally. Barksdale and his friends protested that they could not understand such an attitude, but "he planted the seed in our brains that if we had any ideas of swiping some furniture for our apartment, we would be taking it from Milton, at least in his opinion, and we shouldn't do it. . . . It certainly was effective. At that point we even felt bad about stealing the bricks." Because of their respect and affection for Eisenhower, the students did not begrudge him any of his views, including those that seemed a bit old-hennish.[24]

The chance to meet Eisenhower and talk with him would have been enough to induce virtually any eighteen- or nineteen-year-old to look forward to a dinner invitation. As an added plus, however, his guests always loved the meals themselves. Eisenhower may have enjoyed a good bowl of chili or a juicy hamburger, but he understood that such dishes comprise virtually a student's entire menu. Therefore he liked to serve something special. He invariably did. Back at Penn State, Helen had tutored Margie in the culinary arts. "I have since traveled through many states and to Europe, Latin America, and South America [sic]," William Knowles remarked, "but the food at Dr. Eisenhower's home was comparable only to that of the best restaurants in which I have eaten."[25] Spear, Barksdale, and Watkins "would skip breakfast and lunch so we would be hungrier and devour all the tremendous food Margie would cook. Milton got a big kick out of that."[26]

Eisenhower also got a kick out of the students' reactions to the dinners, especially when they dined at "Chez the President" for the first time. His invitation, albeit formally written, always stressed the informality of the occasion. Grauer recalled that when he received his initial invitation, he fully expected that they would be eating nothing more elaborate than hot dogs. He even brought along a can of sauerkraut as a gag house gift. He was totally taken aback, therefore, when he found the table set with fine silver and crystal and when Margie produced a feast of Cornish hens with pear halves and wild rice. It took a moment for him to recover, and then he practically inhaled everything put before him.[27]

Eisenhower most enjoyed students who shared his interests, or at least liked to learn about them. In addition to politics, they would discuss painting, opera, or classical music; play backgammon or pool together; or work the crossword puzzles. And they would root together for the Baltimore Orioles. Eisenhower was the number-one fan in the city at the time when the Orioles—with Brooks and Frank Robinson, Jim Palmer, and Earl Weaver, as manager—reigned supreme in baseball. He received a lifetime pass to their games (in fact, to all American League games) made of fourteen-karat solid gold. Often he would invite a student friend to share his box at the game, although always on the condition that all studies were completed. Grauer accepted many such invitations. He witnessed firsthand the Hopkins president jumping to his feet and cheering madly for an Oriole home run. Grauer described Eisenhower as a true fanatic. He would go into a deep depression over an Oriole loss, then become highly elated after a victory.[28]

Another enthusiasm was lacrosse, a sport—the only one—at which Hopkins excelled. Eisenhower attended nearly all the lacrosse games until his mid-seventies, when he had to give it up. "I get too excited," he explained. In other sports, he gave his support simply by being in the stands. Sometimes it was embarrassing. Once when Judge and Mrs. Wilkinson were his guests in Baltimore, Eisenhower took them to a football game. Mrs. Wilkinson was "quite a football fan," and Eisenhower warned her as they took their seats, "If this reminds you of a high school game, please keep it to yourself."[29]

Few people showed up for the football games, in sharp contrast to the lacrosse games. Hopkins had no athletic scholarships and did not charge admission to the games, at the insistence of Wilson Shaffer, who for many years ran the athletic program. Shaffer firmly believed in amateur athletics. In his view, universities and colleges that make money off football games ought to be paying a regular salary to the players, for in effect they "worked" for the school. Shaffer saw to it that Hopkins stayed purely amateur, which meant that, except in lacrosse and, to a lesser extent, swimming, Hopkins teams were uniformly bad.[30]

Eisenhower saw the situation somewhat differently. Although he favored amateur athletics, he felt that the school should have a good football team or none at all. "I have felt all along that we ought to quit football," Eisenhower said during his retirement. "It is the most expensive sport we have. Some of the other sports are so poorly financed that the students have to buy their own shoes and some of their own equipment. . . . In a way I wish I had been more vigorous in expressing myself about it when I was president. Hopkins has no business continuing football."[31] Nevertheless, because of his allegiance to the student participants, he went to games "more than any other president we ever had," Wilson Shaffer remarked, "and sat right there in the stands with us. . . . I think he thought we should charge admission. But he honored me for not doing it and stayed with me all the way."[32]

Another hobby was the cinema. "The students came to know that I liked movies," Eisenhower said, "but didn't want to waste my time on bad ones. So they would 'screen' movies for me, and if they were good, take me to them."[33] One night Russell Passarella and a couple of other students took him to a "half-skin flick." Passarella recalled with a chuckle that Eisenhower, always sensitive about compromising the family name, "had his green coat turned up around his head and his hat down because he didn't want anybody to see him leaving it."[34]

A few years later Eisenhower remarked to Grauer, "You know, I've never been in one of those X-rated bookstores, and I wonder what it's like." Grauer promptly volunteered to take him to one. Eisenhower hesitated. He asked Grauer if there were much chance that he would run into someone he knew. Grauer assured him that the chances were remote, and in the unlikely event that he did, he could undoubtedly count on the friend's not wanting it known that he was there either. Satisfied, Eisenhower let Grauer drive him to an adult bookstore on Charles Street, where "he spent about five or ten minutes browsing through the paperbacks and magazines, grimacing at the contents, finally bursting out laughing."[35]

Naturally Eisenhower's relations with the students went beyond socializing with them. He would provide help where and when he could. He wrote scores of recommendations, and obviously a recommendation from Milton Eisenhower carried a lot of weight, whether in an academic, public-service, or professional field. He would use his influence in other ways, too. When Passarella found a desirable apartment near Homewood, he discovered that the bank that owned it would not rent it to him because he was a student. One night, in the course of a conversation at an Oriole game, he mentioned his problem to Eisenhower. By the next day Passarella had his lease. "If he had confidence in you," Passarella commented, "he was always willing to make that phone call, use the personal contacts, the network that he had, to help you."[36]

Eisenhower drew a fine line between expressing his views and prescribing actions. "All my life I have refrained from offering advice to intelligent young people," he wrote Bill Knowles. "Each person must experience both the pain and joy of solving his own problems; further I have never thought myself to be so wise that I know the answers to others' problems." It was frequently impossible, however, to distinguish between Eisenhower's expressions of opinion and his "advice," and he could be forceful and unbending in his convictions.

In Knowles's case, he did not even consider such semantic subtleties. Knowles's heavy schedule outside of the classroom had brought him to the verge of flunking out of Hopkins. "You have a fine mind," Eisenhower wrote Knowles,

an advanced sense of morality, and the ability to learn quickly. But from my long experience I know how young persons can get so caught up in extra-curricular activities that they can become indifferent in their academic pursuits. The human mind is the greatest asset each of us has. Nothing should prevent its maximum development. One should not be satisfied in doing second or third best. Further, the habits you establish now will be with you throughout your lifetime. So, since what you do means so much to me, I hope you will give greater time to your studies and undertake only those outside activities which a rigorous academic program permits.

Knowles did not resent Eisenhower's tone nor his advice. He rearranged his priorities, took a leave of absence to spend two years abroad as a missionary, and decided on a career in medicine.[37]

After Eisenhower's retirement in 1967, when he moved to 12 Bishops Road, just off the Homewood campus, his contacts with students, if anything, increased. The house itself was pastel yellow, spacious inside and out. Eisenhower filled it with the fine antiques he and Helen had acquired over the years. There were so many mementos from his political and educational careers in the house that one student cracked, "Everything Eisenhower has is engraved. I looked in my drink the other night and one of the ice cubes was a gift from Penn State!" On the walls were fine paintings and, as a special touch, collages of snapshots of Eisenhower's friends. Students would stand for hours before one of those collages, trying to pick out all the famous men Eisenhower had worked with or known in five decades.[38]

"Eisenhower thrives on students," George Gorse, a freshman the year Eisenhower moved into the Bishops Road residence, recalled, "on young people who are filled with ideas, youthful idealism, and purpose (as well as the usual confusion about finding themselves). I was amazed at how much he really listened to you."[39] Eisenhower listened to Gorse a lot. As a freshman, Gorse was, in Eisenhower's words, "something of a trouble-maker." He began experimenting with marijuana. This was not unusual for 1968, but his mother wrote Eisenhower "in great distress." That summer Eisenhower visited some friends at Buck Hill Falls in the Pocono Mountains, not far from Gorse's home. "So I wrote and said 'I am here,'" Eisenhower remembered, "'and I always like to see students. Would you like to come over and have lunch with me?' He came over and we started talking. I didn't mention drugs."[40]

Instead, Eisenhower discussed his recent appointment as chairman of the President's Commission on the Causes and Prevention of Violence. Then, to Gorse's astonishment, Eisenhower asked the eighteen-year-old boy to be his personal assistant, primarily to run documents back and forth between Baltimore and Washington. Gorse accepted and the next day moved to Baltimore to live with Eisenhower on Bishops Road.

"Eisenhower worked his tail off," Gorse commented. "I would bring piles of paper, preliminary reading, reports, and memoranda, back from Washington to him every evening. And he would be up to the wee hours of the morning reading, and discussing the important points over breakfast every morning at 6:30 A.M." Yet what impressed Gorse most, as it had Wolk, was the way in which Eisenhower molded the disparate personalities on the commission together in order to produce a quality report. "Eisenhower is a great leader of men," Gorse felt, "a man with a vision, with ideas of his own, who does not compromise them, while being able to lead, moderate, and bring together others in a common cause."[41]

As will be discussed below, the Nixon administration's failure to act positively on the commission's final report lingers as one of Eisenhower's most bitter disappointments. The effects of the commission's work on Gorse, nevertheless, continue to bring him great satisfaction. "Without my ever saying a word to George," he said with unconcealed pride, "the whole drug thing disappeared. He never touched it again." For his part, Gorse discovered from his experience on the commission that he did not want to be a lawyer. Instead, inspired by a course in the history of art taught by Professor Phoebe Stanton, he transferred to a humanities major. "Eisenhower was delighted. He would talk about how Phoebe Stanton was one of the great professors at the university." Gorse went on to Brown University for graduate work in the history of art. "Eisenhower was always prodding me to finish my Ph.D.," he recollected, which Gorse finally did in 1978.[42] He now teaches art history at Pomona College.

The year of his retirement, the Hopkins students began an annual program, the Milton S. Eisenhower Symposium. Eisenhower enjoyed the honor, and he enjoyed the program itself. In his view, it epitomized what he wanted Hopkins students to become. The symposium is run entirely by undergraduates. They select the topic, finance it, obtain the speakers, and manage all the arrangements. Eisenhower is involved only to the extent that after the students have made all the decisions, he writes a follow-up letter to invited speakers urging them to accept. Often his letter is unnecessary. Eisenhower recalled with great pleasure that C. P. Snow, who spoke in 1972, when the topic was "Creativity: The Moving Force of Society," told him that he had come from England (and the House of Lords) to participate "solely because this was the only student-run program of its type in the world, and he was curious to know how the young people did it."[43]

A student who helped plan the program in 1973, Nelson Block, told a typical Eisenhower story. He was working with his classmate Abram Kronsberg. One day he was walking across the campus wearing tattered blue jeans and a tee-shirt when Kronsberg, who was talking with Eisenhower, saw him and called him over. A bit embarrassed at his appearance, Block went nevertheless. To his surprise, Eisenhower paid no attention whatsoever to his dress. "What impressed me was how readily he accepted students, no matter what they looked like and no matter what the circumstances happened to be." He was also impressed to discover that Eisenhower refused to make any decision about the symposium, "even after we came to him for help." Eisenhower did offer some advice, telling Block that "the success of any meeting depended on the chairman allowing all the active members to take the chairman's ideas and bring them forward as if they were their own."[44] Indeed, the symposium has been a huge success. In addition to Snow, the guest participants in 1972 and 1973 alone include Clive Barnes, Jean Piaget, Nathan Glazer, Aaron Copeland, R. Buckminster Fuller, Barry Commoner, Charles Percy, and Isaac Asimov.[45]

After Margie died in 1975, Eisenhower could no longer maintain his Bishops Road house. He moved first to a town house at Cross Keys, in Rowland Mews, and then to a smaller apartment on North Charles Street. He cannot entertain students as frequently or in such numbers as previously, but he still manages to keep his contacts with the student body. Every year he has a Hopkins undergraduate live at his home, providing free room and board in return for the companionship. They play backgammon together, watch television, chat, prepare their meals, and entertain guests. The students, naturally, bring their friends over to meet the venerable man, listen to his stories and views, and share their experiences with him.

Eisenhower also maintains a voluminous correspondence with former students. Some write once or twice a year, some monthly, some once a week. A few are from Kansas State, a good many from Penn State, most from Hopkins. Eisenhower answers every one, usually within twenty-four hours (he spends a full half-day, five days a week, on this correspondence). Many come to visit, and he puts them up in his guest room, takes them out to dinner and the ball game, or spends the evening talking with them.

Following Eisenhower's cancer surgery in the summer of 1979, Neil Grauer spent the first two weeks of the difficult convalescence at the Cross Keys home. Eisenhower, as all his visitors know, is fond of his pre-dinner cocktails (never more than two, always 1½-ounce drinks, usually Old Fashioneds, never before 5:00 P.M.) and looks forward to them. One day Grauer got home from work at about 4:00 P.M. He began to read the paper, and after about a half an hour he happened to glance up. There was Eisenhower looking at him. Somewhat startled, and concerned, he asked Eisenhower if anything was wrong. Grauer recalled that the slightest of grins appeared on Eisenhower's face. "You know," he replied, "it's five o'clock someplace!" Grauer mixed the drinks.[46]

"All of these students I like," Eisenhower wrote in 1980. "I have become very fond of some. A few I say in all candor I love—love to have them with me, love to get their letters. It is not a grandfather-son or father-son feeling. It is a feeling of deep friendship and mutuality of interests."[47]

A crucial feature of all his relationships is his intense concern about the future of America. He has a sense of urgency about contemporary problems and wants desperately to make a contribution to solving them. He has many messages for today's world (to be recounted in chapter 16) and concentrates on getting them across to his young friends. As George Gorse remarked, "His political concerns are central to his human involvements. . . . He is not only personally involved with students as part of his enjoyment of life but also to pass on his experiences and somehow encourage all of us to carry on the torch."[48]

CHAPTER 15

"Goddammit, If I Had Moved to Palm Springs, This Wouldn't Be Happening!"

Retirement and Return

In 1967, when he was nearly sixty-eight years old, Eisenhower retired from the presidency of Johns Hopkins. He had stayed on past the age of normal retirement because he had wanted to be sure that the university was at a healthy plateau when he left.

It was. Hopkins had the fourth highest salary level in the United States, and every important faculty position had been filled. Eisenhower's administration had supervised the institution of many innovative programs that attracted students from among the best in the nation. The prestige of both the Homewood and East Baltimore campuses had never been higher. Over the decade Hopkins had built and paid for $75 million worth of buildings. The endowment had been doubled, the income tripled.

"The place was in apple-pie order," Eisenhower emphasized.[1]

Eisenhower refused to have anything to do with the selection of his successor. He knew that the board of trustees had such confidence in him that it would certainly select any man he named. But unlike the situation at Penn State, where he groomed Eric Walker, he would be unfamiliar with the new man, and "if he turns out to be bad, it is my fault, and yet I am not there to do a damn thing about it." There was also a higher principle involved. In Eisenhower's view, "there is no greater responsibility that the trustees have than to select a president, and if he is good support him to the hilt, and fire him if he isn't."[2]

The man the board selected, after a seven-month search that began with a list of 150 names, was Lincoln Gordon, at the time an assistant secretary of state. "On paper," Eisenhower said later, "this man looked perfect." Gordon had a Ph.D. from Oxford, had been a Rhodes scholar, and had written the critically acclaimed book, *The Public Corporation in Great Britain*. Including a prestigious chair, he had held three professorships at Harvard, one in economics, another in international affairs, and a third in government. He had been a close friend of John F. Kennedy, who had made him ambassador to Brazil; and then Johnson had appointed him as assistant secretary of state for inter-American affairs. He had handled executive duties, personnel duties, and financial duties dealing with large sums of money. Except for working with a faculty and raising money from foundations and other private sources, Gordon had experience in the areas most important to a university president.

Before Gordon accepted the position, the trustees came to Eisenhower to say that their selection was thinking it over and to ask whether Eisenhower would please talk to him. Eisenhower invited Gordon to the president's house for dinner, "and I spent the evening just telling him about the university, what we were doing and what things I saw needed to be done in the future. And I have no doubt that I painted things in pretty glowing terms." Eisenhower was convincing, especially when he promised to try to persuade Charles Garland, chairman of the board, and Thomas Turner, of the School of Medicine, to remain at their posts one more year to help in the transition. Both Garland and Turner agreed, and Gordon accepted.

Due to Eisenhower's initiative, Gordon inherited a specific long-range plan. In 1964, as he had begun to think seriously about retirement, Eisenhower had asked the faculty to nominate members for a committee that would draw up a program for the future. The faculty had done so, and Eisenhower had named William McElroy, head of the biology department, as chairman. Eisenhower had also put his assistant Ron Wolk on the committee "to keep it straight on finances."[3]

The McElroy Committee held more than a hundred meetings over the next two years before submitting its report. In the booming academic market of the sixties, it was perhaps inevitable that the report called for expansion, aggressive expansion. For example, its recommendations included an increase in the Homewood faculty of 140 positions, without a proportionate rise in student enrollment. Similarly, in order to cope with the growing complexity of higher education, the university administration would also be significantly enlarged. Eisenhower, Shaffer, and others were unhappy. Shaffer commented that McElroy was "probably my closest friend on the faculty" (the two men played pocket billiards nearly every day after lunch at the Hopkins Club). But McElroy had come to

Hopkins following World War II, and he represented the thinking that Shaffer so strongly opposed. In the dean's words, "McElroy wanted bigness." Shaffer believed that McElroy and his committee essentially had gone to department after department asking, "How many people do you want?" Most had replied, "About twice what we have now." The report reflected this growth philosophy.[4]

McElroy handed in his report just as Eisenhower was leaving office. A morass of harmful confusion resulted. No one ever officially accepted or approved it; indeed, according to Eisenhower, the trustees "never even heard of it." Eisenhower himself agreed with Shaffer that expansion was inharmonious with Hopkins's history and traditions, but he felt that he should leave it to Gordon to decide what to do with it.[5] Quite possibly, however, Gordon received the impression that Eisenhower at least agreed with the basic thrust of the report—after all, he had created the committee that wrote it. The fact remains that whereas Eisenhower disapproved of the report, Gordon, in what proved to be a monumental mistake, began at once to implement it.

Gordon undoubtedly thought he was acting in Hopkins's best interest. McElroy's committee certainly thought so. Moreover, as the new president, he undoubtedly wanted to leave his own stamp on the university, to do something different from what Eisenhower had done. Unfortunately, not only did Gordon follow a man who had acquired something akin to legendary status on the campus but he came onto the scene as the leader at an especially difficult time. According to Steven Muller, the trustees had "told him [Gordon] something that no board should ever tell an incoming president": that the bulk of the fund-raising had been done, which was why they wanted a scholar as Eisenhower's successor.[6] But the fund-raising at a private institution is never done. To add to Gordon's problems, the stock market broke just as he came to Baltimore. It is relatively easy to raise money in a rising market—and the market rose throughout almost all of Eisenhower's years at Hopkins—but it is nearly impossible when the market falls, since the donor derives few, if any, tax benefits from giving large blocks of stock that are worth less when he gives them than when he bought them. All of which meant that Gordon was rapidly expanding the faculty and staff at precisely the same time that gifts were decreasing.

In addition, Hopkins had a centennial anniversary scheduled for 1976. Everyone agreed that a major drive to increase the endowment should be undertaken in connection with the anniversary, but Eisenhower considered it only appropriate to leave the planning and implementation to his successor. The Gordon administration began gearing up for the drive by increasing the staff. He paid generous salaries as he added people to the administration's payroll, but essentially they had to sit and wait for the campaign to get under way. This meant much higher costs without a corresponding rise in income.[7]

To make matters worse, Gordon took over from Eisenhower at just the moment when the student unrest, even at notoriously apolitical Hopkins, had escalated exponentially. Many observers could hardly believe their eyes when about three thousand students and sympathizers marched through Wyman Quadrangle on Vietnam Moratorium Day. It had become *de rigueur* among students, and some faculty, to be suspicious of *any* administration.

Most Hopkins veterans, however, believed that Eisenhower would have handled student activism differently from, and better than, Gordon. In contrasting the two men, Passarella commented that "the first, and probably most major, difference was that Milton was never surprised, because Milton knew everything that was going on. He would find out by talking with so many students and faculty members."

Passarella related an incident to illustrate his point. It had to do with the question of governance, described by the *Johns Hopkins Journal* as "the top issue on the Homewood campus."[8] The issue boiled down to the extent to which graduates and undergraduates should participate in university decisionmaking. The specific catalyst for the crisis was the Hopkins calendar. Following a longstanding tradition, the calendar began on October 1, and students took their final exams for the fall semester after the Christmas break. For years the students had asked to start school earlier so they could finish exams before Christmas. Then in the spring of 1970, with emotions already running high over controversies concerning military recruitment and R.O.T.C., the student council issued an ultimatum—if the university did not adopt a new calendar in time for the next year, the students would strike.

Passarella was president of the student council. He went to see Gordon. When he could not get an appointment after several attempts, he simply barged into the president's office. "Gordon went through his usual routine, which was to take off his glasses, take out his handkerchief and start to wipe his glasses and talk for half an hour." Passarella told Gordon that all he wanted him to do was promise to take up the issue of the calendar with the Faculty Assembly.

After some equivocation, Gordon said that he supported a calendar change but under no circumstances would he bow to a student threat. Passarella argued that the issue itself, not the way the students presented it, was what mattered. They engaged in a rather heated debate for more than an hour, until Gordon finally agreed to allow Passarella to make his case before the board and the Faculty Assembly. Eventually the students obtained the change, but their perception was that Gordon had let them down, or at least had not paid sufficient attention to their interests. In Passarella's judgment, "Eisenhower would have sensed a lot earlier that this was an issue whose time had come. He would have moved things along faster, so there probably would have been a decision earlier and the whole issue would never have reached the point it did."[9]

There is no proof to substantiate Passarella's assertion. Eisenhower may not have been able to avert the confrontation, and Gordon did side with the student position. Unquestionably, nevertheless, the new president acted differently than his predecessor. Eisenhower had gained their trust, their respect. Those were valuable commodities for a university president in the turbulent 1960s. To weather the crisis ahead, Gordon would have had to earn the same trust and respect, and the incident over the calendar did not help his cause. Eisenhower developed his reputation over eleven years. Gordon would not have the luxury of that much time.

Compounding Gordon's problems further were the sweeping changes that took place at the highest levels of the university. Longtime provost P. Stewart Macaulay had died shortly before Gordon took office. Shaffer left the administration the same year that Eisenhower did. And a year after Gordon took over, Garland retired from the board. Because of his expertise, dedication, and relationship with the former president, Garland's retirement was practically as critical as Eisenhower's. In the opinion of one board member, "The trustees had been lulled into a sense that you don't really have to worry about very much because those two guys at the head of the table take care of everything.'" Garland's successor, Robert D. H. Harvey, did not have Garland's experience or charisma. "Everything ended at the same time, and unfortunately it landed in Lincoln Gordon's lap."[10]

The lap was not big enough to carry the load—perhaps no one's would have been. Eisenhower described Gordon as "an extremely nice gentleman."[11] He was rather slim, with a high forehead, gray hair, large horn-rimmed glasses, a sharp nose, thin lips, and a wide mouth. But Gordon's most recognizable trait had nothing to do with his physical appearance. What distinguished Gordon was that he liked to talk. He talked incessantly, to the point that stories about his chatter at inopportune times spread across the campus.

To illustrate, shortly after Gordon arrived, he called Shaffer on the telephone to ask him to stop by the president's office for a visit. "I came over," Shaffer recalled, "and his opening comment was, 'They tell me if I want to understand Johns Hopkins I should listen to you.' And I was there for an hour and I don't think I said three sentences."[12] Alfred Chandler remembered having lunch at the Hopkins Club one day with some other experienced faculty whom Gordon had called together in order to get their views. Gordon joined them and "talked away. When it was all over we looked at each other and said, 'What was that?' He didn't ask us how we were doing, how funds were, anything like that." The difference between Gordon and Eisenhower, Chandler said in summary, was that "one would listen and act on what he heard, the other would act without listening."[13]

But in the final analysis, Gordon's problems were financial. During his first years in office the faculty in Arts and Sciences increased by approximately seventy professors, with most of the money coming from the reserves left by the preceding administration. The budget for fund-raising rose from $325,000 when Eisenhower left to $1,250,000. Gordon almost doubled the number of administrative personnel, from 150 to 297. Whereas, for example, under Eisenhower the provost's office consisted of the provost and his secretary, under Gordon there was a provost, an assistant to the provost, and an associate provost, each with his own secretary. And whereas Eisenhower had had a part-time dean of students, Gordon had eleven full-time people in that office. All in all, from fiscal year 1967 through fiscal year 1971 total university expenditures rose by nearly $11 million.

Thus, Hopkins raised comparatively less money under Gordon than under Eisenhower, while spending in some areas three times as much. The result was inevitable. By fiscal year 1969 the surplus had turned into a deficit of $530,000. By 1971 that deficit had reached a staggering $4.2 million, a figure to which Eisenhower's accountants later added $800,000 more.[14] When Gordon realized how large a deficit he had produced, he took immediate, drastic, and unexpected action: he ordered a freeze on salaries and a cutback in faculty.

That decision, in late 1970, predictably aroused great consternation among the faculty. Senior members told Gordon that if he cut back the size of the administrative staff first, to show his good faith, they would cooperate. Gordon convened the faculty as a whole and vigorously justified the expansion of the administration that had taken place. He contended that there were no staff positions he could cut, so he would stick to his decision to freeze faculty salaries and eliminate faculty positions.

The faculty had had enough. En masse it revolted. The professors formed a committee of some of their most distinguished members. The committee wrote chairman of the board Harvey saying that it wished to discuss with the board the dangers to the university if Gordon continued in office.

With growing dismay, Eisenhower watched these developments from his home at 12 Bishops Road. Not once did Gordon come to him for advice or help. The former president depended on old friends in the administration and on the faculty, as well as the stream of student visitors, to keep him up-to-date on campus events. He suffered privately through it all, making no public comment, never criticizing Gordon, even in private. He hated to see the reserve fund he had built up over the years disappear, seemingly overnight; he hated even more to see a deficit develop. But he kept quiet.

Then, shortly after the beginning of the 1971 spring semester Harvey paid him a visit, a copy of the faculty committee's letter demanding Gordon's resignation in hand. Eisenhower recalled, "He came tearing over and said, 'What do we do?' "

Eisenhower responded, "Well, as a matter of principle you never see anyone under the president unless they come to you through the president. So tell the committee to see the president first."

Harvey so instructed the professors, and the faculty committee went to see Gordon. Insulated from the university community, he had been unaware how deeply its dissension and concern ran. On March 12, 1971, he submitted his resignation to the board, effective in June unless a successor could be found earlier. According to Eisenhower, Gordon recommended that the board appoint "a young and vigorous man" to meet the challenge of the presidency of Hopkins.[15]

The board accepted Gordon's resignation but not his recommendation. No sooner had the March 12 announcement been made than an overwhelming sentiment surged throughout the Hopkins community to bring Eisenhower back. A committee of trustees, headed by Harvey, virtually marched to Bishops Road to ask Eisenhower to return. Harvey pleaded the case. He said that no one else had the experience and knowledge of Hopkins to step in cold and put the university's affairs back in order. The trustees did not expect Eisenhower to come back indefinitely. They hoped only that he would agree to serve on an interim basis, until the budget could be turned around and a new president found. At this point Eisenhower replied with the query, quoted in chapter 1, "Do you want me to return in a wheelchair?"[16]

They would have taken him back on a stretcher. Faculty flocked to Bishops Road to urge—even beg—Eisenhower to accept. So did students. It became a nuisance. More important, he resented the request. Over drinks one afternoon he growled to Neil Grauer, "Goddammit, if I had moved to Palm Springs, this wouldn't be happening!"[17] As Eisenhower explained years later, since his retirement he had led a very active, and contented, life. He had his many business and cultural interests, he still served on thirteen boards and a host of committees, and he had begun work on a book of memoirs. Moreover, Eisenhower had his reputation to protect. When asked if he felt frustration and anger because Hopkins could not get along without him, or tremendous pride and satisfaction that he had proved to be indispensable, he asserted,

Neither one. I was selfish. I was almost seventy-two years old. I wasn't as agile as I once was, didn't have the stamina and energy. I knew that I had left one of the best records that Hopkins had ever had. Many mean things had to be done, fine people let go, drastic cuts made. My overpowering feeling was, if I go back I'll ruin everything I've ever done as far as my own personal standing at the institution is concerned. It never occurred to me otherwise.

And I thought that was asking a good deal. But as I realized that there was no one else that I knew of who could do it, because it had to be done quickly and therefore you had to know the place intimately, both [sic] personnel and finance and organization, I said, "All right. The institution is more important than any one individual. I'll go back." But I assure you that when I went back I thought that was going to be the end of Milton Eisenhower's reputation.[18]

Most contemporary Americans have become much too cynical to accept at face value Eisenhower's explanation of why he agreed to go back. And indeed, he had repeatedly evidenced his susceptibility to flattery, had an undeniably large ego, and always felt supremely confident about his abilities. Nevertheless, in this case the task before him appeared almost insurmountable, and Eisenhower had always jealously guarded his reputation. In this context, it is instructive to note that the reasons for his reluctance closely paralleled the arguments he presented in opposing his brother's candidacy for a second term as president fifteen years before. Ike, too, had not wanted to jeopardize his reputation. He, too, had wanted to retire, believing he had for decades done all anyone could ask of one individual. Yet Ida and David Eisenhower had instilled in all their sons a sense of duty barely comprehensible outside a devoutly religious household in the rural heartland of America.

Before agreeing to go back, however, Eisenhower exacted a price. "They would have agreed to anything, and I knew they would," he said later. He wanted the board to be broadened to represent a wider spectrum. He wanted a recent faculty member who had the trust of the faculty put on the board. He also wanted a woman on the board. Finally, the most unusual demand, he wanted two recent graduates appointed to the board to represent student opinion, with two more elected later. "I think a few of them thought it was crazy," Eisenhower recalled, but they agreed. In short order, the addition of such standouts as Dr. Marjorie G. Lewisohn, Alfred D. Chandler, Jr., Russell Passarella, and Steven Mahinka transformed the Hopkins board forever.[19]

Harvey announced Eisenhower's decision at a press conference on March 25, 1971, and on Monday, April 5, the "new" president took office. He immediately began making cuts in almost every budgetary category. He made no exceptions. He even pared down his own salary to a third of Gordon's, and saved tens of thousands of dollars by simply eliminating a line in the projected budget for the purchase of new furniture for the administration building. "We can use the old stuff," Eisenhower ruled. After a week of intensive work, Eisenhower went before the Hopkins community, gathered in Shriver Hall, to inform the members of his actions and intentions. The enthusiastic response he received cheered him greatly; he was beginning to think that perhaps this return to duty would not be so bad after all. Already, his reassumption of the presidency had become known on campus as the Second Coming.[20]

That feeling strengthened at an early meeting of the trustees. One of Eisenhower's greatest disappointments during his first term at Hopkins had been his failure to expand Levering Hall into a true student union. When he returned to his post, the trustees "personally reached down in their pockets and gave me $1.5 million and said, 'You do with this what you please. This is for coming back.'" Eisenhower hired an architect to start planning a student union, feeling that the act would show right from the start his commitment to the students' interests. He knew that it would cost more money than Hopkins then had available for capital expansion (" Going ahead with the union was a very gutsy venture," according to Eisenhower's successor), but he did not doubt that he could raise the rest of the money. He did. Eisenhower never forgot where the seed money came from: "I must say, God bless those trustees," he said in summarizing the building of the student union.[21]

In his efforts Eisenhower received incalculable assistance from his new provost. At the end of his tenure, Gordon, after a nationwide search, had hired Steven Muller, of Cornell, to replace the retired William Bevan. Eisenhower talked with Muller before accepting the presidency and persuaded him to agree to so arrange his affairs in Ithaca as to allow him to take up his new duties at the same time that Eisenhower assumed office.

Eisenhower was—and remains—tremendously impressed by Muller. Another Rhodes Scholar with a Ph.D. in political science, Muller was only forty-three years old. He had the looks of a movie actor—sharp facial features, dark hair, an athletic frame, and an abundance of energy—and brains. He had been largely responsible for cooling down an explosive situation at Cornell: as vice-president for public affairs there, he had played a key role in defusing the black students who had emerged from the occupation of Willard Straight Hall carrying rifles and wrapped in bandoleers.

For his part, Muller recalled from his first meeting with Eisenhower, "I found myself tremendously impressed by him. I knew that Milton was venerated on this campus, and he would have the skill to do what needed to be done in the short run to calm everybody down. I immediately got the feeling that I could talk with total candor to him, that I was talking to someone whom I could count on, and who knew what needed doing and would do it, because he had the strength, the experience, and the guts." Furthermore, "he had a marvelous ability to decide what was right and then do it."[22]

Eisenhower and Muller made a formidable team, the kind Eisenhower had grown accustomed to at Hopkins. Together, they slashed away at Gordon's budget, raised money, traveled to talk to alumni and other groups, cut the staff, and carefully monitored faculty attrition. In ten months they obtained nearly $4 million from twelve corporations and foundations and more than $1 million from the state of Maryland. An excited alumni contributed a record roll call of another $1,251,400. Along with other grants and private gifts, the administration reduced the deficit for the 1972 fiscal year to less than $1.8 million, and by fiscal 1973 it had fallen to $700,000. Eisenhower's reputation was preserved forever. Now, in addition to the Eisenhower Library and the Eisenhower Symposium, the trustees established the Milton S. Eisenhower gold medal, awarded to those individuals who have made outstanding contributions to the welfare of the university.[23]

Of course, the literal resurrection of Hopkins pleased Eisenhower equally, as did the cooperative spirit of the community. Everyone pitched in to help. With the student body, Eisenhower immediately renewed his open-house policy, and in the evenings he frequently had as many as twenty-five students at his home discussing the problems. One of the most explosive discussions, as the Vietnam War ground on, concerned the Applied Physics Laboratory, which was institutionally connected to Hopkins but had no relationship to the educational program. Instead, APL carried on research for the government, much of it related to the military. During Gordon's tenure APL became a natural target for protests against the war, with students demanding that Hopkins sever all ties with it, or at least convert it to "socially useful" activities. Eisenhower met on a regular, if informal, basis with the students, carefully explaining to them the work APL had done in World War II, the role it had played in defeating the Nazis, and its nonmilitary functions, such as the development of satellite instrumentation, medical research, and so on. Eisenhower could not satisfy all the protesters. However, he commented, "if there was a diminution of criticism over Hopkins and APL, and I think there was, I think frankly I was using up some of my credit that I had built up with the students over an eleven-year period."[24]

Eisenhower also had to deal with the potentially paralyzing problem of restoring the board's confidence in the institution. His solution was simply to do exactly what he had done during his first administration. His conduct amazed Muller. Eisenhower, accompanied by Ross Jones, would handle all the business in an efficient, fast-paced, two-hour meeting.[25] Alfred Chandler, elected to the board at Eisenhower's insistence, pointed out that Eisenhower would not recommend anything to the board that he did not feel strongly about, nor would he make his recommendation if he foresaw substantial opposition. When he did sense opposition, he would convene the opponents in his office beforehand for a private chat. Once at the formal meeting, he would make sure that each trustee fully understood the proposal, and then he would firmly recommend its approval. The board eagerly accepted Eisenhower's lead, and its confidence was restored. Chandler, with his unique perspective on Gordon's resignation and Eisenhower's return to office, remarked that there "is no way anyone else could have done what Milton did. He had the confidence of the faculty. He had the contacts. . . . I can't imagine anybody who could have done it better than Milton."[26]

Wilbert Locklin, following the events from the president's office at Springfield College, recollected that "Milton astounded the world of higher education with the speed with which he put the place back together, and the thoroughness with which he did it . . . . He proved twice that you can run an institution properly."[27]

When Eisenhower returned to Hopkins in April of 1971 he advised the trustees that he intended to stay on for one year only. And this time, almost unconsciously, he involved himself in the selection of his successor. By the fall of 1971 he and Steve Muller had worked closely enough, and over a long enough period of time, that he could be certain that Muller was the perfect choice for the leadership of Hopkins, just as he had been certain of Walker at Penn State. "We did develop kind of a tutorial relationship," Muller commented about the spring of 1971, "which I vastly enjoyed. I don't think Milton ever planned it that way. He had more important things on his mind than bringing along Steve Muller." At the end of the year, with the crisis over, Eisenhower told Muller that he hoped very much that he would be his successor. He was not quite so explicit with the trustees, but he did not disguise his confidence in and respect for his second in command. On January 20, 1972, the board elected Muller the tenth president of Johns Hopkins. "And," Eisenhower remarked, "that was the end of it."[28]

He had feared that coming back to Hopkins as the oldest university president in the nation would be, if not a disaster, at least damaging to his reputation. Instead, his reputation rose to a new pinnacle. He had feared that slashing away at the budget would make him many enemies, that it would cause people to resist his efforts at balancing the budget or otherwise sabotage his efforts. Instead, he became more popular than ever. In looking back at the entire episode, Eisenhower concluded, "When I think of the wonderful cooperation I received from students and faculty and staff who hated some of the things we had to do (and I hated them too), with never a peep of criticism from anybody, never a confrontation, it just makes me happy."[29]

CHAPTER 16

"Democracy Contains the Seeds of Its Own Destruction"

On the State of the Union

*T*his chapter constitutes a distillation of Eisenhower's views on a cross section of contemporary issues. In order for it to most accurately reflect his thinking, we have, almost exclusively, paraphrased or quoted directly Eisenhower's own words.

Eisenhower's last ten-month tenure as president cf Johns Hopkins was probably the most satisfying period of his exceptionally satisfying life. He had demonstrated to the university community, to the world of higher education, and, by extension, to the entire nation that by careful direction and management America's fundamental institutions, even those on the brink of collapse, can be restored to their former vitality and made to prosper. He had also demonstrated that Americans, when provided with proper leadership, retain their capacity to act cooperatively and resourcefully in order to overcome whatever crisis they confront. Hence, to Eisenhower, those ten months encapsulated what he believed to be the American experience. They epitomized the values instilled in him as a boy in Abilene, values he had sought to instill in others throughout his half-century career in government and education.

Nevertheless, now into his eighties, Eisenhower is no longer as optimistic about the future of the country. It is impossible to spend long periods of time with him, to listen to his speeches, or to read his recent writings without noting a distinct sense of disillusionment, if not outright anger. Eisenhower has remarked on several occasions that as a youth he could

240

not understand a phrase that he believes was written by de Tocqueville: "Democracy contains the seeds of its own destruction." Eisenhower thought of it often as he matured intellectually and politically, and now, some sixty years later, he thinks that he finally understands. He fears that de Tocqueville may have been all too correct, that the American way of life that he so devotedly championed is, indeed, perilously close to destruction.[1]

Once he had left the Hopkins presidency in the capable hands of Steven Muller, Eisenhower, again with Wolk's assistance, returned to the project of writing his memoir. Actually, to use *memoir* to describe *The President Is Calling* is somewhat misleading. Published in 1974, it does cover his association with the eight presidents he served, from Coolidge through Nixon, and it is replete with personal anecdotes. Yet Eisenhower envisaged the book more as a vehicle to advance his recommendations for governmental reform. To his lasting disappointment, it received scant attention beyond the scholarly community, evidently because Watergate exposés dealing with the abuses of power attracted greater public interest than a study concerned with the legitimate and effective uses of that power. Notwithstanding this neglect, Eisenhower regards the difficulties inherent in the governmental machinery as one of the most insidious "seeds" in the potential destruction of American democracy, and he has continued his own crusade. In his view, immediate change is imperative.

Because the presidency is the hub of the U.S. political system, and because Eisenhower worked for more presidents than any other man in the nation's history, his program for reform quite naturally begins in the Oval Office (see appendix B). Having intimately watched the modern presidency develop into an octopuslike complex, he unhesitatingly maintains that "the moment a president is inaugurated he faces an impossible task."[2] He contends that the responsibilities devolving upon the office by the constitution, the endless number of laws, and, especially, the mandates of tradition are beyond the capacities of any individual, no matter how able or robust. As Eisenhower wrote in an article syndicated for *Projects in Education* in 1979, "Our political and governmental structures have simply not been reformed to keep pace with the amazing and dramatic changes of the past century in this nation, and this world.... We are foolish and naive to expect the man in the White House, whoever he may be, to solve problems that we do not fully understand and cannot agree on."[3] Although proud of the fact, he is painfully aware that his older brother has been the only president to serve two full terms in office since the passage of the Twenty-second Amendment. He perceives the defeat of Jimmy Carter as the latest example of America's propensity "to chew up and spit out another of its presidents."[4] Eisenhower does not doubt that many of Carter's problems were of his own making. He emphasizes, nonetheless, that the successive failures of both Republican and Democratic administrations underscore the need to reform the electoral process and reorganize the presidential office.[5]

Eisenhower recoils at the oft-repeated charge that his brother overdelegated his authority. Of course part of his ire stems from filial devotion. But another, larger part pertains to his incomparable perspective on the presidency. At least from the time of Franklin Roosevelt, with the evolution of the so-called modern presidency, Eisenhower observed the U.S. president becoming increasingly inundated with what he considers trivia: signing his name some thirty thousand times a year, greeting groups daily in the Rose Garden, arbitrating interagency disputes, ruling on what air carrier should fly where, to list a relative few. He has witnessed each administration generate more and more papers for "the President's eyes only" and seen them gather more and more dust. President Eisenhower, Milton argues, should have been able to delegate even more of his duties, freeing him to concentrate on those responsibilities most critical to the nation. And compared with the contemporary period, he points out, the 1950s were placid.

Eisenhower abhors the concept of an imperial presidency, and he never shared his brother's enthusiasm for Richard Nixon (Ike did have certain reservations about his vice-president). Still, he did support certain elements of the Nixon reorganization plans, elements which to some extent evolved from Eisenhower's own work with Nelson Rockefeller and Arthur Flemming on the President's Advisory Council on Government Organization in the 1950s. President Eisenhower created PACGO, and Milton served on it for eight years, because both believed fervently that the president, as an institution, required help. Every PACGO proposal was approved. Yet Milton felt in the 1950s, and feels even more strongly now, that more assistance is needed. Basically, he advocates that the principal Cabinet and agency heads charged with implementing executive policy be involved in all deliberations leading to the final decisions.

This recommendation is much more complicated than it may appear. Even with meetings of the Cabinet, the National Security Council, and other advisory organs, the president must rely extensively on his personal staff to coordinate facts from scores of diverse sources in order to keep himself adequately informed. "The trouble with this procedure," Eisenhower posits, "is that Washington protocol—the pecking order— has rigid requirements." Having been a government bureaucrat and a presidential confidant, Eisenhower knows that most White House assistants must work through their counterparts in a department or agency.

Thus they often bring back to the president information or proposals that do not reflect the thinking of, for example, a Cabinet secretary. This leads not only to inefficiency but also, with increasing frequency, to mixed communications and, worse, disloyalty.

Eisenhower's solution, the same as he and his brother advanced decades earlier, is for the president to appoint two supra-Cabinet officials removable only by him but subject to Senate approval and not in line for succession. They would hold the title of executive vice-president, one for international affairs and the other for domestic affairs. This rank would enable them to work directly with the appropriate secretaries and directors, not their subordinates. Moreover, they would have sufficient stature for the president to delegate to them many of the more trivial duties that consume his time. Existing top advisers cannot handle the assignment, Eisenhower explains, because they are already overburdened trying to supervise their own bureaucratic empires and implement policy. In addition, their authority is statutorily limited. As for entrusting the responsibility to the elected vice-president, Eisenhower is quick to indicate that no organizational chief will delegate extensively to someone he cannot discharge. The supra-official must be an arm of the president, not a competitor or opponent, a situation Eisenhower observed many times during his scores of years around the White House.

Eisenhower suggests a number of other reforms, including the line veto, prohibition of legislative riders, and granting to the president permanent authority to reorganize the executive office, unless disapproved by majorities of both the Senate and House. But he adamantly believes that none of his recommendations would resolve the problem of government without a concomitant reform of the process by which officials are initially elected. It should be recalled that despite Eisenhower's lengthy association with Washington, and despite his overused disclaimer that "some of my best friends are ..." (in fact, he is very close to senators Charles Percy and Charles Mathias), he has never felt comfortable with politicians. And in recent years he has become even more convinced "that elected federal officials have become so enamored with reelection that they often seek it at the expense of truly remedial legislation. They vote, not for what is right, but for what will cause their constituents to keep them in office."

This critique of the most fundamental feature of the democratic process has led Eisenhower to devote a large portion of his retirement years to campaigning for electoral change. Beginning with *The President Is Calling*, he has vigorously advocated the enactment of a constitutional amendment that would limit the terms in office of not just the president but also senators and representatives (one six-year term, two six-year terms, and three four-year terms, respectively). Eisenhower is too sophisticated to view the passage of such an amendment, or amendments, as an instant panacea—some elected officials will always cater to particular pressure groups—but he does feel that it would ameliorate what he considers an unmitigated evil: the quest for "electoral immortality." "Public officials," he remarks, "would then be taking a temporary leave from their regular professions or businesses in order to contribute as best they can to the general welfare of the nation, later returning to their private efforts."

Like many of Eisenhower's recommendations, his proposal of a constitutional amendment to limit tenure in office is neither novel nor radical. He concedes that he has borrowed many of his ideas from leading political scientists and even from the founding fathers. Similarly, he does not claim originality when he takes his critique one step farther. Citing such prominent scholars as Aaron Wildavsky and Nelson Polsby, Eisenhower began the twenty-first chapter of his memoir with the aphorism "A society which insists on running its quadrennial conventions like circuses should not be surprised to get tightrope walkers as presidential candidates." Eisenhower attended some half-dozen Republican conventions, twice as a delegate, each time becoming increasingly convinced that their endemic confusion and carnivallike atmosphere perverted the very purpose of the nominating process. The convention is a sham, a transparent charade. Individual positions on the issues are ignored, the party platform virtually forgotten. If the desire for reelection compromises the convictions of the candidates, the conventions practically dictate that they never express them in the first place. "Believe me," Eisenhower once commented, "a prize fight has as much dignity and thought as any of the conventions I have attended."[6]

Eisenhower rejects the notion that primaries provide the solution. Emphasizing that the United States possesses a representative, not democratic, form of government, he argues that the public should elect delegates to the conventions with the same care that it—at least theoretically—elects officials. These delegates should then vote their preferences without any prior restrictions. Moreover, all candidates should be required to participate actively throughout the convention, as opposed to relying on their representatives on the floor. All should present their views before the balloting begins, both in prepared speeches and in response to questions posed by a select panel of delegates. "At the end of that period," Eisenhower concludes, "delegates and the public generally would know more about the relative merits of candidates than they ever did in history."

When Eisenhower starts to talk about the need to reform the political

process, to revamp the executive office, or otherwise to revitalize governing institutions he becomes visibly agitated. One cannot help but sense
that he feels betrayed, not by the American public but by its leaders. One
gets the impression that he is personally hurt by what he sees going on in
Washington. It is as if his nation, his system, and his way of life, all that
he was taught to cherish in Abilene, which he spent so many years trying
to serve, selflessly he believes, has been led astray. He sermonizes, he
lectures; at times he sounds like a broken record of platitudes. Yet his
sincerity is obvious. Eisenhower's criticisms and proposals may not be
startling. They are, nevertheless, legitimate, and equally important, they
reflect the thoughts of an eighty-two-year-old unabashed patriot who is
genuinely concerned about, and fearful for, future generations. "The more
politically sophisticated among us will no doubt think me naive in making
some of these recommendations," Eisenhower wrote of himself and his
program for reform. "I will admit only to being somewhat idealistic. And I
am convinced that because we so often confuse idealism with naiveté, we
frequently accept what *can* be instead of pursuing what *should be*."[7]

Eisenhower's pessimistic view of the government, in particular the
modern presidency, haunts him constantly. He is equally concerned with
the economy (see appendix C). Yet the issue to which he is most emotionally attached and to which he has devoted the most time since his retirement is that of violent crime in America (see appendix D). Before taking
on the chairmanship of Johnson's National Commission on the Causes
and Prevention of Violence, Eisenhower had not paid much attention to
crime. He had not wanted the commission's chairmanship. Like many
Americans, he considered the rising rate pitiful—and then left it to others
to find a solution. However, after working with the commission for a
year and a half; after drawing on the knowledge of some two hundred
authorities in history, law, sociology, criminology, psychiatry, and other
related disciplines; and after gathering evidence from hundreds of
sources, ranging from student radicals to the Federal Bureau of Investigation, Eisenhower became almost obsessed. He has become one of the nation's leading proponents of gun control, advocating an absolute ban on
handguns. When asked why, given all the other ailments that plague
modern society, he has singled out crime, Eisenhower simply quotes the
testimony of Dr. Price M. Cobbs, the black psychiatrist, who told the
commission, "If violence continues at its present pace, we may well witness the end of the grand experiment in democracy."[8]
Eisenhower devoted two chapters of his memoir to the commission's
findings, and he remains unqualifiedly bitter that the Nixon administration did nothing to implement the final report.[9] Thomas Harris, a student

at Hopkins, vividly recalled an evening in 1973 when he joined Eisenhower at Bishops Road for a TV-tray dinner. They turned on the CBS evening news just in time to hear Walter Cronkite announce that Senator John Stennis had been shot in Washington. Immediately afterward came a statement from Press Secretary Ronald Ziegler to the effect that Nixon regretted the incident and that it underlined his stand against handguns. With that, Eisenhower jumped up, tipping over the tray and spilling food all over the floor. Harris had never seen him so angry. "That SOB!" Eisenhower shouted. "Ever since my commission submitted its report [in 1969] he has done nothing but torpedo its recommendations, including the one about handguns. That two-faced. . . ."[10] As far as Eisenhower is concerned, the report is still "filed and forgotten."

Eisenhower has not forgotten, and he reminds as many people as possible of its conclusions. He has memorized the relevant figures: ten million serious crimes are committed in the United States each year; Americans average fifty times as many gun murders a year as do the peoples of England, Germany, and Japan combined; the United States has by far the highest gun-to-population ratio of any nation on earth—more than ninety million Americans own firearms, about twenty-five million of which are concealable handguns, which account for three-fourths of all murders. We live, Eisenhower laments, in "America the Violent."

Because of Eisenhower's stand on gun control, he has been told that he shames his family name and has been called everything from a Fascist to a Communist. These labels and criticisms hurt. What hurt more, he asserts, was the Nixon administration's and its successors' unwillingness to stand up to those pressure groups opposing gun control, groups that Eisenhower believes represent the worst evils of the "democratic" system. He is continually "perplexed by the blind, emotional resistance that greets any proposal to bring this senseless excess under control." He rants that the nation's leaders find it easy to talk about the horrid situation of violence but refuse to do anything about it. "We lag behind every other civilized nation in the world in failing to have a comprehensive, effective national policy of firearms control," Eisenhower told a Johns Hopkins audience. "In the meantime, the senseless tragedies repeat themselves: the domestic quarrel or argument between friends turns into a homicide because a gun is available for acting on the rage. Guns are handy to support the yearnings of the sex maniac. Guns are available to those who hold up banks, filling stations, savings and loan associations. . . . Police in most parts of the country are without an effective legal maneuver against the criminal who possesses a pistol, unless they catch him in the actual act of using it in a crime."[11]

Eisenhower does not delude himself that gun control will eliminate crime and violence. The causes run too deep. In fact, Eisenhower's almost obsessive commitment to gun control and, more generally, to solving the problem of violence is readily understandable through the lens of the commission's report. The commission found that the highest rates of violent crime occur among the young, poor, black, urban male. Most Americans find this conclusion predictable. Indeed, many accept that the criminal is and always will be an indigenous inhabitant of the inner-city ghetto. Eisenhower cannot. He cannot accept that his beloved United States has exposed millions of its citizens to the most socially destructive forces imaginable. He cannot accept that in his beloved city of Baltimore, at least during the period of the commission's existence, each individual's mathematical chance of becoming a victim of a homicide, rape, assault, or robbery exceeded one in fifty each year, a statistic, he interjects, that misleadingly encompasses both the affluent sections and the slums. How painful it is for Eisenhower, with his Horatio Alger saga and ideology, to admit that "for hundreds of years, the realities of American life have made a cruel mockery of the work-for-your-reward ethic for the black segment of our population."[12]

In a sense, therefore, Eisenhower's work on the violence commission forced him to examine or reexamine his most fundamental creeds. He had been taught, and had taught others, that Americans are hard-working people and that success is the inevitable reward for hard work. He had lived among self-reliant farmers, upwardly mobile Washington bureaucrats, and renowned academics. In each community his friends were the most prominent civic and financial leaders. His study of crime compelled him to acknowledge, nevertheless, that whereas he, his brothers, and virtually all his associates experienced virtually nothing but success, millions of blacks and other minorities experience only despair. Eisenhower has not lost faith in American values. Yet he has lost faith, or is losing it, in an American value system that he feels relentlessly impresses upon ghetto youths that they are abject failures. "And why not," Eisenhower asks rhetorically, "use violence to get what he [the ghetto black] needs to be somebody? He has little to gain by playing according to society's rules and little to lose by not. . . . Considering the pressures, frustrations and temptations at work on the youth in our ghettos, the wonder is that violent crime rates in the cities are not higher than they are."[13]

To Eisenhower, violence is more than a criminal act; it is one of democracy's most destructive seeds. It threatens to destroy, not just lives and property, but the fabric of society. Consequently, in his opinion, gun control, reform of the criminal-justice system, improvements in the law-enforcement agencies, and so forth are essential. They can be, however, only partial remedies to an all-pervasive problem. If crime is symptomatic of societal inadequacies, those inadequacies themselves must be rectified.

This analysis, albeit somewhat hackneyed, has positioned Eisenhower firmly at the liberal end of the political spectrum. He admonishes Washington to make the system work once again, to prove to all Americans, particularly blacks and other minorities, that they have everything to gain by living by the rules and everything to lose by defying them. With private cooperation, government must eradicate poverty, improve educational facilities, provide for better health care, build mass-transit systems, renew the inner cities, and ensure decent housing. In sum, America's overriding objective must be to make violence unrewarding and unnecessary.

Eisenhower sounds desperate. He sounds as if everything he and his family have stood for is now in jeopardy. He realizes that his proposals have been proposed before; still, he reiterates them over and over again. His conception of democracy and freedom precludes any other solutions because in his view the only alternatives are revolution, totalitarianism, and more violence. For this reason, he perceives the gravity of the situation as analogous to the most serious crises the United States has confronted, and he speaks in tones and phrases reminiscent of a soapbox orator. "Reordering our national priorities to give new emphasis to the quality of life for every citizen is a realistic goal for this affluent society," he preaches. "It is a worthy new phase for a nation that has subdued a continent physically and accomplished so much technologically."[14]

If Eisenhower were forced to describe in one word the root causes for America's current malaise, he would undoubtedly select *change* (see appendix E). Although it should be clear by now that he is anything but a conservative romantic, he often reminisces nostalgically about his boyhood. In idyllic terms he conjures up an image of "the sleepy town of Abilene, Kansas, a cozy white house, surrounded by colorful hollyhocks, a flourishing orchard, and a generous vegetable garden. My brothers and I sit on the front porch in rocking chairs, observing the drift of seasons and the passing of the small segment of the world we know. There is no war, no domestic turmoil, no protest marches, no complex problems to bother us. . . . All is peaceful and we are quite content." "But the essence of nostalgia," Eisenhower continues, "is an awareness that what has been will never be again."[15]

During his lifetime Eisenhower has witnessed the end of the self-sufficient, isolated community and the rise in its place of a totally integrated and interdependent nation and world; the advent of global warfare and depression; the coming of air, then space travel; mass migration and accelerated industrialization; corporate takeovers and bureaucratic proliferation; and all the other "manifold changes, sometimes defying comprehension and increasing exponentially in volume and velocity." Perched in his metaphoric rocking chair, Eisenhower watched as "in a mere flash of historic time, the predominantly rural society which Jefferson felt was the indispensable bedrock of democracy, gave way to massive urbanization, thus creating those conditions which lead to an increase in crime, a decline in tax bases, inadequate public services, and failures in urban government."[16]

"Changes in every circumstance of life have accelerated, but human attitudes have remained generally inflexible," Eisenhower told the 1967 graduating class at Johns Hopkins. "And so, in most of this century the world has lived in chaotic revolution."[17] In his view, he was addressing the appropriate audience. Even more than in the midst of World War II, when he first became president of Kansas State, he believes that the future of the country—indeed, its salvation—depends upon the broad and comprehensive education of its youth. For more than a quarter of a century Eisenhower oversaw the development and expansion of three major institutions of higher learning, and no man could take greater pride in their accomplishments. Nevertheless, especially with the emphasis on specialization, he castigates the American system of education for failing to keep pace with the rapid transformations that characterize the contemporary world. In 1946 the Presidential Commission on Higher Education, on which Eisenhower served, put the nation on notice with its conclusion that "in a real sense the future of our civilization depends on the direction education takes."[18] Decades later Eisenhower's perspective has not changed. "The supreme social usefulness of a university," he advised those gathered for the opening ceremonies of Hopkins's centennial celebration in 1975, "is not to be measured in program developments but in its search for truth whatever truth may reveal, and in providing the type of liberal, scientific, and professional education which weaves into the fabric of the nation minds capable of the objective, creative, courageous thinking so desperately needed in our evolving and troubled society."[19]

Eisenhower does not doubt that Americans have the ability and the will to solve the problems of government, the economy, crime, and America's myriad other problems. But for them to do so, he counsels, education on all levels must be qualitatively improved. While conceding that "my view of elementary and secondary education is scanty," he does not hesitate to criticize the preparation received by most of the nation's youth during the precollegiate years, even at elite schools. Television, he fears, has replaced the book; drugs and alcohol have replaced baseball and pajama parties. Parents spend increasing amounts of time away from home, leaving their children to find direction and excitement on their own. In his opinion, the majority can find neither. "Young people have no one to help them," he complains. "It is a guarantee of low scholarship."

Under such circumstances, Eisenhower frets, the United States is quickly reaching the stage when only the exceptional young man or woman will regard school as anything more than an unwarranted intrusion upon his or her time. And even those exceptions, if current trends continue, will not receive the education that Eisenhower has for so long advocated. Echoing a common lament, he remarks that "we Americans are the worst linguists in the civilized world. Thousands of students entering college have never learned to write and speak with logic, clarity, and effectiveness, to say nothing of style. Many can hardly read. Their knowledge of history is usually limited to that of the United States, with little comprehension of the interdependence of American history with that of many foreign countries. And few students have mastered mathematics. . . . We suffer from a national inadequacy of communication."

Eisenhower analyzes what he considers a deplorable situation from the same viewpoint that he criticized higher education in the 1940s. Placing most of the blame on parental pressure, he feels that the nation's youth, long before they enter college, have become overly specialized. As early as high school they are encouraged to take more and more electives, neglecting the fundamentals of future learning. Eisenhower goes so far as to question the value of chemistry, biology, or other hard-science requisites at the secondary level. Certainly there is a need for schools to produce scientists, he explains, but there is more than ample time to pursue such studies at the college and graduate levels. He recommends that in the meantime, more emphasis be placed on courses in general science and, more specifically, in the history and philosophy of science and technology. "It is imperative that preparatory students comprehend the enormous influence science and technology have had and continue to have on all societies," he comments. "They do not gain much intellectually by taking a course in biology and cringing as they dissect frogs."

Eisenhower is reluctant to express his views on certain highly volatile issues. In particular, he hesitates to discuss integration, to a large extent because he is personally ambivalent and does not want to be misunderstood. He categorically asserts that integration is long overdue, that "unequal cultures," to use his words, should have been brought together a great many years ago. Yet he also assumes that integration has been a crucial factor in the general decline of preparatory education. On the one hand he affirms that "obviously we must look ahead to the day when all minorities in our society are equal in every respect, including the privilege of being reared in educated families." On the other hand he delineates the inherent difficulties in teaching and maintaining discipline in a classroom composed of students with so diverse and unequal backgrounds. Characteristically, he tries to reconcile the dilemma by striking a balance. "The future demands that we do all we can to provide an education at the highest level of intellectual attainment for those who are so disposed and can profit by it," Eisenhower said in an interview, "but others need to be given vocational and related training so that they are prepared to lead useful and happy lives."

The fundamental contradiction in Eisenhower's proposing that certain minority groups receive vocational training while at the same time advocating universal education in the liberal arts highlights the limitations of this compromise solution. Similarly, he does not provide a systematic method for determining which students will be disposed towards, and can thereby profit most from, "an education at the highest level." Yet Eisenhower does not claim to know all the answers. He only claims that he will never stop trying to find them.

Eisenhower feels more comfortable when discussing college and university education, which he continues to view as the singular most effective mechanism for putting the United States back on the right path. His fundamental recommendations, however, largely reflect the same views that he held forty years ago. They also closely parallel his prescriptions for secondary education. Above all, he insists that it is more important than ever that students be encouraged, and if necessary compelled through breadth requirements, to pursue "the broadest and best possible liberal education, regardless of what area of specialization the student is likely to enter."

Only the smallest minority, according to Eisenhower, should take a restricted curriculum, which would include fundamental courses in the humanities and social sciences but concentrate heavily on vocational ones. These programs, Eisenhower adds, should lead to associate degrees. Conversely, those who seek a B.A. or B.S. should defer their more "technical" training until graduate or professional school. To support his case, Eisenhower points out that even a premedical student needs to take only four required year-long courses. Moreover, he cites a study of sixty-five of the nation's leading scientists which revealed that not one of them decided on a specialization until he or she was a junior in college, and the majority did not decide until the senior year. In addition, a survey of graduate students concluded that over half were specializing in a field different from their undergraduate major.

As he frequently does, in a talk before the Association of American University Presses in 1978 Eisenhower repeated practically verbatim the sentiments he had expressed in previous speeches. He remarked, "I have confidence in our ability to solve the problems that beset us, but to do so will require heroic, courageous, and creative policies and actions, determined within an abiding philosophy that requires men and women to lift their eyes and minds above individual and group selfishness." In his eyes and mind, the responsibility for instilling that philosophy lies with the educational system. "We must educate," he continued, "a new American, many new Americans. Superficial or average understanding among the people will not suffice."[20] Only a broadly educated society, he believes, will be able to comprehend the complexity of current and future problems, to produce capable leaders, and to insist that all private and public agencies operate constructively and in the national interest. "Perhaps the *ordinary* citizen is an anachronism in this perilous age," he told Hopkins graduates. "Perhaps the hope for the future lies in our ability to produce the extraordinary citizen—a new breed of Americans who will devote as much time and energy to being good citizens as they do to being good physicists or good doctors or good engineers."[21]

The preceding pages represent but a cursory distillation, a cross section, of Eisenhower's current thinking. The material reproduced in the appendixes provides further elaboration, as does his own memoir. Many of his criticisms and proposals are relatively simplistic, even clichéd. Some may be interpreted as an attempt, conscious or not, to defend principles and policies long identified with the Eisenhower name. Others reflect the conciliatory, gradualist outlook that has characterized his entire career. Eisenhower has never been an exceptionally original or profound thinker. He has listened carefully to others, studied intently, borrowed generously, and then added his personal imprint. But that imprint is critical. Milton Eisenhower is unquestionably an uncommon and remarkable individual. He has succeeded at all his endeavors, and that success has resulted from concern, intelligence, hard work, and, most important, an abiding dedication to the principles in which he so fervently believes. Distressed over contemporary conditions, he now calls upon Americans to exhibit these same traits, to live up, in a way, to his expectations. Perhaps his critiques are elementary; his expectations are not.

CHAPTER 17

"A Smile on His Face, a Twinkle in His Eyes, and a Forward-looking Attitude"

In Retirement

What I need to do now," Eisenhower wrote one of his student friends in 1976, "is to learn to get as much satisfaction from sheer leisure and play as I have throughout my lifetime from work."[1]

As the previous chapter suggests, Eisenhower's disappointment over the course of contemporary society has put an omnipresent damper on his retirement years. He remains much too emotionally and intellectually involved with current problems to live a carefree life of "sheer leisure and play," even though he certainly has acquired the means to do so. Nevertheless, worrying about America's difficulties and recommending solutions have not occupied all of his time. In between his writings, speeches, and countless other civic activities Eisenhower has enjoyed himself tremendously.

Not surprisingly, his most enduring passion continues to be Johns Hopkins. He basks in the success of the university since his retirement, and he and Muller have developed a warm personal relationship. The two men have lunch together and look forward to chatting at social occasions, and Muller does not hesitate to ask his predecessor's advice. Yet he rarely needs to, which is exactly what Eisenhower wanted and expected. The president emeritus also sees his former faculty and staff on a regular basis, and of course his student friends come to visit whenever they are in Baltimore. He can still often be seen on campus: at the Hopkins Club, at a lacrosse game, or at a university function, where he is always an honored guest and sometimes the principal speaker. He expresses almost childlike pleasure over his special car permit, which allows him to park anywhere on campus. He expresses heartfelt pride in the immediate recognition and respect accorded him everywhere he walks.

Eisenhower's moves to Rowland Mews and then to North Charles Street forced him to sell his organ and pool table. Fortunately, however, most of his hobbies do not require much space. He spends hours on end listening to classical music, and he is all but a fanatic when it comes to opera. He gets to New York much less frequently than he used to, so when he does, it is not unusual for him to attend four operas in a long weekend. Once, while staying at the University Club in New York in the mid-1970s, he found that he just could not stop humming a particular aria. Unable to sleep, he decided to take a walk—in Central Park at two o'clock in the morning! Later he recounted the incident to former student Thomas Harris. Harris forgot their age difference and told Eisenhower quite frankly that he was crazy. "It seemed perfectly safe to me," Eisenhower replied with a rather sheepish grin.[2]

Eisenhower has devoted almost as much energy to understanding music as he did to understanding an academic budget. "I wish you had been at my home at noon today," he wrote Michael McGrael in 1976. "In the mail was the tape you sent me of Artur Rubinstein playing the Polonaise in A Flat and the Military Polonaise; the Minute Waltz which I once played myself, though not at the Rubinstein tempo; a beautiful waltz in C Sharp Minor and seven or eight other delightful pieces. Lunch was delayed while I sat in the big blue and white wing chair and listened, with the volume moderately high in order to get all the resonance of every note. You well know that Chopin is my favorite composer. Successful playing of all his things, from etudes to preludes, requires great clarity of each note. The music is nearly always tuneful but not trite. The changing harmonies are masterpieces. . . . I've heard Paderewski, Cortot, DePachman and others, each different, each great, but none is superior to Rubinstein. Thanks a million."[3]

Eisenhower has also continued his painting, begun at Penn State in response to Ike's encouragement. At first he dabbled only in watercolors. Now he experiments with various mediums. George Gorse, professor of art history at Pomona College, considers Eisenhower "serious about painting, and some of his landscapes are really quite good."[4] His landscapes have benefited from a more recently acquired interest, horticulture, and, as his friend Roy Wilkinson's yard amply illustrates, he has become quite expert with any type of foliage.

As if all these activities were not enough to satisfy his creative impulses, Eisenhower has learned to work miracles in the kitchen (often using his mother's and Ike's recipes). He even tried his hand at writing a novel. The first attempt did not work out; however, he still thinks he has some good ideas and is confident that he will try again.

Long before he finally retired, Eisenhower decided to make Baltimore his permanent home. "I wouldn't consider moving elsewhere," he wrote eight years into his retirement. "I also like San Francisco, Edinburgh, Scotland, and a few other places, but there's only one Baltimore." In his view, Baltimore resembles two of his other favorites, Boston and Philadelphia. "These three cities," he comments, "are dominated by the lives, activities, and attitudes of persons whose families have lived in them since, say, the early 1700s, or late 1600s. They provide stability; they maintain good traditions; they have great pride in the community, and they are wonderful persons to have as intimate friends." In short, what sets Baltimore apart from the others, at least from Eisenhower's perspective, is that he knows and likes so many of its inhabitants. "It is really the people," he concludes, "who cause me to love this place. It is graced by the presence of many persons who have helped shape the city's character, and who are nearly always the leaders who keep the opera, symphony, theaters, libraries, museums, and similar institutions performing exceptionally well."[5]

Muller, who has quickly grown equally attached to the city, believes that it is "like Milton in some ways." Muller explains that Baltimore does not put on airs and that it displays a wholesome recognition of merit when merit is in evidence. In other words, even if one is not blue-blooded and does not come from one of the established families, it is easy to be accepted on the basis of performance. Muller also considers Baltimore a bit old-fashioned, not stylish or trendy, again rather like Eisenhower himself. Finally, it is "knowable," friendly, and approachable, three of Eisenhower's most prevalent traits.[6]

Eisenhower finds Baltimore's location to be ideal—he can get to Washington or New York without difficulty, yet he is sufficiently far away not to be affected by their constant commotion and turmoil. Perhaps more important, his daughter Ruth, her husband, and their three sons live virtually around the corner. Bud (who works for IBM) and his family—Bud has a daughter but no sons, highly unusual for an Eisenhower—now live in Wilton, Connecticut, which is easily accessible from Baltimore by train. They all stay in close touch and have occasionally taken joint vacations to Antigua, where Eisenhower has taken his annual mid-winter vacation for decades.[7]

Along with the city's ambience, Hopkins, family, and friends, Baltimore to Eisenhower also means his beloved Orioles. Their reciprocal love affair has matured with age. On September 15, 1974, the Orioles management opened up Memorial Stadium for Eisenhower's seventy-fifth birth-day party. Five hundred forty guests were served cocktails and dinner in the bull pen, behind left field, and everyone received a blue baseball cap stamped "MSE." Eisenhower still prizes his, along with his picture taken with Earl Weaver, Brooks Robinson, and the other Oriole stars. He has posed with some of the great men of the twentieth century, but from the look on his face in this photograph it appears that he has never been given a greater thrill. He thrilled the Orioles, too, by rattling off each team member's name, current batting average, and, in the case of pitchers, even won-lost records.[8]

Eisenhower has returned his affection for Baltimore by becoming one of its most civic-minded citizens. For some years he was a director of the Baltimore Museum of Art. He made the principal speech at both the groundbreaking ceremony and the formal dedication of the Greater Baltimore Medical Center, then served as one of its directors. He was a long-time trustee of the Johns Hopkins Hospital and is now a trustee emeritus. He helped design a fund-raising campaign for, and contributed other services, to Union Memorial Hospital, where his son-in-law, Dr. Thomas W. Snider, is head of the Department of Radiology and Ruth is president of the volunteer workers.

To continue, he is active in the Central Maryland Cancer Society. As a matter of fact, at the annual dinner he presents the Milton S. Eisenhower award to the person honored for the greatest contribution during the year to cancer research, control, or cure. He served for nearly a decade as president of the Evergreen Foundation and still maintains his office in Evergreen House. He is a valued supporter of the Mechanic Theater, the Baltimore Opera, the Baltimore Symphony, and student productions at Hopkins and Goucher. And outside the city limits, Eisenhower has been a director or trustee of the American Academy of Political Science, the American Red Cross, the National Conference of Christians and Jews (national vice-president), the Pan American Development Foundation, the Society for the Advancement of Management (national vice-president), the National Committee for Economic Development, the Institute of International Education, the National Commission for International Development, the National Council of the U.N. Association, the American Korean Foundation (founder), "and," he adds with a shrug, "some I may have forgotten."[9]

In addition, Eisenhower is a member of numerous prominent Baltimore social organizations, including the Elkridge and Hopkins clubs. He once belonged to the Maryland Club but resigned to protest its discriminatory policies. Conversely, Eisenhower and Charles Garland helped found the Center Club in the then newly built Charles Center in downtown Baltimore. Along with the other charter members, they made it the first fully integrated, "high level" club in the city. A third of its members are Jews, and after Eisenhower personally persuaded two blacks to join, many other minorities quickly followed.[10]

As Eisenhower has gotten older, he has had to give up many of his activities or at least become less involved with them. But he still keeps up with all the city's happenings, and he sees his many friends and associates as often as possible. For Eisenhower it was a long and circuitous route from Abilene to Baltimore. Not for one moment does he regret the trek.

"When I left the university," Eisenhower remarked in 1980, "I didn't want to go to seed. I wanted to be active in affairs. I wanted to learn new things. And I wanted to make a contribution."[11] Unquestionably he has remained active, and contributed, through his writings and speeches. Moreover, three times he has served as honorary chairman of Senator Charles Mathias's state committee, and in the 1980 national campaign he publicly endorsed the presidential candidacy of John Anderson.[12] Actually, due to the vagueness of the electoral laws, Eisenhower temporarily appeared on the tickets of eight states as Anderson's running mate.

Thus, as an octogenarian, Eisenhower finally became a "candidate" for political office. The irony is that he had refused to run for the senate in Kansas, Pennsylvania, and, as late as 1962, in Maryland, largely because he felt obligated to remain at his university posts. Had he been younger in 1980, when he no longer had such responsibilities, he might well have run, not for the vice-presidency but for the Senate. Indeed, he often ruminates that he would have seriously considered a draft candidacy in the late 1960s, when he first began to think of retiring from academia. "I wish," he reflected, "that the offer to run for the Senate of the United States had occurred in 1966 or 1968 instead of 1962. I would have run. If I could have gone into the Senate for the next six, at most twelve years, I would have liked it. Because frankly, the things that I am now saying, things that I am going on TV about from time to time and writing about and making speeches about, I would have been saying right in the Senate of the United States. It is a great forum."[13]

Given his temperament, perhaps it is best that Eisenhower never embarked on a career in politics, where only those with the thickest of skins really flourish. He did manage, however, to find another outlet for his energies in the world of business. His first exposure to business dated back to his days at Kansas State, when the Quaker Oats Company elected him a member of its board of directors. Until 1953, when he began to spend so much time at the White House, he regularly traveled to Chicago for the board meetings each month. He found them fascinating. Furthermore, they provided him with a unique perspective on American agriculture. After all, he had now experienced the problems of the farmer from the point of view of a child in rural Kansas, a bureaucrat in the Department of Agriculture, a president of two land-grant universities, and an officer for one of the nation's largest millers and grain merchants.[14]

In 1962 the New York Stock Exchange invited Eisenhower to become a governor. He consulted with the Hopkins trustees, who urged him to accept, explaining that it would benefit the university because he would meet some of the financial leaders of the nation and learn more about the functioning of the financial community. He served for three years, taking the train to New York once a month. Before each meeting Keith Funston, then president of the exchange, would host a long luncheon for all the governors from out of town. They would cover thoroughly, but informally, the issues on the agenda for the formal meeting. Eisenhower learned a lot, especially from the luncheons. "And I made a fortune out of it," he joked—they paid him a hundred dollars per meeting.

Two years after his term ended he became a director of the Chicago Board of Trade. He held that post until 1970 but found the experience "less interesting" than his period on the exchange. Most of the matters the board dealt with were highly technical—fees, rules of trading, and so forth—and he never felt he could contribute substantively. "The trading floor itself was a madhouse," he remembered. "No stranger could make out what went on in that crazy place."

By the 1960s Eisenhower had expanded his interests in both business and finance, and he maintained most of them after he had left Johns Hopkins. Elected a director of the Commercial Credit Company in 1963, he served until 1975, much of the time as a member of the executive committee. From 1965 to 1972 he sat on the board of directors of the Chesapeake and Potomac Telephone Company, and in 1967 he became a director of the Mercantile-Safe Deposit and Trust Company; Life Insurance of California; and the Insurance and Securities, Inc., Corporation and its two subsidiaries, the ISI Growth Fund and the ISI Income Fund. He continued with ISI until the mid-seventies, almost never missing the monthly meetings in San Francisco. He also made several trips to Windsor, England, where he was a board member of the Windsor Insurance Company.

Notwithstanding these numerous directorships, Eisenhower's most intensive business activities, before and after his retirement, involved the railroad industry. In 1963 he became a director of the Baltimore and Ohio Railroad. His election to the board was quite natural, due to Hopkins's traditional connection with the B&O, a connection personified during Eisenhower's administration by trustees Ben Griswold, Charles Garland, and Douglas Turnbull.[15] Furthermore, because Eisenhower in the 1950s had served for his brother on a Cabinet committee established primarily to study the advisability of constructing the St. Lawrence Seaway, he was already well acquainted with the nation's transportation problems. Then in 1968 he became a director of the Chesapeake and Ohio Railway, which by that time owned nearly all of the B&O stock. Five years later the Chessie System, Inc., set up as a holding company for the B&O, the C&O, and the Western Maryland Railroad, elected him one of its directors.

If anything, Eisenhower's long service on so many boards made him an even more committed fiscal conservative. For example, he became convinced that only by consolidating can the railroad companies hope to attain lasting solvency. He fears that otherwise they will have to rely continually on billions of dollars from the government just to keep going. In addition, he resigned from the board of a non-railroad-related company in opposition to its decision to expand before it had, in his opinion, acquired the financial stability to do so. Not without a certain pride, he notes that the company later went bankrupt. His misgivings aside, however, most of his experiences in business and finance were rewarding ones, both educationally and financially. While he is no longer an active director of any corporation, he does have a standing invitation to resume his membership on the board of every one of them whenever he wishes.

In 1969 Neil Grauer sent Eisenhower a birthday card. In acknowledging it Eisenhower wrote, "I want you to know that while the years continue to roll around, I haven't had a birthday since my fortieth. Jack Benny got ahead of me by one year in this regard, but then he is vain and I'm not."[16]

Eisenhower kids about his age, but as the years have gone by, he has finally had to slow down. In 1975 cobalt radiation treatments cured a small malignancy, and in 1979 he underwent an eight-hour operation for the removal of his bladder. He had to give up his lifelong enjoyment of smoking. Following the surgery, he suffered from a severe depression, confiding to Grauer that he "wasn't sure" that life was worth all the discomfort and inconvenience that accompanied his operations. Yet he bounded back and before long was joking again, now about his "exterior plumbing." Grauer marvels at his spirit. "Eisenhower's most long-lasting impact on me," the former student remarked, "has been to demonstrate how to grow old—not just 'gracefully,' but with strength.... His perseverance in the face of recurring illnesses has been a model to emulate."[17]

Shortly after Eisenhower had recovered from his 1979 operation, Nelson Block came to visit him for the first time in seven years. He was "amazed that he hadn't changed at all." Eisenhower revealed to Block that he had lost all but four of the vital organs in his body. Nevertheless, he said laughingly, the doctors had assured him that he had one lung and one kidney that he could give up, so he still had quite a ways to go. What impressed Block most was that Eisenhower retained his irrepressible energy. To quote Block's description, he had "a smile on his face, a twinkle in his eyes, and a forward-looking attitude."[18]

Another of Eisenhower's closest friends is George Wills, whom he knew first as a Penn State student. Wills later worked for Eisenhower at Homewood House and on the violence commission. Eisenhower is godfather to Wills's youngest child, Kendall. One evening over dinner in 1979 ten-year-old Kendall unexpectedly asked him, "Uncle Milton, with all the things that you've had taken out from inside of you, how do you stay alive?" Eisenhower had his answer ready. "Kendall," he replied in a deadpan tone, "when they take the heart out, I'm in trouble."[19]

That same year Eisenhower wrote to Doug Warren explaining how he felt about his present circumstances. He concluded,

"Let me say that I am relatively unconcerned about all this. I am not apprehensive. I am not worried. I'm more fearful that the Orioles will lose. At my age anything can happen. I may come out of the next operation looking and acting years younger. I may not. The doubtful part of the whole business is immaterial to me.

"You are young. Life is ahead of you. I can wish for you nothing better than what I have enjoyed for a long, long lifetime: A wonderful family situation in youth and maturity; complete satisfaction with my work in education and government. Indeed, if I were starting over I would try to find how to do precisely what I have done."[20]

Eisenhower repeatedly insists that he does not fear death; he only dreads incapacitation or an inability to fend for himself. He has even had special medical equipment installed in his car in case an emergency should arise, and he still loves to drive around Baltimore, even under icy or snowy conditions. When you ring the bell at his home, he is quick to answer, personally. Normally, regardless of the time, he is dressed in a sports jacket and tie. As he makes you comfortable, he barrages you with questions—about your wife and kids, about your work, about your views. He wants to know what you think of a particular senator's latest proposal, or the president's policy on inflation, or the Federal Reserve Board's latest action, or the Orioles' chances to win the pennant. He eagerly responds to everything you say. Reading the newspaper or watching the TV news, he comments freely and knowledgeably about men and events. And after making drinks and serving dinner, he delights in challenging his guest to a few games of backgammon. The world has changed dramatically over the past eight decades. As far as Eisenhower is concerned, however, the more he changes, the more he remains the same.

Appendixes
Notes
Selected Bibliography
Index

Inaugural Address

Kansas State College, September 30, 1943

G overnor Schoeppel, Guests, Members and Friends of the College:
Twenty-five years ago, this month, many of us from the towns and farms of Kansas entered this College as students and members of the students' Army Training Corps. We were at war.

The world we lived in, we felt, had encountered a significant turning point. In our hands we held products of science and technology which we wished to use constructively. But we found ourselves preparing to use them as efficiently as we could to destroy the enemies of human freedom. And so we who entered this College in 1918 developed the notion that civilization had become a race between the machines of man and the wisdom of man. We welcomed the contest. We were convinced that by fighting to save democracy we would give our world a new opportunity to employ the sciences of peace and the machines of man with wisdom, and tolerance, and understanding—for the betterment of ourselves and our neighbors—for the good of all mankind.

Most of the generation that entered our colleges and universities in 1918 touched only the fringes of that war, for the war ended two months later. There was supreme rejoicing when the armistice was signed. With joy in our hearts and an unreasoned conviction that no one again would dare test the strength of a mighty democracy, we went back to our studies and then into the unacademic world. We were young enough to challenge all forces that defied our determination to build, in peace, an abundance and a satisfying culture for all who were willing to work.

In the two decades that followed, we put science to work. With new means of communication fresh from the laboratory, we set out to see to it that the values of education were available to all men and women— everywhere. Urged on by the commercial development of scientific discoveries, we went forth to conquer time and space, and did bring all the world closer to our individual homes. With new knowledge from many laboratories, we determined to conquer malnutrition and other physical perils of mankind. With accumulated knowledge from our great agricultural experiment stations, we launched a drive to heal the wounds the earth had suffered in the exploitive period of American development. We went forth to put science to work—everywhere.

But while our generation was preoccupied with the sciences of peace, men in other countries were not so occupied. They were perfecting the science of war and fashioning instruments of force. They did this with the same knowledge which we of the democracies were using for constructive purposes. We were taking freedom for granted, as if it were inevitable. They were methodically planning to destroy it. When they were fully prepared, they struck.

Suddenly, we faced a grim reality: We had not won the race of 1918. Our enthusiasm for progress in the twenties and the thirties had not been conditioned by sufficient perception of judgment. So, once again, we had to shift our skills from purposes of peace to more urgent purposes of waging and winning a war.

The rapid transition achieved by the people of this country in this war is one of the monumental events in history. The striking power of democracy is now felt on battlefields throughout the world. The lasting power of democracy will bring us victory.

But not merely a victory of our arms. That is not the end for which we fight. We must achieve equally the victory of our minds. War is a physical struggle between the peoples of opposing convictions, and one side will prevail. Our convictions, I think, are relatively simple: Above all else, we have faith in people—in their virtues and in their potentialities. We therefore hold that human beings are more important than the institutions they create. We will not permit any institution or system of whatever political, economic or military complexion to become our master. We believe government must be of the people, by the people and for the people, if the sciences of peace are to contribute to human betterment.

Indeed, the only reason we now wage war is that these beliefs, with all that they mean in terms of human dignity and freedom, shall prevail over the concepts of our enemies. If we were willing to compromise these beliefs, no doubt we could end this war tomorrow.

But our convictions will not prevail even with military victory, if we are complacent and take them for granted, as we did in 1918. Noble concepts worth holding are also worth working for, constantly, tirelessly. The victory of our arms in this war will do no more than offer a new generation a chance to work for a fuller life in an environment of individual liberty and social justice.

Two wars in one generation have convinced many people that knowledge, even though widely diffused, is not in itself enough to guarantee these goals. By no means do I imply that research has fulfilled its mission and that the modern task is to find better methods of applying that knowledge. On the contrary, accelerated research achievements since the last war have merely brought us to a new frontier of knowledge. Each discovery develops potentialities many-fold greater than itself. Any institution or civilization that fails to fight vigorously to push back what is still a vast area of darkness will decay.

But I do mean to say that the fruits of science and technology cannot, in themselves, automatically instil into us the wisdom, the tolerance, the integrated reasoning required for the management of individual and organized affairs in a complex and rapidly changing civilization.

The discovery of knowledge is one vital step. The widest possible dissemination of knowledge is a second vital step. A third vital step, in this modern complexity we have been long building, is the fostering of judgment. Democracy will endure only if responsible citizens are able to arrive at sound judgments in a great multitude of fields.

The discovery of knowledge requires more and more specialization. Sound judgment in making decisions requires more and more integration. Judgment requires a careful fusing of facts from a great many disciplines. It requires a broader and broader understanding of manifold relationships.

Research increases knowledge and makes judgment possible. But, I repeat, neither research nor the mere dissemination of knowledge can guarantee sound decisions by an individual or by society as a whole.

Everyone will agree, I am sure, that the noble concepts which we in this democracy hold cannot be maintained, in the face of economic complications multiplied by social complexities, unless human knowledge is matched by human wisdom. Everyone will also agree, I think, that educational institutions have as great a responsibility for fostering wisdom and tolerance as they have for fostering research and the dissemination of knowledge.

The people of France, of Poland, of the Low Countries, even of Germany and Hungary, have possessed the same fruits of research as we. They have had the same scientific tools to work with. Prior to the dark decade of the thirties, before intellectual repression in the enemy countries became so terribly efficient, they also enjoyed a wide dissemination of the results of research. Yet one nation became strong and ruthless while others became weak, bitterly divided and easy prey to German arms.

I do not want to overstress the point, but if we are not forever vigilant in this country, we could easily drift into some of the difficulties that held France, the Low Countries and Poland so helpless in the late thirties. Bitter disagreements of long standing between great economic groups—in the absence of the restraining hand of simple human tolerance and cool, broad judgment—are the stuff on which revolutions and the monsters of tyranny and repression feed.

One of the heartening things about this war is that, in spite of all kinds of opinions and differences of opinion, we in the United States can unite in a mighty, fighting organization—a global organization built in an incredibly short time, and swung into action to defend our simple, understandable, human concepts.

We can, and I believe we will, do the same thing in our peaceful pursuits when this war is over. Surely we are as capable in peace as in war of defining our objectives, of determining the facts relevant to a solution of the problems involved, of laying our plans intelligently, and of rigorously carrying them out. But the task will not be simple. The generation which goes forth into a peaceful world when this war is won will face problems infinitely more complex than ours when we left College at the end of the last war.

Some of you here today remember when your most difficult economic problem involved the trading of eggs and grain for salt and sugar. The world we shall live in after this war will present to every one of us problems of agriculture, industry, labor, national and international finance and trade, taxation, economic organization, social organization, education, employment and a multitude of other things which will dwarf those of the 1930's as well as those of the 1870's.

It will not be enough for a man to know how to build Grand Coulee dam or the Golden Gate bridge. It will not be enough for a man to know how to till the soil and protect it. It will not be enough for a man to know how to heal the sick. For every man with a useful place in society will have several great responsibilities. He will have the responsibility of using his specialized talent to make a living for himself and his family. As a citizen in a democracy, he will often have the responsibility of applying his specialized talent to the solution of community, state and national problems within his field of special competence. And as a citizen in a democracy, he will always have the responsibility of making manifold decisions on complex problems outside his own discipline—decisions which, if made in ways compatible with our democratic methods, can spread the blessings of democracy, strengthen democracy, and guarantee its future.

American educational institutions, along with our churches, free press, and governmental agencies, have a profound duty to perform if we are to help guarantee that future. There can be no real freedom without sound education. There can be no true education without freedom. The two are inseparable.

All over America, at this moment, practical men and women in our colleges and universities are considering what adjustments may be required of education to have it meet impending problems. They know that thousands of young men, returning from Vella Lavella and North Africa, and France, and Germany, and Japan—with new experiences, new attitudes, and new determinations—will not accept merely what has been offered. They realize that men and women who have fought with guns and struggled with their bare hands for freedom will expect of our educational institutions the kind of help that will enable them to cope with the new problems of their day.

These practical educators know that a heterogeneous lot of studies, in or outside a field of specialization, will not wholly satisfy the returning young people. For these war-experienced men and women will want also to understand many forces and values in their relation to one another, to the individual and to our free society. They will also want to know the relation of all these to the freedom they fought for.

Many of the educators who are thinking along these lines are concerned mainly with the liberal arts. It is necessary to start some place, of course, and it is evident that the liberal arts must be deeply involved. For the liberal arts can provide sequential subjects and teaching methods that will help students understand many basic relationships and will encourage them to become self-educative throughout life.

But the technical schools and colleges have a responsibility, too. Perhaps theirs is the greater responsibility. For in our technical colleges we specialize in scientific disciplines and we therefore face the danger of encouraging a man to become a specialist within one discipline, and a dogmatist in affairs within other disciplines. And lack of understanding between men of varying disciplines is basically no different from lack of understanding between economic groups or nations. Most human misunderstandings stem from a failure of the disagreeing parties to consider objectively the same set of relevant facts and then to reason from those facts toward an agreeable solution.

While our technical institutions have not, so far as I know, given organized attention to this problem, many individual colleges, Kansas State among them, have done so. I have no doubt that the land-grant colleges as a group will function in this regard. Certainly the nationwide system of land-grant colleges has never failed to meet its responsibilities since its inception 81 years ago. The land-grant college system has contributed mightily to our nation's scientific, industrial, economic, social, military and moral strength.

The history of the land-grant colleges is a story of change. The history of Kansas State College, written by our devoted friend, Dr. J. T. Willard, is a story of change—change to help the people of Kansas meet problems presented by onrushing development.

This College is maintained by the people of Kansas and of the entire nation not to serve in all conceivable fields but for this specific purpose: "To promote the liberal and practical education of the industrial classes in the several pursuits and professions in life." This College is obligated to provide a combination of practical and liberal education to the young men and women who enter here.

Under most skillful and devoted leadership, Kansas State College has tried to live up to this obligation. In my judgment and, I believe, in the judgment of the people of the state and nation, it has succeeded. But just as the College has had to change time and again in providing a liberal, practical education for men and women who wished to meet the challenge of their day, so too will it have to keep on changing, growing, developing. The College is not a separate, static thing in our society. It is a living part of society.

Our concern, then, for the immediate future is this: How can Kansas State College maintain and strengthen its excellent research; maintain and improve the quality of its technical and cultural training; and also provide to this generation, including the men and women who will return from the armed services and war industries, those methods of teaching and those broad educational foundations which will yield integrative habits of thinking, a broad understanding of relationships, and sound judgment in a complex society?

Our concern is that men shall conquer machines, that machines shall not conquer men. Our concern is that men and women trained in scientific methods shall also gain tolerance, and understanding, and wisdom. Our concern is with the education of men and women determined to be free.

The precise methods of helping the young men and women of Kansas State along these paths now reside in the collective wisdom of the people of Kansas, the Board of Regents, the faculty, the students, the alumni and the friends of the College.

I conceive my function to be not that of dictating a program for the future but rather that of stimulating all who can help contribute the answers and of integrating their judgments into a useful, attainable program.

It has been my privilege to know my three immediate predecessors. They found it possible to draw upon the cooperative spirit and the collective intelligence of all who wished to aid in having this College stand preeminent as an agency of useful service to the people who support it. That they succeeded is evident in the affection the people of Kansas bestowed upon them and in the educated men and women who developed under their guidance.

I hope I may be able to meet the task of the years ahead as surely and as well as they met theirs.

The Presidency

Can Anyone Do the Job?

T he U.S. is about to chew up and spit out another of its presidents. How often can we do this without crushing the delicate structure of leadership in our democracy and its fragile balance of power?

This is not a defense of President Carter. I am too much a Republican for that. Besides, I believe that much of this President's difficulty is of his own making—the inevitable result of his flawed perception of the demands and the powers of the modern American presidency.

My concern is broader. It is for the office of the presidency, for future holders of that office, and for the Republic itself. Our political and governmental structures have simply not been reformed to keep pace with the amazing and dramatic changes of the past century in this nation, and in the world. My own 80 years span more than a third of the life of this Republic, and I can remember when DuPont was a gun powder factory on the Delaware River and the President of the United States answered his own phone. When the Constitution was adopted 95 per cent of our people were engaged in farming; when Abraham Lincoln was President, half the population was; when I was a boy the total had dropped to 25 percent; today, fewer than 5 per cent of our people produce the food and fiber not only for our own nation, but for much of the rest of the world.

We became an industrialized, urbanized, interdependent society almost before we realized it. Suddenly, we faced problems for which we

Syndicated by *Projects in Education,* this article was first published on October 8, 1979.

had no solutions and on which the individual citizen seemingly could have no influence—inflation, energy, chronic unemployment, pollution, crime, and nuclear arms proliferation, to name a few. So individuals formed organizations to increase their influence, and our society has become the most organized in the world. Many of these organizations have become pressure groups, some of which, majestically housed in marble structures near the nation's Capitol, are extremely powerful and bring enormous pressures to bear on the President and the members of Congress. The National Rifle Association has successfully thwarted effective gun control laws. The Teamsters Union could wreck the economy if it wished. Lobbies in the military-industrial complex will work vigorously to determine the fate of the SALT treaty. And whatever President Carter and the Congress decide to do about the energy crisis, we can be sure that the oil lobby will have a significant influence on the outcome.

We are foolish and naive to expect the man in the White House, whoever he may be, to solve problems we do not fully understand and cannot agree on. The immediate need is not so much for answers to specific problems, but rather for reform of a political system which is now failing us. To cope with the complex problems facing this nation, we need clear and objective study of facts, carefully calculated alternative lines of action, and genuine statesmanship. And we will not get these so long as sheer political partisanship prevails and re-election to office is the first priority of our political leaders.

I offer no quick cures, but I do have some specific recommendations which I think could become the foundation for the kind of structural reform that our political system desperately needs:

The two major political parties should radically reform their quadrennial conventions. It is disgraceful that we select the nominees for the highest position in the nation in a noisy, hectic, manipulated, carnival-like atmosphere. A society that runs its nominating conventions like circuses should not be surprised when its gets tightrope walkers as candidates.

We should elect our Presidents for a single six-year term. This is not very radical or new. A preliminary draft of the Constitution proposed a seven-year term and stipulated that the President "shall not be elected a second time." I believe a President should work only for programs and policies which he is convinced are in the best interest of the nation as a whole—that he should have no incentive to fight for measures mainly to enhance his chances of being re-elected.

Senators should be limited to two terms of six years each and Representatives should be limited to three terms of four years each. The reasoning is much the same as for the presidency, only more compelling. Those who represent limited constituencies are even more likely to put their own career interests or the particular needs of their own local voters above the national interest. And I firmly believe that membership in the House and Senate should not be a career, but a contribution a citizen makes to his country.

The President should have permanent, broader authority to make organizational changes in the executive branch, subject to veto by a majority vote of both houses of Congress. Presently, the Congress can and does dictate, to a considerable extent, how the executive branch is to be organized. Then, having done so, it holds the President responsible for the effective management of the executive branch as required by the Constitution. To keep pace with rapid change and new laws, the President needs the freedom to realign executive departments and move activities from one agency to another.

We should create two supra-cabinet positions in the White House: Executive Vice President for Domestic Affairs and Executive Vice President for International Affairs, appointed by the President, subject to Senate confirmation, *removable by the President and not in the line of succession.* The burdens of the presidency have become so enormous that no one person can redeem them. Wise delegation would not diminish the power of the President.

We should give the President line-veto authority. The framers of the Constitution evidently assumed that each bill sent by Congress to the President would be on a single subject and that the President could either sign it or veto it. Congress soon discovered that it could prevent the President from vetoing a bill he opposed by attaching unrelated but very important legislative riders (such as a critical appropriation) to the main bill. This practice distorts policy and wastes an inordinate amount of the President's time.

By law, presidential commissions should be made an effective method of analyzing complex national problems and proposing solutions to them. When he wishes to create a study commission, the President should be required to send an emergency recommendation to Congress, spelling out the purpose of the commission and seeking specific authorization for it, asking for the necessary funds, and requesting subpoena power. The President should be required within six months to send each commission report to the Congress with his comments and recommendations.

These are just a few examples of the kinds of reforms that are needed to bring the executive branch into harmony with these complex times. Achieving a reasonable level of stability in this incredibly complex age has become an imperative for us. And I am convinced that orderly change deliberately undertaken is the best assurance of stability.

The more politically sophisticated among us will no doubt think me naive in making some of these recommendations. I will admit only to being somewhat idealistic. And I am convinced that because we so often confuse idealism with naiveté, we frequently accept what *can* be instead of pursuing what *should* be.

Eisenhower to Senator Charles McC. Mathias

October 12 and November 9, 1979

Dear Mac: October 12, 1979

As you well know, the several causes of inflation are interrelated and any effort to check the upward spiral must deal with all elements in the picture.

In the period 1953–61, inflation averaged 1¼ percent a year, a condition of stability that carried forward into the early 60's. But in 1965 inflation began with a vengeance.

President Johnson said we could have both guns and butter. Two things happened. The cost of the Vietnam war soared to $25 billion annually and new social programs, some of little use, were started. This caused a huge deficit in Federal finances.

Federal deficits are responsible doubly for inflation. They increase the money supply and thus cause money-pull inflation. I'll label this #1.

But much of the money to cover the deficit comes out of the money market, leaving little for private industry which may wish to build a new plant, renovate an old one, improve research and machinery, and so on. But scarcity in the money market causes interest rates to rise. People borrow at the higher rates and pass on the cost. I label this #2.

In 1965 the General Motors Corporation settled a strike situation with one of the highest wage boosts in history—42 percent over a three-year period, plus an escalation clause which would be operable in harmony with inflation. This set standards for all wage settlements. [Walter] Heller wrote about cost-push inflation at that point. It is now not known and it is immaterial whether prices rise which cause labor to demand higher wages and salaries or whether wages and salary costs force prices to rise. I know in the railroad industry that wages go up every year: ICC grants higher rates. The higher transportation costs are passed on to the consumer. I'll label cost-push inflation #3.

Historically, the United States led the world in increased productivity. These annual increases were not due to men and women working harder. They resulted from research and mechanization. The investment per worker increased. Now, partly because money costs too much, partly because we have lost markets and devote much time to trying to recover, productivity, on the whole, stands still. It increases slightly some years, none other years, and at present is a minus figure. Label this #4.

Government intrusion into private business has been a strong influence which results in loss of productivity, research, creativity, and sheer determination to produce a better product at reasonable cost. There is scarcely an industry in this country that is not badly affected by Federal regulations, thousands of them. It can be demonstrated, as indeed you have done, that the government must accept much of the responsibility for our being outproduced by Japan, Germany, and other countries. Label this #5.

By the time of the energy difficulty, inflation had risen to the 8 or 9 percent figure. The energy problem put the figure in the two-digit field. This in turn caused a recession, which exacerbated some of the influences I have already mentioned, especially Federal deficits. Label OPEC and all it represents #6. (Keep in mind that early in his administration President Carter, speaking about energy, said, "This is the moral equivalent of war.") At that moment we should have instituted rational rationing, not just because supplies might become short, but to keep huge international imbalances from undermining the dollar which had become the world's major means of exchange. By a plan of rationing that would hurt very few, the main attack being on pleasure use, we could have cut energy imports by fifty percent. The cumulative effect would have been significant. The lower the dollar fell, the higher OPEC prices went. But since we continued to import foreign goods and services, the OPEC situation had a dual effect on inflation. However, I'll label this only #6.

Our trade with Japan is disgraceful. Japan with modern research and equipment, with rising levels of productivity, is more efficient than we. But she sells to us [at] less than she sells to her own people, taking into account her cost of transporting to the United States. This is dumping. While Japan does not have a tariff against our goods, her industries force the Japanese government to apply technical requirements, which I am assured by those who know, raises the cost of our goods in Japan about one hundred percent. Thus a Chevrolet that sells for $4,000 here, costs $8,000 in Japan. The deficit in this trade is $13 billion a year. This must be added to the OPEC deficit and its influence is high. I think, therefore, that I am justified in setting this forth as a separate cause that must be dealt with. #7.

I cannot label monetary policy as shaped by the Federal Reserve Board as cause #8, because on the whole, especially under Arthur Burns, the Fed has done as good a job as possible in view of the fact that nothing has been done about the other causes and the Fed by itself is almost helpless.

You did not ask me to say how we should deal with the various causes of inflation. I believe there are acceptable ways to diminish the effect of each, all within the American tradition.

Most elected officials believe that the things which must be done would be unpopular. I dispute this. I am sure that the American people are so worried about the future of this country, including damage to our representative form of government, that if a leader, such as you, would come forth boldly and explain to the people the causes of inflation, imbalances, energy, crime, and so on, and with courage tell the things, popular and unpopular, we must do to save our nation, that person (you can do it) would be swept into office.

But not a single candidate is dealing with the facts or the solutions. They depend upon charisma, criticisms of Carter, good fellow, central position, and emotional gimmicks. I don't know what any Republican candidate would do about our terrible problems if he should become President.

Sincerely and fondly,

Mathias responded with a request for advice on dealing with inflation, which led Eisenhower to write again.

Dear Mac: November 9, 1979

I would much prefer to discuss with you the possible methods we could use to overcome the seven causes of inflation I outlined briefly in my letter of October 12. In writing, I shall omit much essential detail, but will say enough that you will know whether you want additional facts and ideas.

#1: *Federal deficits*: Obviously we can cure a major cause of inflation only by bringing the Federal budget into near-balance. In my judgment, a judgment based on fifty years of work in the Federal executive establishment, the elimination of waste, extravagance, and graft could more than overcome the current deficit which is in the neighborhood of $30 billion.

Otherwise, we must cut appropriations and temporarily diminish good activities. In the reduction process, defense should not be immune. I repeat what I have said to you before and what President Eisenhower constantly emphasized, namely, that our security depends on much more than military hardware and trained soldiers. The total strength and prestige of the nation are essential: Economic strength, unity among our people, respect by foreign nations, and domestic goals of high purpose which transcend the selfish purposes of all the pressure groups whose representatives haunt the halls of the Congress.

#2:   *If #1 is achieved,* then the Federal government will no longer have to invade the money market or have the Federal Reserve banks buy its paper. The Federal Reserve Board could then greatly reduce the rediscount rate, businesses, factories, and others borrowing money would reduce their costs of borrowing, and ultimate costs to consumers would decline. I repeat what I said before: The Federal Reserve Board cannot do anything effective by itself. Indeed, its efforts to stem inflation (without checking the other inflationary influences) are in themselves inflationary. The current discount rate is 15.5 percent. Manufacturers, railroads, and other businesses pay the high cost and pass it on to consumers. The Fed, operating harmoniously in other corrective actions, could be most effective.

#3:   *Cost-push inflation:* I do not advocate wage and price controls, but I want to emphasize that the reason usually given for avoiding such controls is fallacious. It is generally said, "Nixon tried this and it failed." The truth is that Nixon was opposed to controls. But the Congress got panicky and passed a stand-by authority for him to use if he found it necessary. In time he, too, became panicky and instituted controls. But he hated every moment of it. Under phase two of that effort, inflation dropped to 3.4 percent. Then Nixon lifted controls. All the pressures built up by deficit financing and other forces surged forth and prices skyrocketed.

It is important to keep in mind that wage and price controls may be likened to a dam in a river. They will prevent flooding until the waters have reached the top of the dam. If, in the meantime, the fundamental causes of flooding have not been dealt with, then the waters below the dam will be as voluminous and destructive as before. In short, such controls are useful only to buy time to do constructive things.

(You and I lived under controls in World War II and the Korean War. They worked fairly well. We were not hurt.)

My objection to wage and price controls is the bureaucrats who have to be recruited to run the programs are not well trained, some of them are ignorant, and many of them abuse their new importance.

I think there is a better way. On occasions in the past and for other reasons we have employed what we call surtaxes. I would put a surtax on all earnings that resulted from wage, price, dividend, and all other increases of more than, say, three percent a year, this percentage being our goal for increased productivity. Some exceptions to the general regulation would have to be provided. Thus Chrysler, now losing money, ought to be able to get to a profitable situation before a surtax applied.

#4: *Productivity*: Productivity is determined by two elements—the attitude and behavior of workers, and the efficient machinery in production. We have slipped badly in both areas. Sloppy, inefficient work has become normal. Only an effective national leader can rekindle the spirit of all so that we are again willing to do our best to achieve goals we have set for ourselves. The problem of production machinery is quite different. High cost has caused many industries to reduce research and to cease spending funds on improved equipment. There can be no doubt that Japan and Germany, especially, are now more productive per worker than we of the United States. To overcome this deficiency will really take the best leadership our nation can produce.

#5: *Government Interference*: You and some of your colleagues in the Senate have spoken accurately and eloquently of the disaster caused by government interference in business and personal affairs. I need not elaborate. I can tell you that the Federal regulations governing railroad transportation fill half or an entire wall of a modern library.

#6: *OPEC*: When President Carter said, "This is the moral equivalent of war," he was right, but he did nothing about the matter. It is a well known fact that we waste fifty percent of all energy we consume. The real purpose of rationing should not be merely to meet a possible shortage of fuel, but greatly to reduce the current importation and cost of imported energy. In World War II I lived under rationing. I drove to and from my office only once a week; my fellow riders each did the same. Sheer pleasure use was abandoned. There were no yacht races. Seldom did one see a single person driving a car to work. Rationing should hit pleasure uses of energy most, essential uses least. I believe that we could reduce importation of energy by fifty percent by a rationing system that would hurt very few persons.

#7: *Our trade with Japan*: I explained in my previous letter why this trade is unfair and inflationary. I would have the President use his current authority and place serious quotas on imports from Japan, from cars to electronics, cameras and so on. Simultaneously, I would set up a special study commission to determine our own program for making trade with Japan truly fair.

The foregoing actions, thought to be politically unpopular, would, in my judgment, be readily accepted by citizens if they *believed* the man or woman who had the responsibility of telling them the truth about our present dangerous situation. If they believed, they would accept something along the lines I have suggested. With these actions underway, the Federal Reserve Board could take on great importance in maintaining economic stability.

Sincerely,

Violent Crime

An Overview

Ｗe live in an urban society. We live in an affluent society. And we live in a society that is violent.

In the convergence of those three characteristics lies a central problem for America in the 1970's.

In the metropolitan areas, where two-thirds of the American people live, violent crime is rising, and fear is rising in its wake. Fear is manifested in the locked doors, the empty streets, the growing number of guns bought for self-protection, the signs on public buses that say: "Driver does not carry cash." It is the neglected conditions in American cities that help to account for the rise in violent crime, but violent crime is the cancer that may kill the cities and paralyze the suburbs as well.

The potential products of American affluence—flights to other planets, supersonic transports, rebuilt cities, effective systems of mass transit, clean air and water—all these will be hollow achievements if, at the same time, we ignore the despair and alienation of a large portion of our citizens who do not share adequately in America's affluence. The price of ignoring their situation will be ever-mounting rates of violent crimes—and ever-spreading fear, with its paralyzing results.

Dr. Norval Morris, Professor of Law and Criminology, University of Chicago, said to the Commission on Violence: "Crime for the first time is

This text is a transcription of the opening address at the Milton S. Eisenhower Symposium, The Johns Hopkins University, November 10, 1970.

a threat to the quality of life in this country," and Dr. Price M. Cobbs, the distinguished black psychiatrist, said, "If violence continues at its present pace, we may well witness the end of the grand experiment of democracy."

And the Commission on the Causes and Prevention of Violence, after obtaining the unprecedented help of two hundred of the nation's leading scholars in history, law, sociology, criminology, psychiatry, and other fields—after obtaining public evidence from some 150 individuals, ranging from student radicals to police chiefs, from scholars to head of the Federal Bureau of Investigation—and, after considering this complex problem among ourselves for a year and a half, said to the President of the United States: "We solemnly declare our conviction that this nation is entering a period in which our people need to be as concerned by the internal dangers to our free society as by any possible combination of external threats."

II

The best estimate of the number of serious crimes committed in the United States each year is ten million, of which more than 1,200,000 are violent crimes: homicides, aggravated assaults, forcible rapes, and robberies. According to another estimate, more than 1 out of 100 Americans commit a major violent crime in any one year. Many more, of course, commit a serious crime some time in their lives.

This violence in our midst earns us the distinction of being the clear leader in violent crime among the modern, stable nations of the world. Thus, the United States, with 200 million people, averages fifty times as many gun murders a year as do England, Germany, and Japan combined, with their total population of 214 million.

This appalling statistic calls to mind other salient features of our culture. The more than 90 million firearms privately owned by Americans give us the distinction of having the highest—far highest—gun-to-population ratio of any nation on earth. About half of all American homes have a firearm, and many have more than one. About 25 million of those weapons are *concealable handguns*, and these are the firearms used in virtually all aggravated assaults and robberies involving firearms and in three-fourths of all gun murders.

Parenthetically, let me add that I continue to be perplexed by the blind, emotional resistance that greets any proposal to bring this senseless excess under control. We lag behind every other civilized nation in the world in failing to have a comprehensive, effective national policy of firearms control. Yet when the Commission on Violence, after careful weighing of all the relevant facts and arguments, recommended a policy of restrictive licensing of handguns and a simple identification system for long guns, vitriolic mail began to pour into my office in Evergreen House. I was labeled with every epithet I'd ever heard—and some I'd never heard before—from "you shame the Eisenhower name" to "fascist" and even to "Communist" (these last two covering quite a spectrum). Vociferous opposition of this sort has kept this nation from instituting a sane, effective policy of firearms control. In the meantime, the senseless tragedies repeat themselves: the domestic quarrel or argument between friends turns into a homicide because a gun is available for acting on the rage. Guns are handy to support the yearnings of the sex maniac. Guns are available to those who hold up banks, filling stations, savings and loan associations—and too often the guns are used as more than a threat. So merchants are leaving the city in fear of their lives. Residents are fleeing to the suburbs and there installing every known type of protective device. And in the meantime, police in most parts of the country are without an effective legal maneuver against the criminal who possesses a pistol, unless they catch him in the actual act of using it in a crime.

If, on the other hand, we had restrictive licensing of handguns, similar to the Sullivan law of New York State, police could, with the use of modern electronic equipment, spot a metallic object on a suspect and, even under recent Supreme Court rulings, frisk a suspect. If the suspect is found with a gun and lacks a license, he can be convicted and sentenced on that evidence alone. There can be no doubt that in a few years the right law would have a profound effect in reducing the crimes of armed robbery, aggravated assault, and homicide.

Guns *alone* do not give us the distinction of being the most violent of the advanced societies of the world. Controlling firearms would greatly reduce fatalities and discourage many criminal careers, but international comparisons show that our capacity for acts of rage and rapacity is impressive, whether or not firearms are involved. Thus, aggravated assault—which often is just a murder which didn't work out—occurs in the United States at a rate twice that of England and Wales, eighteen times than of Canada. Rape occurs at a rate three times that of Canada, twelve times that of England and Wales. Our robbery rate is double that of Canada, nine times that of England and Wales.

To complete the picture of America the Violent we would have to sketch in the riots that have erupted in American cities in recent years, the firebombings of campus and public buildings by a lunatic radical minority, the attacks by mobs on peaceful demonstrators, and the outrageous killings of students by law enforcement personnel.

By cold statistics, group violence has not been a major problem compared to individual acts of violent crime. A Commission on Violence study looked back over five years and counted 190 deaths and 9,100 injuries from group violence, mostly ghetto riots; in that same five-year period, 53,000 Americans were victims of reported murders; more than a million were injured in aggravated assaults. And if it is fair to extrapolate from a Harris Poll conducted for the Commission, then 62 million Americans have been punched or beaten at some point in their lives, and 24 million have been threatened with a gun or actually shot at.

While group violence is the secondary problem, its prevalence and high visibility in contemporary America does help to shape attitudes which encourage violent crime—a matter I will return to momentarily.

III

We will have to look at the picture of violence in America more closely—to see where violent crime is concentrated—if we are to begin to understand its causes and know where to invest our social resources to reduce its incidence. The National Commission on Violence found:

First, that violent crime is heavily concentrated in the larger cities. There the rate of crime per unit of population is eight times the rural rate, six times the smaller town rate. The 26 cities with more than half a million residents each account for only one-sixth of our nation's population, but almost one-half of our total reported violent crimes. If you live in a metropolitan area today your mathematical chances of becoming a victim of a homicide, a rape, an assault, or a robbery are one in 125 *each year.* If you live in the city of Baltimore, your mathematical chance of becoming a victim of one of these four violent crimes is one in 49 each year. So, during his lifetime, the odds are *in favor* of a Baltimore resident's becoming a victim of a violent crime.

Second, violent crime in cities is overwhelmingly committed by males.

Third, violent crime in cities is concentrated among youthful offenders. By far the highest urban arrest rate for homicide occurs in the 18 to 24 age group. For rape, robbery and aggravated assault, arrests in the 15 to 24 age group far outstrip those of any other group—indeed they are three times as high as for any other age group.

There have been disturbing increases in arrest rates among youngsters 10 to 14—a 300 percent increase in assault between 1958 and 1967, and 200 percent in robbery in the same period.

Fourth, violent crime in the cities is committed primarily by individuals at the lower end of the socio-economic scale.

Fifth, violent crime in the cities stems disproportionately from the ghetto slums where most Negroes live. Where discrimination is added to low socio-economic status, in other words, violent crime rates are especially high. To describe violent crime as primarily a ghetto phenomenon *is to make a statement about social and cultural conditions, not about racial characteristics.* I emphasize that all evidence indicates that one race is no more criminogenic than another. Professor Marvin Wolfgang, the eminent sociologist and criminologist who served as co-director of research for the Commission on Violence, recently published a book on this subject. Solid research conducted over a long period of years shows no correlation between race and crime. The correlation is between the total environmental and human conditions in which some people live and crime.

Sixth, the *victims* of violent crimes in the cities generally have the same characteristics as the offenders—that is, they tend to be males, youths, poor persons, and blacks. Against the dangerous myth that violent crime is a kind of interracial warfare, I cite the fact that nine out of ten urban homicides, aggravated assaults, and rapes *involve victims and offenders of the same race.* An exception is robbery. Our studies showed that 45 percent of urban robberies involve Negroes robbing whites—very often young black males robbing somewhat older white males.

Seventh, with the exception of robbery, violent crimes tend to be acts of passion among intimates and acquaintances. This is true in almost half the cases of rape, and the great majority of cases of assault and homicide. Robbery, on the other hand, is committed by a stranger eight out of ten times.

Finally, the greatest proportion—by far—of all serious violence is committed by repeaters. In a study of 10,000 boys in Philadelphia, 627 boys—*only 6 percent of those studies*—accounted for 53 percent of the homicides, rapes, and assaults known to the police and *71 percent* of the robberies.

In sum, violent crime in the cities is committed primarily by males rather than females, youths rather than older people, by the poor and unskilled rather than the more successful, by ghetto blacks rather than residents of more affluent sections of the city. The highest rates of violent crime occur in the population where these characteristics all intersect: the young, poor, Negro male.

I add the caveat that violent crime is not exclusively a province of ghetto youth. Alcoholics and drug addicts who are a danger to their fellow citizens come from all strata of society. The thin shell of civility that houses our aggressive impulses has been known to crack open and splay violence in some of the so-called "finest families" in America. On the other hand, the social pathology that exists in the ghetto does not turn every poor, young Negro male into a criminal, nor even a majority of them.

We need to focus our attention on the inner-city ghetto because that is where the major problem of violent crime exists. That is where the socially destructive forces are at work breeding violent crime, which hastens the decay of our cities, which in turn breeds more crime.

There are certain dispositions in American thinking that tend to block our understanding of ghetto problems. We are a hard-working people. We believe hard work is important because we believe success—however we choose to define success—is the inevitable reward for hard work. We tend to regard as morally inferior those who are failures. We tend to say: They have only themselves to blame.

We tend also to forget how, for hundreds of years, the realities of American life have made a cruel mockery of the work-for-your-reward ethic for the black segment of our population. We boast of what our immigrant ancestors were able to accomplish while ignoring the fact that their assimilation came easier because they were the "right" color. We forget that they came from Europe with some skills, and at a time when industry thrived on labor, not science and technology, and welcomed all the white workers it could get. We forget that the *white* immigrant ghettos had *their* high rates of crime until they were assimilated into the larger society, a process that often required several generations. Indeed, the success of white immigrants still isn't all we boast it to be; there are still twice as many whites living below the poverty line as non-whites.

Many who acknowledge that blacks have been pounded to despair by discrimination—and many who don't—assume that Negro parents do not bother to discipline their children and take no interest in their moral development. Yet, as Robert Coles, the well-known Harvard psychiatrist, has pointed out, "Negro children probably receive more punitively enforced reminders of what is right and wrong than any other segment of our population."

But consider how hollow the maternal admonitions begin to sound once the realities of the ghetto start to impinge on a black youngster's awareness. Like every American mother, she says: "Work hard in school; it is the only way to get ahead." What measure of reality does that have for the ghetto youth? There are no examples of educated, successful men in his immediate experience. His father—if he has one—and the men up and down the block sweat at menial and intermittent jobs. The one across the street with the fancy convertible isn't working for the sanitation department; he's pushing drugs or robbing corner grocery stores.

In the crowded apartment there are no quiet places for study, no books or serious magazines, no conversations to stimulate the intellect. On the other hand, there is the constant lure of the television set. The average young ghetto resident, by the time he is 18, will have spent more time watching television than he spent in school. There is also the lure of the street where the other children are running and playing, often deep into the night, and where a youngster may have to engage in crime or the use of dope to be accepted by his peers. Here is what Professor Wolfgang calls the sub-culture of violence.

The neighborhood school, dilapidated and poorly equipped, has accommodated itself to defeat. It asks only for a modicum of discipline, ignores the strivings of eager students and the indifference of rebellious students, and automatically promotes to the next higher grade every student just so it can have room for the next crop of undereducated and unmotivated children.

If the ghetto youth has the determination to swim against the tides all the way to a high school diploma—and, of course, many do not—he may find job or further educational opportunities waiting for him. In the past few years, barriers to advancement for high-school educated blacks have been falling. If he drops out, as so many do, he may find the doors to meaningful job opportunities closed to him. In the American value system he is now a full-fledged failure, and he is quite aware of it. All those material comforts displayed and advertised on the television screen are not to be his—at least not by legitimate means.

And why not use violence to get what he needs to be somebody? He has little to gain by playing according to society's rules and little to lose by not. He is familiar with violence. In the disintegrated community of the ghetto, violent quarrels, brawls, and careers in crime are commonplace. Violence is also a way of proving manliness, especially in the street gangs of the inner city. The larger society apparently does not find violence abhorrent; violence is a constant theme in television dramas, and violence is touted in American folklore. Americans love their guns; they have, as I've said, the highest gun-to-population ratio of any nation in the world.

Considering the pressures, frustrations, and temptations at work on the youth in our ghettos, the wonder is that violent crime rates in the cities are not higher than they are.

And yet, *conditions in the ghettos have been improving.* During this past decade incomes of Negroes in cities increased, the percentage of blacks completing high school rose, as did the percentage entering universities, and unemployment rates dropped significantly. We are faced with an apparent paradox: While conditions have been improving for inner-city blacks, rates of violent crime among them have been soaring. As closely as the Commission on Violence could determine, the combined rate of violent crimes—per unit of population—*has increased 100 percent during the last ten years.*

A partial answer to this paradox is that real gains for blacks have still left significant gaps between their conditions and those of whites. Thus, for example, the Negro unemployment rate continues to be about twice that for whites. And unemployment among black teenagers in cities has actually been increasing. Last year it stood at 25 percent, which was two-and-a-half times the unemployment rate for white teenagers.

But secondly, demographic changes in this country would lead one to expect an increase in violent crime. The age group most involved in violent crime, 16 to 24, has soared both in number and proportion of the total population—from 20 million ten years ago to 29 million today, and from 11 percent of the population to almost 15 percent. The increasing urbanization of our society also helps to account for the rise in violent crime. Actually, in the past ten years, the spectacular growth has taken place in the suburbs. Middle-class, mostly affluent whites, have been moving out of the cities, leaving them increasingly to the poor, black population, which suffers inadequate services financed by a declining tax base. Another demographic trend of some bearing is the increasing instability of American families. Divorces and separations are on the rise in every segment of the population, but nowhere as spectacularly as among poor blacks in our cities. At present, only 22 percent of the poor black children in the central cities live with both parents. Ten years ago, half of the children in that category lived with both—a sad circumstance that should have been improved, not permitted to grow worse. This is probably a major consequence of our anachronistic welfare system.

A third factor has been a vast increase in the number of firearms in private hands. Sales of long guns, the Commission on Violence found, doubled from 1962 to 1968. In that same period, sales of *handguns* quadrupled.

Fourthly, we are living in a time of profound changes—technological, occupational, social and cultural. Times of great change alter how we work, think and live. They set us adrift from our moorings and create tensions and uncertainties. If American parents seem unduly permissive, if they appear to be unsure about the values to encourage in their children and the standards to impose, perhaps it is because American society has already changed greatly since their own childhood and is destined to change even more in the future. In the absence of clear-cut expectations and standards, the traditional social controls have lost their grip, and violence is one result of the breakdown. This may explain why violence is rising among youth in affluent, middle-class homes, as well as in the ghettos.

A fifth and related change: Events in the 1960's have served to diminish the respect accorded the institutions of government. The spectacle of governors defying federal court orders, of policemen beating demonstrators, of mobs looting stores with impunity, of some college students destroying property and then demanding amnesty, of elected officials exposed in corruption—all these, and more, have served to encourage a cynical disrespect for law and lawmaking institutions.

Besides encouraging the attitude that lawful behavior is "just for suckers," such events tend to give direct legitimacy to violence. The deep divisions within our country set off tensions and anger, but the readiness with which some groups give violent expression to their anger and impatience creates an appealing, contagious, but very dangerous object lesson. Urban riots had a powerful lesson for ghetto youth: that it is perfectly all right to vent one's dissatisfactions in acts of violence. More recently, violence—as distinguished, of course, from peaceful protest or demonstration—on the nation's campuses has probably had an effect even more powerful. If the most privileged young people can have their violent donnybrooks, a ghetto youth is entitled to ask, "Why shouldn't I?"

Of course the frustrations of ghetto life are very real. The frustrations in recent years have been especially deep because of the so-called revolution of rising expectations. Life for Americans generally has grown more comfortable and rewarding, there have been noticeable improvements for the poor, but delivery of improvements in the ghetto has not kept pace with the *political promises* or with what the poor and disadvantaged have come to expect. It is hardly surprising that the resulting frustrations give rise to violent crime.

There remains one very obvious reason for mounting crime in our society: the increasing failure of law enforcement agencies to cope with it. Consider the grim statistics. Probably ten million serious crimes were committed in the United States last year. About half of these crimes were never reported to the Federal Bureau of Investigation. Only 12 percent of those ten million crimes resulted in the arrest of anyone. Only 6 percent resulted in the conviction of anyone, and this 6 percent included many pleas to lesser offenses. Only $1\frac{1}{2}$ percent resulted in the incarceration of anyone. And of those who were incarcerated, most will return to prison another time for additional offenses.

As Lloyd Cutler, eminent lawyer and Executive Director of the Violence Commission, remarked of these statistics: "It would be hard to argue that crime does not pay. The sad fact is that our criminal justice system, as presently operated, does not deter, does not detect, does not convict, and does not correct."

As crimes go unpunished, and as criminals go through the corrections system, changed for the worse instead of better, it is no wonder crime is on the increase.

IV

Police departments in American cities are understaffed and under-equipped. Police are undereducated and undertrained. Juvenile courts have failed to live up to their humane ideal. The lower courts in which most adults are tried too often have crowded dockets, inadequate procedures for investigating the defendant and circumstances, and necessarily shoddy ways of dispensing justice. The jails in which indigent defendants sit awaiting trial have been aptly described as "rabbit warrens." Prisons have earned the label "schools for criminals." Inside prison walls are terrorist societies ruled more by prisoners themselves than by guards. Lacking equipment and sufficient professional staff, prison training programs are outmoded and rehabilitation services are wholly inadequate. At the end of their terms, most prisoners are thrust out on the street without meaningful help in readjustment.

The Crime Commission studied the deplorable conditions of our criminal justice system and, in its 1967 Report, made dozens of thoughtful recommendations for improving all its aspects—police, courts, corrections. The National Commission on Violence added a few recommendations of its own, mostly having to do with improving coordination among the various agencies of the system. We recommended that urban governments form Offices of Criminal Justice to improve coordination at the local level. We urged citizens to form advisory groups in local areas to help with that effort. We suggested that leading citizens be invited to form a privately financed National Citizens Justice Center to encourage improvements in the criminal justice system at all levels, through private citizens' groups as well as government agencies.

This is not the occasion for detailing the recommendations of either of the two commissions. But I do want to call your attention to one additional recommendation of the Violence Commission—namely, that we as a nation "give concrete expression to our concern about crime by a solemn national commitment to double our investment in the administration of justice as rapidly as such an investment can be wisely planned and utilized."

At present, our entire criminal justice system in this country—federal, state, and local—receives less than 2 percent of all government revenues and less than three-quarters of one percent of our national income. We spend less on this pitifully inadequate system than we do on federal agriculture programs and little more than we do on the space program.

Responsibility for police, courts, and corrections has resided mostly with state and local governments. That is as it should be. But these governments do not have the *financial* resources to deepen their investment in improving the criminal justice system. The financial commitment must be a federal one. The federal government, after all, takes the lion's share of tax revenues; it ought to take the major financial responsibility for deterring crime, administering justice fairly, and bringing wrongdoers back into a productive role in society.

The Council of Economic Advisers estimates that 19 billion dollars annually will be freed for domestic programs once our military engagement ends in Southeast Asia. A host of long-neglected needs at home will be competing for these dollars. The criminal justice system is only one of them. We ought to proceed now to plan the use of those future dollars wisely. A firm commitment now, in the form of the organic legislation, to increase greatly our expenditures on the criminal justice system would permit planners within the system to make effective reforms once the money becomes available.

V

I do not mean to suggest that the criminal justice system should be given priority over all the other competing needs of our society. Quite the contrary. In our report to the President, the National Commission on Violence spoke of the twin objectives of making violence "both unnecessary and unrewarding." Neither corrective approach will succeed without the other. Making violence *unrewarding* is a job for law enforcement agencies. Making violence *unnecessary* is nothing less than the task of giving all Americans a satisfactory stake in the life of the community.

We must seek to eradicate poverty where it persists, improve education where it is deficient, and provide health care in areas of the community where it is inadequate and beyond the financial reach of citizens. Efforts to remake our cities must include steps to eliminate the ghettos, to provide decent housing for everyone, to build effective mass transits (especially for those who cannot afford automobiles), and to assure adequate measures for the upkeep of every neighborhood. Our national goal should be the dignity of work for every citizen capable of work. Our overriding goal, in all such programs, should be to provide every citizen a stake in the community. The citizen who has much to gain by living by the rules and in concert with his fellow citizens has much to lose by defying the rules and rebuking the community.

I add the caution that we ought not to pursue these social measures merely in the name of crime eradication. The high correlation of the outward symbols of deprivation—bad housing, low educational achievement, high unemployment—with violent crime does not mean that improvements in the former will lead inexorably to complete elimination of the latter. Physical conditions can be changed by concerted effort, but attitudes and habits will change only through inner enlightenment. The human animal is complex, and there is more to violent crime than a simple reaction to alienating circumstances.

We ought to undertake these social reform measures, rather, because they are the proper, humane things to do. Reordering our national priorities to give new emphasis to the quality of life for every citizen is a realistic goal for this affluent society. It is a worthy new phase for a nation that has subdued a continent physically and accomplished so much technologically.

These are matters not to be left to government alone. It is the job of all of us, as private citizens, to seek deep understanding of the problem of violence in our society, to voice concern over the deficiencies in our society that give rise to violence, and to help remedy these deficiencies in our private capacities. It is the job of local schools, churches, and citizen-groups to emphasize and transmit, more effectively than they have in the past, the values that will make our society more humane and less violent. It is also their job to lend encouragement to youth to participate creatively in the society. It is the job of our nation's scholars to seek a better understanding of the roots of violence, and to design and evaluate more effective measures for discouraging violence. And it is the job of all of us—but especially of those privileged by education—to repudiate violence and live by the precepts of tolerance, reasonableness, and civility, so that others may see that violence is unnecessary and—measured by the highest standard—truly unrewarding.

I conclude this overview of a troublesome national problem with two quotations from the report of the Violence Commission to the President: We said:

"Order is indispensable to society, law is indispensable to order, and enforcement is indispensable to law."

And then, to make the thought complete, and legitimate, we added:

"The justice and the decency of the law and its enforcement are not simply embellishments, but rather the indispensable condition of respect for law and civil peace in a free society."

Commencement Address

The Johns Hopkins University, June 13, 1967

I consider it a singular honor to have been invited by the Class of 1967 to present the commencement address today.

In at least one sense, it is most appropriate that I join you graduates, for I, too, am completing my formal tenure at Johns Hopkins—and mine, too, has been an educational experience, I assure you.

I can think of no better way to climax a long and fulfilling career in government and education than to bid godspeed to a new generation.

I must disappoint you at the outset, however. Tradition decrees that the commencement speaker should provide the graduates with a vision of the future. But I must confess that the future has become more obscure to me with each passing year.

The speaker is also expected to impart sage advice on how you graduates should cope with the problems and opportunities that lie ahead. I am afraid that I have more questions than answers. In fact, it perplexes me that I had more solutions to life's problems at my own commencement that I have today at yours.

Part of the reason for this, I suppose, is that more awesome changes have taken place in my lifetime than in any previous period and, I sometimes feel, in all of man's earlier time on this earth. And it is not only change that confounds us, it is the *pace* of change, the swiftness with which events move. The more we know, the faster we go. The faster we go, the less we know.

How often have you heard someone say, "You're rushing so fast that you are going to meet yourself coming back." Well, that is the way I often think of this age we live in. And with what the physicists now tell us about anti-matter, we may, indeed, meet ourselves coming back.

II

Occasionally when I contemplate this bewildering era, I reflect upon an earlier time and indulge in the luxury of nostalgia. Then I see in the sleepy town of Abilene, Kansas, a cozy white house, surrounded by colorful hollyhocks, a flourishing orchard, and a generous vegetable garden. My brothers and I sit on the front porch in rocking chairs, observing the drift of the seasons and the passing of the small segment of the world we know. There is no war, no domestic turmoil, no protest marches, no complex problems to bother us. We, like others in our town, are isolated. Our community is self-contained economically, physically, socially. We have not heard of world interdependence. All is peaceful and we are quite content.

But the essence of nostalgia is an awareness that what has been will never be again. The streams of history may be likened to the ceaseless flow of a giant river. Man can work with the river, building dams and dikes, seeking to have its enormous energy serve the good of man rather than to destroy. But he cannot stop the waters from reaching the ocean. So it is with the currents of history which in our time have reached flood stage.

Most of my generation have witnessed these raging currents with astonishment, often in confusion and with serious misgivings.

In Abilene, we had rude awakenings as we came to understand the nature and consequences of modern change.

We had supposed that our economic welfare depended solely upon weather conducive to crop growth and upon hard work, but suddenly, despite perfect weather and efficient work, we found our farmers going broke because Italy raised its tariff on wheat and later because Britain devalued the pound. Soon, and not unrelated to our difficulty, the United States suffered its worst depression. Abilene's economic self-containment—and that of the nation, too—was gone forever.

Our physical isolation also disappeared. I was a freshman in high school before I ventured so far away as Kansas City, Missouri, one hundred and sixty miles down the Union Pacific tracks; alone, I had serious misgivings on that strange trip, and when I got off the train, I was sure Kansas City was the largest metropolitan area in the world and quite possibly a den of iniquity. But in a few years thereafter I was traveling to most of the nations of the world, with greater physical comfort, less fear of the unknown, and in not much more time than I experienced on that first trip away from Abilene.

And our social self-containment was viciously destroyed, for we of Abilene found ourselves in one war, caused not seemingly by anything we of my town had done, but by an explosion in the Balkans; in a few more years we were in another conflict, due to an infamy at Pearl Harbor, and the insane ambitions of a corporal in Germany.

We were forced to recognize that the streams of events were toward the unification of our world, a unification which, to succeed, required genuine intercultural understanding, juridical equality of nations, mutuality in human relations, and a global willingness to forego [*sic*] lesser and more selfish purposes in order to concentrate successfully on the transcendent goal of positive peace and rising levels of well-being for all, wherever they lived, whatever their color, nationality, or basic philosophy.

This was an historical imperative confronting us—as promising as life itself and as inevitable as death. But unhappily, we, as human beings, were not ready for this imperative.

Changes in every circumstance of life have accelerated, but human attitudes have remained generally inflexible. And so, in most of this century the world has lived in chaotic revolution of manifold phases and significance.

III

At the core of revolutionary change are science and technology, in which change is so rapid as to confound all but the most sophisticated. When I was a youngster, there was not a single industrial research laboratory in the United States and fundamental research in our universities was in its infancy. Now we are essentially dominated by scientific and technological developments. Ninety percent of all scientists who ever lived are alive today. Their achievements are monumental. Human knowledge doubles every ten years. Indeed, in a single year, biological and physical scientists alone publish nearly 1,400,000 monographs, technical articles, and books, and the new knowledge is put into use almost instantly. Thus eighty percent of the drugs administered in our hospitals today were unknown a decade ago, and half the products of some of our leading industries have been conceived in industrial research laboratories in the last fifteen years. But the most dramatic example is in the field of national security. For thousands of years a weapons system was valid for five hundred years. In the latter part of the nineteenth century a system was good for fifty years. Now an entire system is essentially obsolete before it is fully operational.

Science and technology, penetrating atoms and genes, exploring space, and mechanizing civilizations, are changing how we work, how we organize, how we think, and how we live. They are profoundly affecting our relations with other free nations, dominating our relations with the center of international communism, and insistently posing the critical question of our time: *Will expanding knowledge and powerful new instruments lead us to the Golden Age which has eluded man since creation, or to mutual annihilation?*

Science, with all its wonders, does not supply the answer. Science tells us what is *possible*, not what is *right*. Science tells us what we *can* do, not what we *should* do. The answer lies not with scientific man, but with all of us—with social man.

A significant sub-element in modern technological change involves rapid transportation, buttressed by world-wide instantaneous communication. These have shrunk the earth, brought peoples closer together. They have enhanced economic interdependence, so much so that today the plants in our great industrial empire would cease to belch smoke, and millions would be out of work, if we could not import vital primary commodities from sixty different nations, and in payment, could not ship to them and others vast quantities of food, fibre, and manufactured goods.

And, needless to say, economic interdependence has made essential solid and dependable political and human relations. *But here is the rub!* The imperative has come too soon. It has preceded mental preparation for it. Most of the peoples of the world grossly misunderstand the United States—its social structure, its philosophy, its global purposes. And our conceptions of others are not much more valid than theirs of us. So, too, often, decisions, profoundly important decisions, are made by us and by other nations not on the basis of what really is, but on the basis of what, in prejudice and ignorance, people think it is. While understanding would not itself guarantee the peaceful conditions modern life demands, it is surely true that there will not be positive peace without better mutual understanding than now prevails.

Concurrently with these measurable changes, and partly because of them—all, I emphasize within one short lifetime—a human revolution has suddenly arisen to confound and haunt us. We are most familiar with the moral conflict between East and West. But in Latin America, where for centuries a few lived amidst fabulous riches while oceans of illiterates lived in squalor, there is at this moment the certainty of massive revolt. The sole question is whether it will be bloody or characterized by rapid, democratic, social change. Radio and television, modest products of the scientific revolution, have reached the minds of the masses who cannot read but can see and hear. So, overnight, they have come to understand that human degradation is neither universal nor inevitable. After a long sleep, the giants of Latin America, Africa, the Middle and Far East, are awake, angrily shaking the archaic social structures that have oppressed them.

Already they have all but eliminated imperialism in the free world, thus reversing several hundred years of history for European nations, about fifty years for us. Unfortunately, this change in the free world, meriting applause, has been paralleled by the development of a new, more vicious imperialism in Eastern Europe and the Far East, involving a third of the three billion persons who inhabit the earth.

These and manifold other rapidly moving historic forces are carrying us to the very brink of critical decision at a time, as I have said, when the minds of men are not prepared to cast out prejudice and to reason together in mutual understanding and respect.

As I seek to shape my own views on these issues, I honestly at moments would welcome a return to the isolation, contentment, and certainties of my youth. Of course I know the futility of such passing thoughts. So I try to consider things as they are now, and without implying any criticism of any action now under way or policy now in effect, I must in candor say that I am persuaded that the time is here when we should reappraise our posture and our methods in the world.

Since World War II, four national administrations have adhered to the policy of opposing, by force when necessary, the coercive spread of communism. This is morally right. But I fear the policy is doomed to ultimate failure unless the other free nations of the world join us in every critical situation in the application of this policy. I believe that the achievement of a dependable alliance, confederation, or transnational compact is the most important single obligation upon statesmen at this moment.

I am also persuaded that foreign aid, as we have conceived and practiced it for a quarter of a century, is little more than a palliative, sometimes self-defeating. But given consistent concerted action by all free nations and especially the industrial nations, I can foresee a successful check upon imperialistic communism, and a type of foreign aid, multilaterally financed and administered, that will help the peoples of the less advanced nations gradually improve their well-being in a world of assured security.

Where do we begin? Highest priority, in any reappraisal of our posture and methods, must in my judgment begin with power. Peace, wherever it exists—in Baltimore, in the United States, or in the larger world around us—is partly the product of power. No one nation possesses sufficient power to enforce peace, nor would its exercise by a single power, even if possessed in abundance, be acceptable to others. So we must, I suggest, moderate preconceptions about absolute sovereignty and address ourselves to the methods by which nations, all believing in human dignity, mutuality in human relations, and the free choice of peoples, may pool their power, or create new power, to enforce global peace. This has been achieved to a limited extent by the United Nations and by NATO. The need now is to expand the NATO concept, which is transnational rather than multinational, to all free nations and eventually, to every country of the world.

The *negative* approach—for this obviously is what it is—must yield us the time so desperately needed by men everywhere to foster education and genuine mutual understanding; to improve health and increase productivity; to develop more enlightened trade, aid and credit relationships; to do all the multitude of things which must be done to build the *positive* peace that will give peoples everywhere the assurance of a better life with dignity, justice, and equality.

This is, as one statesman has said, the century of the common man. The valid aspirations of the oceans of common peoples of all nationalities, colors, religions and circumstances, can be achieved only in a world at peace. The common peoples of East and West, of the advanced and underdeveloped nations, instinctively want to live in a world free of conflict; but governments, influencing the thinking of citizens, stubbornly cling to the outmoded strategy of competitive power, thus dangerously postponing acceptance of the modern imperative.

The awesome task in the years ahead, then, is to preserve the peace until the mind of man is ready to accept the historical imperative.

Can we do it? Or I should ask, "Can *you* do it?" For this is the dubious legacy that my generation makes to yours.

There is a frightening irony at work here. The very scientific revolution that has created the imperative, that has provided mankind with the means to a Golden Age of Peace and Plenty, is at the same time the greatest obstacle to your achieving this objective.

As individual citizens, you will find it increasingly difficult to understand and cope with the incredibly complex problems that this onrushing era is creating. How can you be expected to understand the important facts, circumstances, and complexities of such vital issues as the disarray of the Atlantic Alliance, the conflicts created by divided nationals, the population explosion, the dangers of catastrophic war born of sheer religious differences, air pollution, imbalance of international payments, space exploration, urban blight, civil rights and the depersonalization of automation? How indeed can you expect your elected representatives to know enough about all of them to act wisely?

These are problems greatly compounded by the knowledge explosion and the population explosion, and we have no precedents for dealing with these unique and profound forces.

This situation can easily lead to apathy and a sense of despair. Not long ago I said: "There is a dangerous myth abroad in this land that an ordinary citizen can do nothing to influence the destiny of his country and the world. I have not decided whether this is a rationalization or an epitaph."

Now I see that there may be some substance to that myth. Perhaps the *ordinary* citizen is an anachronism in this perilous age. Perhaps the hope for the future lies in our ability to produce the *extraordinary* citizen—a new breed of Americans who will devote as much time and energy to being good citizens as they do to being good physicists or good doctors or good engineers.

I like to think that *you* are the New Americans the world so desperately needs. I certainly pray that you are.

I close with an anecdote I have told before, for it is most relevant to the phenomenon of accelerating change and to the concept of the New American.

Destiny came down to an island many centuries ago and summoned three of its inhabitants before him.

"What would you do," Destiny asked, "if I told you that tomorrow this island would be inundated by an immense tidal wave?"

The first man, who was a cynic, said, "Why I would eat, drink, and carouse all night long."

The second man, who was a mystic, said, "I would go to the sacred groves with my loved ones and make sacrifices to the gods and pray without ceasing."

And the third man, who loved reason, thought for a while, confused and troubled, and then said, "Why I would assemble our wisest citizens and begin at once to study how to live under water."

This, with poetic license, symbolizes the challenge to you who are receiving a degree today. You must be prepared to cope with change, to deal with problems that have no precedent, to live under a tidal wave of swift-moving and bewildering events.

May you go forth from this campus with the courage, the conviction, and the wisdom to meet this challenge. The best wishes of your University and the hopes of mankind go with you.

Notes

Chapter 1

1. Ronald Wolk, interview with Ambrose, Washington, D.C., April 4, 1980.
2. Milton S. Eisenhower to Dwight D. Eisenhower, January 16, 1956, Milton S. Eisenhower Papers, Dwight D. Eisenhower Library, Abilene, Kansas. Hereinafter their names will be abbreviated as MSE and DDE.
3. MSE, interview with Ambrose, Baltimore, January 22–27, 1980.
4. Steven Muller, interview with Ambrose, Baltimore, April 7, 1980.
5. Ibid.
6. A tape recording and transcript of the speech are in the Ferdinand Hamburger, Jr., Archives, The Johns Hopkins University, Milton S. Eisenhower Library, Baltimore, Maryland.
7. MSE, interview with Ambrose, January 1980.

Chapter 2

1. Bela Kornitzer, *The Great American Heritage: The Story of the Five Eisenhower Brothers* (New York, 1955), 1.
2. MSE, interview with Ambrose, January 1980.
3. Steve Neal, *The Eisenhowers: Reluctant Dynasty* (Garden City, N.Y., 1978), 1–10; MSE, interview with Ambrose, January 1980; Eisenhower family chart, compiled by DDE, located in Dwight D. Eisenhower Papers, Pre-Presidential, 1916–52, Dwight D. Eisenhower Library, Abilene.
4. MSE, interview with Ambrose, January 1980; DDE, interview with Ambrose, Gettysburg, Pa., November 3, 1963.
5. MSE, interview with Ambrose, January 1980.

6. Earl Eisenhower, quoted in Kornitzer, *Great American Heritage*, 9.
7. Ibid., 10–11; Neal, *The Eisenhowers*, 10–11; MSE, interview with Ambrose, January 1980.
8. DDE, speech, Abilene, June 4, 1952, copy in Dwight D. Eisenhower, Records as President, White House Central Files, 1953–61, Pre-Inaugural File. Dwight D. Eisenhower Library, Abilene.
9. MSE, interview with Ambrose, January 1980.
10. Ibid.
11. Ibid.
12. Kornitzer, *Great American Heritage*, 33.
13. Ibid., 20, 53; MSE, interview with Ambrose, January 1980.
14. MSE, interview with Immerman, Baltimore, April 7–8, 1981; Kornitzer, *Great American Heritage*, 16, 23.
15. Kornitzer, *Great American Heritage*, 54.
16. Ibid., 25.
17. MSE, interview with Ambrose, January 1980.
18. Neal, *The Eisenhowers*, 48.
19. MSE, interview with Ambrose, January 1980.
20. Ibid.; Milton S. Eisenhower, *The President Is Calling* (Garden City, N.Y., 1974), 12.
21. Kornitzer, *Great American Heritage*, 37–41; MSE, interview with Ambrose, January 1980; Neal, *The Eisenhowers*, 49.
22. MSE, interview with Ambrose, January 1980.
23. Ibid.
24. Eisenhower, *The President Is Calling*, 15–16.
25. MSE, interview with Ambrose, January 1980; MSE, to Immerman, September 7, 1982.
26. MSE, interview with Ambrose, January 1980.
27. Ibid.; Neal, *The Eisenhowers*, 49–50.
28. MSE, interview with Ambrose, January 1980; Eisenhower, *The President Is Calling*, 17–18.
29. MSE, interview with Ambrose, January 1980; Neal, *The Eisenhowers*, 53.

Chapter 3

1. James C. Carey, *Kansas State University: The Quest for Identity* (Lawrence, Kans., 1977), 133–40.
2. MSE, interview with Ambrose, January 1980.
3. Ibid.
4. Neal, *The Eisenhowers*, 54.
5. Wilbert E. Locklin, interview with Immerman, Springfield, Mass., July 7, 1980.
6. Carey, *Kansas State University*, 138.
7. MSE, interview with Ambrose, January 1980.
8. Ibid.
9. Ibid.
10. Eisenhower, *The President Is Calling*, 22.
11. Neal, *The Eisenhowers*, 55.
12. Eisenhower, *The President Is Calling*, 22; Neal, *The Eisenhowers*, 56.
13. Eisenhower, *The President Is Calling*, 22–23.

14. MSE, interview with Ambrose, January 1980.
15. Eisenhower, *The President Is Calling*, 24–36.
16. Ibid., 34.
17. Kenneth S. Davis, interview with Immerman, Princeton, Mass., July 9, 1980.
18. MSE, interview with Ambrose, January 1980.
19. Ibid.
20. Ibid.
21. Eisenhower, *The President Is Calling*, 37.
22. Neal, *The Eisenhowers*, 60.

Chapter 4

1. Eisenhower, *The President Is Calling*, 55–56.
2. Neal, *The Eisenhowers*, 81–82. For more on the Department of Agriculture see W. D. Rasmussen and Gladys L. Baker, *The Department of Agriculture* (New York, 1972).
3. Eisenhower, *The President Is Calling*, 62.
4. Ibid., 63.
5. Ibid., 66.
6. MSE, interview with Ambrose, January 1980.
7. Ibid.
8. John S. D. Eisenhower, interview with Ambrose, Valley Forge, Pa., February 1, 1980.
9. MSE to Doug Warren, August 20, 1979. Unless otherwise indicated, all correspondence is in the authors' possession.
10. Neal, *The Eisenhowers*, 75–76.
11. Paul Ferris to Ambrose, December 1, 1980.
12. DDE, interview with Ambrose, November 13, 1963.
13. Neal, *The Eisenhowers*, 74.
14. Ibid., 93.
15. MSE, interview with Ambrose, January 1980.
16. Ibid.
17. Eisenhower, *The President Is Calling*, 71.
18. Edward Schapsmeier and Frederick Schapsmeier, *Henry A. Wallace of Iowa: The Agrarian Years, 1910–1940* (Ames, Iowa, 1968); Russell Lord, *The Wallaces of Iowa* (Boston, 1947); Neal, *The Eisenhowers*, 88.
19. Eisenhower, *The President Is Calling*, 72.
20. Ibid.
21. Lord, *The Wallaces of Iowa*, 356; Neal, *The Eisenhowers*, 90.
22. Neal, *The Eisenhowers*, 90–91.
23. Nils A. Olsen, *Journal of a Tamed Bureaucrat: Nils A. Olsen and the BAE, 1925–1935*, ed. Richard Lowitt (Ames, Iowa, 1980), 232. Olsen's journal has many references to Eisenhower's day-to-day work in the department.
24. Neal, *The Eisenhowers*, 89.
25. Eisenhower, *The President Is Calling*, 73–74.
26. Neal, *The Eisenhowers*, 92.
27. Eisenhower, *The President Is Calling*, 75.
28. Ibid., 76.

Chapter 5

1. Eisenhower, *The President Is Calling*, 78-79.
2. Ibid., 80-81.
3. Ibid., 82.
4. Ibid., 83.
5. Ibid., 84.
6. Ibid., 85-86.
7. John S. D. Eisenhower, interview with Ambrose, February 1, 1980.
8. Eisenhower, *The President Is Calling*, 94.
9. Ibid., 96.
10. See Roger Daniels, *Concentration Camps USA: Japanese Americans and World War II* (New York, 1971); idem, *The Decision to Relocate the Japanese Americans* (Philadelphia, 1975); Michi Weglyn, *Years of Infamy: The Untold Story of America's Concentration Camps* (New York, 1976); Bill Hosokawa, *Nisei: The Quiet Americans* (New York, 1969); Morton Grodzins, *Americans Betrayed: Politics and the Japanese Evacuation* (Chicago, 1949).
11. For discussions of the principles and motivations behind the decision to relocate the Japanese-Americans see the sources cited in note 10. The quotes appear in Grodzins, *Americans Betrayed*, 362 and 86, respectively.
12. Daniels, *Concentration Camps*, 68, 76.
13. MSE, interview with Immerman, April 7-8, 1981; Daniels, *Concentration Camps*, 72, 92; Leonard Broom and Ruth Riemer, *Removal and Return: The Socio-Economic Effects of the War on Japanese Americans* (Berkeley and Los Angeles, 1949), 124-26.
14. Daniels, *Concentration Camps*, 92; Hosokawa, *Nisei*, 338; Eisenhower, *The President Is Calling*, 117; Broom and Riemer, *Removal and Return*, 127-30.
15. MSE, interview with Immerman, April 7-8, 1981; Weglyn, *Years of Infamy*, 114.
16. Eisenhower, *The President Is Calling*, 117-19; Hosokawa, *Nisei*, 338; Broom and Riemer, *Removal and Return*, 132; Daniels, *Concentration Camps*, 92-95.
17. Eisenhower, *The President Is Calling*, 118-22; Daniels, *Concentration Camps*, 95-97; Hosokawa, *Nisei*, 339.
18. Eisenhower, *The President Is Calling*, 120-21; Daniels, *Concentration Camps*, 97-100.
19. Daniels, *Concentration Camps*, 101-2; Hosokawa, *Nisei*, 339-44.
20. Henry A. Wallace, *The Price of Vision: The Diary of Henry A. Wallace*, ed. John Morton Blum (Boston, 1973), 88; Weglyn, *Years of Infamy*, 114-19; Eisenhower, *The President Is Calling*, 122-23.
21. Weglyn, *Years of Infamy*, 115; Daniels, *Concentration Camps*, 102; Eisenhower, *The President Is Calling*, 124-27.
22. Eisenhower, *The President Is Calling*, 133.
23. Ibid., 134.
24. MSE, interview with Ambrose, January 1980.
25. Arthur Funk, *The Politics of Torch* (Lawrence, Kans., 1976), 255; MSE, interview with Immerman, April 7-8, 1981.
26. Dwight D. Eisenhower, *The Papers of Dwight David Eisenhower: The War Years*, ed. Alfred D. Chandler, Jr., 5 vols. (Baltimore, 1970), 707, 711 (hereinafter cited as Eisenhower, *Papers*); Funk, *Politics of Torch*, 252.
27. Eisenhower, *Papers*, 789, 795; MSE, interview with Ambrose, January 1980.

28. MSE, interview with Ambrose, January 1980; Robert Murphy, *Diplomat Among Warriors* (Garden City, N.Y., 1964), 150–51.
29. Eisenhower, *Papers*, 860; MSE, interview with Immerman, April 7–8, 1981; Allan M. Winkler, *The Politics of Propaganda: The Office of War Information* (New Haven, 1978), 188–89.
30. Wallace, *The Price of Vision*, 161–62; *PM*, January 26, 1943.
31. Eisenhower, *Papers*, 1079.

Chapter 6

1. DDE to MSE, January 3, 1939, MSE Papers.
2. Eisenhower, *Papers*, 1098.
3. Ibid., 1097, 1148.
4. Eisenhower, *The President Is Calling*, 151; Tom Carlin, "Dr. Milton Eisenhower: Imparting a Broad View of the World," *Kansas Stater*, May 1981, 12; MSE, interview with Immerman, April 7–8, 1981.
5. MSE to Immerman, May 27, 1981; "Interview with Dr. Milton S. Eisenhower," *U.S. News & World Report*, February 21, 1958, 68.
6. Hugh S. Brown and Lewis B. Mahew, *American Higher Education* (New York, 1965), 11; David D. Henry, *Challenges Past, Challenges Present: An Analysis of American Higher Education since 1930* (San Francisco, 1975), 55. In addition to the above, comprehensive surveys of developments in higher education include Frederick Rudolph, *The American College and University: A History* (New York, 1962); and Wilson Logan, ed., *Emerging Patterns in American Higher Education* (Washington, D.C., 1965).
7. Henry, *Challenges*, 47.
8. Presidential Commission on Higher Education, *Higher Education for Democracy: A Report of the President's Commission*, vol. 1, *Establishing the Goals* (New York, 1947).
9. Brown and Mahew, *American Higher Education*, 51; MSE to Immerman, May 27, 1981; Frederick Rudolph, *Curriculum: A History of the American Undergraduate Course of Study since 1636* (San Francisco, 1977), 258–59; Harvard Committee, *General Education in a Free Society: Report of the Harvard Committee* (Cambridge, Mass., 1945), passim.
10. Carey, *Kansas State University*, 151–57; Rufus Cox, interview with Ambrose, Manhattan, Kans., April 1, 1980.
11. Carey, *Kansas State University*, 151; *Kansas State College Bulletin* 27 (January 1, 1943), Kansas State University Archives, Manhattan, Kansas.
12. *The Inauguration of Milton Stover Eisenhower as President of Kansas State College*, Kansas State University Archives.
13. MSE, interview with Ambrose, January 1980.
14. Kenneth S. Davis, interview with Immerman, July 9, 1980.
15. Carey, *Kansas State University*, 163–64.
16. MSE, interview with Ambrose, January 1980.
17. Jeff Peterson, interview with Ambrose, Manhattan, Kans., April 1, 1980.
18. Carey, *Kansas State University*, 176; Rufus Cox, interview with Ambrose, April 1, 1980; Kenneth S. Davis, interview with Immerman, July 9, 1980.
19. MSE, interview with Ambrose, January 1980; Carey, *Kansas State University*, 157.

20. Russell Thackrey, interview with Ambrose, Manhattan, Kans., March 31, 1980.
21. MSE to Deans, August 3, 1946, Kansas State University Archives.
22. Carey, *Kansas State University*, 139.
23. Eisenhower, *Papers*, 1133, 1221.
24. Quoted in Rudolph, *The American College and University*, 419.
25. Quoted in ibid., 424.
26. Itineraries for this and other trips are in the Kansas State University Archives.
27. MSE, interview with Ambrose, January 1980; *Kansas State College Bulletin* 33 (August 15, 1949), Kansas State University Archives.
28. Kenneth S. Davis, interview with Immerman, July 9, 1980.
29. Ibid.; MSE to Davis, April 4, 1947. Davis kindly opened his personal archives to the authors; hereinafter this correspondence will be cited as the Davis Collection.
30. Kenneth S. Davis, interview with Immerman, July 9, 1980; MSE, interview with Immerman, April 7-8, 1981.
31. Kenneth S. Davis, "The Abilene Factor in Eisenhower," *New York Times Magazine*, December 9, 1951, 12 ff.; Kenneth S. Davis, interview with Immerman, July 9, 1980.
32. Kenneth S. Davis, interview with Immerman, July 9, 1980; MSE, memorandum to Davis, n.d., Davis Collection.
33. MSE, interview with Immerman, April 7-8, 1981.
34. Kenneth S. Davis, interview with Immerman, July 9, 1980.
35. MSE to Davis, December 21, 1954, Davis Collection; MSE to DDE, March 16, 1953, MSE Papers.
36. MSE to DDE, March 16, 1953, MSE Papers; MSE to Davis, October 11, 1945, Davis Collection. For Davis's response to Eisenhower's criticisms see Davis to MSE, September 12, 1945, Davis Collection. Two days later Eisenhower replied: "The value of your book is that it is an honest appraisal, containing both good and bad. Your book is important historiographically. I do disagree with your interpretation of North African developments, but I am wholly satisfied merely to have stated my own views to you.... I am a reviewer, not censor" (Davis Collection).
37. MSE, interview with Immerman, April 7-8, 1981.
38. There is a copy of the speech in the Kansas State University Archives.
39. Wilbert E. Locklin, interview with Immerman, July 7, 1980.
40. *Country Gentleman*, November 1946.
41. MSE, interview with Ambrose, January 1980.
42. MSE to Immerman, April 20, 1981; Carey, *Kansas State University*, 1969.
43. Russell Thackrey, interview with Ambrose, March 31, 1980.
44. Ibid.
45. MSE to Immerman, April 20, May 4, 1981; *Kansas State College Bulletin* 27 (January 1, 1943), 33 (August 15, 1949).
46. Russell Thackrey, interview with Ambrose, March 31, 1980.
47. MSE, interview with Ambrose, January 1980.
48. Russell Thackrey, interview with Ambrose, March 31, 1980.
49. Donald Ford, interview with Immerman, Lemont, Pa., June 18, 1980.
50. MSE, interview with Ambrose, January 1980.
51. Russell Thackrey, interview with Ambrose, March 31, 1980.
52. Carey, *Kansas State University*, 172-73.
53. Russell Thackrey, interview with Ambrose, March 31, 1980.
54. *Collier's*, September 3, 1949.
55. MSE, interview with Ambrose, January 1980.

56. MSE to Davis, October 1, 1946, Davis Collection.
57. Russell Thackrey, interview with Ambrose, March 31, 1980.
58. Kenneth S. Davis, interview with Immerman, July 9, 1980.
59. Mrs. Thomas Griffith, interview with Ambrose, Manhattan, Kans., March 31, 1980.
60. Kenneth S. Davis, interview with Immerman, July 9, 1980.
61. Russell Thackrey, interview with Ambrose, March 31, 1980.

Chapter 7

1. MSE, interview with Ambrose, January 1980.
2. Ibid.
3. Carey, *Kansas State University*, 166.
4. MSE, interview with Ambrose, January 1980.
5. Donald Ford, interview with Immerman, June 18, 1980.
6. Ibid.
7. Russell Thackrey, interview with Ambrose, March 31, 1980; Kenneth S. Davis, interview with Immerman, July 9, 1980.
8. Russell Thackrey, interview with Ambrose, March 31, 1980.
9. Eisenhower, *Papers*, 1515.
10. Carey, *Kansas State University*, 166; Kenneth S. Davis, interview with Immerman, July 9, 1980; Russell Thackrey, interview with Ambrose, March 31, 1980.
11. Carey, *Kansas State University*, 165, 166; Kenneth S. Davis, interview with Immerman, July 9, 1980; MSE, interview with Immerman, April 7–8, 1981.
12. Kenneth S. Davis, interview with Immerman, July 9, 1980; MSE, interview with Immerman, April 7–8, 1981.
13. Eisenhower, *The President Is Calling*, 168–69.
14. Kenneth S. Davis, interview with Immerman, July 9, 1980.
15. MSE, interview with Ambrose, January 1980; MSE to Immerman, September 7, 1982.
16. MSE, interview with Ambrose, January 1980.
17. Ibid.
18. Carey, *Kansas State University*, 170; MSE, interview with Ambrose, January 1980.
19. Russell Thackrey, interview with Ambrose, March 31, 1980.
20. MSE, interview with Ambrose, January 1980; Russell Thackrey, interview with Ambrose, March 31, 1980.
21. MSE, interview with Ambrose, January 1980.
22. Donald Ford, interview with Immerman, June 18, 1980.
23. MSE to DDE, March 1, 1948, MSE Papers.
24. Eisenhower, *The President Is Calling*, 175.
25. MSE to Immerman, September 7, 1982; MSE to DDE, February 3, March 16, 1948, MSE Papers.
26. MSE to DDE, c. winter 1948, MSE Papers.
27. MSE interview with Ambrose, January 1980; Jeff Peterson, interview with Ambrose, April 1, 1980.
28. MSE, interview with Ambrose, January 1980.
29. Donald Ford, interview with Immerman, June 18, 1980.
30. Carey, *Kansas State University*, 178–79.

Chapter 8

1. Donald Ford, interview with Immerman, June 18, 1980.
2. Wayland F. Dunaway, *History of the Pennsylvania State College* (Lancaster, Pa., 1946), 236.
3. Ibid., 235-37.
4. Ibid., 492; MSE, interview with Ambrose, January 1980.
5. Roy Wilkinson, interview with Immerman, State College, Pa., June 18, 1980.
6. Wilmer Kenworthy, interview with Immerman, State College, Pa., June 19, 1980.
7. Ibid.
8. Kenneth S. Davis, "Another Eisenhower Takes a New Job," *New York Times Magazine*, October 1, 1950.
9. Donald Ford, interview with Immerman, June 18, 1980.
10. Samuel Vaughan to Ambrose, January 29, 1981.
11. Roy Wilkinson, interview with Immerman, June 18, 1980.
12. Dunaway, *History of Penn State*, 14; Wilmer Kenworthy, interview with Immerman, June 19, 1980.
13. MSE, interview with Ambrose, January 1980.
14. *The Daily Collegian*, November 21, 1953.
15. Samuel Blazer, interview with Immerman, State College, Pa., June 17, 1980.
16. Ibid.
17. MSE, interview with Ambrose, January 1980.
18. Ibid.
19. *The Daily Collegian*, October 10, 1950.
20. Ibid., May 3, 4, 1951; MSE, interview with Ambrose, January 1980.
21. MSE, interview with Ambrose, January 1980; Wilmer Kenworthy, interview with Immerman, June 19, 1980.
22. MSE, interview with Ambrose, January 1980.
23. Roy Wilkinson, interview with Immerman, June 18, 1980.
24. Wilmer Kenworthy, interview with Immerman, June 19, 1980.
25. Vaughan to Ambrose, January 29, 1981.
26. MSE, interview with Ambrose, January 1980.
27. MSE, interview with Immerman, April 7-8, 1981; Roy Wilkinson, interview with Immerman, June 18, 1980.
28. Roy Wilkinson, interview with Immerman, June 18, 1980.
29. MSE, interview with Ambrose, January 1980.
30. Ridge Riley, *Road to Number One: A Personal Chronicle of Penn State Football* (Garden City, N.Y., 1977), 101.
31. Roy Wilkinson, interview with Immerman, June 18, 1980.
32. MSE, interview with Ambrose, January 1980.
33. MSE, interview with Ambrose, January 1980; Roy Wilkinson, interview with Immerman, June 18, 1980.
34. MSE, interview with Ambrose, January 1980.
35. Roy Wilkinson, interview with Immerman, June 18, 1980.
36. Donald Ford, interview with Immerman, June 18, 1980; Vaughan to Ambrose, January 29, 1981.
37. Dunaway, *History of Penn State*, 471-75.
38. MSE, interview with Immerman, April 7-8, 1981; Roy Wilkinson, interview with Immerman, June 18, 1980.

39. Dunaway, *History of Penn State*, 56; *The Daily Collegian*, September 22, 1954.
40. Roy Wilkinson, interview with Immerman, June 18, 1980.
41. MSE, interview with Ambrose, January 1980.
42. Roy Wilkinson, interview with Immerman, June 18, 1980; MSE, interview with Ambrose, January 1980.
43. MSE, interview with Ambrose, January 1980.
44. Roy Wilkinson, interview with Immerman, June 18, 1980.

Chapter 9

1. Donald Ford, interview with Immerman, June 18, 1980.
2. MSE, interview with Ambrose, January 1980; *Pennsylvania State University Bulletin* 50 (January 27, 1956). Pennsylvania State University Archives, University Park, Pennsylvania.
3. Donald Ford, interview with Immerman, June 18, 1980.
4. Ibid.
5. "Interview with Dr. Milton S. Eisenhower, November 30, 1979," Pennsylvania State University Archives (hereinafter cited as Penn State interview).
6. MSE, interview with Ambrose, January 1980.
7. Penn State interview.
8. Roy Wilkinson, interview with Immerman, June 18, 1980.
9. The memorandum, dated February 23, 1954, is in the Richard C. Maloney Papers, Pennsylvania State University Archives.
10. MSE, interview with Ambrose, January 1980; Roy Wilkinson, interview with Immerman, June 18, 1980.
11. Roy Wilkinson, interview with Immerman, June 18, 1980. There is extensive documentation on the Lorch case in the "ABVP/Lorch, Lee" file and in the American Federation of Teachers, Local Union #500 collection (Labor archives), both in the Pennsylvania State University Archives. The *New York Times* editorial appeared on April 11, 1950.
12. MSE to Anthony Luchek, October 14, 1950; "Correspondence and Local Activities, 1942–1951," American Federation of Teachers, Local Union #500.
13. *The Daily Collegian*, December 5, 1950.
14. Roy Wilkinson, interview with Immerman, June 18, 1980.
15. Ibid.
16. Clark Byse, "A Report on the Pennsylvania Loyalty Act," *University of Pennsylvania Law Review* 101, no. 4 (January 1953), 1.
17. *The Daily Collegian*, April 25, May 1, 1951.
18. Byse, "Report," 17; *Teachers Union News*, October 1951; "Loyalty Procedures and Pechan Act," R. Wallace Brewster Papers, Pennsylvania State University Archives.
19. MSE press release, July 26, 1951, in Maloney Papers; see also *The Daily Collegian*, August 1, 1951.
20. Extensive documentation on this subject can be found in the Pennsylvania State University Archives, particularly in the Maloney Papers and the Brewster Papers. Specific references will follow in the notes.
21. Brewster to MSE, March 24, 1952, "MacRae Case," Brewster Papers.
22. MSE to Brewster, March 26, 1952, ibid.
23. Brewster to MSE, March 31, 1952, ibid.

24. Ibid.
25. Byse, "Report," 17–18.
26. MSE to Faculty and Staff, September 9, 1952, "MacRae Case (Pechan Act)," Pennsylvania State University Archives; Roy Wilkinson, interview with Immerman, June 18, 1980; MSE to Brewster, September 13, 1952, "MacRae Case," Brewster Papers.
27. The President's Office, "Tentative Procedures Designed to Enable the Pennsylvania State College to Comply with the Terms of Section 13 of the Pennsylvania Loyalty Act," May 2, 1952, "MacRae Case (Pechan Act)"; idem, "Composition of, and Procedures Followed by, the Loyalty Review Board of the Pennsylvania State College," first released May 10, 1952, phrasing slightly revised, June 30, 1952, "MacRae Case (Pechan Act)"; Byse, "Report," 19.
28. MSE to Faculty and Staff, September 9, 1952, "MacRae Case (Pechan Act)"; Elton Atwater, John Ferguson, Hans Neuberger, Joseph Rayback, and William Werner to MSE, September 15, 1952, "MacRae Case," Brewster Papers; The President's Office, "Composition of . . . the Loyalty Review Board . . ."; MSE, interview with Immerman, April 7–8, 1981.
29. MSE to Faculty and Staff, September 9, 1952, "MacRae Case (Pechan Act)"; MSE to MacRae, August 28, 1952, ibid.
30. "Complete Text of Harrison's Report to Dr. Eisenhower," *Centre Daily Times*, December 8 1952; Wilmer Kenworthy, interview with Immerman, June 19, 1980.
31. MacRae to Louis H. Bell, May 23, 1952, reproduced in "Transcript of Proceedings Had before the Loyalty Review Board of Pennsylvania State College in re: Wendell S. MacRae, August 26, 1952," "MacRae Case (Pechan Act)."
32. Morse to MacRae, June 25, 1952, and MacRae to Morse, July 26, 1952, both reproduced in "Transcript of Proceedings."
33. "Transcript of Proceedings."
34. Morse to MacRae, August 27, 1952, "MacRae Case (Pechan Act)."
35. MacRae to MSE, August 27, 1952, ibid.; Roy Wilkinson, interview with Immerman, June 18, 1980; MSE to Brewster, September 13, 1952, "MacRae Case," Brewster Papers; MSE to MacRae, August 28, 1952, "MacRae Case (Pechan Act)."
36. MacRae to MSE, August 27, 1952, "MacRae Case (Pechan Act)."
37. Brewster to MSE, September 10, 17, 1953, "MacRae Case," Brewster Papers.
38. *Centre Daily Times*, September 16, 17, 1952; Roy Wilkinson, interview with Immerman, June 18, 1980; William Werner to MacRae, August 24, September 1, 1952, "Pennsylvania Loyalty Act (Pechan Act)," Pennsylvania State University Archives; Atwater et al. to Colleague, with attachments, n.d., "MacRae Case (Pechan Act)."
39. MSE to Faculty and Staff, September 9, 1952, "MacRae Case (Pechan Act)"; *Centre Daily Times*, September 16, 1952; Roy Wilkinson, interview with Immerman, June 18, 1980; MSE to Brewster, September 13, 22, 1952, "MacRae Case," Brewster Papers.
40. Byse, "Report," 23–24; Brewster to Charles Kinney, October 2, 1952, "MacRae Case," Brewster Papers.
41. "Complete Text of Harrison's Report."
42. *Centre Daily Times*, December 8, 1952; Roy Wilkinson, interview with Immerman, June 18, 1980.
43. *Centre Daily Times*, May 17, 18, 24, 1955.
44. Ibid., April 11, 1953; April 15, 1975.

Chapter 10

1. *Reader's Digest*, June 1953.
2. For additional information the authors urge the reader to consult Eisenhower, *The President Is Calling*.
3. *Newsweek*, November 21, 1977.
4. Roy Wilkinson, interview with Immerman, June 18, 1980.
5. Ibid.
6. MSE to Doug Warren, July 7, 1976.
7. MSE to DDE, June 18, October 20, 1951, MSE Papers.
8. MSE to DDE, October 20, 1951, ibid.
9. MSE to DDE, April 10, 1952, ibid.; see also the correspondence of May 1 and May 22.
10. MSE, interview with Ambrose, January 1980; Eisenhower, *The President Is Calling*, 248.
11. DDE to MSE, February 2, 1953, MSE Papers.
12. Neal, *The Eisenhowers*, 353.
13. Ibid.
14. *Saturday Evening Post*, September 17, 1955.
15. *New York Times Magazine*, August 23, 1959.
16. MSE, interview with Ambrose, January 1980. Eisenhower analyzes his relations with Perón in *The Wine Is Bitter* (Garden City, N.Y.: Doubleday, 1963), 63–66.
17. For example, see DDE to MSE, September 17, 1955, MSE Papers, in which the President quotes extensively from Milton's previous letter to him and then responds to each point. It would be impractical here to cite all the specific letters; the interested scholar must visit the Dwight D. Eisenhower Library in Abilene to examine the whole correspondence.
18. MSE to DDE, November 5, 1953, MSE Papers.
19. Edgar Eisenhower to MSE, November 8, 1955, ibid.
20. MSE to Edgar Eisenhower, November 17, 1955, ibid.; Bernard Shanley Diary, April 16, 1957, Bernard Shanley Papers, Dwight D. Eisenhower Library.
21. Eisenhower, *The President Is Calling*, 340.
22. MSE to Ambrose, March 19, 1980.
23. MSE to DDE, October 23, 1955, MSE Papers.
24. DDE to MSE, October 25, 1955, ibid.
25. DDE Personal Diary, November 16, 1951, Dwight D. Eisenhower Library.
26. Ibid., May 14, 1953.
27. DDE to Hazlett, December 24, 1953, DDE Papers as President of the United States, 1953–61 (Whitman File), Name Series, "Hazlett, Swede."
28. Roscoe Drummond, "Triumph or Trouble Ahead?" *Collier's*, January 20, 1956.
29. Clipping in "ABVF / Eisenhower, Milton S., News Coverage," Pennsylvania State University Archives.
30. Vance Packard, "Spotlight on Milton Eisenhower," *American Magazine*, November 1955.
31. *American Press*, November 1955.
32. Drummond, "Triumph or Trouble Ahead?"
33. "What Makes Milton Run?" *American Mercury*, February 1956.
34. *New York Herald Tribune*, January 20, 1956.
35. Drummond, "Triumph or Trouble Ahead?"

36. See DDE to MSE, September 17, 1955, and MSE to Walter Williams, September 20, 1955, MSE Papers.
37. Neal, *The Eisenhowers*, 351, 365.
38. Eisenhower, *The President Is Calling*, 345–47.
39. James David Barber, *The Presidential Character* (Englewood Cliffs, N.J., 1977), 159–60.
40. Eisenhower, *The President Is Calling*, 366.

Chapter 11

1. MSE to Ambrose, February 8, 1980.
2. Ibid.
3. Press release, October 2, 1950, "ABVF / Eisenhower, Helen Eakin," Pennsylvania State University Archives.
4. Vaughan to Ambrose, January 29, 1981; Roy Wilkinson, interview with Immerman, June 18, 1980; MSE, interview with Ambrose, January 1980.
5. MSE to Ambrose, February 8, 1980.
6. Samuel Blazer, interview with Immerman, June 17, 1980.
7. *Centre Daily Times*, July 11, 12, 13, 1955; Kenneth S. Davis to MSE, July 20, 1955, Davis Collection.
8. MSE to Davis, August 2, 1955, ibid.
9. *Centre Daily Times*, July 22, 1955.
10. Kenneth S. Davis, interview with Immerman, July 9, 1980; Samuel Blazer, interview with Immerman, June 17, 1980; Roy Wilkinson, interview with Immerman, June 18, 1980.
11. MSE to Ambrose, February 8, 1980.
12. Neal, *The Eisenhowers*, 352.
13. Ibid., 360; Roy Wilkinson, interview with Immerman, June 18, 1980.
14. MSE, interview with Ambrose, January 1980.
15. MSE to George H. Deike, June 9, 1956, Minutes of the Board of Trustees of the Pennsylvania State University, vol. 5, Pennsylvania State University Archives.
16. *Centre Daily Times*, November 26, 1956.
17. Roy Wilkinson, interview with Immerman, June 18, 1980.
18. See Eisenhower's annual report, 1954 / 55, entitled "A Report to the Citizens of Pennsylvania As the Pennsylvania State University Enters Its Second Century of Service to the Commonwealth and the Nation," Pennsylvania State University Archives.
19. Neal, *The Eisenhowers*, 358.
20. Penn State interview.
21. Neal, *The Eisenhowers*, 355.
22. *An Evaluation of the Aims and Affairs of the Pennsylvania State University, Prepared for the Use of the University by the Commission on Institutions of Higher Education of the Middle States Association of Colleges and Secondary Schools* (evaluation dates: November 6–9, 1955), Pennsylvania State University Archives.
23. *The Daily Collegian*, September 21, 1956.
24. Roy Wilkinson, interview with Immerman, June 18, 1980.
25. Ibid.

Chapter 12

1. MSE, interview with Ambrose, January 1980.
2. MSE to Immerman, March 24, 1980; MSE to DDE, May 14, 1956, MSE Papers.
3. Ibid.; MSE, interview with Immerman, Baltimore, March 20, 1980.
4. MSE to Deike, June 9, 1956, Minutes of the Board; MSE to DDE, May 14, 1956, MSE Papers.
5. MSE, interview with Ambrose, January 1980.
6. See Lynn Poole, "Milton Eisenhower Heads Hopkins," *Baltimore Magazine*, August 1956.
7. *New York Times*, July 24, 1956.
8. Poole, "Milton Eisenhower Heads Hopkins."
9. MSE, interview with Ambrose, January 1980.
10. G. Wilson Shaffer, interview with Immerman, Baltimore, March 20, 1980.
11. Ibid.
12. MSE, interview with Ambrose, January 1980.
13. G. Wilson Shaffer, interview with Immerman, March 20, 1980; MSE, interview with Ambrose, January 1980.
14. Charles A. Garland, "A Promise To Keep," *Johns Hopkins Magazine*, special issue, 1967.
15. Ibid.
16. MSE, interview with Ambrose, January 1980.
17. Wilbert E. Locklin, interview with Immerman, July 7, 1980.
18. MSE, interview with Ambrose, January 1980. For a comprehensive analysis of the Hopkins board see Russell S. Passarella, "On Becoming a Trustee" (Paper submitted to the Seminar on University Administration of the Harvard Business School, May 23, 1972).
19. MSE, interview with Ambrose, January 1980.
20. MSE, interview with Ambrose, January 1980; Ross Jones, interview with Ambrose, Baltimore, April 7, 1980.
21. MSE, interview with Ambrose, January 1980.
22. Wilbert E. Locklin, interview with Immerman, July 7, 1980; Russell Passarella, interview with Immerman, Bradley Beach, N.J., March 27, 1980.
23. MSE, interview with Ambrose, January 1980.
24. Ibid.
25. Wilbert E. Locklin, interview with Immerman, July 7, 1980.
26. MSE, interview with Ambrose, January 1980.
27. Wilbert E. Locklin, interview with Immerman, July 7, 1980.
28. Ibid.
29. Garland, "A Promise To Keep."
30. MSE, interview with Ambrose, January 1980.
31. Wilbert E. Locklin, interview with Immerman, July 7, 1980.
32. The original grant proposals, with Eisenhower's editing, are located in the Ferdinand Hamburger, Jr., Archives.
33. Ross Jones, interview with Ambrose, April 7, 1980.
34. Wilbert E. Locklin, interview with Immerman, July 7, 1980.
35. MSE, interview with Ambrose, January 1980; Wilbert E. Locklin, interview with Immerman, July 7, 1980. See also MSE to Dr. Henry T. Heald, President, The Ford Foundation, and enclosures, July 22, 1963, Ferdinand Hamburger, Jr., Archives.

36. MSE, interview with Ambrose, January 1980; Wilbert E. Locklin, interview with Immerman, July 7, 1980.
37. Wilbert E. Locklin, interview with Immerman, July 7, 1980.
38. Garland, "A Promise To Keep."

Chapter 13

1. MSE, interview with Ambrose, January 1980.
2. Ross Jones, interview with Ambrose, April 7, 1980.
3. Wilbert E. Locklin, interview with Immerman, July 7, 1980.
4. MSE, interview with Ambrose, January 1980.
5. Ross Jones, interview with Ambrose, April 7, 1980.
6. MSE, interview with Ambrose, January 1980.
7. Ross Jones, interview with Ambrose, April 7, 1980.
8. MSE, interview with Ambrose, January 1980.
9. Ross Jones, interview with Ambrose, April 7, 1980.
10. Ronald Wolk, interview with Ambrose, April 4, 1980.
11. Wilbert E. Locklin, interview with Immerman, July 7, 1980.
12. Ronald Wolk, interview with Ambrose, April 4, 1980.
13. Ibid.
14. *Political Science Quarterly*, December 1965; *American Political Science Review*, March 1964.
15. *Virginia Quarterly Review*, Autumn 1963.
16. *Time*, July 26, 1963; *Newsweek*, July 29, 1963; *Saturday Review*, July 20, 1963.
17. *New York Times Book Review*, July 21, 1963.
18. *New Republic*, October 26, 1963.
19. *The Progressive*, November 1963.
20. MSE, interview with Ambrose, January 1980. Virtually all the reviews emphasize Eisenhower's claim.
21. Ronald Wolk, interview with Ambrose, April 4, 1980.
22. Ibid.; MSE, interview with Ambrose, January 1980.
23. Ibid.; Ross Jones's comments on draft of Ambrose-Immerman manuscript.
24. Eisenhower, *The President Is Calling*, 385–86; Ronald Wolk, interview with Ambrose, April 4, 1980.
25. Neal, *The Eisenhowers*, 418–40; Eisenhower, *The President Is Calling*, 387–94; Ronald Wolk, interview with Ambrose, April 4, 1980. Wolk asked Eisenhower to autograph the draft. Eisenhower wrote at the top, "This is the speech that Ron Wolk and I wrote at 3:00 in the morning." The draft remains one of Wolk's most prized possessions.
26. MSE, interview with Ambrose, January 1980.
27. Ronald Wolk, interview with Ambrose, April 4, 1980.
28. Ibid.; MSE, interview with Ambrose, January 1980.
29. Ronald Wolk, interview with Ambrose, April 4, 1980.
30. MSE, interview with Ambrose, January 1980.
31. Ibid.
32. Wilbert E. Locklin, interview with Immerman, July 7, 1980.
33. Ibid.
34. Ibid.

35. MSE, interview with Ambrose, January 1980; MSE to Ambrose, December 10, 1980.
36. Ross Jones, interview with Ambrose, April 7, 1980; Ronald Wolk, interview with Ambrose, April 4, 1980.
37. Ross Jones, interview with Ambrose, April 7, 1980. Wolk offered an identical critique of Eisenhower's personnel policy. It should be added that when Eisenhower returned to a financially troubled Hopkins in 1971 he let dozens of employees go.
38. Ross Jones, interview with Ambrose, April 7, 1980.
39. MSE, interview with Ambrose, January 1980.
40. Ronald Wolk, interview with Ambrose, April 4, 1980; Ross Jones, interview with Ambrose, April 7, 1980; MSE, interview with Immerman, April 7–8, 1981.
41. Ronald Wolk, interview with Ambrose, April 4, 1980.
42. MSE, interview with Ambrose, January 1980.
43. Ibid.
44. Ibid.
45. Ibid.
46. Robert P. Sharkey, *Johns Hopkins: Centennial Portrait of a University* (Baltimore, 1975), 36.
47. Ibid., 37; MSE, interview with Ambrose, January 1980.
48. Sharkey, *Hopkins*, 27.
49. MSE, interview with Ambrose, January 1980.
50. Ibid.
51. Ibid.
52. G. Wilson Shaffer, interview with Immerman, March 20, 1980.
53. MSE, interview with Ambrose, January 1980; G. Wilson Shaffer, interview with Immerman, March 20, 1980.
54. MSE, interview with Ambrose, January 1980; Sharkey, *Hopkins*, 33.
55. MSE, interview with Ambrose, January 1980.
56. Alfred D. Chandler, Jr., interview with Immerman, Cambridge, Mass., July 9, 1980.
57. MSE, interview with Ambrose, January 1980.
58. Ibid.
59. G. Wilson Shaffer, interview with Immerman, March 20, 1980.
60. Boas to MSE, April 12, 1966, Ferdinand Hamburger, Jr., Archives.
61. Sharkey, *Hopkins*, 41–42. See also the volumes of *The Johns Hopkins University Circular* for the academic years 1956 / 57 through 1966 / 67.
62. MSE, interview with Ambrose, January 1980.

Chapter 14

1. MSE to William Knowles, April 22, 1975.
2. Neil Grauer to Ambrose, March 2, 1980.
3. MSE, interview with Immerman, March 20, 1980.
4. Russell Passarella, interview with Immerman, March 27, 1980.
5. Garland, "A Promise To Keep."
6. Grauer to Ambrose, March 2, 1980.
7. Russell Passarella, interview with Immerman, March 27, 1980.
8. Grauer to Ambrose, March 2, 1980.
9. Ronald Wolk, interview with Ambrose, April 4, 1980.
10. Grauer to Ambrose, March 2, 1980.

11. George Gorse, "Reminiscences about Milton S. Eisenhower," attached to Gorse to Ambrose, April 6, 1980.
12. Russell Passarella, interview with Immerman, March 27, 1980.
13. Gorse, "Reminiscences."
14. Grauer to Ambrose, February 17, 1980.
15. MSE to Grauer, September 30, 1965.
16. Thomas Harris, "Recollections on Milton Eisenhower," attached to Harris to Ambrose, n.d.
17. William Knowles, "My Friend, Dr. Eisenhower," sent by Knowles to Ambrose, Summer 1980.
18. MSE to Eugene Zeltmann, May 4, 1965.
19. Grauer to Ambrose, February 17, 1980.
20. Ross Jones, interview with Ambrose, April 7, 1980.
21. Gorse, "Reminiscences."
22. Jonathan Krant to Ambrose, April 2, 1980.
23. Grauer to Ambrose, March 2, 1980.
24. Donald Spear provided the authors with a tape recording of his recollections, n.d., hereinafter referred to as Spear tape.
25. Knowles, "My Friend, Dr. Eisenhower,"
26. Spear tape.
27. Grauer to Ambrose, March 2, 1980.
28. Ibid.
29. MSE, interview with Ambrose, January 1980; Roy Wilkinson, interview with Immerman, June 18, 1980.
30. G. Wilson Shaffer, interview with Immerman, March 20, 1980.
31. MSE, interview with Ambrose, January 1980.
32. G. Wilson Shaffer, interview with Immerman, March 20, 1980.
33. MSE, interview with Immerman, March 20, 1980.
34. Russell Passarella, interview with Immerman, March 27, 1980.
35. Grauer to Ambrose, March 2, 1980.
36. Russell Passarella, interview with Immerman, March 27, 1980.
37. MSE to William Knowles, April 22, 1975; MSE, interview with Immerman, April 7–8, 1981.
38. Grauer to Ambrose, March 2, 1980.
39. Gorse, "Reminiscences."
40. MSE, interview with Ambrose, January 1980.
41. Gorse, "Reminiscences."
42. MSE, interview with Ambrose, January 1980; Gorse, "Reminiscences."
43. MSE, interview with Ambrose, 1980.
44. Nelson Block provided the authors with a tape recording of his recollections, July 20, 1980, hereinafter referred to as Block tape.
45. Sharkey, *Hopkins*, 68–69.
46. Grauer to Ambrose, February 17, 1980.
47. MSE to Ambrose, April 1, 1980.
48. Gorse, "Reminiscences."

Chapter 15

1. MSE, interview with Ambrose, January 1980.
2. Ibid.

3. Ibid.
4. Sharkey, *Hopkins*, 59; G. Wilson Shaffer, interview with Immerman, March 20, 1980.
5. MSE, interviews with Immerman, March 20, 1980, and Ambrose, January 1980.
6. Steven Muller, interview with Ambrose, April 7, 1980.
7. Ibid.
8. Quoted in Sharkey, *Hopkins*, 49.
9. Russell Passarella, interview with Immerman, March 27, 1980.
10. Ibid.
11. MSE, interview with Ambrose, January 1980.
12. G. Wilson Shaffer, interview with Immerman, March 20, 1980.
13. Alfred D. Chandler, Jr., interview with Immerman, July 9, 1980.
14. Sharkey, *Hopkins*, 59–60; MSE, interview with Ambrose, January 1980.
15. Neal, *The Eisenhowers*, 465; MSE, interview with Ambrose, January 1980.
16. MSE, interview with Ambrose, January 1980.
17. Grauer to Ambrose, March 2, 1980.
18. MSE, interview with Ambrose, January 1980.
19. Ibid.; see also Passarella, "On Becoming a Trustee."
20. MSE, interview with Ambrose, January 1980; Sharkey, *Hopkins*, 61.
21. MSE, interview with Ambrose, January 1980; Steven Muller, interview with Ambrose, April 7, 1980.
22. Steven Muller, interview with Ambrose, April 7, 1980.
23. Sharkey, *Hopkins*, 62–64.
24. Ibid., 50–51; MSE, interview with Ambrose, January 1980.
25. Steven Muller, interview with Ambrose, April 7, 1980.
26. Alfred D. Chandler, Jr., interview with Immerman, July 9, 1980.
27. Wilbert E. Locklin, interview with Immerman, July 7, 1980.
28. Steven Muller, interview with Ambrose, April 7, 1980; MSE, interview with Ambrose, January 1980.
29. MSE, interview with Ambrose, January 1980.

Chapter 16

1. MSE to Immerman, April 22, 1981.
2. Ibid.
3. Milton S. Eisenhower, "The Presidency: Can Anyone Do the Job?" *Projects in Education*, 1980. For the text see appendix B.
4. Ibid.
5. Unless otherwise noted, the following discussion reflects more than fifty hours of interviews conducted by both authors with Dr. Eisenhower and his thirty-one-page letter to Immerman, April 22, 1981, written at the authors' request. It should be interjected, however, that Eisenhower has repeatedly covered these subjects in his writings and speeches. The authors encourage the reader to study the appendixes.
6. Eisenhower, *The President Is Calling*, 396.
7. Eisenhower, "The Presidency" (emphasis in the original).
8. Milton S. Eisenhower, "Violent Crime: An Overview" (Address delivered at the opening of the Milton S. Eisenhower Symposium, The Johns Hopkins University, November 10, 1970). For the text see appendix D.
9. Eisenhower, *The President Is Calling*, 433–60.
10. Harris, "Recollections."
11. Eisenhower, "Violent Crime."

12. Ibid.
13. Ibid.
14. Ibid.
15. Milton S. Eisenhower, commencement address delivered at the Johns Hopkins University, June 13, 1967. For the text see appendix E.
16. Milton S. Eisenhower, address delivered at the opening of The Johns Hopkins University centennial celebration, September 10, 1975.
17. Eisenhower, commencement address, 1967.
18. Presidential Commission on Higher Education, *Higher Education for Democracy*; see also chapter 6.
19. Eisenhower, centennial address.
20. Milton S. Eisenhower, address delivered to the Association of American University Presses, Baltimore, Maryland, June 13, 1978.
21. Eisenhower, commencement address, 1967.

Chapter 17

1. MSE to Michael McGrael, January 30, 1976.
2. Harris, "Recollections."
3. MSE to McGrael, July 25, 1976.
4. Gorse, "Reminiscences."
5. MSE to Ambrose, July 1, 1980.
6. Steven Muller, interview with Ambrose, April 7, 1980.
7. MSE, interview with Ambrose, January 1980.
8. MSE to Ambrose, July 1, 1980.
9. MSE, interview with Ambrose, January 1980.
10. MSE to Ambrose, July 1, 1980.
11. MSE, interview with Ambrose, January 1980.
12. For example, see MSE to the Editor, *New York Times*, August 31, 1980.
13. MSE, interview with Ambrose, January 1980. In 1962 Eisenhower was offered the Maryland senatorial nomination "without opposition at a time when the Democratic nominee may have been relatively easy to beat." See Eisenhower, *The President Is Calling*, 67.
14. The following account of Eisenhower's business career is derived from Eisenhowers interviews with Ambrose, January 1980, and Immerman, April 7-8, 1981.
15. See chapter 12.
16. MSE to Grauer, October 2, 1969.
17. Grauer to Ambrose, March 2, 1980; see also MSE to McGrael, March 28, 1979.
18. Block tape.
19. George Wills to Ambrose, January 16, 1981.
20. MSE to Warren, June 6, 1979.

Selected
Bibliography

Only those sources that the authors found to be most valuable are listed below. Additional sources are included in the notes.

Unpublished Sources

Archival Sources

Brewster, R. Wallace. Papers. Pennsylvania State University Archives, University Park, Pennsylvania

Eisenhower, Dwight D. Papers as President of the United States (Whitman File). Dwight D. Eisenhower Library, Abilene, Kansas.

———. Personal Diary. Dwight D. Eisenhower Library, Abilene, Kansas.

Eisenhower, Milton S. File. Pennsylvania State University Archives, University Park, Pennsylvania.

———. Papers. Dwight D. Eisenhower Library, Abilene, Kansas.

Ferdinand Hamburger, Jr., Archives. Milton S. Eisenhower Library. The Johns Hopkins University, Baltimore, Maryland.

Kansas State University Archives, Manhattan, Kansas.

Labor Archives. Pennsylvania State University Archives, University Park, Pennsylvania.

Maloney, Richard C. Papers. Pennsylvania State University Archives, University Park, Pennsylvania.

Passarella, Russell. "On Becoming a Trustee." Paper submitted to the Seminar on University Administration of the Harvard Business School, May 23, 1975.

Correspondence

Except for letters in the Davis Collection, all correspondence is in the authors' possession.

317

Eisenhower, Milton S., with the authors.
———, with Kenneth S. Davis (Davis Collection).
———, with Neil Grauer.
———, with William Knowles.
———, with Michael McGrael.
———, with Doug Warren.
———, with Eugene Zeltman.
Ferris, Paul, to Ambrose.
Gorse, George, to Ambrose.
Grauer, Neil, to Ambrose.
Harris, Thomas, to Ambrose.
Knowles, William, to Ambrose.
Krant, Jonathan, to Ambrose.
Vaughan, Samuel, to Ambrose.
Wills, George, to Ambrose.

Interviews
Blazer, Samuel, with Immerman, State College, Pa., June 17, 1980.
Block, Nelson, tape sent to authors, July 20, 1980.
Chandler, Alfred D., Jr., with Immerman, Cambridge, Mass., July 9, 1980.
Cox, Rufus, with Ambrose, Manhattan, Kans., April 1, 1980.
Davis, Kenneth S., with Immerman, Princeton, Mass., July 9, 1980.
Eisenhower, Dwight D., with Ambrose, Gettysburg, Pa., November 3, 1963.
Eisenhower, John S. D., with Ambrose, Valley Forge, Pa., February 1, 1980.
Eisenhower, Milton S., with Ambrose, Baltimore, January 22–27, 1980; with Immerman, Baltimore, March 20, 1980; April 7–8, 1981.
Ford, Donald, with Immerman, Lemont, Pa., June 18, 1980.
Griffith, Mrs. Thomas, Manhattan, Kans., with Ambrose, March 31, 1980.
Jones, Ross, with Ambrose, Baltimore, April 7, 1980.
Kenworthy, Wilmer, with Immerman, State College, Pa., June 19, 1980.
Locklin, Wilbert E., with Immerman, Springfield, Mass., July 7, 1980.
Muller, Steven, with Ambrose, Baltimore, April 7, 1980.
Passarella, Russell, with Immerman, Bradley Beach, N.J., March 27, 1980.
Peterson, Jeff, with Ambrose, Manhattan, Kans., April 1, 1980.
Shaffer, G. Wilson, with Immerman, Baltimore, March 20, 1980.
Spear, Donald, tape sent to authors, summer 1980.
Thackrey, Russell, with Ambrose, Manhattan, Kans., March 31, 1980.
Wilkinson, Roy, with Immerman, State College, Pa., June 18, 1980.
Wolk, Ronald, with Ambrose, Washington, D.C., April 4, 1980.

Published Sources

Barber, James David. *The Presidential Character*. Englewood Cliffs, N.J., 1977.
Broom, Leonard, and Riemer, Ruth. *Removal and Return: The Socio-Economic Effects of the War on Japanese Americans*. Berkeley and Los Angeles, 1949.

Brown, Hugh S. and Mahew, Lewis B. *American Higher Education*. New York, 1965.

Byse, Clark. "A Report on the Pennsylvania Loyalty Act." *University of Pennsylvania Law Review* 101, no. 4 (January 1953).

Carey, James C. *Kansas State University: The Quest for Identity*. Lawrence, Kans., 1977.

Carlin, Tom. "Dr. Milton Eisenhower: Imparting a Broad View of the World." *Kansas Stater*, May 1981.

Centre Daily Times.

Collier's, September 3, 1949.

Country Gentleman, November 1946.

The Daily Collegian.

Daniels, Roger. *Concentration Camps USA: Japanese Americans and World War II*. New York, 1971.

———. *The Decision to Relocate the Japanese Americans*. Philadelphia, 1975.

Davis, Kenneth S. "The Abilene Factor in Eisenhower." *New York Times Magazine*, December 9, 1951.

———. "Another Eisenhower Takes a New Job." *New York Times Magazine*, October 1, 1950.

Drummond, Roscoe. "Triumph or Trouble Ahead?" *Collier's*, January 20, 1956.

Dunaway, Wayland F. *History of the Pennsylvania State College*. Lancaster, Pa., 1946.

Eisenhower, Dwight D. *The Papers of Dwight David Eisenhower: The War Years*. Edited by Alfred D. Chandler, Jr. 5 vols. Baltimore, 1970.

Eisenhower, Milton S. "The Presidency: Can Anyone Do the Job?" syndicated by *Projects in Education*, first published October 8, 1979.

———. *The President Is Calling*. Garden City, N.Y., 1974.

———. *The Wine Is Bitter*. Garden City, N.Y., 1963.

Funk, Arthur. *The Politics of Torch*. Lawrence, Kans., 1976.

Garland, Charles A. "A Promise To Keep." *Johns Hopkins Magazine*, special issue, 1967.

Grodzins, Morton. *Americans Betrayed: Politics and the Japanese Evacuation*. Chicago, 1949.

Harvard Committee. *General Education in a Free Society: Report of the Harvard Committee*. Cambridge, Mass., 1945.

Henry, David D. *Challenges Past, Challenges Present: An Analysis of American Higher Education since 1930*. San Francisco, 1975.

Hosokawa, Bill. *Nisei: The Quiet Americans*. New York, 1969.

"Interview with Dr. Milton S. Eisenhower." *U.S. News & World Report*, February 21, 1958.

Kornitzer, Bela. *The Great American Heritage: The Story of the Five Eisenhower Brothers*. New York, 1955.

Logan, Wilson, ed. *Emerging Patterns in American Higher Education*. Washington, D.C., 1965.

Lord, Russell. *The Wallaces of Iowa*. Boston, 1947.

Murphy, Robert. *Diplomat Among Warriors*. Garden City, N.Y., 1964.

Neal, Steve. *The Eisenhowers: Reluctant Dynasty*. Garden City, N.Y., 1978.

New York Herald Tribune.

New York Times.

Olsen, Nils A. *Journal of a Tamed Bureaucrat: Nils A. Olsen and the BAE, 1925–1935*. Edited by Richard Lowitt. Ames, Iowa, 1980.

Packard, Vance. "Spotlight on Milton Eisenhower." *American Magazine*, November 1955.

PM, January 26, 1943.

Poole, Lynn. "Milton Eisenhower Heads Hopkins." *Baltimore Magazine*, August 1956.

Presidential Commission on Higher Education. *Higher Education for Democracy: A Report of the President's Commission*. New York, 1947.

Rasmussen, W. D., and Baker, Gladys. *The Department of Agriculture*. New York, 1972.

Reader's Digest, June 1953.

Riley, Ridge. *Road to Number One: A Personal Chronicle of Penn State Football*. Garden City, N.Y., 1977.

Rudolph, Frederick. *The American College and University: A History*. New York, 1962.

_____. *Curriculum: A History of the American Undergraduate Course of Study since 1636*. San Francisco, 1977.

Schapsmeier, Edward, and Schapsmeier, Frederick. *Henry A. Wallace of Iowa: The Agrarian Years, 1910–1940*. Ames, Iowa, 1968.

Sharkey, Robert P. *Johns Hopkins: Centennial Portrait of a University*. Baltimore, 1975.

Wallace, Henry A. *The Price of Vision: The Diary of Henry A. Wallace*. Edited by John Morton Blum. Boston, 1973.

"What Makes Milton Run?" *American Mercury*, February 1956.

Weglyn, Michi. *Years of Infamy: The Untold Story of America's Concentration Camps*. New York, 1976.

Winkler, Allan M. *The Politics of Propaganda: The Office of War Information*. New Haven, 1978.

Index

(Italicized page numbers indicate illustrations.)

Abilene, Kans., 8, 10, 24–27; growing up in, 17, 24–26; nostalgia regarding, 248, 293; university presidents from, 88
Abilene Reflector, 26, 30
Academic freedom, 136
Administration by E.: ability for, 5, 54–55, 90; and open-door policy, 97, 115, 215; and organization management views, 127–28; style of, 194, 196, 203–4, 212–14. *See also* Leadership, E.'s, techniques of
Agricultural Adjustment Act (AAA), 49, 53–55
Agricultural Conservation Administration, 55
Agricultural prices, 39, 41
Akerson, George, 43, 44
Alexander, Holmes, 92
Alex. Brown & Sons, 178
Alien Enemy Control Program, 61
Alliance for Progress, 160, 198
Ambition of E., 29, 83–84
American Academy of Political Science, 256
American agriculture, E.'s perspective on, 257–58
American Association of University Professors, 131

American Council on Education, 75
American Friends Service Committee, 64
American Korean Foundation, 256
American Legion, 133, 134, 136
American Magazine, 157
American Mercury, 158
American Press (Sunday supplement), 157
American Red Cross, 256
American Veterinary Medical Association, 102
Anderson, John, as E.'s running mate, 257
Appleby, Paul, 54
Applied Physics Laboratory (Johns Hopkins), 237
Asimov, Isaac, 226
Assistants to E., subsequent careers of, 203
Association of American University Presses, 251
Association of Land Grant Colleges and Universities, 104
Athletics. *See* Sports
Ault, Miss, 25

Baltimore, 255–56
Baltimore Museum of Art, 256
Baltimore & Ohio Railroad, 178, 258
Baltimore Opera Company, 256

Baltimore Orioles, 222, 255-56
Baltimore Symphony Orchestra, 256
Bard Committee at Johns Hopkins, 207-8
Barker, Charles, 211, 212
Barksdale, John, 220-21
Barnes, Clive, 226
Barton, Carlyle, 172-73, 179
Beliefs of E., challenge to, 247
Bell, Louis H., 139-40, 141
Bendetsen, Karl, 59, 61
Bernreuter, Robert, 126-27, 167
Bess, Demaree, 153-54
Bevan, William, 236
Blacks, 99-104, 131, 218-19; Baltimore
  clubs and, 256-57; children of, 285-86; at
  Cornell, 237; crime and violence and,
  247, 284-87; despair of, 247; and honor
  societies, 102; unemployment and, 287;
  as victims of crime, 284; work-for-your-
  reward ethic and, 285
Blazer, Samuel: as E.'s driver, 112-14; as
  Helen's driver during illness, 163
Block, Nelson, 226, 259
Boas, George, 214
Bowman, Isaiah, 174-75
Brewster, R. Wallace, 135-37, 142
Brinkley, David, 201
Bronk, Detlev, 175
Brown Bowl, The (humor magazine), 33
Bryan, William Jennings, 27-28
Bureaucracy, governmental, 55-57, 90-91,
  145, 242-43
Burns, Arthur, 276
Business: and E., 257-59; and educational
  sectors, relationship between, 112-13
Byrnes, James, 57

California Farm Bureau Federation, 60
Carey, James, 79
Carnegie Foundation, 201
Carpenter, C. Raymond, 126
Carr, Ralph, 62
Carter, Jimmy, defeat of, 241-42
Carver, George Washington, 48
Casino incident, 103
Center Club (Baltimore), 256
Central Maryland Cancer Society, 256
Chambers of commerce in California, anti-
  Japanese prejudice and, 60

Chandler, Alfred D., Jr., 212, 232; on E.'s
  achievements at Johns Hopkins, 238
Chautauquas, 29-30
Chesapeake and Ohio Railway, 258
Chesapeake and Potomac Telephone Com-
  pany, 258
Chicago Board of Trade, 258
Childhood of E., 8, 12-17, 24-30
Chronicle of Preparatory Education, 202
Churchill, Winston, 69, 70
Citizens Committee's Critical Issues Coun-
  cil, 200
Citizenship, 252; education for, 74-77, 80-
  81, 97-98, 250
Civil rights: E. and, 218; the MacRae case
  and, 131-39; violations of Japanese-
  American, 59
Clark, Tom, 61
Cobbs, Price M., 245, 281
College presidencies, nature of, 81-82
Colliers (magazine), 91-92, 93, 158
Columbia University, racial discrimination
  and, 103-4
Commercial Credit Company, 258
Commission on the Causes and Prevention
  of Violence, 201-2, 225, 245, 280-81,
  283, 289, 291
Commission on Higher Education, 75, 81,
  104, 249
Commodities, 43, 49
Commoner, Barry, 226
Communists, 132-45. See also McCarthy,
  Joseph R.
Compromise, art of, 137
Conant, James B., 75
Coolidge, Calvin, 39
Cooperatives, farm, 43
Copeland, Aaron, 228
Cox, Richard T., 174
Cox, Rufus, 79
Creel Committee, 58
Crime: in America, 245-48, 280-91; race
  and, 284
Criminal justice system, 289-90
Cronkite, Walter, 201
Cross Keys, Village of (Baltimore), 226-27

Dances, racially mixed, 102
Darlan, Jean: assassination of, 71; Dwight
  and, 68-70

Dartmouth Alumni Magazine, 130
Davis, Elmer, 66
Davis, Kenneth S., 78, 82–87, 98, 104, 194, 199; correspondence of, with E., on Helen's death, 163–64
Davis, Robert, 115
Decker, Alonzo, Jr., 178
Defense, budget and, 277
Deficit spending, 49
Deike, George H., 166
Democracy: alternatives to, 248; violence and future of, 245
Dennis, Larry, 129
Department of Agriculture. *See* U.S. Department of Agriculture
DeWitt, John L., 59, 60, 61
Dickinson County, Kans., 10, 12
Dies, Martin, 59
Domestic life of E., 46, 52, 58, 92–93, 161–62
Donald, David, 211, 212, 213
Donovan, "Wild Bill," 69
Drummond, Roscoe, 157, 158
Dunkards, 9
Dunning, J. H. Fitzgerald, 178
Dunway, Wayland Fuller, 109
Dykstra, R. R., 101–2

Eakin, Helen. *See* Eisenhower, Helen Eakin
Eakin, Jack, 34, 52
Eakin, LeRoy ("Daddy Roy"), 24, 34–35, 58, 67–68
Edinburgh, Scotland. *See* U.S. consultate in Edinburgh, Scotland
Editorial Projects for Education, Wolk and, 202
Education: changes in choice of major on graduate level, 251; E.'s early, 13, 17, 25; E.'s views on, 74–77, 80–81, 94, 97–98, 209, 249; failure of system of (in U.S.), 249–50; federal involvement in, 89; importance of college and university to, 251; institutions for, 265; medical, 208; philosophy of, 74–77, 80–81; radio and television in, 126; science in secondary, 250; specialization and, 251. *See also* Students
Education and the People's Peace, 75
Eisenhauer. *See* Eisenhower family
Eisenhower, Arthur (brother), 12, 18, 74, 181

Eisenhower, Buddy. *See* Eisenhower, Milton, Jr.
Eisenhower, David (father), 8, 10–15, 18, 19
Eisenhower, Dwight D. (brother), 12, 13, 17, 18, 40, 47, 50, 181, 182, 184; advice to E. on academic positions, 72–74; Darlan in North Africa and, 68–70; decision of, to buy Gettysburg home, 168; E. as adviser to, 3–4, 103–4, 148–49, 160; E. as speech writer for, 151, 160; emergency surgery for, 147–48; first biography of, 78; heart attack of, 156; insights of, into workings of Congress, 47; as MacArthur's assistant, 46–47, 58; need of, for political advice, 71; North Africa and, 67–71; papers of, 211–12; relationship of, with E., 46–48, 68–71, 73, 146–60; relationship of, with E. and Helen, 47, 52; Republican leaders and, 154; sensitivity of, to criticism, 154; Adlai Stevenson and, 153; views of, on E., 156–57; visits of, to Penn State, 155; in War Department's Operations Division, 66; as world figure, 67–68
Eisenhower, Earl (brother), 12, 15, 18, 20, 40, 181
Eisenhower, Edgar (brother), 12, 16, 18, 154–55, 159, 181, 200
Eisenhower, Hans Nicol (ancestor), 9
Eisenhower, Helen Eakin (wife), 23, 34, 35–36, 58; cancer of, 162–63; chapel at Penn State named for; 164; death of, 163–64; and E.'s work, 46, 93, 162; engagement of, to E., 39; hobbies of, 93; and Latin American tour with E., 162; marriage of, 40; and parental chores, responsibilities for, 52, 93; portrait of, 164; as president's wife at Kansas State College, 92–93; as president's wife at Penn State, 161–62; relationship of, with Dwight and Mamie, 47, 52, 162; social lfe of, 92–93, 161–62
Eisenhower, Ida Stover (mother), 10–15, 18, 19, 92
Eisenhower, Jacob (grandfather), 9–12
Eisenhower, John (nephew), 58; as cadet at West Point, 66
Eisenhower, Mamie (wife of Dwight), 40, 58, 66; relationship of, with E. and Helen, 47, 52, 162
Eisenhower, Milton Stover, 18, 20, 21, 22,

Eisenhower, Milton Stover (*continued*)
23, 24, *180, 181, 182, 183, 184, 185, 186,
187. See also related topics*
Eisenhower, Milton, Jr. ("Buddy") (son),
46, 52, 58, 66, 93, 255; at Penn State, 113,
117, 163
Eisenhower, Paul (brother), 12
Eisenhower Project (at Johns Hopkins),
211–12
Eisenhower, Roy (brother), *18*
Eisenhower, Ruth (daughter), 66, 93, 163,
184; birth of, 58; after Helen's death, 164;
marriage reception for, 118; E. in retire-
ment and, 255; Union Memorial Hospital
and, 256
Eisenhower family: athletic ability in, 12;
career choices in, 10; duty and, 4, 235;
move to Kansas of, 9–10; origin of name
of, 9; religion of, 9, 13, 14
Eisenhower Symposium, 225–26
Electoral changes, proposed by E., 242–44
Eliot, Charles W., 81–82
Elkridge Club, 256
Engle, Charles ("Rip"), 120
Episcopal Church, 40
Evans, G. Heberton, 174, 212
Evergreen Foundation, 256

Faculty: affairs of, 87, 89, 117, 129–30, 131–
45, 177, 204–8, 210–11; on board of directors at Johns Hopkins, 235–36; communication with, 130; communist hysteria
and, 132–45; E.'s respect for, 203; E.'s
rapport with (at Johns Hopkins), 213,
214; E. and younger members of, 130; under Gordon at Johns Hopkins, 230, 233;
loyalty oaths and, 133–45; promotions
of, 129–30; revolt of, at Johns Hopkins,
233; salaries of, 129, 173, 228; tenure of,
131. *See also* Johns Hopkins University;
Kansas State College; Pennsylvania State
University
Falls Church, Va., 52, 66
Famine Emergency Relief Commission, 104
Farm commodity policy, 43
Farmers, subsidies to, 154
Farm School, Pa., 122
Farm Security Administration, 52
Farrell, Francis David, 73, 76
Federal Farm Board, 42–43

Federal government. *See* U.S. government
Firearms. *See* Gun control
Fiscal views of E., 218, 259
Flemming, Arthur S., 41, 43, 152, 242
Ford, Donald, 89, 96–97, 111, 120; counsel-
ing unit at Penn State and, 126–27
Ford Foundation, 191
Foreign aid, 296
Frank, Jerome, 209
Franklin and Marshall College, 194–95, 198
French, the, in North Africa, 68–71
Friendships of E., 161, 177–78, 227, 247
Fritsche, Milton, 117
Fuller, R. Buckminster, 226
Fund raising, 189–92, 237
Funk, Arthur, 68
Funston, Keith, 258

Galambos, Louis, 212
Gardner, Hy, 157
Garland, Aurelia, 179
Garland, Charles, 176, 179, 188, 229, 232,
258
Garrett family, 216
General Motors strike, E. on mediation
board during, 104
German immigrants, 9
Ghettos, inner city, 284–86, 290
G. I. Bill of Rights, 91, 101
Gilman, Daniel Coit, 82
Gireau, Henri, 68, 69
Glazer, Nathan, 226
Goldwater, Barry, 200
Good, Milton, 11–12
Gordon, Lincoln, 2, 228, 229–34
Gorse, George, 217, 224–25, 254
Government. *See* U.S. government
Grants from foundations, 190–92
Grauer, Neil, 217, 219, 220, 259
Greater Baltimore Medical Center, 256
Griswold, Benjamin, 178, 258
Grower-Shipper Vegetable Association, 60
Gullion, Allen W., 59
Gun control, 245–47, 286–87

Hammond, Harry P., 128
Harger, Charles Moreau, 24, 26–27, 28–30,
73, 76
Harger, Ruth, 26–27

Harris, Thomas, 219-20, 245-46, 254
Harrison, Earl G., 143-44
Harrison, Pat, 44
Harvard Report (on general education), 76
Harvey, Robert D. H., 232
Hatfield, Mark, 157
Hayes, Rutherford B., 81
Hazlett, "Swede," 157
Health of E., 53, 227, 259-60
Held, Victor, 141
Helen Eakin Eisenhower Memorial Chapel (Penn State), 164, 166
Heller, George, 127-28
Herter, Christian, 191
Hetzel, Ralph, 166
Hetzel, Ralph Dorn, 109-10, 117
Hill, Howard H. T., 33
Honor societies, minorities and, 102
Hoover, Herbert, 42-45
Hopkins, Annie, 25
Hopkins Scholarship Fund, E.'s royalties paid to, 198
Hopkins University. *See* Johns Hopkins University
Houghton, Amory, 104
Housing, off-campus, integration of, 199-200
Hughes, Charles Evans, 37
Hughes, John B., 60
Hunt, Ruth, 26
Huntley, Chet, 201
Hyde, Arthur M., 42-45

Ickes, Harold, 51, 64
Industrialist, The (Kansas State College), 33
Inflation, 274-76
Insurance and Securities, Inc., Corporation, 258
International relations, E.'s introduction to, 37-38
Issei, 59. *See also* Japanese-Americans

Jackson, C. D., 70-71
Janney, Stuart, 178
Japan, trade with, 275
Japanese American Citizen League, 65
Japanese-Americans: advisory council of leaders of, 61; civil rights of, 59; as college students, 63-64, 95; economic motives for relocation of, 60; E.'s efforts on

behalf of, 61-64, 65; E.'s views of treatment of, 59, 60, 61; as farm laborers, 64; financial losses to, 61; perceived threat of, 60; protection of rights and assets of, 61; racists and, 59-60; relocation camps of, 62-63; relocation decisions regarding, 59; threat of attacks on, 61; western states' governors and, 62
Jardine, William M., 33-34, 37, 39-41, 76; as head of Federal Farm Bureau, 43; as President Coolidge's Secretary of Agriculture, 39
Jarrett, Edwin, 178
Jews: Baltimore clubs and, 256-57; at Columbia University, 103-4; at Kansas State College, 99
John F. Kennedy Institute for the Habilitation of the Mentally and Physically Handicapped Child, 208
Johns Hopkins Club, 256
Johns Hopkins Hospital, 256
Johns Hopkins University, 1-7, 170-92, 193-214, 215-27, 228-39, 253; Applied Physics Laboratory, 237; board meetings of, 177; budget cuts of, 5-6, 188; budget deficits of, 4-5, 188, 237; budget surpluses of, 192; buildings of, 228; commencement address for class of 1967, 292-98; condition of, upon E.'s return, 1-7, 229-34; doctors at, E.'s views on, 209; institutions at, 205-9; E.-Muller team at, 237; endowment of, 228; E.'s accomplishments at, 211; E.'s assistants at, 193-204; E.'s demands about new board for, 235-36; E.'s greatest failure at, 204; E.'s open-door policy at, 7, 215; E.'s return to, 1-7, 235-39; faculty-administration relations at, 174, 177, 204-5, 214; faculty salaries at, 173, 175, 228; fund raising at, 175-76, 188-90, 228, 230, 233, 236; high school teachers at, 213; ingrown nature of, 174; library for, 175, 178; long-range plan for, 229; and McElroy committee, 229; neglected economic infrastructure at, 125; original endowment of, 178; responsibilities of board and president of, 177, 204; School of Advanced International Studies (SAIS), 191-92, 211; selection of new president for, 228; student-faculty relations at, 216; students at, 216; student

Johns Hopkins University (*continued*) union at, 236; tradition of smallness at, 174–75, 229–30; trustees of, 176–79; undergraduate education at, 6, 209–11, 214; undergraduate responsibilities of faculty at, 204

Johnson, Lyndon B., *186*, 201

Jones, Ross, 4, *185*, 199; appointment of, as university secretary at Johns Hopkins, 198; as E.'s assistant at Johns Hopkins, 195–96; in Muller administration at Johns Hopkins, 203; opinion of, of E., 203–4; as vice president at Johns Hopkins, 203

Justin, Margaret, 89

Kane, Robert, 145

Kansas, Eisenhower family's move to, 9–10

Kansas City Star, 33

Kansas State College, 31–37, 73–93, 94–107; agricultural research funds for, 88; appointment of E. to faculty of, 36; appropriations for, 88; assemblies at, 95; attracting good students to, 82; blacks at, 98–104; chapel at, 99; curriculum changes at (under E.), 76–80; Department of Citizenship at, 97–98; desegregation at, 99–104; educational environment at, 95–96; Eisenhower Hall at, 107; E.'s achievements at, 98; E.'s inaugural address at, 263–69; E.'s last commencement at, 106; E.'s leadership at, 79, 87–89; E.'s matriculation at, 29; E.'s popularity at, 88; E. as president of, 74–93, 94–107; as student at, 31–36; faculty relations at, with E., 77–80, 87–89, 98, 107; faculty and staff size at, 88; foreign students at, 95; general education at, 76–77; honorary doctorate for E. from, 107; Japanese-American students at, 95; Jews at, 99; opposition to E. at, 78–80; presidency of, offered to E., 73; racial discrimination at, 98–104; research at, 91; salaries at, 87–88; students at, 31, 87–89; student-teacher ratio at, 87, 88; veterans at, 87–89; Veterans Administration funds for, 91

Kansas State College Endowment Association, 97

Kansas State Collegian, 32

Kansas State Republican Club, 37

Kansas State University. *See* Kansas State College

Kellogg Foundation, 192

Kennedy, John F., 198

Kenworthy, Wilmer, 110, 116

Kerr, Clark, 201

Khrushchev, Nikita, *185*

Kibei, 59. *See also* Japanese-Americans

King, Martin Luther, 218

Klein, Philip, 143; and assessment of E.'s impact at Penn State, 164

Knowles, William, 220

Krant, Jonathan, 220

Kronsberg, Abram, 226

Kurzman, Dan, 198

Lancaster County, Pa., 9

Lane College, 10–11

Lane, Frederick, 211, 212

Latin America: certainty of revolt in, 295–96; E. as president's representative in, 152, 160

Lattimore, Owen, 213

Leadership, E.'s, techniques of, 54–55, 100–101, 111, 120, 137, 202, 212. *See also* Administration by E.

Leisure activities of E., 93, 222–23, 254–56

Life Insurance of California, 258

Lion's Paw fraternity (Penn State), 116–17

Lippmann, Walter, 60

Locklin, Wilbert E., *187*, 188, 189–90, 192, 193; on E.'s achievements at Johns Hopkins, 238; influence of E. on, 203; Springfield College and, 203

Lorch, Lee, 131

Lord, Russell, 49

"Love Life of the Bullfrog," 44–45

Loyalty oaths and hearings, 133–45

Loyalty Review Board (Penn State), 138, 140, 142–45

Lykens Valley River Brethren, 9

MacArthur, Douglas, 46–47

Macaulay, P. Stewart, 232

McCain, James A., 107

McCarthy, Joseph R., 132, 144, 213. *See also* Loyalty oaths and hearings; MacRae, Wendell Scott

McCloy, John, 61, 63

McCoy, Ernest B., 119–20

McElvoy, William, 229–30
McGael, Michael, 254
MacKenzie, Ossian, 125
MacLeish, Archibald, 58
McNary-Haugen bill, 39, 41
MacRae, Wendell Scott, 131–45
Malott, Deane W., 88
Mandelbaum, Maurice, 212, 219
Manhattan, Kans., 29, 30, 31; desegrega-
    tion in, 99–103; E.'s return to, 74
Margie (housekeeper), 219, 221, 222, 226
Marriage of E., 40
Marshall, George Catlett, 66, 70
Maryland Club, E.'s resignation from, 256
Masaoka, Michael, 65
Mathias, Charles McC., 243, 274–79
Mauthe, Lester ("Pete"), 119–20
Meiklejohn, Alexander, 84
Mennonites, 9. *See also* River Brethren
Mercantile-Safe Deposit and Trust Com-
    pany, 258
Middle States Association of Colleges and
    Secondary Schools, 167–68
Middleton, Drew, 68, 71
Milholland, James, 106, 110, 117, *183*
"Milton for President" boom, 156–58
Milton S. Eisenhower Auditorium (Penn
    State), 169
Milton S. Eisenhower gold medal, 237
Minorities, 98–104, 131, 218–19, 237, 247,
    284–87; in Baltimore's Center Club, 256–
    57; education and, 250; honor societies
    and, 102. *See also* Race relations; *names
    of specific minority groups*
Missouri Valley Conference athletics, racial
    integration and, 103
Mont Alto, Pa., 116
Montgomery, Bernard, 70
Moos, Malcolm, 200
Morris, Emery, 192
Morris, Norval, 280–81
Morris Mechanic Theater, 256
Morrison, Donald, 130
Morse, A. D., 140
Moscow, E.'s trip to, 160
Mt. Sidney, Va., 10–11
Muller, Steven, 4; estimation of E. by, 237;
    as new provost at Johns Hopkins, 236; re-
    lationship of, with E., 253; as successor to
    E. at Johns Hopkins, 238–39

Murphy, Franklin, 171
Murphy, Robert, 70
Music, 13, 93, 254
Musser, Cris, 12
Myer, Dillon, 64

National Collegiate Athletic Conference,
    119
National Commission for International De-
    velopment, 256
National Commission on the Causes and
    Prevention of Violence, 201–2, 225, 245,
    283. *See also* Crime; Violence
National Conference of Christians and
    Jews, 256
National Council of the U.N. Association,
    256
National Farm and Home Hour, 43
Native Sons and Daughters of Kansas, 85
NATO concept, need to expand, 297
Nelson, Russell, 208
New Deal, 48, 49, 52
Newton H. White, Jr., Athletic Center
    (Johns Hopkins), 179
New York Herald Tribune, 158
New York Stock Exchange, 258
New York Times Magazine, on estimates of
    E.'s role in White House, 153
Nichols, Thomas, 171, 176
Nisei. *See* Japanese-Americans
Nitze, Paul, 191
Nixon reorganization plans, 242
Nixon, Richard M., 160, *185,* 225, 243; gun
    control and, 246; price controls and, 277
Nonviolence, 218–19
North Africa: news of invasion of, 67; polit-
    ical and diplomatic aspects of invasion
    of, 68–71; preparations for invasion of,
    68

Office of Facts and Figures, 58
Office of Land Use Planning, 54–58
Office of Strategic Services (OSS), 69
Office of War Information (OWI): Dwight's
    military decisions and, 68–71; E. and, 58,
    66, 73–74
One Nation: Indivisible (pamphlet), 87
Organization of American States meeting,
    173
Overseas Information Agency, 58

Pacifism, 13
Painter, Sidney, 212
Panama, 172
Pan American Development Foundation, 256
Papers of Dwight D. Eisenhower, The: The War Years, 212
Passarella, Russell, 223, 231
Patchell, Walter W., 117
Paterno, Joseph, 120
Peace, power and, 296–97
Pearl Harbor, 58, 60
Pechan Act, 133–36, 143; declared unconstitutional, 145
Peek, George, 49–50
Pegler, Westbrook, 60
Pennsylvania Dutch, 9, 13
Pennsylvania legislature, budget sessions with, 167
Pennsylvania Loyalty Act, 133
Pennsylvania State University, 108–24, 125–45, 161–69; advantages of, for E., 106; athletics at, 119–20; atomic research at, 128; board of trustees at, 106, 117–21; business enterprises and, 112–13; campus radio station at, 117; change of, from college to university, 121–24; chapel at, 164; College of Business Administration at, 125–26; Communists and, 132–45; counseling at, 126–27; Dwight's visits to, 155–56; E. offered deanship at, 72; E.'s goal at, 111; E.'s impact on, 166–68; E.'s interest in, 105; E.'s offer to resign from, 151; and evaluation by Middle States Association of Colleges and Secondary Schools, 167–68; Faculty Advisory Council at, 130; faculty characteristics and problems at, 129–30; faculty recruitment at, 126; faculty's request for representation on board of, 110; food service at, 117–18; Hetzel Union Building at, 166; historical background of, 121; legislature's financial support of, 167; location of, 112; loyalty reviews and oaths at, 133–45; name of, 121–24; negative self-image at, 108–9, 110; nuclear reactor at, 128; orientation of students and parents at, 127; post office address of, 124; public relations at, 112; salaries at, 129; student encampments at, 116–17; student suicides at, 127; tenure policy at, 131–32

Percy, Charles, 226, 243
Pershing, John J., 47
Pétain, Henri, 68
Peterson, Jeff, 105
Piaget, Jean, 226
Pi Beta Phi, 161
Political conventions, 244
Political process, reforms of, 242–45
Politics and E., 147, 151, 156–59, 164–67, 200–201, 243, 248, 257
Polsby, Nelson, 244
Populists, 12, 25
Presidency (U.S.), 270–73; concept of imperial, 242; E.'s pessimism about, 245; problems of, 242–43, 271
President Is Calling, The, 241, 243
Presidential Advisory Committee on Government Organization (PACGO), 153, 242
Professors. *See* Faculty
Propaganda, 58
Public Broadcasting System, 126
Publish-or-perish policy, 130

Quaker Oats Company, 257
Quakers, 64

Race, crime and, 284
Race relations, 59–60, 98–104, 199–200, 218, 250–51. *See also* Blacks; Japanese-Americans
Radio Maroc (Free French station), 69–71
Ramsay Lodge (Edinburgh), 38
Rankin, John, 60, 94
Ratner, Payne, 95
Reed, Lowell Jacob, 170–71
Reform: of electoral process, 242–44; recommendations for governmental, 241–45
Religion. *See* Eisenhower family, religion of; Episcopal Church; Mennonites; River Brethren
Reporter, E. as, 27–30
Representatives (U.S. Congress), terms of office for, 243–44, 271
Republican National Committee, E. and (during college years), 36
Reputation of E., 85, 88–89, 91, 155, 204
Retirement of E., 218, 224–27, 240–60
River Brethren (sect), 9, 13, 98
Robbins, Charles Burton, 50
Robinson, Brooks, *187*, 256

Rockefeller Foundation, 191–92
Rockefeller, Nelson, 151–52; plans for governmental reorganization and, 242
Roosevelt, Franklin D: change in (1942), 59; confidence of, in E., 65; Dwight Eisenhower's North African arrangements with French and, 69–70; E.'s rapport with, 50–52; E.'s tribute to, 97; Office of War information and, 58; personal relationships in administration of, 70; reorganization of Department of Agriculture and, 56–58; Wallace and, 48, 50–52; War Relocation Authority (WRA) and, 59–61, 64–65
Rowland, Roger ("Cappy"), 118, 166
Roy, Robert H., 174, 212
Rudolph, Frederick, 82
Rural Electrification Administration, 52
Rusk, Dean, 191

Saturday Evening Post, 152
Scholarship: E.'s respect for, 203–4, 205, 252; respect for (among Eisenhowers), 17
School of Advanced International Studies (Johns Hopkins), 191–92, 211
Scientists, 294–95
Scotland, E. in, 37, 38
Scranton, William, 200–201
Senators, terms of office for, 243–44, 271
Shaffer, G. Wilson, 174–75, 209–11, 212, 214, 232; and football at Johns Hopkins, 222–23; plans to enlarge Johns Hopkins and, 229–30
Shanley, Bernard, 155
Shapiro, Samuel, 198
Sharkey, Robert, 208
Sherwood, Robert, 58
Sigma Alpha Epsilon, 32
Singleton, Charles, 212
Smith, Harold, 59
Snider, Ruth Eisenhower. *See* Eisenhower, Ruth
Snider, Thomas W., 256
Snow, C. P., 227
Snyder, Howard, 148
Social affairs in Washington, 50
Society for the Advancement of Management, 256
Soil Conservation Service, 52, 53–57
Soldier of Democracy (Davis), 78

Spaulding, Keith, 167, 188–89, 192, 194–95, 198
Spear, Donald, 220–21
Specialization, E. on, 251, 265
Sports, 114, 119–20, 222–23, 255–56
Springfield College, 202–3
Sproul, Gordon, 63
Staff members working for E., 193–94, 203, 204
Stanton, Phoebe, 212, 225
State College, Pa., 122–24. *See also* Pennsylvania State University
Stebbins, Ernest, 208
Stevenson, Adlai, 153
Stewart, Tom, 60
Stimson, Henry L., 70
Stone, I. F., 71
Stover, Bud. *See* Eisenhower, Milton, Jr.
Stover, Ida. *See* Eisenhower, Ida Stover
Student encampments: at Johns Hopkins, 216; at Kansas State, 95–96; at Penn State, 116–17
Student housing, discrimination and (in Baltimore), 199–200
Students: advice to, 223–24; black, 99–104; coffee hours at Johns Hopkins and, 216; E. and, 97, 115, 215, 219–23, 227; E.'s goals for, 94–95; E.'s relations with, 95, 97, 113–17, 215–27; Eisenhower Symposium and, 225–26; encampments for, 95–96, 116–17, 216; faculty relations with, 95–96, 216; foreign, 95; integrated housing for, 101; involvement in decisionmaking at Johns Hopkins, 231–32; Jewish, 99, 103; Johns Hopkins' board excluded from affairs of, 177; meals with E., 219–22; open-door policy for, 97, 115, 215; over-specialization of, 250; parochialism of, 95; protests and civil disobedience of, 218–19; recommendations for, 223; segregation and discrimination and, 99–104, 199–200; stolen items of, 221; theatrical productions by, 252; visits of, with E., 218–22
Szulc, Ted, 198

Taft, Robert, 150
Taft, William Howard, 25
Teachers of E., 25–26
Television, education and, 126, 249
Tenure for faculty, 131

Thackrey, Russell, 80, 90, 102, 204
Truman, Harry, 75, 81, 150
Tugwell, Rexford G., 52, 54
Turnbull, Douglas, 258
Turner, Thomas, 208, 209, 229

UNESCO, 95; E. as chairman of U.S. National Commission for, 104
Union Memorial Hospital, 256
United States: change in, 248, 270; failure of educational system in, 249; form of government of, 244; future of, 240–41; misunderstanding of, 295; national priorities in, 248; recommendations regarding vice presidency of, 243. *See also specific topics relating to, e.g.*, Democracy; Electoral changes
University, social usefulness of, 249
University of Edinburgh, 38
University of Michigan, 105
University Park, Pa., 125
University of Pennsylvania, 108, 121
University of Tennessee, offer of presidency of, 105
Urbanization, 249
U.S. consulate in Edinburgh, Scotland, E.'s post at, 37–39
U.S. Department of Agriculture: AAA and, 49; conflicting programs within, 53–57; conservative economic views of, 49; E. in, 39, 40–41, 42–45, 48–52, 53–58; E. and reorganization of, 104; Hyde as head of, 42–45; Jardine as head of, 39; New Deal and, 48, 49, 52, 53–54; and Office of Land Use Planning, 54–58; research funds from, 90; Wallace as head of, 48–51
U.S. Department of Agriculture, The: Its Structure and Function (Eisenhower), 43
U.S. government: and bureaucracy, 55–57; and demand for E.'s services, 67; and elected officials, 242–45; executive branch of, 272; and industry regulations, 275
U.S. National Commission for UNESCO, 83

Vaughan, Samuel, 117, 120
Veterans Administration, 91
Vichy government, 68
Vietnam War, 218

Violence: statistics on, 283–84; steps to prevent, 248; as threat to democracy, 245, 247. *See also* Crime; National Commission on Causes and Prevention of Violence
Volker Charities Fund, 97, 98

Wage Stabilization Board, 150–51
Walker, Eric, 110, 129; chosen as successor to E. at Penn State, 166
Walker, Robert, 98
Wallace, Henry A., 71; E. and, 48–52, *180*
Wallace's Farmer, 48
Waring, Fred, 118
Warren, Doug, 260
Warren, Earl, 60
Washington Symphony Orchestra, 46
Watchtower Society, 13
Watkins, Jack, 220–21
Weaver, Earl, 256
Weil, Frank, 104
Western Growers Protective Association, 60
Western Maryland Railroad, 259
White, Mrs. Newton H., Jr., 178–79
White, Newton H., Jr., 178–79
Whitman, Ann, 153
Wickard, Claude, 61
Wilcox, Francis O., 191
Wildavsky, Aaron, 244
Wilkinson, Roy, 109, 111, 147–48, 254; and proposed change of name of State College, 121–22, 123–24; faculty loyalty oaths and, 137; MacRae case and, 140–42, 144; views of, on E., 168–69
Willard, J. T., 268
Wills, George, 260
Wills, Kendall, 260
Wilson, Woodrow, 25, 28–29
Windsor Insurance Company, 258
Wine Is Bitter, The, 197–98
Wolfe, Theodore, 178
Wolk, Ron, 197; Brown University appointment of, 202; on Commission on the Causes and Prevention of Violence, 202; as editor of E.'s *The Wine Is Bitter*, 196–97; Editorial Projects for Education and, 202; as E.'s assistant at Johns Hopkins, 198–201; integration in off-campus student housing at Johns Hopkins and, 199;

Scranton nominating speech and, 200–201

Wolman, Abel, 174

Wood, W. Barry, Jr., 171, 206–7, 209

Writings by E., 254–55; articles (college years), 33; memoir (*The President Is Calling*), 241, 243; speeches and articles, 82, 83, 85–87, 97, 112–13, 198–99, 200–201, 257; *The U.S. Department of Agriculture: Its Structure and Function*, 43; *The Wine Is Bitter*, 197–98

Yearbook of U.S. Agriculture, 43

Young, Philip, 125

Zeltmann, Eugene, 220

Zook, George F., 75

STEPHEN E. AMBROSE is professor of history at the
University of New Orleans. His many books include
Duty, Honor, Country: A History of West Point and
*The Supreme Commander: The War Years of General
Dwight D. Eisenhower*. He is presently at work on a
full-length biography of Dwight Eisenhower.

RICHARD H. IMMERMAN is assistant professor of history
at the University of Hawaii at Manoa. He is the author
of *The CIA in Guatemala: The Foreign Policy of
Intervention* and he collaborated with Stephen
Ambrose on *Ike's Spies*. He is currently writing a book
on the Eisenhower administration.

The Johns Hopkins University Press

Milton S. Eisenhower
EDUCATIONAL STATESMAN

*This book was composed in Paladium text and display
type by Action Comp Co., Inc., from a design by
Susan P. Fillion. It was printed on 50-lb. Sebago Egg-
shell Cream Offset paper and bound in Holliston Rox-
ite A by the Maple Press Company.*